ESSENTIAL DOCUMENTS IN THE HISTORY
OF AMERICAN HIGHER EDUCATION

Essential Documents in the History of American Higher Education

John R. Thelin

JOHNS HOPKINS UNIVERSITY PRESS

Baltimore

Johns Hopkins University Press
2715 North Charles Street
Baltimore, Maryland 21218-4363
www.press.jhu.edu

Library of Congress Cataloging-in-Publication Data

Thelin, John R., 1947–
    Essential documents in the history of American higher education /
John R. Thelin.
        pages cm
    Includes bibliographical references and index.
    ISBN 978-1-4214-1421-8 (hardcover : alk. paper) — ISBN
978-1-4214-1422-5 (pbk. : alk. paper) — ISBN 978-1-4214-1423-2
(electronic) — ISBN 1-4214-1421-x (hardcover : alk. paper) — ISBN
1-4214-1422-8 (pbk. : alk. paper) — ISBN 1-4214-1423-6 (electronic)
    1. Education, Higher—United States—History. 2. Universities and
colleges—United States—History. 3. Education—History—Sources. I. Title.
    LA226.T43 2014
    378.73—dc23   2013043572

A catalog record for this book is available from the British Library.

*Special discounts are available for bulk purchases of this book. For
more information, please contact Special Sales at 410-516-6936 or
specialsales@press.jhu.edu.*

Johns Hopkins University Press uses environmentally friendly book
materials, including recycled text paper that is composed of at least
30 percent post-consumer waste, whenever possible.

For Sharon
Writer, Editor, Muse

Contents

Acknowledgments

I am indebted to Gregory Britton, Editorial Director of Johns Hopkins University Press, for having suggested this project in March 2013—and for being its advocate from start to finish. Assistant Editor Greg Nicholl provided expertise on matters of format, presentation, design, and graphics. Assistant Editor Sara Cleary provided editorial expertise and reassurance in the final, finishing stages of the project. And, as has been my grateful experience for over a quarter century, I have had the benefit of the support and expertise of Executive Editor Jacqueline Wehmueller.

David M. Brown and Jillian Faith, graduate students in the Higher Education program in the Educational Policy Studies Department at the University of Kentucky, were excellent researchers who worked thoughtfully and skillfully in numerous aspects, such as selecting, transcribing, annotating, and decoding disparate historical documents. Their suggestions at each stage of editing and writing greatly enhanced this work. I am fortunate to have had the dedication and skill of such ascending new higher education scholars. I thank Johns Hopkins University Press and the University of Kentucky's Educational Policy Studies Department for having provided funding for research assistantships.

A. Sharon Thelin, who has carefully read and commented on my writings for four decades, once again brought a keen eye for style and substance to this particular historical project, as she reviewed the book proposal and the evolving manuscript. Her combination of critique and care has made this and all of my writing projects fulfilling.

At the start of the following introductory essay I invoke the example of Edwin Slosson, the acclaimed higher education writer and editor who pleaded in 1908 that each institution assign one person to be responsible for documents. College and university archivists fulfill this charge—and researchers' dreams. In fact, thanks to the advice and expertise of academic archivists, I have been able to carry out in this anthology some good approaches. In October 2007 I had the honor of being the keynote speaker for the annual conference of the New England Archivists (NEA) association. I was invited by Tom Rosko, Archivist for the Massachusetts Institute of Technology—with whom I had worked on projects over several years. Elizabeth Slomba, Archivist for the University of New Hampshire, tended to program arrangements. I am indebted to them and their fellow college and university archivists of NEA for the opportunity to learn from them about recent innovations at campus archives—and for mutual discussion of research prospects and problems involving primary sources and historical documents for the study of higher education. This has influenced my approach to editing this book and led to my writing the article "Archives and the Campus: Past, Present and Future," published in the April 2008 issue of the *New England Archivists Newsletter*. Responses from and additional conversations with university archivists led me to expand my analysis, eventually published as "Archives and the Cure for Institutional Amnesia: College and University Saga as Part of the Cure for Institutional Amnesia," published in the *Journal of Archival Organization* (2009).

The following archivists have been supportive colleagues on this and related projects over many years: Richard Lieberman, Archivist at the City University of New York's La Guardia Community College campus, who was Project Director for the 2010 CUNY calendar and website project devoted to *Investing in Futures: Public Higher Education in America*; Frank Stanger, Director of Special Collections at the University of Kentucky, who has assisted me and many of my graduate students in archival research; J. R. K. Kantor, Archivist Emeritus of the University of California, Berkeley, who has provided both documents and thoughtful advice over many years; and Jay Gaidmore, Director of Special Collections at the College of William and Mary and, previously, University Archivist and Head of University Archives and Records Management at the University of North Carolina, Chapel Hill, and Archivist at Brown University, who helped me with photographs and sources, especially those dealing with college sports.

I also am grateful for the assistance of the following college and university archivists who made possible my inclusion of specific historical documents published in the anthology: Jennifer Betts, University Archivist, Brown University, for the 1764 Charter and the 1783 Laws of the College of Rhode Island; Caroline A.

Killens, University of Georgia Archivist, and the Board of the *Georgia Review* for advice on archival holdings; the *Georgia Review* for allowing me to reproduce the memorable 1785 Charter for the University of Georgia; and Leslie Fields, College Archivist for Mount Holyoke College, who gave me access to and permission to reprint the original 1836 Charter for Mount-Holyoke Female Seminary.

Compilation and publication of this historical document anthology would not have been possible without the generous, enthusiastic cooperation of the agents and heirs of authors, as well as the directors of research institutes, associations, and foundations whose respective studies and reports are at the heart of debate and analysis about higher education. So, in addition to the formal recognition of official and formal permissions for me to reprint documents, I wish to thank personally and individually the following who have made this anthology possible—and the work enjoyable.

Memoirs of college and university life are a distinctive and particularly enjoyable feature of this anthology about higher education. The following executors, trustees, and authors have helped bring higher education to life through a rich literary heritage.

Nat Benchley, grandson and literary executor for the late Robert Benchley, kindly provided permission to include the legendary 1927 memoir "What College Did to Me."

Lori Styler, Contracts Manager for the Barbara Hogenson Agency in New York City, took time to respond to my inquiry and request and then arranged with Rosemary Thurber, daughter of the late James Thurber, permission for reprinting "University Days."

James Galbraith, Professor at the Lyndon B. Johnson School of Public Affairs at the University of Texas, Austin, administers his late father's literary rights. In this role he was supportive and prompt in graciously allowing permission to include John Kenneth Galbraith's 1968 memoir about being a graduate student at the University of California, Berkeley, in the 1930s.

Lynn Hollander Savio kindly granted permission for me to reprint her late husband's December 2, 1964, speech, which he delivered on the steps of Sproul Hall at the University of California, Berkeley. Her enthusiasm for and interest in the historical document anthology was best demonstrated by her suggestion that she send me a copy of the heretofore unpublished original transcript of this legendary public address.

Editor Wendy Miller of *California* magazine, published by the Alumni Association of the University of California, Berkeley, took time to put me in touch with contributing author Russell Schoch and with interviewee Professor Laura Nader. The happy ending for me was that both enthusiastically agreed to allow me to publish their articles and interviews as historical documents.

Rosa Maria Pegueros, Professor of History at the University of Rhode Island, gave permission for inclusion of her 1995 student memoir about the University of San Francisco and her doctoral studies at UCLA, "Todos Vuelven: From Potrero Hill to UCLA." Steven J. Kelman, the Albert J. Weatherhead III and Richard W. Weatherhead Professor of Public Management at Harvard's John F. Kennedy School of Government, allowed me to reprint his 1982 memoir of his undergraduate days and student activism at Harvard from 1966 to 1970. Greta Lindquist of the University of California Press patiently reviewed numerous copyright files held by the Regents of the University of California related to the 1970 memoir by former Cal student-athlete Jackie Jensen. Marylou Ferry, Vice President for Communication and Marketing for Scripps College, not only granted permission to reprint the distinctive Scripps College seal featuring "La Semeuse" but also arranged for Johns Hopkins University Press to receive a high-quality image, including its motto, *Incipit Vita Nova*.

American higher education is distinctive in the high-quality reports that foundations have published periodically. Gay M. Clyburn, Associate Vice President for Public Affairs at the Carnegie Foundation for the Advancement of Teaching, gave me permission to reprint excerpts from two landmark reports: Abraham Flexner's 1910 report on medical education and Howard Savage's 1929 report on American college athletics. Jane Kulow, Assistant to the President of the Virginia Foundation for the Humanities, assisted me in gaining permission to reprint Stephen J. Wright's 1987 essay about the historically black colleges and universities. Amy Perko, Executive Director of the Knight Commission on College Sports, arranged for me to have access to and publication permission for two landmark reports from, respectively, 1990 and 2010—central to the national forum on reform in intercollegiate athletics. Dr. Rita J. Kirshstein, Director of the American Institutes for Research in Washington, D.C., gave permission to reprint the 2012 AIR Delta Cost Project report, *College Spending in a Turbulent Decade*.

I have relied on the high-quality reporting in the *Chronicle of Higher Education* for over thirty years, both as a source of daily information about higher education and as a source of historical coverage of landmark debates. Jessica Stremmel of the YGS Group was most considerate in arranging copyright permissions for

Chronicle articles. Over the past decade Douglas Lederman, Editor of *Inside Higher Ed*, has provided me a sounding board and forum for connecting past and present in the serious analysis of higher education issues.

The cooperation of executors, trustees, editors, and authors indicated serious interest in this project. It shows that for higher education, history matters. Remembering the essential characters, actions, and events that have shaped our colleges and universities for over four hundred years provides information and inspiration that allow us to connect past and present in how we look at, probe, and think about what is important in higher education. Illustrative of the cooperation and interest these executors, officials, agents, and authors showed toward my requests and inquiries was that they each and all were curious about when the book would be published—and requested a copy. That is a request with which I am happy and grateful to comply.

Introduction
Documents and Higher Education's Heritage

In 1908 Edwin Slosson, editor of *The Independent* magazine, concluded his year-long study of emerging universities throughout the nation with a visit to Phila-delphia. There, he praised the University of Pennsylvania for its unique Bureau of Publicity, which collected diverse artifacts of campus life. Slosson exclaimed, "No other university, so far as I have found, has such a complete and convenient collection of materials for the present and future study of the institution." He concluded, "In particular, let me suggest that there should be in each university a society or preferably a person whose duty is to collect fugitive publications of all kinds, programs of clubs and festivities, snapshots of student life, and mete-oric periodicals. A file of catalogues and doctors' dissertations will not satisfy the needs for future historians and biographers. They must have something more if they are to make these dry bones live."

This anthology, published a little more than a century after Slosson's pro-posal, is intended to help fulfill his goal by providing a new generation of higher education scholars with selected documents "to make these dry bones live." It attempts to do so by animating higher education's lively past by deliberately se-lecting diverse documents—each of which has been chosen for a particular pur-pose or message. As such it is a tribute to college and university archivists nation-wide who have thoughtfully gathered and systematically preserved and organized disparate records and mementos of our academic institutions.

My approach to writing and editing this book is indebted to some important, earlier works that have provided guides to and collections of documents from and about colleges and universities. Foremost is the 1961 volume edited by Richard Hofstadter and Wilson Smith, *American Higher Education: A Documentary History*.

A more recent successor is Wilson Smith and Thomas Bender's 2008 anthology, *American Higher Education Transformed, 1940–2005: Documenting the National Discourse.* Also worthy of special tribute is A. C. Spectorsky's 1958 collection of fiction, memoirs, essays, and photographs, *The College Years.* Another influential genre that has flourished over the past decade has been that of oral history and campus life, exemplified by the work of Carolyn B. Matalene and Katherine Chaddock Reynolds, editors of *Carolina Voices: Two Hundred Years of Student Experiences.*

Paying tribute to these memorable, influential works does not at all signal that this book replicates or mimics them. My charge is distinctive and selective: to provide readers, many of whom are graduate students and researchers, with a small number of documents whose cumulative contribution is to capture and convey essential features of life within colleges and universities. It includes both landmark events and less dramatic yet enduring episodes from the round of life. In some cases I have relied on accounts or articles written long after an event in order to show how different generations resurrect and rediscover an incident— and then incorporate this rediscovery into a new round of claims and deliberations. Nowhere is this better illustrated than in Document 2.2, in which a 1985 article by Jeanne Evangelauf, published in the *Chronicle of Higher Education*, captures the strong feelings that two institutions—the University of Georgia and the University of North Carolina—elicit about historic claims as part of the University of Georgia's bicentennial celebration of its 1785 charter. Some historians may object that by including such an article the anthology is providing secondary sources, not original documents or primary sources. My response is that I am trying to promote in readers an appreciation for the ways in which historical memory is passed on and revived—and altered—over time and according to diverse, often conflicting and polemical perspectives. The challenge is for the contemporary scholar to sort out these multiple layers and interpretations. In fact, these partisan accounts and reinterpretations have long been a part of historical writing about higher education. A good example is Document 1.1, Anthony Wood's essay about the 1354 riot at Oxford, which Wood wrote in the mid-seventeenth century—three centuries removed from the actual events and yet probably the most informative source available then or now.

Also, one important consideration is that I have arranged the documents so that they are in harmony with the organization and chapter structure of my book *A History of American Higher Education*, published by Johns Hopkins University Press in 2004, with an expanded second edition in 2011. The aim is to provide readers with readily available sources that expand and illuminate topics I have analyzed in detail in the original book. No doubt some readers will object that one of their favorite documents was omitted. I do not deny this, but offer the following reasons: First, the need to contain this anthology to a single, portable volume imposed one limit. Second, some documents my editors and research assistants and I had in mind were not available, either because materials had been destroyed in fires or floods or, in some cases, reprint permission was unobtainable—or, charges were simply prohibitive. This was especially so with some visual sources, including some historic photographs and film clips. For disappointed readers the editors and I offer consolation and an invitation: see this anthology as essential without being exhaustive. I hope it encourages readers to try their own hand at searching, sorting, and editing their own anthologies about higher education's exciting, complex heritage.

This anthology differs markedly from the scope and size of the Hofstadter and Smith work, which spans 1,016 pages over two volumes and tends to focus on "top-down" history as shaped by official reports and documents by influential leaders and college and university presidents. In contrast, *Essential Documents for the History of American Higher Education* is confined to a single volume. Despite this limit, its scope is different and in some ways more extensive than that of Hofstadter and Smith. Whereas Hofstadter and Smith stop their documents around 1950, this anthology extends to 2012. It includes student memoirs—with attention to diversity shaped by gender, race, age, social class, and geography. Graduate students constitute a group usually overlooked in histories of colleges and universities. I have attempted to correct that omission by including John Kenneth Galbraith's account of his graduate student years at Berkeley in the 1930s. In addition to including documents by and about presidents and professors, I have deliberately included coverage of other roles often underappreciated, such as the faculty spouse. The documents include samples from Hollywood movies, journalism, short stories, real estate advertisements, historical monuments, and other materials that connect American colleges to American popular culture. A good example of this novel perspective is in the recurrent attention I have deliberately given to intercollegiate athletics, starting with the 1929 report by Howard Savage for the Carnegie Foundation for the Advancement of Teaching and continuing in 1990, and then again in 2010, with reports sponsored by the Knight Commission. The rationale for this addition is that intercollegiate athletics are sufficiently pervasive, visible, and controversial to be included in serious discussions about American higher education. My inclusion of student memoirs and artifacts from popular culture supplements official documents such as charters, legislation, presidential reports, and public policies.

Wilson Smith and Thomas Bender's recent anthology devotes 450 pages to an important yet short and recent past—the decades from 1940 to 2005. Furthermore, it places the spotlight on the intense debates about the purposes and shape of higher education as carried out by scholars and expert analysts as published in scholarly journals or in the public forum associated with the intelligentsia. Their work is sufficiently comprehensive and substantive in its domain that I have shown my respect by not trying to replicate their distinctive focus.

In presenting documents that are synchronized with the narrative text of *A History of American Higher Education*, my aim is to invite—and to tempt—readers to go beyond a secondary source and to sample firsthand the myriad primary sources and ephemera that make colleges and universities simultaneously exciting and perplexing. Perusal of the table of contents will show that the selected documents vary in length. The caveat is that length in itself is no indicator of historical significance one way or the other. In chapter 2, for example, Document 2.4, the 1836 Commonwealth Charter for Mount-Holyoke Female Seminary, is a single page in length. The following item, Document 2.5, the President's Address to students at the College of William and Mary from the same year, is twenty pages long and represents a reprinting of the entire two-hour speech. Its prose is inflated; some of its passages are predictable liturgy and may even put a reader to sleep. That is not necessarily a bad experience that calls for severe pruning of the text—mainly because the intact document probably recaptures for contemporary readers the experiences of generations of students who constituted a captive audience for long-winded college presidential oratory. That is in large part what it meant to be a restless, impatient undergraduate in the nineteenth century—and perhaps in the twenty-first century as well. The overarching point is that whether a document is one page or twenty, each warrants careful consideration in its own right. Each is important for understanding higher education, and each conveys distinctive insights about characters in the drama of college and university life.

The message is that reading and analyzing historical documents is an acquired skill. I have found it helpful to provide concise guidelines to promote a sequential systematic list of questions whose cumulative impact is to understand—and appreciate—the numerous layers of the document. The logic of analysis applies comparably to concise and lengthy documents. It starts with identifying straight-

GUIDELINES FOR ANALYZING HISTORICAL DOCUMENTS

1. Date of the document: Is this original? Is it republished in a secondary source?
2. Origins: place of publication. If reprinted, where and when?
3. Author: any significant biographical background that influences the document?
4. Audience: for whom is the author writing? What is the author's main purpose in creating the document?
5. Tone: what is the author's perspective and attitude toward the work?
6. Alterations: has the document been edited? If so, how have various editions changed the content or substance?
7. Publisher or sponsor: does the document reflect the sponsorship or point of view of some particular orthodoxy or group? If so, what is that perspective?
8. Language: are there distinctive words or phrases the author uses which call for careful definition?
9. Brief summary of the document's content.
10. Significance of the document at the time of its publication. How was it received?
11. Historical significance of the document.
12. Triangulation: are there other sources that are useful for making sense out of the document?
13. Context: place the document in its historical setting.
14. Missing information: are there puzzles or gaps in the document which render it incomplete or its meaning uncertain?
15. Additional comments or questions.

forward data about a document and moves progressively toward more substantive questions associated with interpretation.

The rationale of these guidelines is that they break down an unwieldy, amorphous exploration of a document into a systematic, step-by-step concise report that makes clear the findings and the unanswered portions of the analysis. Eventually, after practice, the itemized list of questions becomes second nature as one sifts and sorts the layers and levels of information and images. My observation is that readers who venture into the domain of documents often follow with visits to a college or university archive. The experience of working with primary sources often is sufficiently intriguing and enjoyable that their neutrality toward historical research about higher education is transformed into genuine, enduring enthusiasm and commitment.

ESSENTIAL DOCUMENTS IN THE HISTORY
OF AMERICAN HIGHER EDUCATION

CHAPTER ONE

Colleges in the Colonial Era

Why—and how—did the civil and religious leaders who joined with prosperous merchants in the New World take time, trouble, and money to build enduring colleges between 1636 and 1781? Neither the question nor its answers are obvious, even though we take for granted today in the United States the prevalence of colleges and universities nationwide. The precedents of Oxford and Cambridge Universities in England, along with the examples of the charters of the University of Paris and other institutions in Europe, provide some clues to and continuity with college founding in the American colonies. Ultimately, however, Americans acquired their own commitments and innovations that made their colonial college distinctive.

Acquiring a charter from a royal, civil, or ecclesiastic authority was a difficult, necessary step to assure the legal rights and protections that would allow an educational institution to survive external conflicts—such as the infamous "Town and Gown" riots that threatened Oxford University in 1354. It also conferred a rare power: the right to grant academic degrees. The likelihood of a college to survive was further enhanced because host governments, whether colony or crown, made certain that these academic corporations enjoyed exemption from taxation, as spelled out in Document 1.2. The reciprocity was that college officials and trustees agreed to create and administer detailed codes of conduct and college laws that assured a responsible, well-behaved academic community (Document 1.3). Given this intricate legal structure and incorporation, colleges in the colonial era combined revenues from government subsidies with tuition payments and philanthropic gifts to cobble a financing strategy that required continual vigilance to keep expenses lean (Document 1.4). On balance, the corporate and legal structures that defined the academic and community life of the colleges were stronger than the provisions and plans for yearly and long-term financing of these special institutions.

1.1: Town and Gown: Anthony Wood's "Riot at Oxford"

Tensions between university scholars and local merchants and landlords in 1354 led to a violent, lengthy confrontation, resulting in serious injuries and numerous deaths in Oxford, England. This account, written more than three centuries after the event by Anthony Wood of Oxford University, provides a detailed yet partisan report. The important legacy for colleges and universities in England and in the American colonies was the affirmation of the power of a charter conferred by a monarchy or ecclesiastic body to uphold privileges and protections for the university and its scholars against external adversaries, including townspeople and even the local sheriff. The grievances and altercations had little to do with academic freedom and scholarship. Rather, the crucial issues dealt with jurisdiction over scholars in matters of personal movement, consumer rights, and privileged exemptions from local civil authorities. The flash point involved literally "bread and butter issues"—namely, university scholars' accusations about bad wine, stale food, and price gouging by vendors and merchants.

Not only did the university and its scholars prevail with its charter and legal protections being upheld in the wake of this epic conflict with the town, but the episode also put into motion a new plan for the university as an architectural and residential entity outside the town—a development that contrasted with the urban universities on the European continent. Oxford University, comparable to the Universities of Bologna and Paris, had no "campus" or exclusive buildings, having long relied on rented halls and hostels, with scholars lodging in various sites, all of which had been marbled into the motley buildings and streets of the town. The new, emerging Oxford University arrangement consisted of using endowments and donations to build magnificent quadrangles for residential colleges, henceforth creating a buffer between "Town" and "Gown."

Howbeit seeing that divers Chronicles do remember a very grievous discord to have hapned this year between the Scholars and Townsmen, and that divers were

Anthony Wood, *The History and Antiquities of the Colleges and Halls in the University of Oxford* (Oxford: John Gutch, 1796).

at St. Mary's to be rung out, whereupon the Scholars got bows and arrows, and maintained the fight with the Townsman till dark night, at which time the fray ceased, no one Scholar or Townsman being killed or mortally wounded or maimed.

On the next day being wednesday, albeit the Chancellor of the University caused public proclamation to be made in the morning both at St. Mary's church in the presence of the Scholars there assembled in a great multitude, and also at Quatervois among the Townsmen, that no Scholar or Townsman should wear or bear any offensive weapons or assault any man, or otherwise disturb the peace (upon which the Scholars did in humble obedience to that proclamation, repaired to the Schools, and demeaned themselves peaceably till after dinner) yet the very same morning 'circa horam ordinariam' (as I find it exprest) the Townsmen came with their bows and arrows, and drave away a certain Master in Divinity and his auditors, who was then determining in the Augustine Schools. The Ballives of the Town also had given particular warning to every Townsman at his respective house in the morning that they should make themselves ready to fight with the Scholars against the time when the Town bell should ring out, and also given notice before to the country round about, and had hired people to come in and assist the Townsmen in their intended conflict with the Scholars. In dinner time the Townsmen subtilly and secretly sent about fourscore men armed with bows and arrows, and other manner of weapons into the parish of St. Giles in the north suburb; who, after a little expectation, having discovered certain Scholars walking after dinner in Beaumont (being the same place we now call St. Giles's fields) issued out of St. Giles's church, shooting at the said Scholars for the space of three furlongs: some of them they drove into the Augustine Priory, and others into the Town. One Scholar they killed without the walls, some they wounded mortally, others grievously and used the rest basely. All which being done without any mercy, caused an horrible outcry in the Town: whereupon the Town bell being rung out first and after that the University bell, divers Scholars issued out armed with bows and arrows in their own defence and of their companions, and having first shut and blocked up some of the Gates of the Town (least the country people who were then gathered together in innumerable multitudes might suddenly break in upon their rear in a hostile manner and assist the Townsmen who were now ready prepared in battle array, and armed with their targets also) they fought with them and defended themselves till after Vesper tide; a little after which time, entered into the Town by the west gate about two thousand countrymen with a black dismal flag, erect and displayed. Of which the Scholars having notice, and being unable to resist so great and fierce a company, they withdrew themselves to their lodgings . . .

But the Townsmen finding no Scholars in the streets to make any opposition, pursued them, and that day they broke open five Inns, or Hostles of Scholars with fire and sword . . .

Such Scholars as they found in the said Halls or Inns they killed or maimed, or grievously wounded. Their books and all their goods which they could find, they spoiled, plundered and carried away. All their victuals, wine, and other drink they poured out; their bread, fish &c. they trod under foot. After this the night came on and the conflict ceased for that day, and the same even public proclamation was made in Oxon in the King's name, "that no man should injure the Scholars or their goods under pain of forfeiture."

The next day being Thursday (after the Chancellor and some principal persons of the University were set out towards Woodstock to the King, who had sent for them thither) no one Scholar or Scholar's servant so much as appearing out of their Houses with any intention to harm the Townsmen, or offer any injury to them (as they themselves confessed) yet the said Townsmen about sun rising, having rung out their bell, assembled themselves together in a numberless multitude, desiring to heap mischief upon mischief, and to perfect by a more terrible conclusion that wicked enterprise which they had began. This being done they with hideous noises and clamours came and invaded the Scholars' Houses in a wretchless fort, which they forced open with iron bars and other engines; and entering into them, those that resisted and stood upon their defence (particularly some Chaplains) they killed or else in a grievous sort maimed. Some innocent wretches, after they had killed, they scornfully cast into houses of easement, others they buried in dunghills, and some they let lie above ground. The crowns of some Chaplains, viz. all the skin so far as the tonsure went, these diabolical imps flayed off in scorn of their Clergy. Divers others whom they had mortally wounded, they haled to prison, carrying their entrails in their hands in a most lamentable manner. They plundred and carried away all the goods out of fourteen Inns or Halls, which they spoiled that Thursday. They broke open and dashed to pieces the Scholars' Chests and left not any moveable thing which might stand them in any stead; and which was yet more horrid, some poor innocents that were flying with all speed to the Body of Christ for succour (then honorably carried in procession by the Brethren through the Town for the appeasing of this slaughter) and striving to embrace and come as near as they could to the repository wherein the glorious Body was with great devotion put, these confounded sons of Satan knocked them down, beat and most cruelly wounded. The Crosses also of certain Brethren (the Fryers) which were erected on the ground for the present time with a *procul hinc ite profani*, they overthrew and laid flat with the cheynell. This wickedness and outrage continuing the said day from the rising of the sun till noon tide and a little after without any ceasing, and thereupon all the Scholars (besides those of the Colleges) being fled divers ways, our mother the University of Oxon, which had but two days [before] many sons is now almost forsaken and left forlorn. The names of the Clerks or Scholars that were killed which were the next day or two days after known and told to the Bishop of Lincoln were

Thomas Mestologie, Robert Morbogard, Priests, of Ireland, as I suppose.

Roger Grenham, Henry Havecate, Scholars.

John Walleys, Servitor, Philip Beauchampe, Clerk.

The names of the wounded Clerks, whose lives were then despaired of, were

Malachie Murbanan, Priest	Charles Ogormulyn
Malachie Magnigir	Dionysius Ohagagan, Priest
Patrick Magbradardie	Maurice Odeorogean

All Irish men, as I conceive.

The last of which was wounded to death in the head in procession with the Brethren.

Gilbert Osserir	William Deerley
John Salton	Mr. Hugh de Breynton M. of A.
Hugh Middleham	and Priest
Barthelm. Wellyngton	John Harald, Priest
Roger Blaby	Roger of Wales, a Deacon
William Godeshale	Richard Haryngton.

Which last (Haryngton) fled to the body of our Lord and was thence dragged, grievously wounded and imprisoned. Then

Roger Bourgh;	Cote of St. Mary Hall.
Salamon Tirie, Priest,	Gilbert Harmach.

With divers others who were run into the country and could not be as yet known whether they were dead or alive. Some died in their flight, or rather creeping away, into the country; and others not yet known that were wounded, killed, cast into privies and buried in dunghills.

The slaughter being thus finished (albeit a thirst continued still after blood on the Town part) the Sages or the chief Magistrates with the company of Regents that were remaining gathered privately together, and drawing up a diary of these proceedings (such mostly that I have already repeated) inclosed it in a Latin Epistle written by them, and dated 16 Febr; which being done they sent it to the Bishop of Lincoln by the hands of Mr. John de Staunton; M. of A. who on the 18 of the said month wherein this conflict fell out, arriving at Buckden in Huntingdonshire, the seat belonging to the said Bishop, delivered it into his own hands with the diary inclosed, attested by the subscriptions of such that were spectators of the said outrage: the former beginneth thus *Reverendo in Christo patri, D. Johanni Episcopo Lyncolniæ &c.* the other thus – *Die Martis in sesto S. Scholasticæ Virginis proxima prædicta &c.* The particulars of all which, the Bishop hearing, not without grief and astonishment, caused forthwith letters of excommunication to be drawn up. In which, in the first place, praising the University of Oxford with this elogie – *super omnia Studia per cuncta mundi climate landabilis &c.* and others, and then inserting the chief particulars of the said Conflict, he interdicted the Town, and caused the same letters of excommunication to be read in each parish church in Oxon for several (both Lord's and Festival) days, with ringing of bells, crosses erected, lighted and extinguished candles, by the Priests or Chaplains of the said churches in their sacerdotal vestments and robes. So that the Townsmen being utterly deprived of all ecclesiastical benefit in hearing Service, receiving the Sacraments, Burial, Marriage, &c. caused such good people that made a conscience of religion (such I mean that were not accessary to the conflict) to be full of grief and sorrow, especially when they considered if death in the mean time should arrest them.

1.2: A College Charter in the Colonial Era: The College of Rhode Island (1764)

The 1764 charter of the College of Rhode Island is the predecessor of Brown University—an institutional name change in 1804 which reflected the philanthropy and support of the college by the Brown family of Providence, whose wealth came from generations of commerce and shipping, including the slave trade. In the colonial era a college charter was granted by a governing body—the Crown or the governor of a colony—only after serious consideration of a detailed petition. The following docu-

Charter of the College of Rhode Island of 1764. Reprinted by permission of the Brown University Archives. Transcribed as published in Walter C. Bronson, *The History of Brown University, 1764–1914* (Providence, RI: Brown University, 1914) pp. 500–507.

ment is typical among the seventeenth- and eighteenth-century charters in its attention to legal rights and responsibilities. It is also particular to the College and Colony of Rhode Island in its configuration of religious denominations as part of governance and legal structures. In short, Rhode Island leaned toward accommodation of numerous Protestant denominations in the composition of its trustees and fellows—and in its admission of students. In some instances this was expressed by generous terms of tolerance. In determining the configuration of governing bodies, such as the trustees, the strategy was one of apportionment and accommodation of each of the major Protestant denominations—groups whose relationships often were characterized by animosity and bitter distrust. The Rhode Island approach as set forth in the college charter was in marked contrast to some of the extremely strict terms of denominational exclusion elsewhere in the colonial colleges and civil life. It showed far more tolerance than usually was the case at Oxford and Cambridge, where scholars and masters were required to swear an oath of allegiance to the Church of England. Even though diplomatic accommodation of religious denominations was central to the charter, the interesting codicil was that trustees were pledged to encourage and protect academic freedom within the college. Within the context of essential Christian principles, education and discourse were to be civil and reasonable. Logic and science, not the polemics of a particular denomination's religious orthodoxy, were the standards by which college discussions and inquiry were to be conducted and evaluated.

The colonial college charters have been durable, with relatively few changes over three hundred years. One defining feature that contrasts the college charters of the New World with those of Oxford and Cambridge Universities is the deliberate decision to place ultimate institutional authority in an external board, designated as "trustees," in conjunction with a strong office of the president and delegation of fellows. This locus of ultimate authority in an external board departed significantly from the Oxford and Cambridge custom of almost total control by masters and faculty scholars in the historic English universities. The attention to details by the petitioners is impressive in that the terms suggest that founding a college was not undertaken casually or quickly. Perhaps more important than the legal details, however, is the statement of purpose, in which the education of an elite group of students is cast in a serious tone, characterized by invoking high principles and noble mission. The college charter was both thorough and thoughtful.

At the General Assembly of the Governor and Company of the English Colony of Rhode Island and Providence-Plantations in New England in America, begun and held at East Greenwich within & for said Colony by adjournment upon the last Monday of Febr:, one Thousand Seven Hundred and Sixty-four, and in the fourth Year of the Reign of His Most Sacred Majesty George the Third, by the Grace of God, King of Great Britain, and so forth

Whereas Institutions for liberal Education are highly beneficial to Society, by forming the rising Generation to Virtue Knowledge & useful Literature & thus preserving in the Community a Succession of Men duly qualify'd for discharging the Offices of Life with usefulness & reputation they have therefore justly merited & received the attention & Encouragement of every wise and well regulated State, and whereas a Public School or Seminary erected for that purpose witlun this Colony, to which the Youth may freely resort for Education in the Vernacular & Learned Languages & in the liberal Arts and Sciences, would be for the general Advantage & Honor of the Government, and whereas

Mr. Gideon Hoxsey	Mr. Ezekiel Gardner	Daniel Jenckes Esqr.
		Nicholas Tillinghast Esqr.
Mr. Thomas Eyres	Mr. John Waterman	Nicholas Gardiner Esqr.
Mr. Thomas Potter Junr.	Mr. James Barker Junr	Col. Josias Lyndon
Mr. Peleg Barker	Mr. John Holmes	Col. Elisha Reynolds
Mr. Edwd. Thurston	Solomon Drown Esqr.	
Mr. Wm Redwood	Mr. Saml Windsor	Peleg Thurston Esqr.
		Simon Pease Esqr.
Joseph Clarke Esqr.	Mr. Joseph Sheldon	
Mr. John G Wanton	Charles Rhodes Esqre.	John Tillinghast Esqr.
		George Haszard Esqr.
Mr. Thos. Robinson	Mr Nicholas Brown	Col Job Bennet
	Col. Barzilla Richmond	Nicholas Easton Esqr.
	Mr John Brown	Arthur Fenner Esqr.

with many other Persons appear as undertakers in the valuable design, & thereupon a Petition has been prefer'd to this Assembly praying that full liberty and Power may be granted unto such of them with others as are hereafter mentioned to found endow, order & govern a College or University within this Colony & that for the more effectual execution of this design they may be incorporated into one Body Politic to be known in the law with the powers priviledges & franchises necessary for the purpose aforesaid —

Now, therefore know ye that being willing to encourage and patronize such an honorable and useful Institution, we the said Governor & Company in General Assembly convened do for ourselves and our Successors in and by virtue of the Power and Authority within the Jurisdiction of this Colony to us by the Royal Charter granted & committed enact grant constitute ordain & declare & it is hereby enacted granted constituted ordained and declared that the

Revd. James Manning	Joshua Babcock Esqre:	Hon'ble Stephen Hopkins Esqre:
Revd. Russel Mason	Mr: John G Wanton	Hon'ble Joseph Wanton Junr Esqr:
Colo. Elisha Reynolds	Revd: Edward Upham	
Colo. Josias Lyndon	Revd: Jeremiah Condy	Hon'ble Samuel Ward Esqre:
Colo. Job Bennet	Revd: Marmaduke Brown.	Hon'ble William Ellery Esqr:
Mr. Ephraim Bowen	Revd: Gardner Thurston.	" John Tillinghast Esqre:
Joshua Clarke Esqre:	Revd: Ezra Stiles	" Simon Pease Esqre:
Capt. Jona Slade	Revd: John Greaves	" James Honyman Esqre:
John Taylor Esqre:	Revd: John Maxson	" Nicholas Easton Esqre:
Mr: Robert Strettell Jones	Revd: Saml: Winsor	" Nicholas Tillinghast Esqre:
Azariah Dunham Esqre:	Revd: John Gano	" Darius Sessions Esqre:
Mr. Edward Thurston Jr.	Revd: Morgan Edwards.	" Joseph Harris Esqre:
Mr. Thomas Eyres	Revd: Isaac Eaton	" Francis Willet Esqre:
Mr. Thomas Haszard	Revd: Saml: Stillman	Wm: Logan Esqr:
Mr. Peleg Barker	Revd: Saml: Jones	" Daniel Jencks Esqre:
		George Hazard Esqr.
		Nicholas Brown Esqr.
		Jeremiah Niles Esqre:

or such or so many of them as shall within twelve Months from the date hereof, accept of this trust and qualify themselves as herein after directed, and their Successors shall be for ever hereafter one Body Corporate & Politic in Fact and Name to be known in Law by the Name of Trustees, and Fellows of the College or University in the English Colony of Rhode Island and Providence Plantations in New England in America the Trustees and Fellows at any Time hereafter giving such more particular Name to the College in Honor of the greatest & most distinguished Benefactor or otherwise as they shall think proper which Name so given shall in all Acts, Instruments and Doings of said Body Politic be superadded to their corporate Name aforesaid, and become a part of their legal Appellation, by which it shall be for ever known and distinguished, and that by the same Name, they and their Successors chosen by themselves as hereafter prescribed shall and may have perpetual Succession, and shall & may be Persons able and capable in the Law to Sue, & to be Sued to Plead and to be impleaded to Answer, and to be Answered unto, to defend and to be defended in all and singular Suits Causes Matters Actions and Doings of what kind so ever & also to have take possess purchase acquire or otherwise receive & hold Lands Tenements Hereditaments, Goods Chattles or other Estates of all which they may and shall stand and be seized notwithstanding any Misnomer of the College or the Corporation hereof and by what ever Name or however imperfectly the same shall be described in Gift, Bequests and Assignments provided the true intent of the Assigner or Benefactor be evident. Also the same to grant demise alien lease use manage and improve according to the Tenor of the Donations, and to the Purposes Trusts & Uses to which they shall be seized there of and full Liberty Power & Authority is hereby granted unto the said Trustees & Fellows and their Successors to found a College or University within this Colony for promoting the Liberal Arts and Universal Literature, and with the Monies Estates & Revenues of which they shall from time to time become legally Seized as aforesaid to Endow the same and erect the necessary Buildings & Edifices thereof on such Place within this Colony as they shall think Convenient : And Generally to regulate Order & Govern the same Appoint Officers & make Laws as herein after prescribed & hold use & enjoy all the Liberties Priviliges exemptions. Dignities & Immunities enjoy'd by any College or University whatever. And furthermore that the sd. Trustees & fellows & their Successors shall and may forever hereafter have a public Seal to use for all Causes matters & affairs whatever of them and their Successors and the same Seal to alter Break & make anew from time to time at their Will and Pleasure which Seal shall always be deposited with the President or Senior fellow and furthermore by the Authority afforesaid it is hereby enacted Ordained & declared that it is now and at all Times hereafter shall continue to be the unalterable Constitution of this College or University that the Corporation thereof shall consist of two Branches Vizt : that of the Trustees & that of the fellowship with distinct seperate & respective powers, and that the Number of the Trustees shall and may be thirty six of which twenty two shall forever be Elected of the Denomination called Baptists or Antipedobaptis Five shall for ever be elected of the Denomination called Friends or Quakers, four shall for ever be elected of the Denomination called Congregationalists, & Five shall for ever be elected of the Denomination called Episcopalians & that the Succession in this Branch shall be for ever chosen & filled up from the respective Denominations in this proportion and according to these Numbers which are hereby fixt & shall remain to perpetuity imutably the same and that the said

Revd. Isaac Eaton	Francis Willet Esq.	Hon'ble Stephen Hopkins Esqre.
Revd. Saml. Stillman	Daniel Jencks Esq.	Hon'ble Joseph Wanton Jun Esqr.
Revd. Russcl Mason	George Haszard Esqr.	
Colo. Elisha Reynolds	Nicholas Brown Esqr.	Hon'ble Samuel Ward Esqr
Colo. Josias Lyndon	Jeremiah Niles Esq.	Hon'ble William Ellery Esqre
Colo. Job Bennet	Mr. John G Wanton	John Tillinghast Esq.
Mr. Ephraim Bowen	Joshua Clark. Esqr.	Simon Pease Esqre
John Taylor Esqre.	Revd. Gardner Thurston	James Honyman Esqre.
Capt. Jona. Slade	Revd. John Greaves	Nicholas Easton Esqre.
Mr. Robert Strettell Jones	Revd. John Maxson	Nicholas Tillinghast Esq.
Azariah Dunham Esqre.	Revd. John Gano	Darius Sessions Esqre.
Mr. Edward Thurston Junr.	Revd. Saml. Winsor	Joseph Harris Esq.
Mr. Peleg Barker		

or such or so many of them as shall qualify themselves as aforesaid shall be and they are hereby declared and established the first and present Trustees. — And that the Number of the Fellows inclusive of the President who shall always be a Fellow, shall and may be Twelve of which eight shall be for ever elected of the Denomination called Baptists or Antipaedobaptists, and the rest indifferently of any or all Denominations and that the

Joshua Babcock Esq.	Revd. Ezra Stiles	Revd. Edward Upham
Mr. Thomas Eyres	Revd. Saml: Jones	Revd. Jeremiah Condy
Mr. Thomas Haszard	Revd. James Manning	Revd. Marmaduke Brown
	Wm. Logan Esqr.	Revd. Morgan Edwards

or such or so many of them as shall qualify themselves as aforesaid shall be, and they are hereby declared the first and present Fellows and Fellowship to whom the President when hereafter elected who shall forever be of the Denomination called Baptist or Antepedo Baptist shall be Joined to compleat the Number. And furthermore it is declared and ordained that the Succession in both Branches shall at all times hereafter be filled up and supplied according to these Numbers and this established and invariable Proportion from the respective Denominations by the seperate Election of both Branches of this Corporation which shall at all Times sett and Act by seperate and distinct Powers, and in general in order to the validity and consummation of all Acts there shall be in the Exercise of their respective seperate and distinct Powers, the Joint concurrence of the Trustees and the Fellows by their respective Majorities except in adjudging and conferring the Academical Degrees which shall for ever belong exclusively to the Fellowship as a Learned Faculty And further it is constituted that the Instruction and immediate Government of the College shall for ever be and Rest in the President and Fellows or Fellowship — And furthermore it be ordained that there shall be a General Meeting of the Corporation on the first Wednesday of September Annually within the College Edifice, and untill the same be Built at such Place as they shall appoint to consult Advise and transact the Affairs of the College or University at which or at any other time the Public Commencement may be held and Celebrated and that on any special Emergencies the President with any two of the Fellows or any Three of the Fellows exclusive of the President may convoke and they are hereby impowered to convoke an Assembly of the Corporation on twenty Days Notice and that in all Meetings the Major Vote of those Present of the two Branches respectively shall be deemed their respective Majorities aforesaid, provided that not less than twelve of the Trustees & five of the Fellows be a Quorum of their Respective Branches — That the President or in his Absence the Senior Fellow present shall always be Moderator of the Fellows, that the Corporation at their Annual Meetings once in three Years or oftner in Case of Death or Removal shall and may chose a Chancellor of the University and Treasurer from among the Trustees, and a Secretary from among the Fellows, that the Nomination of the Chancellor shall be in the Trustees whose Office shall be only to Preside as a Moderator of the Trustees and that in his Absence the Trustees shall choose a Moderator for the time being by the Name of Vice Chancellor and at any of their Meetings duly formed as aforesaid shall and may be elected a Trustee or Fellow, or Trustees or Fellows in the Room of those Nominated in this Charter who may refuse to accept or in the Room of those who may Die, Resign or be Removed — And furthermore it is enacted ordained and declared that this Corporation at any of their Meetings regularly convened as aforesaid shall and may Elect and appoint the President and Professors of Languages and the several Parts of Literature, and upon the demise of him or them or either of them their Resignation or Removal from his or their Office for Misdemeanor Incapacity or Unfaithfulness, for which he or they are hereby declared removeable by this Corporation others to Elect and Appoint in their Room and Stead, & at such meeting upon the Nomination of the Fellows to Elect and Appoint Tutors Stewards Butlers and all such other Officers usually appointed in Colleges or Universities as they shall find necessary and think fitt to appoint for the promoting Liberal Education

for Tuition Fines and Incidental Expences to be collected by the Steward or such other Officer as they shall appoint to Collect the same, and the same with their Revenues and other College Estates in the Hands of the Treasurer to appropriate, in discharging Salaries and other College Debts and the College Accounts shall be Annually Audited and Adjusted in the Meeting of the Corporation and furthermore it is hereby enacted and declared that into this Liberal & Catholic Institution shall never be admitted any Religious Tests but on the Contrary all the Members hereof shall for ever enjoy full free Absolute and uninterrupted Liberty of Conscience and that the Places of Professors, Tutors and all other Officers the President alone excepted shall be free and open for all denominations of Protestants and that Youths of all Religious Denominations shall and may be freely admitted to the Equal Advantages Emoluments & Honors of the College or University and shall Receive a like fair generous & equal Treatment, during their Residence therein, they conducting themselves peaceably and conforming to the Laws and Statutes thereof: And that the Public teaching shall in general Respect the Sciences and that the Sectarian differences of opinions, shall not make any Part of the Public and Classical Instruction, altho' all Religious Controversies may be studied freely examined and explained by the President Professors and Tutors in a personal seperate and distinct manner, to the Youth of any or each Denomination and above all a constant Regard be paid to and effectual Care taken of the Morals of the College and furthermore for the honour & encouragement of Literature we constitute and declare the fellowship aforesaid a learned faculty and do hereby give grant unto and invest them & their Successors with full Power & Authority, and they are hereby Authoriz'd & impowered by their President & in his Absence by the Senior Fellow or one of the Fellows appointed by themselves at the Anniversary Commencements or at any other times and at all Times hereafter to Admit to & Conferr any & all the Learned Degrees which can or ought to be *given and conferred in any of the Colleges & Universities in America* or any such other Degrees of Literary Honor as they shall devise upon any and all such Candidates and Persons as the President and Fellows or Fellowship shall Judge worthy of the Academical Honors, which Power of conferring Degrees is hereby restricted to the Learned Faculty, who shall or may Issue Diplomas or Certificates of such Degrees or conferr Degrees by Diplomas and Authenticate them with the Public Seal of the Corporation, and the Hands of the President and Secretary, and of all the Professors as Witnesses and deliver them to the Graduates as Honorable and Perpetual Testimonies, and furthemore for the greater Encouragement of this Semi-

cation thereof shall be a sufficient Warrant to the said Corporation to hold, use and exercise all the Powers, Franchises, and Immunities herein contained —
March 2d : 1764   To the House of Magsts —
Gent. Resolvd that the aforewritten Pass as an Act of this Assembly

Voted & passd Nemine Contradicente

Pr Ordr. Josias Lyndon Cler

In the Upper House
Read (on the Third) and concurred Nemine Contradicente

By Ordr. Henry Ward Secr'y

1.3: A College's Laws and Code of Conduct (1783)

Whereas a charter defines the legal structure of rights and responsibilities that enable a board of trustees and president to assure the interests and well-being of the institution in its external affairs, the following detailed document deals with the responsibilities—and rights—of students and other members of the college community. It is in large measure *intramural* in character. Reading these regulations provides an estimate of how college officials viewed student life inside and out of the classroom. Explicit requirements of conduct suggest that presidents and tutors drew from years of experience (including student protests about bad food) to anticipate situations and sources of conflict which might arise in the course of a typical academic year. One also gains at least an approximation of the broad code of conduct that defined in the eighteenth century a "gentleman and scholar." Although many of the provisions emphasize penalties students might face if they were disobedient, there also are explicit statements about what students could expect to receive in good faith from college officials. Not the least important matter was that of compacts about dining halls, meals served by the college steward, and cleaning of dormitory rooms. One has no less than formal statements dealing with what today we call "student consumerism."

The college was exclusive in that student enrollment was limited to white men, most of whom came from prosperous families and belonged to one of the major Protestant denominations. Within this limited constituency, there were pockets of tolerance

The Laws of the College in Providence in the State of Rhode Island, Enacted by the Fellowship and Approved by the Trustees of Sd. College [From the Corporation Records of 1783]. Reprinted by permission of the Brown University Archives. Transcribed as published in Walter C. Bronson, *The History of Brown University, 1764–1914* (Providence, RI: Brown University, 1914) pp. 508–519.

for minorities, including allowance for *their* distinctive beliefs. Quaker students, often excluded from some colleges, were admitted. Furthermore, in deference to the customs of the Friends Meetings, they were the only group of students exempted from college regulations about removing one's hat inside college walls. Jewish students were offered admission and, once enrolled, were not required to profess belief in all facets of Protestant theology, as the college laws explicitly stated that "Young Gentlemen of the Hebrew Nation are to be exempted from this law, so far as it relates to the New Testament and its authenticity."

The college laws of 1783, drafted after the Revolutionary War, show important differences from the Charter of 1764 (Document 1.1). For example, institutional fealty is no longer directed to the monarchy of Great Britain. Second, students enrolled in the college are advised of and granted specific conditions about being drafted for military service in the event of war or insurrection. In sum, both college officials and students had learned from past events, as reflected in this codification of proper conduct within a campus community—and in student behavior when interacting with townspeople. The net result from the College Laws document is that readers today learn about an educational community that is both familiar and alien to us. The laws are unabashed about the privileges that come with high social rank. Yet this is tempered by comparable provision for the primacy of civil behavior and the responsibilities and requirements that accompanied rights and privileges within the elite world of students in the eighteenth-century college and university. A good example of this balance was demonstrated in the penalty of "degradation"—in which a misbehaving student was admonished by lowering his social rank within the roster of fellow students. The college regulations codified the dictum that for young gentlemen scholars, rank had its privileges—and responsibilities.

Chapter. 1st.

Concerning admission —

1. No Person may expect to be admitted into this College, unless, upon examination by the President and Tutors, he shall be found able to read accurately construe and parse *Tully* and the Greek Testament, and Virgil; and shall be able to write true Latin in prose, and hath learned the rules of Prosody and Vulgar Arithmatic; and shall bring suitable Testimony of a blameless life & conversation —

2. No Person shall be admitted under-Graduate into this College until his father or Guardian or some other person of property shall have given to the Steward a sufficient bond for the payment of his quarter Bills, approved of by the Au-

thority of the College from time to time, so long as he shall continue to be a member of College, which bond the Steward shall keep until the said Scholar shall have taken his second Degree, unless it should be given up sooner by the order of the President. And the Steward is obliged to produce and transmit to his father or guardian, a general state or account of the several sums or dues to be charged in the quarter bill. —

3. No student shall be admitted into this College until he shall have written out a correct copy of the Laws of the College, or have otherwise obtained them, and had them signed by the President, & one, or more of the Tutors, as the Evidence of his admission, which copy he shall keep by him during his residence in College —

4. Every scholar, thus admitted, whether he be present or absent, shall be obliged to pay all College dues, except for victualling, until he shall be regularly dismissed ; or at least, until he shall, by the advice of his parents or guardians, if under age, ask a dismission of the President —

5. After admission, every Student shall reside in the College Edefice, and there pursue his Studies, lodge & board in Commons, except the Inhabitants of the town and its vicinity, who are permitted to victual at home; also such indigent Scholars to whom the Faculty may grant any indulgence; and also such young Gentlemen as the President may think proper to receive into his own family as boarders —

Chapter. 2D.

Concerning academic exercises —

1. The hours of study betwen the fall & spring vacations shall be from morning prayers one hour before breakfast, and, from 9 OClock A.M. until 12 OClock; — from 2. OClock P.M. until sunset; and from 7. until 9 OClock in the Evening; — And between the Spring and Fall vacations, one hour after morning prayers; from 8 OClock A.M. until 12; from 2 OClock P.M until 6. OClok; and no Student shall be out of his Chamber after 9 OClock in the Evening

2. Both before and afternoon, and after 9 OClock in the Evening the Tutors in their turns shall duly visit the rooms of the Students, to observe whether they be within and pursuing their Studies; and shall punish all those who are absent without liberty, or necessity —

3. The President and Tutors, according to their judments, shall teach and instruct the several Classes in the learned Languages and in the liberal Arts and Sciences, together with the vernacular Tongus — The following are the clasics

appointed for the first year, in Latin, Virgil, Cicero's Orations and Horace, all in usum Delphini. In Greek, the new Testament, Lucians Dialogues & Zenophon's Cyropaedia; — For the second year, in Latin, Cicero de Oratore & Caesars Commentaries; — In Greek Homer's Iliad & Longinus on the Sublime, together with Lowth's vernacular Grammar, Rhetoric, Wards Oratory, Sheridan's Lectures on Elocution, Guthrie's Geography, Kaims Elements of Criticism, Watts's and Duncan's Logic. — For the third year, Hutchinsons moral Philosophy, Dodridges Lectures, Fennings Arithmatic, Hammonds Algebra, Stones Euclid, Martins Trigonometry, Loves Surveying, Wilsons Navigation, Martins Philosophia Britannica, & Ferguson's Astronomy, with Martin on the Globes. —In the last year Locke on the Understanding, Kennedy's Chronology and Bollingbroke on History, and the Languages, Arts & Sciences, studied in the foregoing years, to be accurately reviewed.

4. During the two first years, such Latin Exercises shall be exhibited as shall be directed by their respective Teachers; and, throughout the two last years weekly disputations shall be held on such subjects as shall be previously assigned them, both in the forensic and syllogistick way, as shall be judged most conducive to their improvement —

5. Two of the Students, in rotation, shall every Evening, after prayers, pronounce a piece upon the Stage; and all the members of the College shall meet every Wednesday afternoon in the Hall, at the ringing of the Bell at 2 OClock, to pronounce before the President & Tutors, pieces well committed to memory, that they may receive such corrections in their manner, as shall be judged necessary —

6th. On the last Wednesday in every month, every Student in College shall pronounce publikly on the Stage, memoriter, such an Oration or piece as shall be previously approved by the President, on which occasion the two upper classes shall make use of their own compositions —

7. No student may read any book in the hours of study, excepting the Classics, or such as tend to illustrate the subject matter of his recitation, for the time being —

8. No. one may enter anothers Chamber without knocking and obtaining liberty; nor shall he even do this in study hours, except to do an errand, in which he shall be speedy —

9. Each student shall be duly prepared for, and duly attend on recitations, at such times and places as their Instructors shall appoint, during which no one shall suggest any thing to his Class-Mates, or by any means interrupt their Attention —

10. It is not permitted any one, in the hours of study to speak to another, except in Latin, either in the College, or College Yard —

11. The Senior Class shall attend recitations, and other public exercises, until the second Wednesday in July, on which they shall appear in the Hall to be examined by the President, Fellows, Tutors, or any other Gentlemen of liberal Education, touching their knowledge and proficiency in the learned Languages, the liberal Arts and Sciences, and other qualifications requisite for the Degree of Bachellor in the Arts; and upon approbation they shall not leave the College before they have compleated their necessary preparations for the public Commencement; nor then with-out the Liberty of the President —

12. On the last Wednesday in every quarter there shall be a public examination of the three lower classes on the studies they shall have pursued during that quarter; and if it shall appear that any one has neglected his business, so as not to have made such proficiency in them as his opportunity and abilities would admit of, the President and Tutors may put him upon a conditional standing with his Class, which shall continue to the end of the Year (unless by his better conduct he shall merit an exemption therefrom at a future examination) and then if there appear no hopeful signs of reformation, they may degrade him to a lower class —

Chapter 3d.

Concerning a religious & moral & decent conduct —

1. On ringing of the Bell for morning and evening prayers, all the members of the College shall immediately, without unnecessary noise repair to the hall, and behave with decency, during the time of the exercises —

2. The senior class, when required, shall read a chapter out of the Greek Testament into english before morning prayers, the President or Tutors calling on whom they think proper of the class to perform this duty —

3. Every student shall attend public worship every first day of the week, where he, his parents or Guardians shall think proper; provided that any who do not attend with any officer of instruction, produce vouchers, when demanded, of his steady and orderly attendance —

N.B. Such as regularly and statedly observe the seventh day as a Sabbath, are exempted from the Law; and are only required to abstain from secular employments, which would interrupt their fellow Students —

4. When any student attends public worship at any religious Society whatever, he shall behave with suitable gravity and decency —

5. No student, boarding in commons, is permitted on the first day of the week to go out of the College Yard, unless to public worship; nor those who board in Town except to public worship and to meals; but the whole of the day is to be observed by abstaining from all secular concerns, recreation and diversion. —

6. Agreeably to the Charter of this College, which enacts that Christians of every denomination, shall, without the least molestation, in the peculiarities of their religious principles, enjoy free Liberty, &c.

It is ordered that if any Student of this College shall deny the being of a God, the existence of Virtue & Vice; or that the books of the old and New Testament are of divine authority, or suggest any scruples of that nature, or circulate books of such pernicious tendency; or frequent the company of those who are known to favour such fatal errors; or harrass and disquiet the minds of his fellow Students, respecting any of the peculiarities of their christian faith, by ridicule, sneers, scoffing, Infidel Suggestions, or in any other way; and shall continue obstinate therein after the first & second admonition, he shall be expelled from the College —

Young Gentlemen of the Hebrew Nation are to be exempted from this Law, so far as it relates to the New Testament and its authenticity —

7. If any scholar shall be guilty of Blasphemy, Robbery, fornication, forgery, or any such attrocious crime he shall be forthwith expelled —

8. Every scholar be strictly forbidden to play at cards, or any unlawful Games; — to swear, lye, steal, get drunk, or use obscene or idle words, strike his fellow Students or others; or keep company with persons of a known bad Character; or attend at places of idle or vain Sports —

9. The conduct of the students with respect to morality and good manners, in the times of Vacation, shall be cognizable equally as when present at the College —

10. Every scholar be required to shew all due honour & reverence, both in words & behaviour, to all his superiors, viz, to Parents, Magistrates, Ministers; and, especially to the Trustees, Fellows, President & Tutors of the College; nor shall in any case use any reproachful, reviling, disrespectful or contumacious language; but shall show them all proper tokens of reverence and obedience —

11. No student, excepting those who statedly attend the Friends Meeting, is permitted to wear his hat within the College walls; nor when speaking to, or spoken to by, or is in company with an officer of instruction, unless he be permitted by them to put it on —

12. All due respect shall be paid, by inferiors, to those of a superior standing, by giving them the precedence and choice of seats —

13. Every student be required to treat the Inhabitants of the Town and all others with whom they converse with civility and good manners —

14. No student shall refuse to open the door when he shall hear the stamp of the foot or staff at his door in the entry, which shall be a token that an officer of instruction desires admission, which token every student is forbid to counterfiet, or imitate under any pretence whatever —

15. No one is permitted to make any stay in any room or meddle with any thing in it belonging to the occupant in his absence —

16. No one is permitted to make a practice of receiving company in his room in study hours; or keep spirituous Liquors in his room with-out liberty obtained of the President —

17. No student may at any time make any unnecessary noise or tumult either in his room or in the Entries; but each one shall endeavor to preserve tranquility and decency in words & actions—

18. No one when in anothers room shall meddle with or examine his books and writings —

19. No one is permitted to be absent from collegiate exercises without first rendering his excuse to his instructor, or go out of the College yard, in the time of study without Liberty —

20. If any student shall do damage to the College edefice, or the Goods of others, he shall repair the same; nor shall any attempt to throw anything over or against the College

21. No student is permitted to make use of any boards, timber, or any other materials, boarding to the College Edefice, for any purpose whatever, without first obtaining Liberty of the Conmiittee for the furnishing or repairs of the Edefice —

22. Every student in College shall take a particular care of fire, not carrying it needlessly out of his room in pipes or otherwise; and shall carefully cover or quench his fire when retireing to bed or leaving his room.

23. The chimney of every inhabited room shall be swept at the expence of the occupants, once every year —

24. The senior Class are authorized to detain in the Hall, after evening prayers, such of the under classes as they shall observe violating any of the Laws of College, and there admonish them for such offences; as well as to correct and instruct them in their general Deportment; correcting their manners in such minute particulars of a geenteel carriage and good breeding as does not come within any express written Law of the College, which corrections, &. are to be strictly observed

Chapter. 4.

Concerning the Library —

1. The oldest Tutor, in case of no other Appointment, shall be the Librarian, who shall open the Library once a week, at an hour appointed and attend and deliver out such books as shall be called for by such of the students as are permitted the use of them —

2. All students, except the members of the freshman Class shall be permitted the use of the Library —

3. The following conditions of taking out books shall be strictly regarded; — Each one shall sign a receipt for every book he shall take out, engaging to return it in the like good order with in the time he is permitted the use of it, which shall be four weeks for a Folio; three weeks for a Quarto; two weeks for an Octavo; & one week for a Duodecimo. —

4. In case any book, so taken out, shall be lost, or unnecessarily damaged, the delinquent shall replace it by a new one, within three months, or pay the Librarian double the price which it cost, the Librarian being the judge, in the Case —

5. No student shall lend a book which he has taken out unto another; nor take out more than one book at a time, except Duodecimos, of which he may take two. —

6. Every new, or neatly bound book, shall be covered, so as to defend the binding from injury, during the time of using it —

7. No person shall be allowed to take any book out of the Library with out the knowledge of the Librarian, and the Librarian shall enter, in the receipt the title and size of the book taken out, & the time when taken & returned. —

8. For every book not returned, agreeably to his receipt, the delinquent shall pay for one month, for a Folio, one Shilling, and so in proportion for a longer or shorter time; — Two thirds as much for a Quarto; — half as much for an Octavo, and one quarter the sum for a Duodecimo —

Chapter 5th.

Concerning the rooms in College

1. The senior class shall always have the choice of rooms; — The junior next, & the Sophimore next, except where a student of the lower Classes shall have been at the expence of painting & papering a room; or shall offer to do so, in that case such scholar shall have the preference; and be not only permitted to reside in it during his stay at College; but on leaving the same, shall have the Liberty of

disposing of his property therin to any member of the senior or junior classes, who shall thereby become possessed of the same right —

2. If any scholar shall be absent from College beyond the time allowed him; or shall be guilty of any great misdemeanour, the President at discretion may take away the chamber assgned him, and may dispose of it to another —

3. When a Chamber shall be assigned to a student he shall immediately certify the Steward of all the Damages already done, who shall enter the same in a Book and carry it to the President, in order that he who lived last therin, or did the damages, may be obliged to make restitution.

And during the time that any room shall stand assigned to any one, he (whether present or absent) shall be accountable for all the damages done therein, unless he shall prove that it was done in such a manner, as implies no carelessness of his own —

4. When any Glass shall be broken in the hall, Entry, in any public room, or in any room not inhabited, the expense of mending the same shall be born equally by all the Scholars. —

5. No student when permitted to be absent from College; or when he leaves the same, shall carry away the Keys of his doors; but shall fasten a piece of wood to each key, with his name, and the number of his door theron, and deposit it in the hands of the President or Steward.

Chapter. 6th.

Concerning the Steward and Commons

1. The Steward shall cause all the rooms, inhabited by the Students, who board in commons, together with the Entries, to be swept once pr day; and cause all the beds, in said rooms, to be decently made every fore-noon —

2. The Steward shall furnish three good meals of victuals pr: day, sufficient for those who board in Commons, agreeably, or nearly so, to the following prescriptions —

For Dinners every week, two meals of salt Beef & Pork, with Peas, Beans, Greens, Roots, &c. — For drink good small Beer or Cyder. — Two meals of fresh meat roasted, baked, broiled or fried with proper Sauce or Vegetables. — One meal of Soup & Fragments. — One meal of boiled fresh meat, with proper vegetables & broth. — One meal of salt or fresh Fish, with brown bread for dinner. —

For Breakfast Tea, Coffee, Chocolate, or milk; with Tea or Coffee white Bread, with Butter; with Chocolate or Milk, white Bread without Butter. With Tea Coffee, Chocolate, brown Sugar —

For Supper, milk with hasty Pudding, Rice, Samp, with bread, &c. or Milk, Tea, Coffee, Chocolate, as for Breakfast —

3. The several Articles and provisions abovementioned, especially dinners, are to be diversified & changed, as to their Succession through-out the week, as much as may be convenient & agreeable —

4. All the articles of Provision shall be good, genuine and unadulterated —

5. The meals shall be appointed at stated times; and, the Cookery well, neatly, and decently executed —

6. The Steward shall sit at meals with the Students, unless prevented by company or Business, and exercise the same authority as is customary or needful for the head of a family at his Table —

7. The Steward shall be exemplary in his moral Conduct, and not fail to give Information to the Authority of College against any of the Students who shall transgress any of the College orders and regulations; and for this purpose he, as well as every other Officer of College, shall constantly keep by him a copy of the College Laws —

8. The Students who board in Commons, shall observe order in going into & coming out of the dining room, as of the Hall; and at Table each Class shall sit together in alphabetical order, and while there, shall behave decently, making no unnecessary noise or disturbance, by either abusing the Table Furniture, or ungenerously complaining of the Provisions, &c. Notwithstanding which, should any be dissatisfied, they may mention it decently to the Steward in private, and, if he does not redress any supposed grievances, they may then apply to the President —

9. Those who neglect to attend at the stated Mealtimes, shall forfeit such meals, unless sufficient reasons of absence appear to the Steward, who shall be judge in that case —

10. No allowance shall be made to any Student for absence from Commons for any Term under a week —

11. Whoever shall stay beyond the limitted term of Vacation, or the expiration of the term for which he had liberty to be absent, shall pay his commons Bill to the Steward, in the same manner as though present, unless he shall bring a certificate from some reputable Physician, that his state of health would not permit him to prosecute his Studies; or shall assign such just reasons of his detention as shall be deemed sufficient by, at least, three of the Fellowship & four of the Trustees —

12. The scholars shall all treat the Steward as an officer of College, & his family with all due respect —

13. No scholar shall be permitted to rise to a higher standing, or be admitted to the Honours of the College, who shall have neglected to pay the Bills against him, to the Satisfaction of the Steward.

The Steward shall be permitted to sell to the Students, in the times allowed for Recreation, Cyder, Strong Beer, Small Beer, Candles, Bread, Butter, Sugar, Milk, Tea, Cheese, Coffee, Chocolate & Apples; and any other necessaries which the Students are allowed the use of in the Hours of play, — provided he has the Permission of their Parents or Guardians for so doing; and that they be sold at a reasonable profit, and not in such quantities as may lead them to neglect their Studies. —

14. As a Compensation to the Steward, it is agreed that he be allowed the use of three rooms on the lower Floor, and one, in an upper Story rent free; and while the whole of the rooms are not occupied by the Students, more if he needs them, he paying the rent, which shall be eight Dollars pr: year for each Room. He shall also have the use of both the Cellar-Kitchens, together with sufficient room in the cellar, free from Rent. He shall be permitted the use of the Garden at the South west part of the College Lot, and the Stable at the South East part of it —

15. Every student shall pay for his board in Commons, making his Bed & sweeping his room, pr: week such Sum, or sums as the Corporation shall from time to time direct the Steward to take; also, each scholar shall pay to the Steward four Dollars pr: Quarter Tuition Money —

16. Each student shall pay 6 / pr: Quarter Room rent, for the use of one half a Chamber —

17. The Steward at the close of each quarter, shall make out a regular bill, containing the several quarterly Sums, payable by each Student, with a duplicate thereof; in which shall be charged Fines, the Sums for broken Glass & all other Damages; and shall show both these Bills to the President, which, being by him approved, and one of the Tutors, shall be signed by the President; one of which the President shall deliver to the Steward, and keep the other himself, together with a Bond signed by the Steward, acknowledging the receipt of the other Bill; and engaging himself to be accountable to the President & Faculty, for the whole Sum contained therein; And the Steward shall collect all the money contained in the quarter Bills, and pay out the whole Sum (except for Commons & the Butlers Bill, according to orders given by the President and Faculty —

Chapter. 7.

Of Monitors & the duties of the Freshman Class —

1. A weekly bill shall be kept in rotation, beginning and proceding alphabetically, by all except the senior Class, in which shall be noted, nonattendance at prayers, unbecoming conduct when there, or any breach of the Laws of the College, of which the monitor shall take strict notice —

2. There shall be a quarterly monitor appointed, who shall take the weekly bills, after they are examined; & shall take a particular account of all the transgressions which shall not be excused, & of all the fines which shall be imposed; which bill shall be produced at the quarterly examination before the gentlemen who may attend the same as matter of conviction of those who shall be tardy or deficient; he shall also collect the money for fines & deliver it to the Steward; of which, if not paid, he shall, at the end of his quarter, put the Account into the hands of the Steward —

3. All the money ariseing from fines, shall be converted into Premiums, to be awarded to those who shall excel at the public examinations, always observing that the Premiums of each Class shall be made up of the fines of that Class —

4. In order to perpetuate the infamy of the transgressions of the Laws, all the punishments, excepting pecuniory, publickly inflicted on any delinquent, shall be registered in a book for that purpose, together with an account of the crime for which it was inflicted; and, every Student who shall be recorded therin, as a transgressor, shall be excluded from being chosen by the President, or his Class, to any of the orations at Commencement: however, in consequence of extraordinary & continued reformation, the Authority may erase such censures before the time of choosing Orators —

5. The Freshman Class shall, in rotation, ring the bell (beginning, and proceeding through the Class, in alphabetical order) at all the seasons of ringing it, except for meals, & the recitation of the upper Classes —

6. In the same order the Freshman Class shall kindle a fire seasonably before morning prayers in the room where they may be attended, during the winter season —

Chapter: 8th:

Of Commencements, Degres and Vacations —

1. All scholars who have been regularly admitted into College, and have diligently attended their Studies, & performed the duties prescribed them in the Laws, and made good proficiency in the several branches of Learning pursued in

this College; and after they have given proof of this at the public examination, on the second Wednesday in July, may expect to be honoured with the Degree of Bachelor in the Arts. —

2. All such as shall have applied themselves to their Studies, or any honourable profession in Life for the space of three years from the time of their taking their first Degree, and have been guilty of no gross crime, may expect to receive the honour of a second degree, provided they apply for it one week before Commencement —

3. Every Candidate shall pay the President four Dollars for every degree conferred on him —

4. No Scholar shall have his Degree unless the Steward on the morning of Commencement, or before, shall certify the President that he has paid all his College dues. This Law is to be read publickly in in the hall in the beginning of the Month of July, and on monday before the public Commencement —

5. No student shall presume to exhibit anything at the public Commencement, which has not been previously approved by the President —

6. The times of Vacation shall be from Septr: 6th: to October 20th; — From December 24th: to January 10th; — and from April 21st: to June 1st: —

7. No scholar shall presume to leave College at the time of Vacation, before the Vacation be publicly notified in the Hall ; nor at any other time leave the College, without previously obtaining Liberty from the President —
Chapter. 9th.
Concerning the Authority of College —

1. The legislative Authority of this College is, by the Charter, vested in the President & Fellowship, who have Authority to make & give Sanction to all such Statutes, Laws, Rules & Orders (not repugnant to the Laws of this Government) which they shall think proper for the well ordering the College, which shall also be approved by the Trustees of the College —

2. The executive Authority is vested principally in the President, who, in concurrence with the advice of the Professors & Tutors hath power to rule govern & direct the College, and all matters relating thereto — in concurrence with the advice of the Professors & Tutors hath power to rule govern & direct the College, and all, matters relating thereto —

3. The penalties annexed to the foregoing Laws, where not expressed, shall be proportioned to the Nature, circumstances, & Agravations, attending the several offences – After private admonition, pecuniary Penalties shall be from two Pence

Lawful money, to three Shillings. The highest & last, excepting absence from the College, shall be six Shillings or a Dollar; — after which they shall be publicly admonished before the College & Corporation, which proving ineffectual, the offenders shall be degraded if judged necessary; — for the last & concluding punishment, they shall be totally & forever expelled from the College —

4. And whereas the Statutes are few & general, there must necessarily be lodged with the President & Tutors a discretional, or parental Authority; & therefore, where no Statute is particularly & expressly provided for a case that may occur, they are to exercise this discretionary authority according to the known customs of similar institutions, & the plain, general rules of the moral Law. And, in general the penalties are to be of the more humane kind, such as are at once expressive of compassion to the offender, & indignation at the offence. Such as are adapted to work upon the nobler principles of humanity, & to move the more honourable Springs of good order and submission to Government —

5. And in case any person or persons shall judge themselves injured by any heavy punishment inflicted by the President & Tutors, such as expulsion, dismission or Rustication for a year, they have Liberty to bring a Petition to the Corporation for relief therin, setting forth the grounds & reasons of their petition, provided the persons apprehending themselves to be injured, their Parents or Guardians shall previously have desired, a rehearing before the President & Tutors —

Finis Legum

1.4: Finances of the Colonial Colleges

Colonial colleges reflected their standing as one of the most formal and privileged organizations of their time and place by keeping detailed records of annual revenues and expenses. It was no less than a requirement of fiduciary responsibility for trustees of the academic corporation. Since colleges enjoyed tax exemptions on real property and income, governors and the public from time to time expected accounting for the commonwealth. The problem for researchers today is that many ledgers were lost in fires and floods. Surviving financial documents are often fragmentary. Hence, we are indebted to the original and exhaustive reconstruction of financial records from sev-

Jesse Brundage Sears, "Finances of the Early Colleges," in *Philanthropy in the History of American Higher Education* (Washington, DC: U.S. Government Printing Office, 1922) pp. 16–19.

eral colonial colleges which Jesse Brundage Sears undertook. His detailed profiles of trends and practices were published in his 1922 book, *Philanthropy in the History of American Higher Education.* In addition to summarizing financial trends, Sears also provided annotations about terms and customs of the seventeenth and eighteenth centuries which help to make the collegiate records comprehensible for scholars in the twenty-first century.

Sears's 1922 study, of course, is *not* a primary source in the strict definition of the term. It is now historic in its own right, having remained useful for ninety years because it has brought together disparate documents on a difficult topic that is both time-consuming and expensive to pursue. Note, for example, that there have been few intensive, original studies of colonial college finance. Margery Somers Foster's 1962 book, *Out of Smalle Beginnings . . . An Economic History of Harvard College in the Puritan Period*, endures as a model of scholarship. Unfortunately, in the half century since the publication of Foster's remarkable book, few historians have completed comparable studies for other colleges. Hence, Sears's 1922 profile persists as a good introduction to reconstructing the finances of the colonial colleges.

Finances of the Early Colleges
1. Scarcity of Money.

Down to 1693 we had but one college, that founded at Cambridge in 1635. There is probably nowhere available to-day a complete record of all the early gifts to Harvard, but what have been brought together here will doubtless give a fairly satisfactory exhibit of the nature and extent of the earliest philanthropy devoted to higher education in this country.

There is one thing so characteristic of the early gifts to all the colonial colleges that it must receive brief notice at the outset. That is, the size and kind of gifts. Harvard records the receipt "of a number of sheep bequeathed by one man, of a quantity of cotton cloth, worth 9 shillings, presented by another of a pewter flagon, worth 10 shillings, by a third, of a fruit dish, a sugar spoon, a silver-tipt jug, one great salt, and some small trecher salt, by others." From Yale's early history the sentiment attaching to the words: "I give these books for founding a college in Connecticut," pronounced by each of the trustees as he placed his little contribution upon the table, could not be spared, and before a charter had been granted a formal gift of the "glass and nails which should be necessary to erect a college and hall" had been made, Eleazar Wheelock, the founder and first president of Dartmouth, in a letter replying to criticisms of the "plainness of the surroundings" at the college, says: "As to the college, it owns but one (tablecloth), that was lately given by a generous lady in Connecticut, and of her own manufacture," and again in a letter to the Honorable Commissioners for Indian Affairs, etc., he says, after indicating the impossible financial condition in which the college finds itself: "I have, with the assistance of a number of those who have contributed their old put-off clothing, supported them (the scholars) along hitherto." Doubtless similar examples could be taken from the subscription lists that yielded relatively large amounts to Princeton, Queen's, Brown, and William and Mary if these were extant.

In these gifts there is reflected much of the simplicity of the social and economic life of that time. Actual money was scarce, as shown by the repeated issues of currency by the various Colonies, hence such gifts as Dartmouth's sawmills and blacksmith shop and Harvard's printing press entered most naturally and effectively into the making of colleges in those days.

2. Use of the Subscription Method.

These colleges were all active in gathering funds by the subscription plan both in England and in America. Princeton received a subscription of £1,000 proclamation, given in produce and money, in the southern Colonies in 1769, another £1,000 from Boston in the same year, and £2,000 in England. Brown received $4,500 by subscription in England and Ireland in 1764. Blair brought home from England £2,500 which he had gathered by subscription for William and Mary in 1693. Dartmouth collected £10,000 in England in 1769, while King's and Pennsylvania shared equally a subscription fund of £10,000 gathered in England. These are only the most striking instances of the use of this method of collecting the gifts of the people. Through the churches this method was repeatedly used and frequently the colonial court or the town officials would name a day on which a subscription for the college would be asked from every citizen.

3. Few Large Gifts.

In that day of small gifts a few names of great benefactors stand out. Whatever the "moiety" of Harvard's estate was, it was a princely sum in the year 1638 for a college with one or two teachers and a half dozen students. This was the first great gift to education in America, and it is worthy of note that it was not tied up with conditions which might make it useless to the Harvard College of the future. It was given by request to the college outright, and constituted half of the fortune and the entire library of one of the wealthiest and most noted men in New England.

The immediate influence of this was great, and is well recorded by the historians of the college, Quincy and Peirce. During the next few decades several gifts of £100 were received, and in 1650 Richard Saltonstall, of England, gave "to the college" goods and money worth 320 pounds sterling. In 1681 Sir Matthew Holworthy bequeathed "to be disposed of by the directors as they shall judge best for the promotion of learning and promulgation of the Gospel" £1,000. The Hon. William Stoughton erected a building in 1699 which cost £1,000 Massachusetts currency. These are the large gifts of the seventeenth century, with the exception of the gift of William and Mary, of England, to the college of Virginia.

During the next century Thomas Hollis established a professorship of divinity at Harvard (1721). In his "orders" he asks "that the interest of the funds be used, £10 annually for help to a needy student for the ministry – as many of these as the funds will bear." He reserves the right to sanction all appointments during his lifetime, then leaves it to the "President and Fellows of Harvard College," and asks "that none be refused on account of his belief and practice of adult baptism." The conditions which he places upon this, the first professorship established in America by private donation, are of interest. These are his words: "I order and appoint a Professor of Divinity, to read lectures in the Hall of the College unto the students; the said Professor to be nominated and appointed from time to time by the President and Fellows of Harvard College, and that the Treasurer pay to him forty pounds per annum for his service, and that when choice is made of a fitting person, to be recommended to me for my approbation, if I be yet living."

In that day of fierce theological controversies these seem to be very liberal conditions.

A few years later Hollis established a professorship of mathematics and natural philosophy. In all, his donations total over £5,000, a sum which far exceeded any single gift to education in America up to that time. Aside from books and goods the purposes of all his gifts were stipulated, but in such general terms and, as his letters show, so fully in terms of the wishes of the president and overseers, that it constitutes an example of educational philanthropy that is worthy of note.

Madam Mary Saltonstall, who bequeathed £1,000 in 1730 for educating young men "of bright parts and good diligence for service of the Christian Church"; Thomas Hancock, who founded the professorship of Hebrew and other oriental languages in 1764 with a gift of £1,000; John Alford, whose executors, acting in accordance with his wish that his money should be used to aid "pious and charitable purposes," gave £1,300 to establish a professorship "of some particular science of public utility"; Nicholas Boylston, who bequeathed £1,500 for the support of a professor of rhetoric in 1772; and Dr. Ezekiel Hersey, whose gift established a professorship of anatomy and physic in 1772, are other pre-revolutionary names which figure on the list of Harvard's greatest benefactors.

At the Collegiate School of Connecticut the names Elihu Yale and Rev. Dr. George Berkeley, with gifts of £500 and £400, respectively; at the College of New Jersey the names of Tennent and Davy, of England, with a gift of over £2,000; at King's the name of Joseph Murray with a bequest of his library and his estate worth £9,000 in 1762; and at William and Mary the names of James Blair and Robert Boyle give us other instances of educational philanthropy on a liberal scale in the colonial days.

4. Gifts from Towns, Churches, and Societies.

In addition to these gifts from private individuals there is frequent evidence of support coming from towns, churches, and societies. In 1764 the town of Boston collected £476 by subscription, which it gave to Harvard to repair the loss occasioned by the destruction of Harvard Hall by fire. Nine other towns made smaller contributions to the same end, while two years previously 44 towns had made contributions to the college. Wheelock received funds from public collections taken in several eastern towns between 1762 and 1765 which were of great value to his struggling school, soon to be known as Dartmouth College. In the cases of Princeton, Queen's, King's, and Brown the donations from churches were large and frequent.

The Society for the Propagation of the Gospel in Foreign Parts found the colleges appropriate agencies through which to operate in the Colonies. As early as 1714 reference is made to a gift of books to the Yale library; in 1747 the society made a large donation of books to Harvard, and £100 in money in 1764. From the same society King's received £500 sterling and in 1762 a library of 1,500 books. The society also assisted in getting a collection made in England which raised nearly £6,000 sterling for the college in 1762. The Society for Propagating the Gospel in New England and parts adjacent gave to Harvard 1,101 volumes and £300 sterling to repair the loss of its library in 1764. The Edinburgh Society for Promoting Religious Knowledge presented Harvard with some books in 1766, and the Society for Propagating Christian Knowledge, in Scotland, gave £30 for the purchase of books in 1769.

5. Gifts of Books, Buildings, and Land.

It is noticeable in the early years that many gifts of books were made to the colleges. However strongly the titles of the books may suggest the religious and theological nature of higher education, in those days such gifts were of the greatest importance when both the bounds and the methods of knowledge lay almost wholly within books alone.

There is an occasional gift of a building, and frequent reference is made to gifts of land. During the colonial period Harvard received from towns and individuals over 2,000 acres; Yale received over 1,000 acres, including 300 acres from the general assembly; King's received 5 acres in the heart of New York City, and 34,000 acres more from the State which were lost to the college and the State as well at the close of the Revolution; Dartmouth received 400 acres from proprietors of the town of Hanover; the College of New Jersey received 210 acres from the town and people of Princeton; and a large portion of Queen's campus was the gift of a private citizen. Gifts of real estate were for many years of little productive value however; so the chief support had to be money or something that could be exchanged at any time.

Analysis of Gifts to the Four Colonial Colleges.

To get the full meaning of the philanthropy of this period, however, complete lists of all the gifts to Harvard, Yale, King's, and the College of New Jersey, four of the nine colonial colleges, have been made and appear in tables 3, 4, 5, and 6.

Remembering that it is not the absolute amount of a gift, but rather what the gift will purchase, that measures its value, we may ask, first: What was the size of the problem the philanthropy had undertaken and what did education cost?

1. Size of the Colonial Colleges.

The numbers of students attending these colleges can be judged by the number of their graduates. Harvard rarely if ever had over 100 students before the year 1700, and at no time in the colonial period did she have over 350 or 400 students, while Yale and King's had fewer still. Pennsylvania graduated in all only 135 students before 1776, Brown 60, and Dartmouth 31.

The teaching staff was also small. The president's administrative duties were insignificant, his chief function being that of instructor. Before 1720 Harvard's faculty consisted of a president and from 1 to 4 tutors. At Yale the president was assisted by from 1 to 4 tutors, rarely more than 3, before the year 1755. After 1720 Harvard's faculty gradually increased to 9; Yale's to 8; and King's to 11. In the case of King's a much larger percentage were from the start of professorial rank.

Thus, judged by the size of student body and faculty, the actual work done in the colonial colleges was small, and great sums of money were not needed.

2. The Cost of a College Education.

The cost of a college education at Harvard in its early days is shown in an old account book from the period 1649–50 to 1659, from which it appears that for those graduating from 1653 to 1659 the total expense ranged from £30 25s. 1 ¼ d. to £61 11s. 8 ¾ d., or from about $100 to about $200 for four years' residence in college.

An itemized account of a student, Thomas Graves, of the class of 1656, by quarters, shows that he paid about 32s. for tuition. His first quarter's expenses appear as follows:

	Pounds.	S.	D.	Qr.
8, 10, 54 Commones and siznges..................................	2	8	9	2
Tuition, 8 s; study, rente, and bed, 4 s; fyer...............				
and candelle 2 s	14	0	0	
Fower loode of wood..	17	4	0	

The other three quarters' expenses were similar to this. In 1797 this cost, according to an account of Judge Daniel Appleton White, given in volume 6 of the Massachusetts Historical Society Proceedings, page 272, would have been about $480 for the four years.

Students' bills were often paid in butter, rye, malt, hog, lamb, eggs, etc. At Princeton, Maclean tells us that a student's entire expenses in 1761 were £25 6s. proclamation money.

A fairly complete account of the tuition cost at Yale, as set forth in Table 2, data for which were gathered from Dexter's Annals, shows the tuition not to have been much different at the beginning from the above account of tuition cost at Harvard a half century earlier.

Table 2. Cost of education at Yale College.

Date.	Tuition.	Room.	Board.	President's salary.	Salary of tutor.
	Shillings.			*C.P.*[1]	*C.P.*[1]
1701..	30	.....	.....	120	50
1704..	30	.....	.....	.....	50
1712..	30	.....	.....	100	.....
1718..	30	.....	.....	140	.....
1719..	.....	20s.	4s. 4d.	.....	.....
1725..	30	.....	.....	.....	.....
1726..	40	.....	4s. 8d.	140	.....
1727..	50	.....	.....	212	65
1728..	50	.....	.....	250	60
1729..	50	.....	.....	300	65
1734..	50	.....	.....	300	65
1737..	60	.....	.....	.....	.....
1738..	60	.....	.....	300	.....
1740..	60	.....	.....	320	.....
1742..	24	.....	.....	.....	.....
1745..	17	.....	.....	.....	.....
1748..	17	.....	.....	.....	.....
1749..	20	(22 to 26s.)		.....	.....
1754..	24	3s. or 4s. 8d.	.....	.....	.....
1755..	24	.....	.....	.....	.....
1759..	26	.....	.....	.....	.....
1764..	30	.....	.....	.....	.....
1767..	.....	.....	.....	200	.....
1768..	.....	.....	.....	200	(2)
1769..	48	6s.	.....	.....	.....
1777..	.....	.....	.....	160	.....

[1]In country pay 120 equaled about £60 sterling or one-third.
[2]£57 6s. 8d.

At Dartmouth in 1773 tuition and board together were £20 a year. At William and Mary the tuition in 1724 was "20s. entrance and 20s. a year for pupilage for each scholar." A woman offered to "undertake the keeping of the college table at the rate of £11 per annum for each scholar, with the other advantages allowed to Mr. Jackson." At Princeton tuition was £3 in 1754, £4 in 1761, £5 in 1773, and board in 1761 was £15 a year, according to Maclean.

Reference to the prices of a few well-known commodities will help one to appreciate the apparently small gifts which we are to examine. In 1641 common labor was worth 1s. 6d. per day, the next year corn was worth 2s. 6d. and wheat and barley 4s. per bushel. In 1670 wheat was worth 5s., corn 3s.; the year following labor was worth from 1s. 3d. to 1s. 8d. In 1704 corn was worth 2s. and wheat 3s. 8d. In 1727 wheat was worth 6s. 6d. to 8s. In 1752 corn was worth 4s. and wheat 6s. In 1776 corn was 3s. and wheat 6s. 8d.

3. Salaries of College Professors.

One further item of interest in this connection is the salary of the teaching staff. This was the chief item of expenditure in every college and is a fair index to the value of any gift or to the value of the funds available for the use of the college at any time. As shown in Table 2, Yale's president received from £60 to £300, while the salary of a tutor was very much less. Maclean thinks that Princeton's president did not receive over £50 annually before 1754. In that year his salary was fixed at £150 proclamation, rising to £200 proclamation in 1757 and to £400 in 1766, only to be reduced again to £250 with the usual perquisites, and finally to £200 in 1767. In 1768 it rose again to £350 proclamation, or about £206 sterling. In 1752 MacLean states the salary of a tutor to have been £20 sterling and £66 in 1767. The three professors at Princeton in 1767 received: Divinity, £175; mathematics, £150; language and logic, £125. In 1654 the overseers of Harvard College offered Rev. Mr. Charles Channing the presidency of the college at a salary of £100 per annum. From Judge Sewell's diary the salary in 1698 appears to have been £200.

At the close of the colonial period Harvard's president was receiving £300, a professor about £200, and the librarian £60. In October, 1766, a committee of the colonial assembly of Connecticut reported that Yale ought to have:

1. A president, at £150 per annum.
2. A professor of divinity, at £113 6s. 8d. per annum.

3. A senior tutor, at £65 1s. 4d. per annum.
4. Three junior tutors, at £51 1s. 4d. per annum.

Salaries at William and Mary were little different. President Blair, the first president, received £150 at first, and later only £100, increasing in 1755 to £200. During the same period a professor received £80 and fees of 20s. per student. In 1729 each professor received £150, but no fees. In 1770 the president received £200, each of two divinity professors £200, two other professors each £100, master of grammar school £150, first usher £75, second usher £40.

When one considers that the entire expenditures of Harvard for the year 1777 were but £1,086 18s. 2d. and that the college had but £386 18s. 2d. to pay it with, the residue being paid by assessments on the scholars for study-rent, tuition, and other necessary charges, amounting *communibus annis* to about £700; or that the average annual income of William and Mary College during the decade 1754 to 1764 was £1,936 14s. 6 ¾ d., these salaries appear relatively high.

CHAPTER TWO

Creating the "American Way" in Higher Education
College Building, 1785 to 1860

Creation of the new United States of America ushered in a bold, new—and frightening—world of institutions and governance. Nowhere was this combination of optimism and concern more evident than in the creation of colleges and universities. In a new nation that gave its federal government scant jurisdiction over or involvement in education, college building was a state and local endeavor. The serious purpose and good intentions of college building commitment were shown in the mottos among the newly founded institutions:

Transylvania University: *In Lumine Ilo Tradimus Lumen* (In That Light, We Pass on the Light)

Bowdoin College: *Ut Aquila Versus Coelum* (As an Eagle Toward the Sky)

University of North Carolina: *Lux Libertas* (Light and Liberty)

University of South Carolina: *Emollit mores nec sinit esse feros* (Learning humanizes character and does not permit it to be cruel)

Amherst College: *Terras Irradient* (Let Them Give Light to the World)

University of Michigan: *Artes, scientia, veritas* (The arts, knowledge, truth)

The states were generous in granting charters to various petitioning religious or civic groups—but markedly frugal in their funding of the new institutions. Legislatures imposed few taxes that would provide stable funding for public education at any level. Only in America would one find a flourishing of state-granted charters for colleges and universities with few provisions for elementary and secondary schooling. Testimony to this American optimism in higher education was the subsequent extension into charters for constituencies heretofore denied access to higher education—namely, women—along with various ethnic and religious denominations. Charters from state governments provided a license to proceed—without much assurance of state support. As such, higher education as a growing, innovative enterprise mirrored the spirit and unregulated character of business and other ventures in the enticing national environment; during the first half of the nineteenth century, it was marked by a high rate of attrition, mortality, and mergers. The motto for a group seeking to found a new college might have been translated into English as "Good Luck—and Fat Chance!"

2.1: A Charter for a New State University: The University of Georgia Charter (1785)

This charter is a model of serious commitment to genuine educational values. It is especially remarkable in that it was a voluntary initiative undertaken in a new state whose immediate concerns hardly required such thoughtful investment in higher learning. The nascent state universities faced a new situation, namely, the power to grant charters—an act that previously had been under the jurisdiction of the monarchy of Great Britain or colonial governments. With little if any provision for the federal government to be involved in founding or funding educational institutions, state governments were a new source of charters for colleges and universities. In addition to the charter's opening emphasis on education characterized by civility and the public good, the University of Georgia founders incorporated novel features, such as establishing the state university as the linchpin of any present or future statewide educational system. Minds and morals, not profits or economic development, were foremost among university advocates' priorities. This inclination was reinforced in its motto: *Et docere et rerum exquirere causas*—translated from Latin to English as "To teach, to serve, and to inquire into the nature of things."

One complication of this new arrangement was that state governments had great discretion in how to provide funding—and how much—for their new state universities. In most cases appropriations were sporadic, with grants of land or the annual proceeds from a state lottery being more palatable to legislatures than were recurring monetary subsidies based on tax revenues. Little wonder, then, that the new state universities' lofty goals faced a wide gulf owing to financial uncertainties and shortfalls.

The University of Georgia Charter (1785). Reprinted by permission of the University of Georgia Archives and with special thanks for permission from the *Georgia Review*.

By the Representatives of the Freemen of the State of Georgia in General Assembly and by the Authority of the Same.

An Act for the more full and complete Establishment of a public seat of Learning in this State

As it is the distinguishing happiness of free governments that civil Order should be the Result of choice and not necessity, and the common wishes of the People become the Laws of the Land, their public prosperity and even existence very much depends upon suitably forming the minds and morals of their Citizens. When the Minds of people in general are viciously disposed and unprincipled and their Conduct disorderly, a free government will be attended with greater Confusions and with Evils more horrid than the wild, uncultivated State of Nature. It can only be happy where the public principles and Opinions are properly directed and their Manners regulated. This is an influence beyond the Stretch of Laws and punishments and can be claimed only by Religion and Education. It should therefore be among the first objects of those who wish well to the national prosperity to encourage and support the principles of Religion and morality, and early to place the youth under the forming hand of Society that by instruction they may be moulded to the love of Virtue and good Order. Sending them abroad to other countries for their education will not answer these purposes, - is too humiliating an acknowledgment of the Ignorance or Inferiority of our own, and will always be the Cause of so great foreign attachments that upon principles of policy it is not admissible. This Country in the times of our common danger and distress found such Security in the principles and abilities which wise regulations had before established in the minds of our countrymen, that our present happiness joined to pleasing prospects should conspire to make us feel ourselves under the strongest obligation to form the youth, the rising hope of our Land to render the like glorious & essential Services to our country. And whereas for the great purpose of internal education, divers allotments of land have, at different times, been made, particularly by the Legislature at their Session in July One thousand seven hundred and eighty three, and February One thousand seven hundred and eighty four, all of which my be comprehended and made the basis of one general and complete establishment.

Therefore the Representatives of the Freemen of the State of Georgia in general Assembly met this twenty seventh day of January in the Year of our Lord One thousand seven hundred & eighty five enact, ordain & declare, and by these presents, it is Enacted, Ordained, and Declared

1st The general superintendence and regulation of the Literature of the State and in particular of the public seat of learning, shall be committed and entrusted to the Governor & Council, the Speaker of the house of Assembly, and the Chief Justice of the State for the time being, who shall, ex officio, compose one board, denominated The Board of Visitors hereby vested with all the powers of visitation to see that the intent of this institution is carried into effect, and John Houston, James Habersham, William Few, Joseph Clay, Abraham Baldwin, William Houston, Nathan Brownson, John Habersham, Abiel Holmes, Jenkin Davis, Hugh Lawson, William Glascock, and Benjamin Talliaferro esquires who shall compose another board, denominated The Board of Trustees. These two boards united, or a majority of each of them shall compose the Senatus Academicus of the University of Georgia.

2nd All Statutes, laws and Ordinances for the Government of the University shall be made, and enacted by the two boards united or a majority of each of them, subject always to be laid before the General Assembly, as often as required, and to be repealed, or disallowed, as the General Assembly shall think proper.

3rd Property vested in the University shall never be sold, without the joint concurrence of the two boards, and by act of the Legislature; but the Leasing farming & managing of the property of the University for its constant support shall be the business of the board of Trustees. For this purpose they are hereby constituted a body corporate, and politic, by the name of Trustees Of The University of Georgia: by which they shall have perpetual succession, and shall and may be a person in Law, capable to plead, and be impleaded, defend, and be defended, answer, and be answered unto, also to have, take, possess, acquire, purchase or otherwise receive Lands, tenements, hereditaments, goods, Chattels, or other estates, and the same to lease, use, manage, or improve for the good, and benefit of said University, and all property given, or granted to or by the Government of this State for the advancement of learning in general, is hereby vested in such Trustees in Trust as herein described.

4th As the appointment of a person to be the President and head of the University is one of the first and most important concerns, on which its respect, and usefulness greatly depend, the board of Trustees shall first examine, and nominate, but the Appointment of the President shall be by the two boards jointly, who shall also have the power of removing him from Office, for misdemeanor unfaithfulness or incapacity.

5th There shall be a stated annual meeting of the Senatus Academicus at the

University, or at any other place, or time to be appointed by themselves, at which the Governor of the State, or in his absence the President of Council shall preside, their records to be kept by the Secretary of the University.

6th As the affairs, and business of the University may make more frequent Meetings of the Trustees necessary, The President and two of the members are impowered to appoint a meeting of the board, notice always to be given to the rest, or letters left at the usual places of their abode, at least fourteen days before said meeting, seven of the Trustees thus convened shall be a legal Meeting, in case of the Death absence or incapacity of the President, the senior Trustee shall preside, the Majority of the Members present shall be considered a Vote of the whole, and where the Members are divided, the President shall have a casting Vote;

Provided always that nothing done, at these special meetings, shall have any force, or efficacy after the rising of the then next annual Meeting of the Trustees.

7th The Trustees shall have the power, of filling up all Vacancies of their own board, and appointing Professors, Tutors, Secretary, Treasurers, Steward, and any other Officers which they may think necessary, and the same to discontinue, or remove as they may think fit, but not without seven of their Number, at least, concurring in such Act.

8th The Trustees shall prescribe the Course of public Studies, appoint the Salaries of the different Officers, form and use a public Seal, adjust, and determine the expenses, and adopt such regulations, not otherwise provided for, which the good of the University may render necessary.

9th All Officers appointed to the instruction, and government of the University, shall be of the Christian Religion, and within three months after they enter upon the execution of their Trust, shall publicly take the Oath of Allegiance and Fidelity, and the Oaths of office prescribed in the Statutes of the University the President, before the Governor or President of Council, and all other Officers, before the President of the University.

10th The President, Professors, Tutors, students and all Officers and Servants of the University whose Office requires their constant attendance shall be and they are hereby excused Military Duty and from all other such like Duties and services; And all Lands and other property of the University is hereby exempted from taxation.

11th The Trustees shall not exclude any person of any religious denomination, whatsoever, from free, and equal liberty, and advantages of education, or from any of the Liberties Priviledges and Immunities of the University in his education, on account of his or their speculative sentiments in Religion or being of different Religious Profession.

12ᵗʰ The President of the University, with consent of the Trustees, shall have power to give, and confer all such honors, degrees & licenses as are usually conferred in Colleges, or Universities, and shall always preside at the Meeting of the Trustees & at all the public exercises of the University.

13ᵗʰ The Senatus Academicus at their stated annual meetings shall consult, & advise, not only upon the Affairs of the University, but also to remedy the Defects, and advance the Interests of Literature through the State in general. For this purpose it shall be the business of the Members, previous to their Meeting, to obtain an acquaintance with the State, and regulations of the Schools, and places of education in their respective Counties, that they may thus be possessed of the whole, and have it lie before them for mutual Assistance, and deliberation. Upon this Information they shall recommend what kind of Schools, and Academies shall be instituted, agreably to the Constitution, in the several parts of the State, and prescribe what branches of Instruction shall be taught, and inculcated in each. They shall also examine, and recommend the Instructors to be imployed in them, or appoint persons for that purpose. The President of the University, as often as the duties of his station will permit, and some of the Members, at least once in a year, shall visit them, and examine into their Order and performances.

All public schools – instituted or to be supported by funds or public monies in this State shall be considered as parts or members of the University and shall be under the foregoing directions and regulations.

Whatsoever public measures are necessary to be adopted, for accomplishing these great and important designs, the Trustees shall from time to time, represent, and lay before the General Assembly.

All laws and ordinances heretofore passed in any-wise contrary to the true intent, and meaning of the premises, and hereby repealed, and declared to be null and void.

In Full Testimony, and confirmation of this Charter, ordinance and Constitution and all the articles therein contained, the Representatives of the freemen of the State of Georgia in general Assembly hereby Order, that this Act shall be signed by Honble Joseph Habersham Esquire Speaker of the House of Assembly, and Sealed with the public Seal of this State, and the same, or the enrollment thereof in the Records of the State, shall be good and effectual in Law.

To Have and to Hold the powers, privileges, and immunities, and all and singular, the premises herein given, or which are meant, mentioned, or intended to be hereby given to the said boards of Visitors, and Trustees, and to their successors in Office for-ever.

Joseph Habersham, Speaker

2.2: Founding State Universities: The Great Bicentennial Debate, 1785 to 1985

State universities are justifiably central to state pride. No wonder that such historic state universities as the University of Georgia and the University of North Carolina take seriously their founding dates—and bragging rights for such anniversaries as the bicentennial. On balance this is healthy and good for the entire nation, as it reminds institutions new and old of the importance of heritage—and the historic missions of our colleges and universities. For all the rivalries and even animosities among the states and their flagship universities, the tensions are held in check, civility prevails, and all states reaffirm the American commitment to investment in higher education as a public good. Perhaps intercollegiate athletics have provided a safety valve of sorts in which each year institutional rivalries are renewed and respected on the gridiron or basketball court—and not on the battlefield or in the courtroom. Illustrative of this American accommodation is that it has become customary for governors of rival state universities to wager one another distinctive state products, with the governer of the winning state university, for example, taking home a home-grown agricultural product while leaving the governor of the losing state university to eat crow—at least until the game in the coming year!

The University of North Carolina is making big plans to celebrate its 200th birthday in 1995, and officials there are billing the festivities as the "bicentennial of the founding of American public higher education."

Meanwhile, the University of Georgia has been celebrating the bicentennial of American public higher education for the past 17 months. Georgia officials are careful to note, though, that what they are actually commemorating is the bicentennial of the university's charter. Sixteen years passed before Georgia opened its doors to students in 1801, according to Thomas G. Dyer, who, in addition to his

Jean Evangelauf, "Where Did U.S. Public Higher Education Begin? Georgia and North Carolina Claim the Honor," *Chronicle of Higher Education* (October 23, 1985). Reprinted by permission of The YGS Group.

responsibilities as professor of history and education and associate vice-chancellor for academic affairs, is in charge of Georgia's bicentennial celebration.

The University of North Carolina was chartered in 1789, and its early leaders laid the cornerstone of Old East – "the first public university building in America" – in 1793. In 1795, Hinton James – "the first public university student in America" – started his studies. "Georgia has been celebrating a piece of paper," says Ted Bonus, North Carolina's director of public information. "We like to celebrate the teacher and the student."

Carolina's Motto: North Carolina intends to celebrate its charter, too, but Mr. Bonus thinks that Georgia's bicentennial implies, to the casual observer, at least, that the university has been in continuous operation for 200 years. "Here in North Carolina," he says, "our state motto is 'To be rather than to seem . . .'"

Georgia's Mr. Dyer holds that piece of paper in greater esteem. "The charter was extremely important in our state, and for American higher education generally," he says. Of his rival, Mr. Dyer says: "We regard ourselves as a sister institution of North Carolina. We admire it. It's a great university."

The government of the United States has weighed in on the side of Georgia and its "piece of paper." The National Center for Education Statistics, which keeps tabs on such things, ranks Georgia as the 23rd oldest operating university in the nation. North Carolina holds the 28th slot. Four public institutions are older than Georgia, but they started as private colleges. Despite that, North Carolina considers the arrival of Hinton James to Old East the true founding of public higher education.

"It's like your birthday," Mr. Bonus explains. "Do you celebrate it on the day you were born, or on that marvelous date of creation some nine months before?"

2.3: Philanthropy and Student Financial Aid: The American Education Society (1815)

Highly organized, systematic student financial aid has a long history in our nation, starting with the colonial colleges and then flourishing in the early nineteenth century of the new United States. The impetus came from private, voluntary associations—not from the state or federal government. The American Educational Society's (AES)

Eliphalet Pearson, *Constitution & Address of the American Society for Educating Pious Youth* (Boston, 1816).

scholarship program, launched in 1815, was both a pioneer and a model in focused, effective student aid. The AES scholarship fund provided generous funding that made going to college accessible to academically able yet impoverished young men. The reciprocal effect was that AES scholarship funds helped a constituency work to achieve its goal of fostering a sustained flow of college-educated young men into the learned profession of Protestant ministry, with a pledge to serve as assigned missionaries. Between 1815 and 1835 the AES funded on average more than one thousand college students per year—often constituting between 10 and 15 percent of college student enrollments nationwide. This model of funding students who then agreed to serve in designated professional fields and underserved geographic areas has been used in the twentieth century by the federal government in such fields as medicine, health care, law, and teaching.

Taking into serious consideration the deplorable condition of the inhabitants of these United States, the greater part of whom, as appears from authentic documents and well supported estimates, are either destitute of competent religious instruction, or exposed to the errors and enthusiasm of unlearned men, we, whose names are underwritten, do hereby, in the fear of God and love of man, form ourselves into a Society for the benevolent purposing of aiding, and of exciting others to aid, indigent young men of talents and hopeful piety, in acquiring a learned and competent education for the Gospel Ministry, upon the principles and in the manner following, viz.

VII. Qualified candidates for this charity may be aided in each of the several stages of preparatory education for the ministry. But, except in very singular cases, no applicant shall be assisted, even in the first stage, who is not fifteen years of age; nor in either stage, shall any candidate receive assistance, who shall not produce, from serious and respectable characters, unequivocal testimonials of real indigence, promising talents, and hopeful piety; nor shall any person be continued on this foundation, whose Instructor or Instructors shall not annual exhibit to the Directors satisfactory evidence, that in point of genius, diligence, literary progress, morals, and piety, he is a proper character to receive this sacred charity; in addition to which, each beneficiary, after his admission into any College, shall annually exhibit to the Directors a written declaration, that it continues to be his serious purpose, if his life be spared, to devote that life to the gospel ministry.

IX. If any person, who has been assisted by the Society, with a view to the

gospel ministry, shall not devote himself to that work; he shall within a reasonable time refund the sum, expended for his education, with lawful interest for the
same, whenever required by the Directors.

2.4: Higher Education for Women: Charter for Mount-Holyoke Female Seminary (1836)

Access and admission to college for women represents a historic breakthrough that
has changed for the better the composition and character of higher education in the
United States on all fronts and by all counts. This one-page, handwritten document
is deceptive in its strength, energy, and innovation. It also demonstrates an American
approach to expanding educational and professional opportunities—separate but not
necessarily equal—to such underserved constituencies according to gender, religion,
race, and ethnicity. The college's motto captures its distinctive educational mission,
quoting from Psalms 144:12: "That our daughters may be as corner stones, polished
after the similitude of a palace."

A good source to track the institutional innovation and expansion of colleges for
women is Helen Lefkowitz Horowitz's 1984 book, *Alma Mater: Design and Experience
in the Women's Colleges from Their Nineteenth-Century Beginnings to the 1930s*. Against
all odds, the founders and pioneers at Mount Holyoke and its subsequent sister institutions pursued academic excellence with pragmatic innovation. Their educational gains
were achieved with great difficulty and often begrudgingly from established groups
in government and civil society. As such, Mount Holyoke was a pioneering institution
truly in the American grain.

Commonwealth of Massachusetts

In the Year of our Lord one thousand eight hundred and thirty-six

An Act to incorporate Mount-Holyoke Female Seminary.

Be it enacted by the Senate and the House of Representatives in General Court
assembled and by the authority of the same, that William Bowdoin, John Todd,
Joseph D. Condit, David Choate, and Samuel Williston, their associates and successors be and are hereby incorporated by the name of the Trustees of the Mount-
Holyoke Female Seminary, to be established in South-Hadley in the County of

An Act to Incorporate Mount-Holyoke Female Seminary (Boston: Commonwealth of Massachusetts,
1836). Reprinted by permission of the Archives of Mount Holyoke College.

Hampshire, with the powers and privileges and subject to the duties and liabilities provided in "Chapter forty-fourth of the Revised Statutes passed November fourth in the year one thousand eight hundred and thirty-five," and with power to hold real and personal estate not exceeding in value one Hundred thousand dollars, to be devoted exclusively to the purposes of education.

House of Reps, Feb. 10, 1836

Passed to be enacted.

Julius Rockwell Speaker,

In Senate Feb 10, 1836

Passed to be enacted.

Council – Chamber 11th February 1836   Horace Mann, President

       Approved

         Edward Everett

2.5: College Presidents and Their Students: Thomas R. Dew's Address before the Students of the College of William and Mary (1836)

College presidents in the nineteenth century had to be skilled orators. Their students, in turn, had to be patient, polite listeners, who, as a captive audience at official college gatherings, often had to sit still for over two hours. Reprinting the president's opening speech word for word for readers today gives some approximation of this collegiate arrangement. William and Mary had a reasonably large enrollment for the era—about 148 students, a substantial recovery from its dip to sixty-eight students in the 1820s. A staple of college life was to gather for convocations throughout the academic term—with some colleges having daily chapel. The opening of the academic year address by the president is typical of colleges nationwide in several features: the president justifies a classical education as fitting for modern life; he shows gratitude to former presidents and to the board; he inspires entering students to be serious and well behaved; and, quickly, he reminds students that misconduct and discourtesy will be punished. Further, the president demonstrated a crucial role as one who reconciles religion and science. For Dew, this meant putting in a good word about the college's new "civil engineering" course of study—a pragmatic innovation that, unfortunately, was never met with enthusiasm or large enrollments by William and Mary students.

Thomas R. Dew, "An Address Delivered before the Students of William & Mary at the Opening of the College, on Monday, October 10th, 1836," as published in the *Southern Literary Messenger* (November 1836) vol. 2, issue 12, pp. 760–769.

In addition to this familiar liturgy and ritualized oratory, Thomas Dew's lengthy remarks warrant particular attention for their association with contentious issues facing this college and its region and society. The president, for example, matter-of-factly speaks to the students as being the sons of slaveholders—indicative of the demands of a college education for future leaders in Virginia and in the South. Dew also makes a direct case for support of state plans for "internal improvements"—the canals, road-ways, and other transportation systems that would enhance economic development— a proposal that faced bitter opposition from some constituents who did not wish to pay taxes for projects outside their own locales. Shifting from matters of state and national policies, President Dew devoted a lot of time to scoldings and warnings about the dangers of personal misconduct, including abuse of liquor, gambling, and run-ning up huge debts. These were not mere "boys-will-be-boys" admonishments. In fact, William and Mary—along with other elite colleges in the South—had a serious problem with a student culture that often was disrespectful of the faculty and of the college laws. "Honor," for the young college gentlemen in the South, emphasized chivalry and manhood—in particular, the defense of honor as manifested in duels and challenges associated with slights and disrespect. At William and Mary, one under-graduate challenged his professor to a duel with pistols because the professor had insulted the student's honor by correcting him for a wrong response to a question in class. By contrast, at colleges in the North, the term "honor" tended to refer to adher-ence to the academic honor code and compliance with college rules.

Thomas Dew represented the influence of a college president as a public figure in the nineteenth century. Outside the classroom or campus convocation, he had gained regional fame and national renown for having provided the definitive intellectual defense of slavery, tied to his academic standing as a professor of moral and political philosophy. This role was a companion to the state and regional leadership of other well-known college presidents of the era—such as Thomas Cooper, president of the University of South Carolina, whose emphasis on teaching skills of oratory, combined with a political economy curriculum that championed nullification theory and states' rights, shaped the college education of numerous future governors and United States senators. If President Dew of William and Mary, along with Thomas Cooper of South Carolina, embodied the character of leadership and undergraduate education in the South, important to keep in mind is that their approach—oratory and appeals to duty and honor—had their counterparts at colleges in New England, the Mid-Atlantic, and the Western Reserve. Each college president used his position as a bully pulpit to so-cialize future leaders into established sets of beliefs that were central to public affairs

and the national discourse. Regardless of the particular political polemics or orthodoxy of a particular college president, all college presidents of the era shared a common fate: a year-by-year quest for adequate revenues, whether from tuition or gifts,
to allow the college to pay its bills and operate for another academic term.

Gentlemen:—In obedience to the customs of our institution, I proceed to address
you on the present occasion; and I do it, I assure you, with feelings of no ordinary
character. When I reflect upon the antiquity and reputation of this venerable
institution,-upon the numerous alumni who have been sent forth from its halls,
so many of whom have graced the walks of private life, or risen into the high
places of our government, and shed around them the benign influence of their
talents and statesmanship,-when I reflect upon the long line of efficient and
distinguished men who have preceded me in this office, and upon the character
and virtues of him who was my predecessor, I cannot but feel a weight of responsibility which excites in me a deep and painful solicitude. For eight years it was
my pleasure to be associated with him whose place I have been called to fill. His
learning, his piety, his conscientiousness in the discharge of his duties, however
onerous, will long be remembered by all who knew him well; and the regret
manifested in the countenances of the citizens of our town when he bade them
an affectionate farewell, marks conclusively the deep impression which his virtues and usefulness had made upon their hearts, and the loss which our society
has sustained by the departure from among us of one, who, with his amiable
family, constituted so interesting a portion of our social circle. Again, then, let
me say, I enter upon the duties of my station with deep and painful solicitude,
sustained alone by the consciousness, that I shall yield to none who have gone
before me in this office, in zeal, fidelity, and love for our venerated Alma Mater.

I shall not, on the present occasion, endeavor to present to your view an
exposition of the general advantages resulting from education; the limits which
I have prescribed to myself in this address, together with the necessity of introducing other topics, will, of course, prevent me from such an effort. Nor is it
necessary;—your presence in this hall—your determination to subscribe to our
laws, and to obey the requisitions of our statutes, prove that you have already
comprehended the inestimable benefits of education, and have come up here to
pursue your collegiate career.

As it is probable there may be students in every department of our college,
and each one may be anxious to know something of our entire system previous

to the selection which he may make of the courses of study for his attendance, I will, in the first place, give you some information as to our general plan. Our plan embraces a course of general study, which may be pursued to great advantage by all having the time and means, no matter what may be their professions in after life. Besides this course of general study, it embraces the subject of law, and aims at accomplishing the student in one of the learned professions.

Let me then commence with the subject of the classics. In this school we have a preparatory department, in which the student may acquire that elementary instruction requisite for the successful study of the higher classics. As but few of you, however, will, in all probability, wish to enter this school, I shall confine the remarks which I have to make on this subject to the higher classical studies. In one department of this higher school, the attention of the student will be confined to the following authors: Horace, Cicero de Oratore, Terence, Juvenal, Livy and Tacitus, in Latin—and to Xenophon's Anabasis, Aeschylus, Herodotus, Euripides, Sophocles, Thucydides, and Homer in Greek.

He will be required to read them with facility—to construe them—to explain their meaning—to master portions of history which may be referred to, and to acquire a thorough and intimate acquaintance with the whole philosophy of the Latin and Greek Grammars. In this school it is expected that the classic student shall complete his knowledge of the ancient languages. I would therefore recommend it to all who may have the time and inclination to pursue such studies, or whose profession in after life may demand deep classical learning.

The knowledge of the ancient languages is far more important to us than that of any other, save our own. At the time that the barbarians from the north and east broke up the Roman Empire, and engrafted the feudal system on its fragments, whence the nations of modern Europe have arisen, the Latin and Greek languages were the two great languages of the civilized portion of the ancient world. It is necessary to study them in order that we may be enabled to understand their transition into the modern languages; the latter are derivations from the former. It has been well observed that there is not a single nation from the north to the south of Europe, from the shores of the Baltic to the plains of Italy, whose literature is not imbedded in the very elements of classical learning, and this remark applies particularly to the literature of England. But again, in order that you may understand well the classical authors put into your hands, it is necessary that you should become acquainted with the manners, customs, institutions and religion of the ancient world. Great and mighty changes have taken place in the condition of man since the fall of the vast fabric of the Roman Empire. The whole interior economy of nations has been changed. The complex system of polytheism, with its thousands of forms, and ceremonies, and sacred mysteries, has all been overthrown, and the beautiful and simple religion of the meek and humble Saviour of the world traced, as with the pencil of light, upon the sacred page, and revealed even unto babes, has been established in its stead. This great and salutary change alone has stamped a new character upon the age in which we live. How vast the difference between a Priest of Jupiter and a Minister of the Gospel! How great the difference between the Eleusinian mysteries of the Polytheist and the communion service of the Christian! In order then that you may be enabled to read the classic authors to advantage, and apply with skill the lessons which you may draw from the page of ancient history, it is necessary that you should study the laws, customs, institutions, religion, and polity of Greece and Rome. For this reason, there has been recently attached to our classical department, a school of Roman and Grecian Antiquities, and Heathen Mythology, in which you will be enabled to derive full and complete information on all these topics.

The degree in the classical department has been placed upon a high footing. It is necessary that the candidate for this honor should not only be a proficient in the studies just mentioned, but that he should obtain a certificate of qualification on the junior, mathematical, rhetorical, and historical courses. With this additional information, our classic graduate goes into the world not a mere Latin and Greek scholar, but an elegant classic. This course of study has been devised principally for the benefit of that large and respectable class of students who propose to follow the profession of teaching. To all students of this description, I would recommend the attainment of this degree—a degree which will at once give its owner a high standing in our community, and be a most ample certificate of his merits and qualifications.

Besides the degree in the classical school, there are three others of a high order given in our institution; these are the degrees of A. B., B. L., and A. M. With regard to the first, you will find in our laws a detail of the courses of study necessary to its attainment. These courses you will find full and well selected, bearing an advantageous comparison with similar courses in any other college of our Union. They embrace the four great departments of mathematics, physics, morals and politics. These studies I would recommend to all who may have the time and the means to pursue them, no matter what profession they may follow in after life. Independently of the pleasure which each of them imparts to the mind of the zealous student, there is a utility arising from them far beyond the conception of ordinary minds—a utility which springs both from the enlargement of the understanding by the salutary exercise which they afford to it, and from the light which they respectively cast on each other. One of the most beautiful and interesting facts in relation to literature, is, that all its departments are connected and associated with each other; the study of one perfects the mind in the comprehension of another. The acquisition of a new idea sometimes revolutionizes the little republic of the mind, and gives a new cast to all our thoughts. Hence the division of labor in science is not productive of the same advantage as in physics, but we should always extend the range of our studies in proportion to the enlargement of mind and the facilities for acquiring information, no matter what may be our profession or occupation hereafter.

If the time or means of the student, however, should constrain him to limit his course of studies whilst here, then it would be certainly proper that he should make a selection of those subjects which may have the closest and most intimate connection with the profession which he may follow, or the station in life which he may expect to fill. His own judgment will readily inform him of the selection which should be made, taking care always, according to the requisition of our statutes, to enter a sufficient number of classes to afford him full occupation. Every young man should task himself fully, lest want of employment, while here, should induce idle habits. For the peculiar advantages of each course of studies, I must refer you to the introductory lectures of the Professors, all of which will be open to your attendance, and will give you much more complete information on each department than I could possibly impart, even if not confined within the limits of an opening address.

The degree in law is of a professional character, and consequently we can generally expect that those alone will aim at its attainment who propose to follow the profession of the law. This profession, in all countries, but particularly in our own, is one of elevated standing, of superior learning, and, I may add, of great moral and political power. The habits of his profession ensure the lawyer, in every country, an honorable station among statesmen, and the foremost rank in deliberative councils. Law, said Dr. Johnson, is the science in which the greatest powers of the understanding are applied to the greatest number of facts. The common law of England, with the great modifications which it has undergone in our own country from the operations of our government and republican institutions, will form the principal text to which your attention will be directed in this department. "This law," it has well been said, "is not the product of the wisdom of some one man, or society of men, in any one age; but of the wisdom, counsel, experience and observation of many ages of wise and observing men." It is, emphatically, "the gathered wisdom of a thousand years." And you, gentlemen, who propose to accomplish its study, must devote yourselves to it with unremitting ardor. You must not study the mere statutes and prescriptions of the law alone, but you must examine, with the eye of philosophy, the whole foundation on which the great superstructure is raised. It is necessary that you should examine the principles of the science of government; that you should look into the wants of our nature; examine the beautiful structure of the human mind, with all our feelings, principles, propensities and instincts. In fine, you must, in the language of one who has risen to the highest eminence in his profession, "Drink in the lessons and spirit of philosophy. Not that philosophy described by Milton, as 'A perpetual feast of nectared sweets where no crude surfeit reigns;' but that philosophy which is conversant with men's business and interests, with the policy and welfare of nations; that philosophy which dwells not in vain imaginations and platonic dreams, but which stoops to life, and enlarges the boundaries of human happiness; that philosophy which sits by us in the closet, cheers us by the fireside, walks with us in the fields and highways, kneels with us at the altars, and lights up the enduring flame of patriotism."

Deep and extensive knowledge is, above all things, requisite for the success of him who aspires to an elevated stand in this honorable profession. Well, then, have the officers of our institution ordained that the degree in this department shall not be conferred for a mere knowledge of laws. The candidate for this honor must have studied, beside the municipal law, the subject of government and national law, together with some exposition of our own system of government, all of which subjects are taught by the Law Professor. He must, moreover, have obtained the Baccalaureate honor in this, or some other institution, or if not, must have attended a full course of lectures in some one of the scientific departments of this institution. With the collateral information thus obtained, the graduate in law will go forth, not a mere lawyer, equipped only with the forms and technicalities of his profession, but with a mind deeply imbued by the principles of science and the spirit of philosophy. With a mind thus furnished, every hour of study in his profession becomes efficient, and moves him forward with ease and rapidity in his career, enabling him to encounter all the difficulties and obstacles which beset him on his way. For a full exposition of the courses of study in the law department, I must refer you to the introductory lecture of the Professor, which will impart all the information which you may desire on this subject.

Before speaking of our Master's degree, I will say a few words on the school of civil engineering, lately established by the visitors in this institution. The United States of North America present at this moment one of the most sublime spectacles which has ever been offered to the eye of the philanthropist—the spectacle of a people few in numbers at first—rapidly increasing and spreading over one of the fairest quarters of the world; building up institutions, the admiration of the age in which we live; and rearing up, by the mere development of internal resources, a fabric of greatness and empire, unparalleled in the annals of history. The original heterogeneous interests of the different portions of our Union are made to harmonize more and more, from day to day, by the magic influence of internal improvement. The canal and the rail road, the steam boat and steam car, constitute in fact the great and characteristic powers of the age in which we live. Throughout our extensive territory, covering so many degrees of latitude and longitude, embracing every climate and yielding every production, nature calls on art to aid her. Although we have already executed works of improvement within the limits of our system of republics, which rival in splendor and grandeur the boasted monuments of Egypt, Rome or China, and far surpass them in usefulness and profit, yet the work is still in a state of incipiency—a boundless field is opening to the enterprise of individuals and states. In the peculiar phraseology of a favorite science, there at this moment exists a vast demand for internal improvements. From one side to the other of our immense territory, turnpikes, rail roads and canals are constructing every where; the engineer is abroad in the land, almost annihilating by his skill, time and space. Yet his labors are not commensurate with the demand. There is, at this time, scarcely any profession in our country which rewards its successful follower more highly and certainly than that of civil engineering. The visitors of our institution have therefore very wisely attached a school of this description to our college, placing it under the direction of an individual who combines, most happily, profound scientific knowledge with great practical skill—an individual who for years zealously and successfully pursued the business of engineering in another country, until called off by other employments. I would therefore warmly recommend this school to all who are anxious to follow this profession, as soon as their attainments will enable them to join it with advantage.

In the supplemental laws, published since the last session of our board of visitors, you will find a detail of the studies requisite for the attainment of the degree of A. M. This is the highest honor in our institution which can be won by the student during his collegiate career. It will require generally two years additional study after obtaining the Bachelor's degree; few of you, consequently, can be expected to aim at its attainment. Those however who shall have an opportunity, will find themselves amply rewarded by the advantages which may be derived from it. In this course, all the studies which are pursued in the first portion of your collegiate career, are extended and amplified. In the first portion of your studies, you master the great principles of science; in the latter, you enter more fully into your subjects, and begin the great work of applying your principles to facts. He who shall have the good fortune to obtain this degree, will have amassed a fund of knowledge which will enable him to grace and ornament any of the walks of life into which he may choose to enter. His mind will have been trained in the most important of all arts—that of acquiring knowledge and generalizing facts. He will almost necessarily have attained the great desideratum of literary men— love of study and the power of discrimination. So that in his case there will be afterwards no waste of labor and time, no useless expenditure of frivolous and unprofitable thought. To a mind thus trained, all nature furnishes lessons of instruction and philosophy, from her least to her greatest operations—from the falling of an apple, to the complex movements of worlds innumerable, all is harmony, concord and wisdom. Such a mind can draw the lesson of philosophy alike from the prattle of the innocent babe, or the deeply studied conversation of a Bacon or a Newton.

I have thus, gentlemen, endeavored briefly to present an exposé of the several departments of study in our college. I have given you the bill of fare, and we hope that you may make your selections with judgment, and spring from relations of universal existence throughout afterwards prosecute your studies with energy and perseverance. By the late arrangement of the visitors in regard to the Master's degree, our scientific courses are as extensive as at any other institution in this country, and one of them, the moral and political, is believed to be more extensive than in any other institution known to us. And this will lead me to say a few words on policy of our board of visitors in establishing so extensive a course.

Many persons are under the impression that moral and political studies need not be prosecuted at college—that the physical and mathematical sciences are the most important subjects, and should be studied to their exclusion. This opinion seems to be based upon the popular notion that moral and political subjects may be comprehended without the assistance of a teacher, may consequently be prosecuted to most advantage when the student has finished his collegiate career and entered upon the great theatre of life. This impression is certainly erroneous and highly pernicious; and in justification of the system which we have adopted in our own college I must employ a few moments in attempting to explain its thorough fallacy. I have no hesitation in affirming that moral and political studies are the most important of all. These subjects are of universal application; they concern every member of the human family. We cannot escape their influence or connection, no matter what may be our destiny through life. The great *high-ways*, and the little *by-ways*, of our existence, if I may be allowed the expression, alike pass through the regions of morals and politics. From the village gossip who tells the tale of her neighbor's equivocal conduct, and significantly hints that it was no better than it ought to be, to him who watches the movements of empires and penetrates the secret designs of statesmen, all are concerned in these universally applicable subjects. It is a matter of very little practical consequence to us what may be the opinions of our neighbor in mathematics or physics—whether he believes two sides of a triangle may be less than the third, or that the earth is the centre of our system, and that the sun, moon and stars revolve around it. We may laugh at him once or twice during the year for his ignorance wound none of our sensibilities and run counter to none of our interests. But the moment opinions clash upon the subjects of morals and politics, that moment the case is altered. The opinions of my neighbor are no longer indifferent to me. If he has notions of morality under which he is constantly condemning my course of life, or a system of politics entirely at war with mine, then does the collision become indeed a serious one. It was a matter of very little moment to Castile that King Alphonso should believe the solar system miserably defective in its arrangements, and that he could suggest some most important improvements in it. But the case was seriously altered when he believed that he was responsible to God alone, and not to his subjects, in the administration of his government, and that his wisdom was sufficient to make and unmake the laws of his country. The fact is, morals, politics and religion are the great concerns of human nature. They spring from the relations of universal existence throughout the human family—relations from whose influence none of us can possibly escape.

But it is said that even if these subjects be of such universal application, they may easily be acquired in after life when we have appeared as actors upon the great stage of the world. Then it is affirmed we may begin the study of morals and politics to most advantage, when theory and experiment may go hand in hand—when we may correct the visions of an over-wrought imagination by the plain and palpable realities that exist around us. This opinion is certainly erroneous. The period of youth is the proper time to commence these studies. You have come up here, gentlemen, with minds and feelings not yet hackneyed in the beaten walks of a business life. You are now enlisted in no mere party warfare. Your hopes have not yet been damped by disappointment, nor your energies been the student has finished his collegiate career and entered deadened by adversity. All your affections and sympathies are warm and generous. Your hearts and heads have not been besieged by cold, inveterate selfishness, or perverted by unreasonable and noxious prejudices. You have as yet set up no false idols in the temple of the mind. Addicti jurare in verba nullius magistri. You stand committed to the cause of truth and justice alone. Under such circumstances you are in the best possible condition for the reception of pure and virtuous principles. Now is the time to imbibe the great lessons of morality and to study the general and elementary doctrines of government and politics. A little time hence you will have entered upon the bustling, busy theatre of the world. Your private interests and party prejudices will then rise up at every step to cloud your minds and pervert your judgments. Your moral and political researches will no longer be conducted with a single eye to truth and justice, but the demon of party will too probably exert an irresistible control over the little republics of the mind and heart.

There are no sciences which require the same full, free, and generous exercises of the feelings of the heart, as morals and politics. In the fixed sciences, it is a matter of very little concern to us what the character of the fact may be; all aim at is mere truth. We do not care whether a triangle should have two, three, four or five right angles; all we are in search of, is the mere fact, the real truth. Whilst we are conducting the inquiry, all the passions and active feelings of our nature are laid to rest, and the intellect is left alone and unbiased to move directly to its results. But when we have reached the region of morals and politics, then do we find that all the passions, propensities and principles of our nature are brought into full play. The whole human being, as he has been made by our Creator, becomes the important subject of our researches, and we can never arrive at just conclusions without a due consideration of all the forces which are in action. And this is one reason why these are really the most difficult of all sciences.

Hence, gentlemen, the wisest and greatest statesmen have been generally found among those who have directed their minds at an early period of their lives to morals and politics. Such men become deeply imbued with the great principles of those sciences in their youth. They are early taught to worship at the shrine of truth, while the ardent feeling of devoted patriotism banishes from the mind all narrow considerations of selfishness and shields it against the intolerable prejudices of party spirit. A mind thus early and correctly impressed with the great elementary principles of morals and politics, will ever be well balanced and considerate in its conclusions, and rarely surprised into hasty and rash decisions. In looking to the speeches which emanate from our deliberative bodies, I have often been struck with the exemplification which they afford of the truth of this remark.

There is nothing in which our speakers are more defective than in comprehension of view. They seem too often to seize but one single point of a subject; and although they may move with a giant's strength in that direction, yet the mind remains unsatisfied. One of the principal causes of this defect is the want of a proper moral and political education in early life. They have not received elementary instruction sufficient to give the proper impulse to the mind. They are capable of taking but one view of a subject and that is dictated by local and partial interests, or by too intense a consideration of but one set of circumstances. Such politicians, however brilliant they may be in mere detail, are incapable of taking the length, breadth and depth of a great subject; they lack scope and comprehension of idea, and cannot dive down to the bottom—where truth is always found. Such men may be efficient instruments when directed by the genius and the skill of the great politician, but are totally incapable of taking the lead in difficult times, because incapable of forming the conception of great plans and the means by which they are to be executed.

Of all the states in the Union, I may perhaps affirm without fear of contradiction, that Virginia has produced the greatest number of able and profound statesmen and of eloquent and efficient debaters. And to this fact, no doubt, has been owing principally that preponderating influence which she has so happily exerted in by-gone times upon the destiny of our confederacy. One great reason of the superiority of our orators and statesmen, is the fact that the mind of the Virginia youth has always been easily directed to the study of politics and morals. Our whole state hitherto has been one great political nursery, and I hesitate not to affirm that our old and venerable Alma Mater has had a powerful agency in the achievement of this result. The law, political and moral departments of this college have always been upon a high and respectable footing, and moral and political subjects have here always received a due consideration. Hence it is that old William and Mary can boast of so astonishing a number of distinguished statesmen in proportion to her alumni—statesmen with whom she might boldly challenge any other institution in this country, or even in the world—statesmen who, whilst they have woven the chaplet of her glory and engraven her name on the page of our country's history, have illustrated by their eloquence and statesmanship the national legislature and federal government, and carried their pervasive influence into the councils of every state in our wide-spread confederacy. So that we may well say of our Alma Mater in view of these brilliant results, in the language of one of the Trojan wanderers,

Quis jam locus,
Quae regio in terris nostri non plena laboris?

It is surely then a subject for congratulation, rather than censure, that the governors of our institution, whilst they have enlarged the course of studies in every department, have been particularly attentive to morals and politics, and have prescribed such a course on those subjects as will, I am in hopes, insure advantages never before enjoyed in this institution. The great mass of high intellect in all countries, must be employed in morals and politics, and no mind can have received its greatest enlargement, or be fully prepared for a faithful discharge of the great duties of life, without their study. This applies forcibly to our own country, but particularly to the slave-holding portion of it, and will lead me to make a few remarks on the inducements which should urge you, gentlemen, as Americans and Virginians, to make, whilst here, the greatest possible proficiency in all your studies.

The establishment of our federative system of government has justly been considered as the commencement of a new era in the history of nations. It is emphatically the great experiment of the age in which we live; to it the eyes of all are directed, and upon its issue must the cause of liberty and republican institutions throughout the world, mainly depend. The great and distinguishing characteristic of our system is, that the sovereignty resides in the people—that they constitute the source of all political power, and the only check on the misconduct of rulers. Where such a system prevails, all must depend on the general intelligence and virtue of the mass. If the mainspring of our system is the sovereignty of the people, then does it follow that the people must be enlightened. In the language of the great author of the Declaration of Independence, "power is always stealing from the many to the few;" and nothing can prevent the gradual decay and final loss of our liberties, but unceasing vigilance on the part of the people. We must ever be upon the watch-tower, ready to give the alarm, not only when the citadel of our liberties is openly and violently attacked by the arm of bold and ruthless usurpation, but when we behold those secret and artful approaches to despotism, which gradually undermine the fabric of our institutions, and give no signs of coming mischief, until we are involved in irremediable ruin.

Every man throughout our wide-spread republic, must take his share of responsibility in the result of the great experiment which is now going forward. There is no privileged class here to rule by the right divine. Far different is our case from the despotisms of the ancient world, or the monarchies of the modern. Sovereignty resided formerly at Babylon, at Thebes, at Persepolis. Now we find it at Paris, Vienna, and London. But in our own more happy country, it pervades our territory like the very air we breathe, reaching the farthest, and binding the most distant together. Politics here is the business of every man, no matter how humble his condition may be. We have it in commission to instruct the world in the science and the art of government. We must, if we succeed, exhibit the extraordinary phenomenon of a well-educated, virtuous, intelligent people, "free without licentiousness—religious without a religious establishment—obedient to laws administered by citizen magistrates, without the show of official lictors or fasces, and without the aid of mercenary legions or janissaries." As a nation, a glorious charge has devolved upon us. Our condition prescribes to each one the salutary law of Solon, that there shall be no neutrals here. Each one must play his part in the great political drama; and you, gentlemen, who have assembled here for the purpose of receiving a liberal education, must recollect that fortunate circumstances have placed you among the privileged few. Every motive of honor, of patriotism, and a laudable ambition, should stimulate to the utmost exertion. Neglect not the precious opportunity which is afforded you. The *five talents* are entrusted to your care; beware lest you bury or throw them away. This is the most important era of your life—the very seedtime of your existence; success now may insure you success hereafter.

The age in which you live, and the circumstances by which you are surrounded, as inhabitants of the south, create a special demand for your utmost exertions. The times are indeed interesting and momentous. We seem to have arrived at one of those great periods in the history of man, when fearful and important changes are threatened in the destiny of the world. In the prophetic language of the boldest of philosophers, we may perhaps with truth affirm, that "the crisis of revolutions is at hand." Never were the opinions of the world more unsettled and more clashing than at this moment. Monarchists and democrats, conservatives and radicals, whigs and tories, agrarians and aristocrats, slaveholders and non-slaveholders, are all now in the great field of contention. What will be the result of this awful conflict, none can say. England's most eloquent and learned divine tells us, that there now sits an unnatural scowl on the aspect of the population—a resolved sturdiness in their attitude and gait; and whether we look to the profane recklessness of their habits, or to the deep and settled hatred which rankles in their hearts, we cannot but read in these moral characteristics the omens of some great and impending overthrow. The whole continent of Europe is agitated by the conflicts of opinions and principles; and we are far, very far from the calm and quiet condition which betokens the undoubted safety of the republic.

When the times are so interesting and exciting; when clouds are lowering above the political horizon, portending fearful storms; when the lapse of time is every day disclosing great and startling events, can you, gentlemen, fold your arms in inglorious indolence—throw away the opportunity that is now offered you—fail to prepare for the important part which should devolve on, you, and add yourselves to the great mass of the unaspiring, illiterate citizens, who have been in all ages and all countries the blind instruments with which despotism has achieved its results. I hope—yes, I know, that at this moment a worthier and a nobler impulse actuates every one of you. And you must recollect too, that you are generally members of that portion of our confederacy whose domestic institutions have been called in question by the meddling spirit of the age. You are slaveholders, or the sons of slaveholders, and as such your duties and responsibilities are greatly increased. He who governs and directs the action of others, needs especially intelligence and virtue. Prepare yourselves, then, for this important relation, so as to be able to discharge its duties with humanity and wisdom. Then can we exhibit to the world the most convincing evidence of the justice of our cause; then may we stand up with boldness and confidence against the frowns of the world; and if the demon of fanaticism shall at last array its thousands of deluded victims against us, threatening to involve us in universal ruin by the overthrow of our institutions, we may rally under our principles undivided and undismayed— firm and resolute as the Spartan band at Thermopylae; and such a spirit, guided by that intelligence which should be possessed by slaveholders, will ever insure the triumph of our cause. I will not dwell longer at present on the high motives which should urge you to exertion; but let me call your attention to some of the evils and temptations which will beset you in your collegiate career, and against which I must now warn you to be on your guard.

There are many persons opposed to a college education, because it is supposed to subject the youth to strong temptations, and in the end, to lead many into dissipation and vice, who might otherwise pass through life moral and correct citizens. I will not say that temptation does not exist here—that evil may not arise to some from their connection with college. But I do affirm unhesitatingly, that there is no better preparation for the great world into which you are soon to enter, than a proper discharge of your duties in the little one with which you are now about to connect yourselves. The individual who passes through a college life with honor and credit to himself, resisting the little temptations which beset him, has already been tried and tested, and his virtue is of a much more stern and genuine character than that of him who has never gone forth from the paternal roof, and consequently never been disciplined in the school of his equals. You may rest assured that every one of you who shall pass safely through this ordeal, will be a better and a more useful citizen, because of the very temptations which you may have triumphantly resisted whilst here.

Let me then call on each of you to guard against all excesses which may lure you from the path of your duties—remember that one transgression tempts to another, until the individual becomes hardened and reckless in his course. Beware of the very beginnings of vice; a little indulgence at first, believed even to be harmless, may lead to melancholy ruin in the end. Never forget the great purpose for which your parents have sent you here, and never permit, for a moment, any circumstances to divert you from it. Be firm, be determined in your course; listen not to the Syren voice of pleasure and dissipation, but acquire at once that manliness and resolution which will enable you to say NO! when pressed to do wrong; and you may rest assured that you will meet with your recompense not only in after life, but here, even whilst you are students. I may claim to have some experience in this matter. I have been myself a student in this college, and for some years past have been connected with it, and have been no inattentive observer of passing events; and it gives me pleasure to assure you, that the economical, moral, and diligent students have always been the most popular, and the most highly esteemed by their companions. Are there any honors to be conferred?—those are the gentlemen to receive them. Are there any distinguished duties to perform?—those are the individuals invited to discharge them. It is their names which are sounded with praise by their fellow-students, wherever they go in society; and their reputation survives and is cherished, while those who have spent their time in idleness and dissipation are forgotten; or if remembered, remembered to be condemned.

It too often happens that the youth at college imagines that he has rights and interests to defend adverse to those of his instructors. This false impression is pregnant with the most mischievous consequences. It arrays the student against the professor, introduces disorder and idleness into the institution, and in the end becomes, perhaps, the cause of the student's dismission, and consequently of irreparable injury to himself, and of pain and mortification to his friends and relatives. Now, gentlemen, I beg you to reflect a moment on the absurdity of this opinion. Where can there be any hostility of interest between your instructors and yourselves? Is it not our interest, as well as yours, that you should be diligent in your studies, correct and moral in your deportment? Does not the student, who makes the greatest proficiency in his studies, earn the greatest honor for himself, while he reflects the greatest renown upon the college? and I can assure you that we feel proud indeed when we behold those who have received our instruction gracing and adorning the spheres in which they move. Where, then, is the hostility of interest? There is none; the belief is vain and idle. The right for which the student is induced to contend, is often nothing more than the *right* to do *wrong*, the exercise of which always proves more destructive to himself than detrimental to us. If the student would only take a correct view of this subject, there would be nothing more endearing and harmonious than the relation of professor and pupil. The complexion of his whole future life may depend upon his acquirements and conduct whilst here. It is our duty, and it is his interest, that we should guard and restrain when he would run into excess. It has been my fortune to meet with several in the world who have spent their collegiate lives in reckless dissipation and idleness. I have beheld them while reaping the bitter fruits of their conduct; have heard their confessions of deep regret, and seen them shed the tear of heartfelt repentance; and I have not met with one who did not wish that he could run his race again, that he might avoid the errors of his youth.

But, independently of the motives of interest which should operate on you, there are others, of an elevated character, which must ever stimulate the generous and the virtuous. The friends and relatives, who dwell around the enchanted spot of your nativity and boyhood, and seem associated with your very existence, are looking with interest to your career whilst here, and calling upon you for exertion

more universally complained of in all our southern institutions than the unreasonable and absurd extravagance of many of the students who attend them. This evil, in some cases, has been enormous, and I have known many parents to be so much discontented with the conduct of their sons in this respect, as to cut short their education, and to become so disgusted with a college life as to resolve never more to subject a son to the same temptation. Now, the principal cause of this lavish expenditure of money has been the facility with which credit has been obtained. The facility of obtaining credit has ruined even many a cautious man, by the temptations which have been thrown in his way, and the consequent inducements which have been offered to him to run into debt. During the ardent and too often thoughtless period of youth, experience has shown that this privilege becomes too dangerous to be trusted to the individual. He adds expense to expense—proceeds from one extravagance to another, until he becomes perfectly reckless in his career. Prices, of course, will be enhanced in proportion to the risk which the creditor runs. Those who are honest are made to pay for those who are not. And thus many a student, before he has had a pausing season for reflection, finds an aggregate of items arrayed against him, which draws down the displeasure of his parent, or materially embarrasses his own little property.

The resolution of the Board of Visitors is intended, if possible, to eradicate this evil. The student's expenses now must be known to his parents and guardians, or they must give their express consent to his obtaining credit. If he shall be still extravagant, the responsibility must rest with him and his parents; we shall have done our duty. But we hope, most sincerely, that you will keep in view both your own and the college interests in this particular. Strict economy on the part of the student at college is a great virtue. Let each one remember that the money which he spends here has not been wrung from his brow, but from that of another. Liberality with that which is mine may be generous, but with that which is another's, is often selfish and culpable. I beg you to reflect upon the consequences of extravagance while here: it leads the student into idle, dissipated habits, and defeats the great purposes for which he has entered our institution; it blights his future prospects, and draws down upon him the displeasure of his parents. But, above all, gentlemen, let me bid you remember that which must always move the generous heart of youth. Your extravagance here extends beyond yourselves; it may reach your innocent brothers and sisters—your parents may become disgusted, or their resources may be contracted, and a Bacon or a Newton may be made to follow the plough, because the thoughtless, prodigal son has gone before them. And thus may it be affirmed, but too truly, that every increase of collegiate expense necessarily inflicts an injury on the great cause of science and education. There may be those whose ample resources may place them far above the necessity of strict economy. To them I would say, that it is selfish, or thoughtless at least, to indulge, before those with whom they must associate, in a style of expenditure which they cannot imitate without ruin to themselves and their parents. Liberality, under such circumstances, ceases to be generous—it becomes a species of selfish ostentation, which reflects no credit on him who displays it, and does great injury to his associates. To every one of you, then, let me recommend rigid economy, and you may be sure of reaping your reward in more steady habits, increased diligence, and a more perfect preparation for the great theatre of life on which you expect to enter.

Upon the subject of drinking and gambling, I shall say but a few words; the melancholy consequences of these vices are known to all—how the one stupifies and benumbs the faculties of the mind and the body, while the other reaches the citadel of the heart, and generates a train of the blackest vices which human nature is heir to. Let me beg you to beware of these vices, which have plunged so many families into distress and mourning, and have generated so large a portion of the misery of the world. Take care how far you indulge, lest your ruin come before you are aware of it. Our laws are severe against these vices, and experience has convinced us that we must rigidly execute them. But I hope the propriety of your course here will furnish us with no occasion for the enforcement of our laws.

In conclusion upon this subject, I will say to you, that if the students of William and Mary shall bind themselves, during their residence at college, not to spend more than a certain amount of pocket money, which should be moderate—not to taste ardent spirits any where, nor wine, or any other intoxicating liquor, except in private families, and not to touch a card, or play for money at any game of hazard, and shall strictly conform to these resolutions—then you will indeed have formed a temperance society, of which you may be justly proud—one that will do the greatest honor to yourselves, establish the reputation of our college, and set an example to the world whose benefit may extend throughout our country; and the students of '36 and '37 will long be remembered in the College of William and Mary. How far superior will such a reputation as this be to that short-lived notoriety purchased by extravagance and dissipation, and terminating too often in mortification and ruin. The case of the student is a very peculiar one; if he can pass through his short career at college, with all due diligence and propriety, he will have achieved for himself a great result. Full success in his studies during the few brief months that he remains within our college walls, may accomplish more for his future standing, and future happiness, than many years of hard toil and labor in after life, without the advantages which he might have reaped whilst here. It is for this reason that a society of the kind which I have just recommended must succeed here, if it can succeed any where. For you have only to adhere to your temperance vow for a few months, and the benefit is attained. But whether you shall form such a society as this or not, let every one of you endeavor, whilst here, to be economical, temperate and diligent; and such as persevere in this course, whatever may be said to the contrary, are most respected and honored by their fellow-students, make the greatest proficiency in their studies, and turn out at last the most valuable and distinguished members of society.

There are many other subjects to which I would wish to call your attention; but the limits which I have prescribed myself in this address, compel me to be brief. Our laws forbid your entry into taverns, and likewise all drinking parties and suppers among yourselves. Experience has shown these things to be ruinous to the students, and highly pernicious to the interests of the institution. You are to respect the college premises—not to deface or injure the college buildings. Each one of you is to be responsible for the injury done to his room, and to pay for all the injury which he may do to the buildings—always bearing in recollection that you come here not to exercise your knives, but your heads.

I would advise you particularly to be punctual in your attendance on divine service every Sabbath, and to be respectful and attentive whilst in church. He who disturbs a religious congregation, not only manifests a censurable disregard of religion, but exhibits an unfeeling heart, and is guilty of conduct which is not gentlemanly. An enlightened pulpit is not only the source of religious instruction, but of morality and civilization; and a truly pious clergyman merits the respect, the love, and gratitude of the world, for he is one of the greatest of its benefactors. Be always respectful in your conversation towards religion, not only from regard to the feelings of others, but for the sake of your own reputation. Avowed infidelity is now considered by the enlightened portion of the world as a reflection both on the head and heart. The Atheist has long since been overthrown by the light of nature and the Deist by that of revelation. The Infidel and the Christian have fought the battle, and the latter has won the victory. The Humes and Voltaires have been vanquished from the field, and the Bacons, Lockes, and

Newtons have given in their adhesion. The argument is closed forever, and he who now obtrudes on the social circle his infidel notions, manifests the arrogance of a literary coxcomb, or that want of refinement which distinguishes the polished gentleman. If there be among you any ministers of the gospel, or professors of religion studying with a view to the ministry, to them we cheerfully open our lecture-rooms, free of all expense, and shall consider ourselves as highly recompensed, if the instruction which we may communicate shall be made instrumental in promoting virtue and true religion.

A copy of our laws will be placed in the hands of each one of you: read and respect them. On the part of the Faculty, with which I have the honor to be connected, I have to state that the discipline of the college must and will be enforced. The oath of office, the reputation of the institution, your own welfare and success, all demand vigilance and promptness on our part. From your instructors you will always receive kind, affectionate, and parental treatment, and you may well believe it will ever be painful to us to animadvert on your conduct, or to inflict the penalties required by our laws. Nothing but a high sense of duty could lead us to proceed against those for whom the bare relation which subsists between us must generate feelings of the kindest character. The professor, who is kind to the student, and attentive to his interests, while he nerves himself upon all occasions to a discharge of his duty, is always his greatest benefactor; and the student will acknowledge it as soon as he has left the college walls.

Be diligent, be perseveringly attentive to your studies, and you have the antidote against all the evils and temptations to which college life is incident. And let me advise you, particularly in your evening rambles and social gatherings, to direct your thoughts and conversation to subjects of importance, particularly to the subject of your lectures. Enlightened, intelligent conversation is a source of great mental improvement; it brings mind into conflict with mind, sharpens the faculties, gives increased relish for study, and greatly enlarges the stock of information by an interchange of ideas. It is for this reason that a few intelligent men in a county will be found quickly to raise its intellectual level; and a few inquiring, successful students in a college, will in like manner quickly inspire the whole number with ardor and devotion to study. Hence the fact which the statistics of all long established colleges will prove, that great men are not sent out from their walls one by one, from year to year, in regular succession, but they come at longer intervals, and always in little platoons. Thus are we convinced of the interesting fact, that genius is rarely solitary—it delights in company. The example and conversation of the successful student arouse and stimulate his companions, and lead them along with himself to distinction.

Let me advise you by all means to discard at once that absurd notion, which has made an illiterate man of many a vain student—that genius delights not in labor. Very different is the fact; love of study, and unshaken perseverance in the pursuit of its object, is the true characteristic of genius every where. The men of genius who have built up the great systems of philosophy, and laid the foundation of civilization, have all been laborious students, as well as deep thinkers; they have been the true working-men of the world. Such men were Socrates and Plato, Demosthenes and Cicero, of antiquity, and such have been the Luthers, the Bacons, and Newtons of modern times, and such all men are compelled to be, who possess a laudable ambition for distinction and usefulness. In the language of Doctor Johnson we may assert, that "all the performances of human art, at which we look with praise and wonder, are the results of perseverance. It is by this that the quarry becomes a pyramid, and that distant countries are united by canals. It is therefore of the utmost importance that those who have any intention of deviating from the beaten track of life, and of acquiring a reputation superior to names hourly swept away by time among the refuse of fame, should add to their reason and their spirit the power of persisting in their purposes, acquire the art of sapping what they cannot batter, and the habit of vanquishing obstinate resistance by obstinate attacks."

There is even a great deal of labor requisite on your part to place yourselves on the intellectual level of the age in which you live. In the beautiful language of one of the ablest writers of our country, we can truly say, "it is not with us as it was in former times, when science belonged to solitary studies, or philosophical ease, or antiquarian curiosity. It has escaped from the closet, and become an habitual accompaniment of every department of life. It accosts us equally in the high ways and byways. We meet it in the idle walk, and in the crowded street; in the very atmosphere we breathe, in the earth we tread on, in the ocean we traverse, and on the rivers we navigate. It visits the workshop of the mechanic, the laboratory of the apothecary, the chambers of the engraver, the vats of the dyer, the noisy haunts of the spinning-jenny, and the noiseless retreats of the bleachery. It crosses our paths in the long-winding canal, in the busy rail-road, in the flying steamboat, and in the gay and gallant merchant-ship, wafting its products to every clime. It enters our houses, sits down at our firesides, lights up our conversations and revels at our banquets. One is almost tempted to say that the whole world seems in a blaze, and that the professors in science, and the dealers in the arts surround us by their magical circles, and compel us to remain captives in the spells of their witchcraft." And can you consent to waste your time in inglorious repose and idleness, while the whole world is blazing with philosophy? No, gentlemen, you cannot. Arouse all your energies, waken up your faculties, enter on your career like the combatant at the Olympic Games, resolved to win the prize, and in advance I tell you, the victory will be yours.

You are here placed amid scenes which may well excite a noble and a laudable ambition, and make the bosom of the patriot throb. You tread on classic soil—a soil connected with associations which carry the imagination back to bygone days, and fix it on the noble achievements of philanthropists, heroes, statesmen, and sages. There is every thing here to excite generous aspirations. On the one side of you is the almost hallowed island where our hardy forefathers made the first lodgment of civilization on our portion of the western world, in face of the wilderness and the savage foe. On another side, not far removed, is the spot where the father of his country wound up the drama of the revolution, by that great and signal victory which gave us peace, and ensured us so important a station among the nations of the earth. You will assemble daily in these classic halls, which have witnessed the collegiate labors of some of the greatest and noblest men who have ever lived in the tide of time; men who have raised up their country's glory, and gone down to their graves covered with the laurels which their genius and their virtues won. Fronting this building, at the other end of our street, and in full view, stand the interesting remains of the Old Capitol of Virginia, which every true Virginian must gaze on with mingled emotions of pride and pleasure—a building in which the chivalry and talent of our state were assembled during the dark days of the revolution, when Wythe, Pendleton, and Jefferson displayed their wisdom in council, and Lee, Mason and the matchless Henry poured forth those strains of sublime eloquence which animated and cheered the drooping spirit of the land, and warmed the heart and braced up the nerve of the patriot. Looking on such scenes as these—contemplating the great minds that have been nursed in our institution, and the intellectual Titans who have won their trophies on this interesting theatre, can you fail to be inspired with a noble ambition?—an ambition to imitate those mighty men who have gone before you, and whom the genius of the place in silent eloquence summons to your recollection. The author of the Decline and Fall of the Roman Empire tells us, that he first caught the inspiration which gave rise to his great work, while gazing from the modern capitol of Rome on the ruins that lie scattered over the vallies and the seven hills. May we not hope then that many of you will catch a similar inspiration amid the interesting objects which surround you while breathing, in this old and hospitable city, a political atmosphere that still retains all the ardor and patriotism of former days? Again then, gentlemen, I call on you for perseverance and unremitting exertion; and in view of all the circumstances which surround and stimulate you while here, may I not say to you, in conclusion, that your friends, your parents, your instructors, expect every one to do his duty.

CHAPTER THREE

Diversity and Adversity
Resilience in American Higher Education, 1860 to 1890

Between 1860 and 1890, higher education in the United States was characterized by the entry of the federal government into selected areas of policies and programs. Foremost in this category were the Morrill Acts of 1862 and 1890. These represented, with varying degrees of success, nationwide initiatives to promote an extension of higher education—both in terms of available institutions geographically and in fields of study. The practical arts and sciences of agriculture, mechanics, and military were now supported along with the liberal arts. The 1890 act also was a significant breakthrough in providing access and institutions for African American students. These three decades also marked a period of innovation and funding for new women's colleges—and with some established institutions arranging for coeducation of men and women. These initiatives and their gains, however, were muted by the stark realities of exclusion and limits within American culture at the local, state, and national levels. This meant for many groups that higher education was separate and unequal. In addition, in contrast to England and European nations, the absence of a federal ministry of education in the United States, combined with the norm of low taxation by state governments, meant that most colleges and universities, whether public or private, depended each year on attracting a sufficient number of tuition-paying students, whose enrollments constituted the fragile lifeline of operating budgets.

3.1: Federal Land Grant Legislation: The Morrill Act of 1862

The year 2012 marked the sesquicentennial of this historic, influential legislation, which has been integral to extending public higher education—and to broadening the curricula associated with state universities. Named in honor of Vermont legislator Justin Morrill, who served both in the House of Representatives and, later, as a U.S. senator, the Morrill Act also illustrates how higher education in the United States often has been enhanced owing to its role as a secondary character in some larger national dramas of public policy. In this case, the primary concern of the U.S. Congress was promoting the settlement and sale of vast amounts of land in the territories of the West. Legislators such as Justin Morrill understood how the land settlement question could be used beneficially to achieve other goals—namely, helping to make higher education affordable and accessible. The legislation represented one of the early and few times that the federal government became involved in higher education—a matter that the Constitution reserved for state governments and voluntary associations. The Morrill Act respected this deference to the states, as indicated by its deliberate provisions to promote voluntary cooperation between federal and state agencies and to curb federal intrusion. The 1862 legislation was the first in a long series of related bills that promoted useful arts and learning, especially in the agricultural sciences.

Chap. CXXX.—An Act Donating Public Lands to the several States and Territories which may provide Colleges for the Benefit of Agriculture and Mechanic Arts.
Be it enacted by the Senate and House of Representatives of the United States of America in Congress assembled, That there be granted to the several States, for the purposes hereinafter mentioned, an amount of public land, to be apportioned to each State a quantity equal to thirty thousand acres for each senator and representative in Congress to which the States are respectively entitled by the apportionment under the census of eighteen hundred and sixty: *Provided*, That no mineral lands shall be selected or purchased under the provisions of this Act.
SEC. 2. And be it further enacted, That the land aforesaid, after being surveyed, shall be apportioned to the several States in sections or subdivisions of sections, not less than one quarter of a section; and whenever there are public lands in a State subject to sale at private entry at one dollar and twenty-five cents per acre,

The Morrill Act (1862) Public Law 37-108, which established land grant colleges, 07/02/1862; Enrolled Acts and Resolutions of Congress, 1789–1996; Record Group 11; General Records of the United States Government; National Archives.

the quantity to which said State shall be entitled shall be selected from such lands within the limits of such State, and the Secretary of the Interior is hereby directed to issue to each of the States in which there is not the quantity of public lands subject to sale at private entry at one dollar and twenty-five cents per acre, to which said State may be entitled under the provisions of this act, land scrip to the amount in acres for the deficiency of its distributive share: said scrip to be sold by said States and the proceeds thereof applied to the uses and purposes prescribed in this act, and for no other use or purpose whatsoever: *Provided*, That in no case shall any State to which land scrip may thus be issued be allowed to locate the same within the limits of any other State, or of any Territory of the United States, but their assignees may thus locate said land scrip upon any of the unappropriated lands of the United States subject to sale at private entry at one dollar and twenty-five cents, or less, per acre: *And provided, further*, That not more than one million acres shall be located by such assignees in any one of the States: *And provided, further*, That no such location shall be made before one year from the passage of this Act.

SEC. 3. And be it further enacted, That all the expenses of management, superintendence, and taxes from date of selection of said lands, previous to their sales, and all expenses incurred in the management and disbursement of the moneys which may be received therefrom, shall be paid by the States to which they may belong, out of the Treasury of said States, so that the entire proceeds of the sale of said lands shall be applied without any diminution whatever to the purposes hereinafter mentioned.

SEC. 4. And be it further enacted, That all moneys derived from the sale of the lands aforesaid by the States to which the lands are apportioned, and from the sales of land scrip hereinbefore provided for, shall be invested in stocks of the United States, or of the States, or some other safe stocks, yielding not less than five per centum upon the par value of said stocks; and that the moneys so invested shall constitute a perpetual fund, the capital of which shall remain forever undiminished, (except so far as may be provided in section fifth of this act,) and the interest of which shall be inviolably appropriated, by each State which may take and claim the benefit of this act, to the endowment, support, and maintenance of at least one college where the leading object shall be, without excluding other scientific and classical studies, and including military tactics, to teach such branches of learning as are related to agriculture and the mechanic arts, in such manner as the legislatures of the States may respectively prescribe, in order to promote the liberal and practical education of the industrial classes in the several pursuits and professions in life.

SEC. 5. *And be it further enacted*, That the grant of land and land scrip hereby authorized shall be made on the following conditions, to which, as well as to the provisions hereinbefore contained, the previous assent of the several States shall be signified by legislative acts:

First. If any portion of the fund invested, as provided by the foregoing section, or any portion of the interest thereon, shall, by any action or contingency, be diminished or lost, it shall be replaced by the State to which it belongs, so that the capital of the fund shall remain forever undiminished; and the annual interest shall be regularly applied without diminution to the purposes mentioned in the fourth section of this act, except that a sum, not exceeding ten per centum upon the amount received by any State under the provisions of this act may be expended for the purchase of lands for sites or experimental farms, whenever authorized by the respective legislatures of said States.

Second. No portion of said fund, nor the interest thereon, shall be applied, directly or indirectly, under any pretence whatever, to the purchase, erection, preservation, or repair of any building or buildings.

Third. Any State which may take and claim the benefit of the provisions of this act shall provide, within five years from the time of its acceptance as provided in subdivision seven of this section, at least not less than one college, as described in the fourth section of this act, or the grant to such State shall cease; and said State shall be bound to pay the United States the amount received of any lands previously sold; and that the title to purchasers under the State shall be valid.

Fourth. An annual report shall be made regarding the progress of each college, recording any improvements and experiments made, with their cost and results, and such other matters, including State industrial and economical statistics, as may be supposed useful; one copy of which shall be transmitted by mail [free] by each, to all the other colleges which may be endowed under the provisions of this act, and also one copy to the Secretary of the Interior.

Fifth. When lands shall be selected from those which have been raised to double the minimum price, in consequence of railroad grants, they shall be computed to the States at the maximum price, and the number of acres proportionally diminished.

Sixth. No State while in a condition of rebellion or insurrection against the government of the United States shall be entitled to the benefit of this act.

Seventh. No State shall be entitled to the benefits of this act unless it shall express its acceptance thereof by its legislature within three years from July 23, 1866: *Provided*, That when any Territory shall become a State and be admitted into the Union, such new State shall be entitled to the benefits of the said act of July two, eighteen hundred and sixty-two, by expressing the acceptance therein required within three years from the date of its admission into the Union, and providing the college or colleges within five years after such acceptance, as prescribed in this act.

SEC. 6. And be it further enacted, That land scrip issued under the provisions of this act shall not be subject to location until after the first day of January, one thousand eight hundred and sixty-three.

SEC. 7. *And be it further enacted*, That the land officers shall receive the same fees for locating land scrip issued under the provisions of this act as is now allowed for the location of military bounty land warrants under existing laws: *Provided*, their maximum compensation shall not be thereby increased.

SEC. 8. *And be it further enacted*, That the Governors of the several States to which scrip shall be issued under this act shall be required to report annually to Congress all sales made of such scrip until the whole shall be disposed of, the amount for the same, and what appropriation has been made of the proceeds.

3.2: Student Memoir: Lyman C. Bagg's *Four Years at Yale* (1871)

Published in 1871, Lyman C. Bagg's *Four Years at Yale* is an epic chronicle of the day-to-day lives of students at that institution in the mid-nineteenth century. At over seven hundred pages, Bagg's descriptions sometimes blur the line between meticulous and obsessive; yet for a work written in an era before databases and digitized records, the depth and breadth of his research are nothing short of astounding. Readers willing to bear Bagg's occasional descents into tediousness are rewarded with a snapshot of student life so intimate and comprehensive that few before or since have matched its scope.

The following excerpts are but a small sampling of what *Four Years at Yale* has to offer modern scholars. The first passage, from the book's preface, acquaints the reader with the author's motivations for writing the book. The subsequent sections offer glimpses into three significant aspects of life at Yale in Bagg's era: the joining of fresh-

Lyman C. Bagg, *Four Years at Yale: By a Graduate of '69* (New Haven, CT: Charles C. Chatfield, 1871).

man societies, academics, and the vices to which college men of the time were inclined. The final passage, which is the book's concluding paragraph, is Lyman Bagg's unequivocal charge to his readers to give their money freely to the institutions for which (in his view) it would do the most good—a charge that, if heeded, would have left American higher education looking very different than it does today.

The erroneous and absurd ideas which very many intelligent people, who have not chanced to experience it, entertain upon the subject of college life, have led me to believe that a minute account of affairs as they exist to-day at one of the chief American colleges would not be without value to the general public, nor without interest to the alumni and undergraduates of other colleges as well as of the one described. Hence, though not without some little diffidence, I venture to offer this compilation of facts, which no one has ever yet taken the trouble to group together, with the hope that it may be of service as a corrector of opinion and of interest as an aid to the memory.

Looking at things from the undergraduate in distinction firm the official stand-point, I have given as little attention as possible to those matters which a formal historian would render prominent, and have gone into the smallest details in cases which he would take no notice of. I have accounted no fact too trivial or insignificant to be unworthy of record. I have attached no moral to the most important one. I have simply endeavored to place every scrap of evidence fairly before the reader, leaving him to decide for himself how much of it to use in making up his judgment. I have studiously refrained from urging any idea or theory of my own, and have endeavored, in cases where some expression of opinion seemed necessary, to offer simply the prevailing sentiment of college. Yet, that my position may not be misunderstood, I have added a Concluding Chapter, for the expression of my personal beliefs, and I respectfully ask that no one represent anything in the book as an "opinion" of mine until he has read that chapter. Facts are facts, and because I see fit to describe them in cold blood, without comment of any sort, I do not wish to be quoted either as approving of or as condemning them.

Some of my statements will doubtless be distasteful to many. Some may be called untrue or unfair. Especially will the facts I offered in regard to the Society System be likely to arouse ill-will. Now, I have never gone out of my way to pry into society secrets; nor have I attempted any betrayal of them. I have simply repeated the current beliefs and rumors, without pretending to vouch for their correctness. Indeed, as a society man, I know that some of the things reported are not true in fact; but I have taken an outside view of matters, and reported nothing save what a man learns—or at least might easily learn—who never enters a society-hall. My narrations, I think, on the whole, tend to the societies' advantage; and if any fierce partisan blames me for having, in some instances, said too much, let him at least give me the credit for having, in every instance, kept back much which I might have said. As I was left a neutral in senior year, I can hardly be accused of having much prejudice in favor of the senior societies, and if I have treated them with fairness, the fact may perhaps induce some to believe in my ability to take an impersonal, unprejudiced, outside view of the others which make up the system.

****

When "the candidate for admission to the freshman class in Yale College" draws near to New Haven, for the purpose of attending the dread entrance examination, he is usually accosted with the utmost politeness by a jaunty young gentleman, resplendent with mystic insignia, who, after some introductory commonplaces, "presumes he may be intending to enter Yale?" "Yes." "Perhaps he has heard of some remarkable societies existing in that neighborhood?" If he has, and says at once that he's "pledged" to this or that society, our affable friend congratulates him on the wisdom of his choice, if it be *his* society, or quickly turns the subject if it happens to be its opponent, and in either case soon bids him good day. But if he wants information on the subject, the jaunty young gentleman is most happy to supply it. "He chances to have in his pocket a prize list, recently published by the college authorities, which shows exactly how the thing now stands." This list of course places one society far ahead of the rest in the matter of "honors," and other desirable things; which society our friend at length confesses he had the honor of belonging to last year, and thinks he has still enough influence there to secure the unanimous election of his new acquaintance, if he decides to work for it. "Will he pledge to accept the election, in case he is so lucky as to get it for him?" Perhaps the sub-Freshman says Yes, forthwith. More likely, he "wants to think about it," and would rather "wait till he gets to the city, and looks around for himself, a little." But no, that would be useless. His time will then be taken up with other things. Besides, this list contains all the facts. Hasn't President Woolsey authorized it? Presume *his* word isn't doubted? Oh, dear, no! Well, the whole ground is gone over, and some sort of a pledge is at last exacted. "If you won't pledge to Sigma Eps, you'll at least promise not to go to Gamma Nu?"

Yes, subFresh will promise that. "And you won't pledge to Delta Kap till you talk with me again?" "No." And so they part. This is supposed to happen before the train or boat reaches the station or landing. By that time our Sigma Eps partisan—for as such we now recognize him—is in the midst of his argument with another "candidate." They are just preparing to alight, when other Sigma Eps men surround them. At a sign from the first, one takes his valise, another his umbrella, a third his bundle. "This way if you please, Mr. —." And before the sub-Fresh has time to protest, he is rolling along in a hack, and his new found friends are enquiring the number of his boarding house, or the name of the hotel he wishes to go to? Very likely they treat him to dinner or supper, but at any rate they are very attentive to his wants and do not leave him until he is "pledged." Sometimes the transfer to the hack is not so easily accomplished, for the runners of another society may scent the prey, rush for it, and bear it off in triumph. There are plenty of representatives from all three societies hanging about the railroad station on the arrival of the important trains, and rarely does a sub-Freshman run the gauntlet of their eyes without detection. They jump upon the platforms of the moving cars, they fight the brakemen, they incommode the travelers, they defy the policemen,—but they *will* offer the advantages of "the best freshman society" to every individual "candidate." And they do. "Pledged" is the magic word, and the only one, that secures the new comer an immunity from their attentions. Amusing mistakes often happen in these contests. A quiet Senior, or resident graduate, mistaken by a society runner for a sub-Freshman, may "play off verdant," allow himself to be electioneered, accept a free ride to the hotel, and possibly a supper, and at last, carelessly displaying a senior-society pin upon his shirt-front, inform his terror stricken entertainers that he "belonged to Delta Kap about four years ago," and wish them a very good evening.

Within a week from the commencement of the term, about every Freshman has been pledged, and preparations are being made for the "initiation." The term opens on Thursday, and the traditional time of initiation is Friday night of the following week. As the darkness approaches, the discordant blasts of tin horns and the rattle of bangers upon the pavement admonish the expectant Freshmen that the hour of their trial is rapidly drawing near. Each one has received during the day a black-edged envelope, covering a black-edged card or sheet of paper, bearing the society badge and this fearful summons: "Freshman [or "Mr."] So and So: You will be waited upon at your room this evening, and be presented for initiation into the dark and awful mysteries of the — fraternity. Per order." The half of a card of fantastic design and peculiarly notched edge is also enclosed, and the Freshman is instructed to surrender himself only to the personage who presents him with the other half of that particular card, which will be identified by the "matching" of the edges,—no two cards of the many given out having been notched exactly alike. Sometime between the hours of seven and ten our Freshman is called for, identifies the card presented to him, and gives himself up to his conductor, who may very likely have a companion, wearing a mask, like himself, or otherwise disguised. Perhaps they visit some eating house where the Freshman treats to an oyster supper; or perhaps he promises to give the supper on the following evening; or perhaps he doesn't care to treat at all. Possibly he has been blindfolded from the time he left his room, and has had a tin horn blown close to his ear occasionally, on the way, though this is unusual. But at length they draw near some public building, from within which proceed sounds as of pandemonium itself. The Freshman is blindfolded for a minute or two, is shoved forward, hears a door open and close behind him with a bang, and opens his eyes to find himself in pitch darkness. However, he at once perceives that he is not alone, but in the midst of other Freshmen, like him "waiting their turn." The noise meanwhile seems louder and louder, and when an inner door opens and a name is called, it becomes almost deafening. Soon our Fresh is wanted. A red devil in the passage way, assisted by a living skeleton, redolent of phosphorus, quickly blindfolds him, and he is hurried upward. When he has reached an elevation apparently of several hundred feet, a new element in the continual din assures him that he is at last in the inquisitorial hall. But just as he begins a reply to the last nonsensical question put by an attendant fiend, some one jostles against him, and down, down, down he falls until he strikes—a blanket, held in readiness for him. Then up he flies into the air again, amid admiring shrieks of "Go it, Freshie!" "Well done, Sub!" "*Shake* him up!" until a new candidate demands the attention of the tossers. Then he is officiously told to rest himself in a chair, the seat of which lets him into a pail of water, beneath, though a large sponge probably saves him from an actual wetting; his head and hands are thrust through a pillory, and he is reviled in that awkward position; he is rolled in an exaggerated squirrel wheel; a noose is thrown around his neck, and he is dragged beneath the guillotine, when the bandage is pulled from his eyes, and he glares upon the glittering knife of block-tin, which falls within a foot of his throat, and cannot possibly go further. Being thus executed, he is thrust into a coffin, which is hammered upon with such energy that he is at length recalled to life, pulled out again, and

whole. Blackboards and maps line the walls, which are whitewashed, and rows of hat hooks also extend around them. In winter the rooms are lighted by gas and supplied with furnace heat. The same general description applies to all the recitation rooms of college, though those devoted to the upper classes, except in the fact of having the floor covered with hemp matting, are not as good as those held by the Freshmen since the remodeling of the Athenaeum in 1870. In '69's time the freshman rooms were the poorest of all, being badly ventilated and heated with cylinder coal-stoves. Then, too, the arm-rests or writing-boards, attached to the benches for the benefit of each sitter, were quite a novelty, though now supplied to almost all the recitation rooms of college. In the upper classes, where the officer is familiar with the names and faces of the men, the alphabetical arrangement is not so closely insisted upon, and the "corner seats" of the benches are taken by the first who arrived. Once in a while, when by this means a division has become very much disarranged, the regular order of sittings is enforced again, to be followed in due season by another relapse. All this depends much upon the temper of the officer in charge. Some insist upon a uniform order of sittings to the very last. But in general, though the rule is always theoretically regarded, it is enforced less and less rigidly as the course advances.

The recitations are held daily—the first immediately after prayers in the morning, the second at half-past eleven, and the third at 5 in the afternoon—except on Wednesday and Saturday, when the latter is omitted. Each is an hour in length, and as there are 35 or 40 in a division (in senior year, when the four divisions become two, there are 50 or more in each), of course less than half can be individually called upon, each time. In all the classes, therefore, most of the officers call up their men, by lot,—drawing their names, hap-hazard, from a box which contains them,—and so making each individual liable to be examined on every day's lesson. For the early part of the first freshman term, however, the officers usually call upon the names in their order that they may the sooner become acquainted with the abilities as well as faces of the different members of the class. For the latter purpose, also, the roll is called at the beginning or end of the recitation. This likewise happens in after years whenever new officers take charge of the class. As soon, however, as the faces are connected with the names by an officer, he notes the absences by glancing about the room at the close of the recitation or before, and marks them in his book. It is chiefly to expediate this process that the alphabetical or some other settled order of sittings is required. In senior year, as the divisions are very large, the roll call is oftener resorted to than the marking at sight. The names of those who have not recited are the only ones called. Each recitation save the morning one is announced by the ringing of the bell, which continues two or three minutes, at the end of which time every one is expected to be in his seat. The officers unlock the rooms and take their places in them a few minutes beforehand, but no students enter until the ringing begins, though crowds of them may have assembled about the entrance of the building. The latter practice is most noticeable in the Freshmen, who gather about the Athenaeum steps five or ten minutes in advance of time. It is less common among the Sophomores, still less among the Juniors, and a Senior rarely leaves his room for recitation until urged by the sound of the bell.

In a Latin or Greek recitation one may be asked to read or scan a short passage, another to translate it, a third to answer questions as to its construction, and so on; or all this and more may be required of the same individual. The reciter is expected simply to answer the questions which are put to him, but not to ask any of his instructor, or dispute his assertions. If he has any enquiries to make, or controversy to carry on, it must be done informally, after the division has been dismissed. Sometimes, when a wrong translation is made or a wrong answer given, the instructor corrects it forthwith, but more frequently he makes no sign, though if the failure be almost complete he may call upon another to go over the ground again. Perhaps after the lesson has been recited the instructor may translate it, comment upon it, point out the mistakes which have been made, and so on. The "advance" of one day is always the "review" of the next, and a more perfect recitation is always expected on the second occasion;—a remark which is not confined to the languages but applies equally well to all the studies of the course. In '69's time, many or most used to interline their text books with notes, hints and translations, brought out by the advance lesson, and put them to good service in the daily and term reviews; and text books, specially interleaved with blank pages for taking notes, were quite common, but latterly these practices have been put an end to. In construing a sentence, one is only required to refer to general grammatical principles, and is not obliged to repeat the rules at length. Distinct grammar lessons—especially in Greek—have to be given out through a large part of freshman year, and sometimes even later. These are generally recited at the beginning of the recitation. Andrews & Stoddard in Latin, and Hadley in Greek, are the recognized grammatical authorities, though at the entrance examination no question is raised as to the grammars previously employed, and none are named in the official catalogue. In reading Greek, too, stu-

fore its own division-master. In the first term, the first "subs" of all the divisions are released soonest; in the second term the second, and the first subs the latest; in the third term, there are no term examinations. The last examinations are held on Tuesday morning, with which day the term officially closes; but two subs of each division finish *their* last examinations at two different hours the day before, and forthwith disperse to their homes. The examinations are held in the usual recitation rooms, and at the appointed hour the sub-division enter and take seats upon the rear bench. Each one is twice called upon, and the same order is usually observed on the second round as on the first, whether this be decided by the alphabet or arbitrarily. The questions are written upon slips of paper, no two of which are alike, and are distributed by the officer, or drawn hap-hazard from his hands. The first one who takes a paper is allowed a reasonable time, say five or ten minutes, to "think up" on it before reciting. Meanwhile a second has drawn a paper, and as the first signifies his readiness to recite, a third paper is given out. Thenceforth as each finishes with his paper, another person draws one, and so each is allowed to cram during the time occupied by two others in reciting. In the interval between drawing the paper and reciting it each person sits upon the front bench, out of the reach of anyone else. Sometimes, all the members of a subdivision are seated at a distance from each other and supplied with papers at the outset. As soon as one is ready to recite, he hands in his paper, and the recitations are heard in the order in which the papers are handed in. The second paper is given to each one as he finishes with his first, but it cannot be attended to until every one else's first paper has been recited, no matter how soon it be handed in. Each one's examination concludes with the recitation of his second paper. Thus the first man is usually released in about an hour's time, and others keep following him at short intervals until the close of the second hour, when the last finishes his work. If a paper is flunked, a second or even third may be drawn, but a recitation on these substitute papers counts for much less than if made on the original ones. No books of any sort can be brought into the room. Where any are required, as in translating the languages, the instructor supplies them. With the paper—on which is indicated the passage to be translated, grammatical questions, etc.—he hands a text-book, the printed "notes" of which have been sealed up, and the penciled additions, if any, erased. In the examination in geometry, the paper contains simply the number of the proposition to be proved. The one who is examined must draw the figure and give the caption, unassisted. In all departments, the examiner consults his own judgment in the asking of general questions, not indicated upon the paper. Those who fail upon examination are conditioned, unless their "term-stand" in the study is high enough to counterbalance the low examination mark. Conditions have to be made up at the opening of the following term.

At the close of the third term, is held the "Annual" examination, on all the studies of the year. This generally comprises four sessions, covering a period of about ten days, and ending on the Thursday or Friday before Commencement. The senior Annual, which has hitherto ended on the Friday before Presentation, will henceforth be no exception to this rule. The last session of every Annual is a forenoon one, ending at twelve o'clock. Nine in the morning and three in the afternoon are the hours of assembling at Alumni Hall, where all the Annuals are held. An entire class go in together, and are seated alphabetically at the little octagonal tables, no two of which are placed within eight feet of each other. An ink-bottle, fixed in a square standard of cork, a blotter, and a dozen or twenty half-sheets of quarto post, lie upon every table. Pen and penholder each man brings for himself. The students being seated, the entrance door is closed, and the officers begin to distribute the printed papers, which are all alike, and often come damp from the press. Having completed the distribution, they take their seats on small raised platforms, situated close beside the walls on opposite sides of the apartment. There are four of these watching-places for overlooking the hall, and if more than that number of the faculty be present, which is not often, they spend the time in passing about from one to the other of them. The students meantime have carefully read through the paper, and begun to write out the answers to it, using only one side of the sheets, numbering them in order, and putting their names at the head of each one. Upon a mathematical paper, the figure, as well as the caption or statement of the thing to be proved, is always supplied; and upon a paper in the languages, all the passages from the text which are to be translated are printed in full, so that no text-books are required. Occasionally, a perplexed student walks up to an officer, to enquire if there is not a misprint or ambiguity in the paper, in hopes of gaining a few "useful hints"; or an industrious one asks for more paper; or a thirsty one goes up to the water jug for a drink; but except this the monotonous scratching of pens is the only sound heard for the space of two hours. At the end of that time the senior officer rises to announce that "in fifteen minutes more, papers may be handed in, and in an hour more, papers must be handed in." In fifteen minutes, after telling the time of the next examination and making any other general announcements, he gives notice that "papers may now be handed in." Forthwith a few—who have floored their papers, or been floored by them—hand in their work to the proper officer, and hasten from the hall, and their example is continuously followed by stragglers to the very end of the session. Five minutes before its close, notice is given that all writing must cease at the stroke of the clock. Even then, after three hours' writing, many complain of want of time, but all hand in their work, and rush forth to compare notes with others as to what they have accomplished. "How'd ye get through?" is the ordinary salutation for the next half-day; and then the past examination becomes an old story, and cramming is begun for the next one. The result of a man's failure on "Annual," unless his "general stand" makes up for it, is that he is conditioned on one or more of the third term's studies; or suspended for a term and obliged to pass a new examination on all the studies of the year; or dropped altogether. A condition on Annual must be made up at the first trial, if at all.

****

Public sentiment in college inclines favorably towards moderate drinking, and does not disapprove of one's "getting comfortably tight," occasionally. To chaff a man for participating in some well-known drinking bout is accounted rather complimentary than otherwise, and the laughable antics of one who was then over excited by liquor are often related in his presence, and accepted in the light of a joke. Drunkenness, however, is frowned down upon, and cases of it are not common. It is seldom that a Yale man, while "on a bum," so far loses his wits as to be unable to reach his room unassisted and instances of arrest by the police of drunken students are almost unheard of. A hard drinker or habitual drunkard would not be tolerated by his classmates, even were it possible to keep his habits from the notice of the faculty. Quite a large portion of college are total abstinence men, a very great majority never drink to excess, and the number even of moderate "bummers" —who perhaps "get tight" once or twice a year, at the time of a society supper or some special celebration—is comparatively small. It should be said that the drinking exploits in New Haven of visitors from outside colleges, where the standard of morality is supposed to be higher than at Yale, often exceed anything which the hardiest Yale "bummer" is accustomed to.

Licentiousness must of course prevail to some extent among so large a body of men; yet it is not regarded as leniently as over indulgence in drink is by them. A man's doings in this direction are not, in his presence, talked about as a pleasant jest, even by his friends. Faults of the kind are of course forgiven and overlooked often enough, but they are always regarded as faults and as disreputable ones, and, when known, they rather tend to lower the subject of them in popular esteem. Once in a while a man—perhaps, on an average, one man in a class— is said to keep a mistress of his own; and once in a while—perhaps a little less often—a man's hurried withdrawal from college gives notice of an unfortunate intrigue with some damsel of the city; but were cases of the sort, among the same class of men, no more common elsewhere, the world might be purer than it now is. Swearing is to a certain extent a very prevalent habit; but other forms of vulgarity and foulness in speech are less approved of, though gatherings where "Venus rules o'er all that's said," as well as "Bacchus o'er all that's done," are not altogether unknown. It is the Freshmen who go to the greatest excess in all sorts of indulgences; and the representatives of college to be found at the concert rooms and dance halls are almost wholly drawn from among their number.

Smoking is of course very common,—two thirds of the '69 graduates being smokers, and the proportion probably being very nearly an average one. On the same basis, one-third of the smokers also chew tobacco, and one-half of all college play billiards. "Eli's," close beside the post-office, has long been the favorite billiard room, and "Rood's," on Union street, is equally popular as a drinking resort for the more fiery beverages, while "Träger's" and "Moriarty's" are the chief headquarters of undergraduate beer-guzzlers. Card playing is almost universal, whilst and euchre being the games chiefly affected. In '69, out of 117 men only a baker's dozen refused to be classed as card-players. The gambling dens of the city are not often visited except in curiosity, and "the tiger is fought" for very small stakes, if at all. A member of '70, however, "ran a faro bank," in a modest way, in his college room, for a while. The game of chess usually has quite a number of votaries, and class or college chess-clubs have occasionally figured in the *Banner* for fifteen years or more. In 1861 it was spoken of as customary for the college club to hold an annual "chess tournament," wherein the "championship" was decided as follows: The Seniors played against the Juniors and the Sophomores against the Freshmen, and the winners of these preliminary games then engaged in the third and decisive trial. The class of '61 were the champions for three successive years. Three matches have been played against Harvard, —at the time of the regattas of '59, '60 and '66,—and the two latter were won by Yale, though in each case the game was unfinished. Harvard also won a billiard match in 1859; and endeavored without avail at that time to extemporize with Yale a champion trial in the manly game of "checkers"! A year later, the Yale Freshmen accepted a challenge for a billiard match from those of Harvard, but if the game

education was energized and expanded by what came to be known as the Second Morrill Act, passed in 1890. In addition to extending various programs and paving the way for subsequent funding of research and development, the 1890 act marked an important initiative in federal policy: dealing with former Confederate states that had been readmitted to the Union, and, concurrently, questions of federal policies for those states with laws prohibiting the coeducation of the races. What one finds is a partial move toward equity and social justice. Seventeen states, ranging from as far north as Delaware and stretching to Oklahoma and Texas, maintained segregated public education systems. The compromise offered by Congress was that if a state government refused to provide equal access on the basis of race to the established land grant college in the state, it would be eligible for federal land grant funding only if the state demonstrated its provision for a separate public college that enrolled and educated African Americans. This option was the wellspring for the nation's public historically black colleges and universities (HBCUs). Some details of this development are found in Document 3.4 by Dr. Stephen J. Wright.

Chap. 841.—AN ACT To apply a portion of the proceeds of the public lands to the more complete endowment and support of the colleges for the benefit of agriculture and the mechanic arts established under the provisions of an act of Congress approved July second, eighteen hundred and sixty-two.

Be it enacted by the Senate and House of Representatives of the United States of America in Congress assembled, That there shall be and hereby is, annually appropriated, out of any money in the Treasury not otherwise appropriated, arising from the sales of public lands; to be paid as hereinafter provided to each State and Territory for the more complete endowment and maintenance of colleges for the benefit of agriculture and the mechanic arts now established, or which may be hereafter established, in accordance with an act of Congress approved July second, eighteen hundred and sixty-two, the sum of fifteen thousand dollars for the year ending June thirtieth, eighteen hundred and ninety, and an annual increase of the amount of such appropriation thereafter for ten years by an additional sum of one thousand dollars over the preceding year, and the annual amount to be paid thereafter to each State and Territory shall be fifty thousand dollars to be applied only to instruction in food and agricultural sciences and to the facilities for such instruction: *Provided*, That said colleges may use a portion of this money for providing courses for the special preparation of instructors for teaching the elements of agriculture and the mechanic arts: *Provided*, That no money shall be paid out under this act to any State or Territory for the support and maintenance of a college where a distinction of race or color is made in the admission of students, but the establishment and maintenance of such colleges separately for white and colored students shall be held to be a compliance with the provisions of this act if the funds received in such State or Territory be equitably divided as hereinafter set forth: *Provided*, That in any State in which there has been one college established in pursuance of the act of July second, eighteen hundred and sixty-two, and also in which an educational institution of like character has been established, or may be hereafter established, and is now aided by such State from its own revenue, for the education of colored students in agriculture and the mechanic arts, however named or styled, or whether or not it has received money heretofore under the act to which this act is an amendment, the legislature of such State may propose and report to the Secretary of Education a just and equitable division of the fund to be received under this act between one college for white students and one institution for colored students established as aforesaid which shall be divided into two parts and paid accordingly, and thereupon such institution for colored students shall be entitled to the benefits of this act and subject to its provisions, as much as it would have been if it had been included under the act of eighteen hundred and sixty-two, and the fulfillment of the foregoing provisions shall be taken as a compliance with the provision in reference to separate colleges for white and colored students.

SEC. 2. That the sums hereby appropriated to the States and Territories for the further endowment and support of colleges shall be annually paid on or before the thirty-first day of October of each year, by the Secretary of the Treasury, upon the warrant of the Secretary of Education, out of the Treasury of the United States, to the State or Territorial treasurer, or to such officer as shall be designated by the laws of such State or Territory to receive the same, who shall, upon the order of the trustees of the college, or the institution for colored students, immediately pay over said sums to the treasurers of the respective colleges or other institutions entitled to the Secretary of Agriculture and to the Secretary of Education, on or before the first day of December of each year, a detailed statement of the amount so received and of its disbursement. The grants of moneys authorized by this act are made subject to the legislative assent of the several States and Territories to the purpose of said grants: Provided, That payments of such installments of the appropriation herein made as shall become due to any State before the adjournment of the regular session of legislature meeting next after the passage of this act shall be made upon the assent of the governor thereof, duly certified to the Secretary of the Treasury.

SEC. 3. That if any portion of the moneys received by the designated officer of the State or Territory for the further and more complete endowment, support, and maintenance of colleges, or of institutions for colored students, as provided in this act, shall by any action or contingency, be diminished or lost, or be misapplied, it shall be replaced by the State or Territory to which it belongs, and until so replaced no subsequent appropriation shall be apportioned or paid to such State or Territory; and no portion of said moneys shall be applied, directly or indirectly, under any pretense whatever, to the purchase, erection, preservation, or repair of any building or buildings. An annual report by the president of each of said colleges shall be made to the Secretary of Agriculture, as well as to the Secretary of Education, regarding the condition and progress of each college, including statistical information in relation to its receipts and expenditures, its library, the number of its students and professors, and also as to any improvements and experiments made under the direction of any experiment stations attached to said colleges, with their cost and results, and such other industrial and economical statistics as may be regarded as useful, one copy of which shall be transmitted by mail free to all other colleges further endowed under this Act.

SEC. 4. That on or before the first day of October in each year, after the passage of this act, the Secretary of Education shall ascertain and certify to the Secretary of the Treasury as to each State and Territory whether it is entitled to receive its share of the annual appropriation for colleges, or of institutions for colored students, under this act, and the amount which thereupon each is entitled, respectively, to receive. If the Secretary of Education shall withhold a certificate from any State or Territory of its appropriation the facts and reasons therefor shall be reported to the President, and the amount involved shall be kept separate in the Treasury until the close of the next Congress, in order that the State or Territory may, if it should so desire, appeal to Congress from the determination of the Secretary of Education. If the next Congress shall not direct such sum to be paid it shall be covered into the Treasury. And the Secretary of Health, Education, and Welfare is hereby charged with the proper administration of this law.

SEC. 5. There is authorized to be appropriated annually for payment to the Virgin Islands, American Samoa, Guam, the Northern Mariana Islands, and the Trust Territory of the Pacific Islands (other than the Northern Mariana Islands) the amount they would receive under this Act if they were States. Sums appropriated

under this section shall be treated in the same manner and be subject to the same
provisions of law, as would be the case if they had been appropriated by the first
sentence of this Act.

SEC. 6. Congress may at any time amend, suspend, or repeal any or all of the
provisions of this Act.

3.4: Stephen J. Wright on the Historical Background and Future Prospects of Black Colleges and Universities (1987)

Stephen J. Wright originally presented this as a talk in 1987 sponsored by the State
Council of Higher Education for Virginia. Born in North Carolina, he received his
bachelor's degree in chemistry from Hampton Institute, a master's degree at Howard
University, and later a doctorate from Columbia University. Wright was well qualified
to write about the breadth and details of the HBCUs given his experience as a professor and dean at his alma mater, Hampton Institute. He was later president of Bluefield
State University in West Virginia and Fisk University in Nashville. In 1966 he was named
president of the United Negro College Fund. A remarkable feature of his essay is his
balance and candor in connecting institutions to larger public policies and court cases.
His historical survey does not gloss over the problems and difficulties African American students, faculty, presidents, and their institutions have faced historically in a situation of both informal and formal exclusion and segregation.

Let me begin with a very brief historical overview because it helps us, I think, to
understand the present status of the black colleges and universities and the public policies affecting them.

With two exceptions – Lincoln and Wilberforce Universities – the black colleges and universities were established after the Civil War. They were established,
in the main, by three different groups: The predominantly white northern church
denominations and organizations, the black church denominations, and the southern states.[1]

The white northern denominations and organizations established the majority of their colleges and universities during the first decade following the war,
1865–1875. Included in this group of institutions were Atlanta University, Fisk,

Stephen J. Wright, "The Black Colleges and Universities: Historical Background and Future Prospects," *Virginia Foundation for the Humanities Newsletter* (1987). Reprinted by permission of the
Virginia Foundation for the Humanities.

Howard, Johnson C. Smith, Shaw University, St. Augustine's, Talledega, Virginia Union, among others.

It is important to recall that when the Civil War ended, 96 percent of the 4 million newly freed blacks were illiterate and that there were no schools to provide the college preparatory work. The newly established institutions were thus colleges and universities in name only – the hopes and dreams of their founders. They had pitifully few facilities, having begun their work in churches, hospital barracks, abandoned railroad cars and various other temporary accommodations.[2]

Instruction in these institutions necessarily began at the elementary school level. But most of these institutions went on to develop academies to provide college preparatory work. These academies were gradually phased out as black public schools were established. This did not occur on any large scale until the 1920's and 30's. I am, for example, a 1930 graduate of the Hampton Institute Academy, in next to its last class.

The next major group of colleges to be established were those established by the black church denominations. This group was established for the most part in the second decade following the Civil War, 1875–1885. The group included such institutions as Allen University, Morris Brown, Lane, Livingstone, Philander Smith, among others.

Beginning also about 1875, the southern states began the establishment of colleges for blacks and continued to do so until by 1891, every southern state except South Carolina and Tennessee had at least one public college for blacks. South Carolina and Tennessee established their black institutions in 1896 and 1912, respectively. Black public colleges have, of course, been added since that time. North Carolina Central University for example, was purchased by the State in the 1920's; Fort Valley State College, Morgan and Jackson State Universities were purchased during the 1930's by Georgia, Maryland, and Mississippi, respectively. Mississippi Valley State College and Texas Southern Universities were established as late as 1946 and 1947 respectively.

II

Let us turn briefly to the missions of these new institutions. The principal mission of the private black colleges was the development of leaders, especially teachers – a critically urgent need at the time. The content of the programs, however, emphasized the liberal arts. In other words, they were patterned basically after the colleges from which their northern missionary teachers came, especially those institutions established during the first decade following the Civil War. The conspicuous exception was Hampton Institution which introduced a strong vocational emphasis they called "Industrial Education."

Hampton with its "industrial education" philosophy was later joined by Tuskegee under the leadership of the eloquent Booker T. Washington, a graduate of Hampton, a member of the class of 1875. The influence of Hampton and Tuskegee so dominated the education of blacks that many of the institutions attempted to emulate them in order to share the philanthropic generosity which Hampton and Tuskegee enjoyed. As late as 1950, the combined endowments of Hampton and Tuskegee exceeded the endowments of all of the other black institutions combined!

It was the spread of the idea of vocational education as the best type of education for blacks, which was also embraced by the southern states, that gave rise to the so-called Booker T. Washington – W.E.B. DuBois controversy – DuBois believing essentially in the higher education of the "Talented Tenth" by means of the liberal arts.[3]

The mission of the public black institutions reflected the deep reservations that southern whites held, at the time, concerning the educability of blacks and was limited almost entirely to teacher training. With the designation of the 17 land-grant colleges, following the passage of the second Morrill Act in 1890, the second emphasis was vocational – "agricultural and mechanical," the mechanical meaning primary trades. In fact, the only public black institutions with strong liberal arts until about 1940 were North Carolina Central and Morgan State Universities, both purchased as ongoing institutions as already indicated.

Until the Supreme Court's Gaines decision was handed down in 1938 – a decision to which we will return – no black public college offered any graduate or professional work. Nor did any public black college have a school of engineering. The policy of the southern states was to operate the black colleges as cheaply as possible. There was no real pretense about separate being equal.

But even after Gaines, the degree programs in public black colleges were extremely limited. Until 1983, only four states – North Carolina, Louisiana, Tennessee and Texas – provided schools of engineering in black colleges. Maryland joined the group in 1983 with a school at Morgan State University. The fact that degree programs were so limited makes the enhancement of these institutions difficult and expensive, not to mention the duplication involved.

III

The development of the black colleges and universities over the years and particularly those located in the South, has been greatly influenced by seven major events: The Jones Study of 1917, the Klein Study of 1928, the decision of the Southern Association of Colleges and Schools to accredit these institutions, the Gaines decision of 1938, the Brown decision of 1954, the Civil Rights Act of 1964 and the Adams Case, filed in 1970.

The Jones Study

The first systematic study of the black educational institutions was conducted by Thomas Jesse Jones and published by the U.S. Bureau of Education in 1917.[4] The devastating conclusion of the study was that only three of the institutions – Fisk University, Howard University and Meharry Medical College were even worthy of the name college.

Unfortunately, the report was essentially correct. The trouble was that the report became obsolete shortly after World War I but was still being used as the "Bible" on black colleges as late as 1925 and served as the authority for excluding black students from graduate and professional schools. This situation led to a successful appeal by the leaders of the black colleges for a new study. This new, 964 page study, conducted by Arthur Klein of the U.S. Bureau of Education, was published in 1928. Apart from updating the data on black colleges and universities and thus superceding the Jones' study, the most important result of the Klein study was that it led to the decision, in 1930, by the Southern Association of Colleges and Schools to accredit black institutions for the first time. They did so by creating a special committee for the purpose, but did not admit the colleges to membership. This did not occur until 1957 – 27 years later. Negotiations incident to membership extended over a number of years. During the 1950's, I served on the Liaison Committee of the Black Association of Colleges and Secondary Schools which worked with a comparable committee of the Southern Association of Colleges and Schools in effecting the admission of black institutions to membership in the Southern Association.[5]

Accreditation of Black Colleges and Universities

The decision by the Southern Association in 1930 to accredit black colleges and universities did three very important things: (1) it cleared the way for blacks to gain admission, without conditions or penalties, to the graduate and professional schools of the North and West, the principal sources of faculty for the black colleges and universities; (2) it gave the black institutions a strong rationale for some increase in financial support from both the states and private sources; (3) it stimulated the institutions in their pursuit of accreditation to improve their educational programs.

The Gaines Decision

The event that brought the first really major changes in the degree programs of the public black colleges and universities was the decision of the U.S. Supreme Court in the Gaines Case in 1938, to which I alluded earlier.[6] In essence, the court held, in a class action suit brought by the NAACP, that the State of Missouri had to admit Lloyd Gaines, a Black, to the University of Missouri Law School or provide him an equal legal education within the State.

The Gaines decision had reverberations throughout the South. One example will illustrate the nature of the changes. I joined the faculty of North Carolina Central University in the fall of 1939. That fall, North Carolina Central University opened a law school (with 3 students), a school of library science and began graduate work at the master's level, primarily in Education. But North Carolina Central was not alone. Other law schools were established at Lincoln University in Missouri (actually located in St. Louis), Florida A and M College, South Carolina State College, Southern University and later at Texas Southern University. Furthermore, graduate work at the master's level was begun in selected black institutions in most of the southern states. The Gaines decision also reminded the South of the doctrine of "separate but equal" and this doubtless improved, modestly, the financial support of the black institutions.

The Brown Decision

The well known Brown decision handed down by the U.S. Supreme Court in 1954 held that . . . "in the field of public education the doctrine of 'separate but equal' has no place. Separate educational facilities are inherently unequal. Therefore we hold that the plaintiff and others similarly situated for whom the actions have been brought are, by reason of the segregation complained of, deprived of the equal protection of the laws guaranteed by the Fourteenth Amendment."

This decision did not have as great an impact on the colleges as on the public schools during the years immediately following 1954. What it did do, however, was to begin the long process of desegregating both the traditionally black and traditionally white institutions, despite strong opposition at several institutions and the violence that erupted with the admission of James Meredith to the University of Mississippi in 1961.

In any event, the opening of the traditionally white institutions has, in later years, begun to have an adverse effect on the enrollments in the majority of the black colleges.

The Civil Rights Act of 1964

The Civil Rights Act of 1964, in outlawing segregation, helped to encourage the modest flow of white students into the traditionally black institutions in the border states of West Virginia, Kentucky, Delaware and Missouri, changing the racial character of these institutions – particularly in West Virginia and Missouri. At the same time, the flow of black students into the traditionally white institutions has become substantial, even in the deep southern states of South Carolina and Alabama.

The Civil Rights Act of 1964 also includes Title VI which prohibits racial discrimination where federal funds are involved – the legal basis for the Adams case.

The Adams Case

The Adams case, filed by the legal Defense Fund had as its purpose requiring the Department of Health, Education and Welfare to enforce the provisions of Title VI of the Civil Rights Act of 1964, mentioned above – in effect to eliminate the vestiges of segregation in those institutions which had practiced *de jure* segregation.

Filed in 1970 (and still continuing), the principal emphasis in the case has been desegregation of the governing boards, the administrations, faculty, staffs and student bodies in both black and white institutions and the enhancement of the black institutions. The efforts to desegregate student enrollments have adversely affected the enrollments in the black institutions as mentioned above but the Adams litigation has had a positive impact on these institutions where the efforts to enhance them are concerned – i.e., improving these institutions to the end that they "will have the facilities, quality, and range of programs, degree offerings, faculties, students assistance and other resources which are least comparable at those at traditionally white institutions."[7]

Taken seriously, the enhancement efforts could make the critical difference in the quality of the black institutions. For the current biennium in Virginia, for example, the legislature appropriated some $12.8 million above and beyond their normal budgets for the enhancement of Virginia State and Norfolk State Universities. These funds are for such things as the academic programs, the elimination of historical deficits and the improvement of teacher education programs.

In the case of Alabama, for another example, as the result of a Justice Department suit in the Adams case, the State has promised to provide, over the next five years, some $35,200,000 in capital funds, $17,760,000 in non-capital funds, along with a number of smaller enabling grants and very substantial student financial aid funds for the enhancement of Alabama A and M and Alabama State Universities. Furthermore, as a part of Alabama A and M's program enhancement, the University has been authorized to offer a doctoral degree in physics with an emphasis on optics. The relevant question is, of course, whether the state's commitments are enough. Or in a larger context, whether the affected states have made a commitment equal to the dimensions of the enhancement problem of bringing the black institutions to the required level. In the meanwhile, what has happened is that appropriation formulas now tend to be applied equitably where the black institutions are concerned, if one accepts the classifications given these institutions. But equitable current appropriations will not, of course, remove historical deficits.

IV

With respect to the future of the black colleges and universities, let us look first at the private institutions. This is a group of institutions born with what might be called a fatal flaw, like the fatal flaw in the main character in a classical Greek tragedy. That flaw is the fact that these institutions are dedicated to the higher education of one of the most economically disadvantaged groups in our society and that they simply cannot charge the level of tuition that other American private colleges charge and unless they have very strong endowments or very substantial operating funds from external sources, or both, the quality of their educational programs will almost inevitably be compromised.

According to the College Entrance Examination Board, the average tuition charged by the private college for the academic year 1986–87 was $5793. I doubt seriously whether *any* private black college can charge the average without pricing itself out of the black student market – barring dramatic increases in federal or state aid, or both. Take Hampton University, for example, one of the strongest, if not *the* strongest of the black private institutions. Its tuition for the academic year 1986–87 was $4335 – or $1458 below the national average. If Hampton were able to charge the average, collect it and maintain its enrollment, it would have more than $6,000,000 additional dollars to invest in its educational program.

The seriousness of this fatal flaw is reflected, in part, by the fact that during the past decade, five of the weaker black colleges closed their doors and last December, three institutions lost their Southern Association accreditation. Moreover, a number of others are in serious trouble.[8]

Beyond the problem of the fatal flaw is the problem of enrollment. For the academic year 1986–87, 13 of the private black colleges had enrollments of fewer than 600, with apparently little or no prospect of growth, since they are compelled to deal with two counter forces: The increasing number enrolling in public institutions because they are less expensive and frequently have superior educational programs; and [the fact that] increasing numbers of students are enrolling in traditionally white institutions.

For the reasons given above, the majority of black colleges face a troubled future. But we know by now, that colleges and universities do not suffer heart attacks or strokes and die suddenly. On the contrary, they die slowly of chronic ailments like financial malnutrition, or "anemia" resulting from a decrease in the life blood of institutions: an adequate flow of students.

In the meanwhile, one of the most, if not the most effective public policies for private institutions are state tuition assistance grant programs. Virginia, for example, makes a grant in the amount of $1150 per F.T.E. Virginia student enrolled in a Virginia private college. Several other states in the region have similar programs but the amount varies: Alabama $600, Florida $1000, North Carolina $1500, and Georgia $1237.

The public black institutions present, I think, a more complex but a less troubled future. Among the major factors that will influence their future are:

1. The number and percent of blacks in a given state. In West Virginia, for example, where blacks constitute less than 3 percent of the population, the historically black institutions are now 85 and 95 percent white. For all intents and purposes, the desegregation issue in West Virginia is dead. In such a state, blacks have very little political power. And while not as imbalanced as West

Virginia racially, Kentucky, Oklahoma and Missouri may face somewhat similar problems.

2. The number of black institutions in a given state. This varies from one to five,
but eight of the southern states have only one. However, those states with the
larger number of black colleges obviously have the larger problems of historical deficits. This could affect the speed with which they are desegregated.

3. The locations of the black college(s) within the state. Kentucky State and Lincoln Universities, for example are located in cities with no approximate, public, traditionally white institutions and the high probability is that they will
become predominantly white within a decade.

4. The existence of a large amount of unnecessary duplication, particularly where
there are two proximate institutions – one black and the other white. Examples
would include Alabama State and Auburn University at Montgomery; Florida
State and Florida A and M Universities and Texas Southern and the University
of Houston. In such situations, the high probability is that the predominantly black institutions will lose enrollment – unless, of course, they attract
white students in numbers at least comparable to the enrollments of blacks
in the traditionally white institutions. Jackson State University with no undergraduate public competition will, in all probability, grow substantially in
both total enrollment and in the number and percentage of white students.

5. The vigor and sincerity with which the OCR criteria are pursued by OCR
and the affected states and particularly the vigor and sincerity with which the
enhancement of the black colleges is pursued. We know that several states
have preferred long and costly lawsuits to compliance. Whether their resistance will carry over into their implementation of the court decrees remains
to be seen.

Important as it is, public policy, in and of itself, will not totally determine the
future of the public black colleges. Student enrollment choices, for example, will
be a major factor. And no one can predict how the enrollment patterns will develop, since college attendance is neither compulsory nor free.

I like to think of public policy as being a definite course of action, carefully
selected among options by appropriate government bodies to guide decisions with
respect to perceived problems and needs. Where the black colleges and universities are concerned, we cannot formulate sound policy without understanding
thoroughly their problems, needs and potential.

1. The denominations and organizations included in the following: The American Missionary Association, the Freedman's Aid Society of the M.E. Church, the American Baptist Home Missionary Society, the Presbyterian General Assembly of Pittsburgh, the Protestant Episcopal Freedmen's Commission, the A.M.E., A.M.E.Z. and P.M.E. Churches – the latter three being black.

2. The hospital barrack associated with the founding of Fisk University has been preserved and is still being used.

3. In an essay entitled, "Of Mr. Booker T. Washington and Others," DuBois drew national attention to the issue. See: DuBois, W.E.B., *Souls of Black Folk*. Chicago: A.C. McClurg and Company, 1903. Washington never formally responded to DuBois.

4. Jones, Thomas Jesse, *Negro Education: A Study of the Private and Higher Schools for Colored People in the United States*. U.S. Bureau of Education, 1916, Nos. 38 and 39. Washington: U.S. Government Printing Office, 1919; see also Klein, Arthur J. (Dir.) *Survey of Negro Colleges and Universities*. U.S. Bureau of Education, Bulletin, 1928, No.7.

5. See: Cozart, Leland S. *A History of the Association of Colleges and Secondary Schools, 1934–1965*. Charlotte, N.C.: Heritage Printers, 1967.

6. Missouri *et rel*. Gaines v. Canada

7. "Amended Criteria Specifying Ingredients of Acceptable Plans to Desegregate State Systems of Public Higher Education." *Federal Register*, Vol. 42, No. 155, August 11, 1977.

8. The institutions that closed their doors were Mississippi Industrial College, Payne College, Friendship Junior College, Natchez Junior College and Virginia College. The institutions that lost their accreditation were Bishop, Knoxville, and Morristown. Knoxville has appealed the decision.

3.5: College Admissions and Student Consumerism: "The Oldest and Cheapest College in the South" (1892)

American colleges and universities have always been dependent on revenues from student tuition payments. Little wonder, then, that there has been a long tradition of vigorous recruitment of students. This document features an admissions poster from 1892 in which the College of William and Mary in Virginia, America's second-oldest college, relied on both its heritage and its low price to persuade young white men to apply and enroll. Broadside posters have been replaced or supplemented by magazine advertisements, elaborate view books, direct mailings, and social network media

"The Oldest and Cheapest College in the South," Admissions poster for the College of William and Mary (1892).

WILLIAM AND MARY COLLEGE,

WILLIAMSBURG, VIRGINIA.

Session Begins First Thursday in October, Closes
June 28th.

The Oldest and Cheapest College in the South.

Provides a thorough Normal and Academic Training. Historical Surroundings. Healthy climate. Forty-eight miles from Richmond. on the C. & O. Railroad.

EXPENSES

FOR STUDENTS PLEDGED TO TEACH AS REQUIRED
BY LAW.

(Tuition, board, fuel, lights and washing) . . $10 per month.
Other Students, from $12 to $14 per month.
Tuition fee chargeable against pay Students $17.50 half session.

SEND FOR CATALOGUE.

LYON G. TYLER, President.

"Oldest and Cheapest College in the South": Admissions Brochure of 1892
for the College of William and Mary (Document 3.5)

as college admissions officers persist in attempting to reach high school students who are potential college applicants. Students, in turn, participate in the elaborate ritual of courtship, application, and acceptance—or rejection—by colleges. Reliance on new enrollments each academic term persists as a staple of campus organization and operation.

pendent, were based on Slosson's year-long tour of American campuses nationwide. Included here are excerpts from the preface, six of the book's fourteen campus profiles, and the final chapter, "Comparisons and Conclusions." Slosson wrote about the peculiarities of higher education from experience, having taught chemistry at the University of Wyoming for over a decade before accepting the editorship of *The Independent*. With wry wit and uncommon candor, Slosson named several afflictions that had befallen higher education in the late nineteenth and early twentieth centuries—many of which still await a cure.

The unprecedented growth of American universities in recent years and their efforts to conform or to resist conformity with the demands of the times have effected such a transformation it is difficult to get a clear idea of their present condition and relative standing. A list of the larger universities arranged in the order of their size, wealth, scholarly productivity, or other objective criterion has surprises for almost every reader. He finds in the list and near the head of it names of institutions about which he knows little, and probably some of those whose names are most familiar to him are really very different from his conception of them, derived from their history or from early acquaintance. The alumnus who returns for the decennial reunion finds his Alma Mater greatly changed. Usually he is inclined to think that the change has not been altogether for the better in spite of the new buildings and crowds of students. He can, in fact, name the date when his Alma Mater began to decline and to lose the real old college spirit. It was ten years ago, when was graduated what is universally conceded by all its members to be the brightest class that ever came forth from its walls.

The present work is the result of an effort to find out for myself what our leading universities are now doing. I was aware of the fact that university catalogues and annual reports alone do not always give an adequate and satisfactory picture of actual conditions, for I once had a share in writing them. So in order to make the acquaintance of the fourteen universities selected and to catch something of that most important and most intangible thing called "the college spirit," I spent a week in residence at each of them, living in some club or boarding house, attending classes and talking with as many of the faculty and students as I could. Such an acquaintance is of course superficial, and this volume would have been more authoritative if each chapter had been written by the president or the president's secretary, but I trust that there is some compensating advantage in the comparative point of view; that I have been able by passing in such quick succession from one university to another, with my mind sensitized by the previous exposure, to discover some similarities and contrasts unrealized by those who have not had the benefit of such an experience.

As these chapters appeared month by month in *The Independent* from January, 1909, to March, 1910, they have had the benefit of a very searching criticism from the college press and numerous correspondents, so I venture to hope they are reasonably free from errors of misstatement. From errors of misjudgment and mistaken emphasis it cannot be expected that they should be free. I discovered early in my tour that very few things could be said about a university which would not be contradicted by some one else upon the same campus. What one person would claim as a virtue of the institution another would disavow as a defect. Consequently most of these pages would have been blank, except where filled with bare description, if I had not assumed the responsibility for the frank expression of opinions based upon the best evidence I could obtain. The value of impressions and criticism is inevitably somewhat dependent upon the standpoint of the observer, so in order that the reader may make due allowance for the personal equation, I have not attempted to conceal my own views upon the questions considered.

The choice of the universities to be visited was an embarrassing one, for the number must be limited and any method of selection would be open to objection. It was intended to confine the study to the large universities, not because small colleges were thought unimportant, for there are many signs indicating that they will have a more definite field of usefulness in the future than in the recent past, but because the larger institutions present more novel features and unsettled problems. After much consideration it was decided to include nine endowed universities: Harvard, Columbia, Chicago, Yale, Cornell, Princeton, Pennsylvania, Stanford, and Johns Hopkins, and five State universities, those of Michigan, Minnesota, Wisconsin, California, and Illinois.

Princeton University: The favorite lie of the old grad is "nothing I learned from books was any help to me." And he acts in accordance with this by throwing the weight of his influence, money, and applause mostly on the side of the various activities which divert the undergraduate from his books. Consequently college life everywhere becomes increasingly pleasant, luxurious, and alienated from legitimate collegiate aims. No one has better described this condition of affairs or has done more to remedy it than President Wilson. The college to which he was called as president was popularly known as "the pleasantest country club in the United States," but that was not the kind of institution he wanted to preside over. His "Report on the Social Coordination of the University" [*Princeton Alumni Weekly*, June 12, 1907] exploded like a bombshell on the peaceful Princeton campus and shook its historic buildings to their foundations. The opposition of the alumni checked the agitation of his proposal to substitute "residential quads" for the upper-class clubs, and in deference to their protests he consented to lay the motion on the table for a time and give them a chance to work out a remedy for the conditions in their own way. His description of these conditions is worth quoting because it applies in some degree to many other or all other colleges, but not every president has had the courage to point it out so plainly: —

"We realized that, for all its subtle charm and beguiling air of academic distinction, Princeton, so far as her undergraduates were concerned, had come to be merely a delightful place of residence, where young men, for the most part happily occupied by other things, were made to perform certain academic tasks; that, although we demanded at stated times a certain part of the attention of our pupils for intellectual things, their life and consciousness were for the rest wholly unacademic and detached from the interests which in theory were the all-important interests of the place. For a great majority of them residence here meant a happy life of comradeship and sport interrupted by the grind of perfunctory 'lessons' and examinations, to which they attended rather because of the fear of being cut off from the life than because they were seriously engaged in getting the training which would fit their faculties and their spirits for the tasks of the world which they knew they must face after their happy freedom was over."

Leland Stanford Junior University: The students of California take naturally to outdoor spectacles, to parades and pageants. Why should not this tendency be encouraged and developed, instead of being allowed to run wild and make trouble? Could not the artistic instinct be combined with the athletic impulse, as once it was in Greece? Why need our sport be both brutal and ugly? Why should Stanford students imitate the games of a remote and foggy isle? Could they not invent a novel form of athletic contest which would be worth coming across the continent to see?

The demolition of their great gymnasium at the moment of its completion gives them a chance to try. I climbed up one afternoon to the top of a pile of sculptured rocks, a heap of broken capitals and lintels, of heads, limbs, and torsos, looking like a Babylonian ruin. From this vantage point I could imagine a spectacle such as I had never seen, a whole school at open-air play, not forced gymnastics, but spontaneous movement for the joy of movement, not drilled to mechanical maneuvers, but trained to voluntary cooperation. The sunny plain, the lake, the woods, and the hillsides seemed alive with people, old and young, youths and maidens, each group with its appropriate part to play, each person with all his faculties engaged. It seemed half a pageant and half a game, spectacular and yet competitive. It was on a California scale, in tune with the big trees, appropriate to Palo Alto and possible nowhere else, on an athletic field of 9000 acres, miles of rough running, mass plays in three dimensions up and down the steep hillsides. And there was music of many instruments, timed to the play, and inspiring the players, and from the scattered groups of those who were for the moment idle came a sort of rhythmic chanting, apparently a musical development of the old drilled rooting. These choruses, while waiting their turn to come into the active game again, sang songs, Stanford songs, outdoor music of a new form, answering each other, challenging from opposing hillsides. I could not follow the game, not knowing the rules, but I could see that it brought into use every muscle and gave scope at unexpected moments to the most diverse individual talents. The young men were utilizing all their strength and endurance, while the young women were neither their competitors nor imitators, but played a part of their own, calling more for agility and finesse. The men were not dressed in the ugly or ridiculous costume we associate with athletics, but artistically and appropriately, evidently with some individual freedom which found expression in the fanciful and the fantastic. The girls ran like the Winged Victory, free-limbed and free-bodied, their robes fluttering behind them seeming to hasten rather than to impede their flight. Theirs was not the dull uniform of the gymnasium, but bright and varied as the flowers and leaves. They were mostly bare-headed, with streaming hair, and I noticed they did not stop every few minutes, as they do in basket ball, to pick up shed celluloid. There was in the game an element of pursuit and capture, reminding me dimly of some tribal custom, a suggestion of symbolism which gave a deeper meaning and undefined interest to the play. The maidens played the part they play in life, the triple role of spectators, participants, and prizes. None but the brave deserve the fair I saw exemplified as in a tourney or folk game.

I turned my kodak at the scene and pressed the button. I realized that it was imaginary drama conjured up by the stage setting, yet I remembered reading an article ["The Sympsychograph," *Pop. Sci. Mon.*, 49, p. 597] that Dr. Jordan wrote, not many years ago, but when he was very much younger than he is now. It purported to be an account of a seance of the Astral Camera Club of Alcalde on April 1, at which a photographic plate had been placed in the center of the circle and each member fixed his mind upon it and thought of a cat. The experiment was successful in demonstrating the influence of mind over matter, but the resulting photograph was very confused, owing to the fact that each person had thought of a different kind of a cat or of one in a different position. The article excited a great deal of discussion at the time, and I presume Dr. Jordan is still explaining it to anxious correspondents whose intelligence he had overestimated. But my imagination was apparently not strong enough to reduce the silver bromide on this film or else the effect was counteracted by a plunge into reality. For as I climbed down from the ruins I went into the surrounding woods and came out at a large wooden grand stand on which a crowd of idle students were sitting with their elbows on their knees, watching fifteen men going through some mechanical exercises. Their costumes were, to say the least, not esthetically gratifying, and all they did was to form in line, and then at a word of command rush forward and fall down in the dirt on top of a football, this over and over again, so spending all the afternoon "play period." And I knew that somewhere around the neighborhood, behind some hedge, was a group of young women, solemnly engaged in a similar absurd occupation, conscientiously working at manly sports in an unmanly way. I think it was the feeling of despair and skepticism of any improvement in athletics, induced by this, which fogged the films in my camera, so I cannot present as definite a plan of reform as I should like, for how can a man develop a faint mental impression in the light of common day?

University of California: Established customs of disorder, such as hazing, roughhousing, and rushing, have been abolished or reduced to comparatively innocuous forms. In place of hazing a certain mild penalism is imposed on Freshmen, such as serving refreshments, moving the grand stand, etc. The class rush, formerly rather a brutal affair, has been done away with, and, as the sign of its abolition and the seal of the perpetual treaty of peace between the warring classes, a gigantic "C" has been laid in concrete on the highest hill of the campus, visible across the bay and for miles down the valley. The University of Utah boys have put a "U" that is still bigger on a mountain near Salt Lake, but it does not mean any more. Every year the Sophomores with great ceremony turn over the guardianship of the C to the Freshmen, who keep vigil over it around a campfire all night and pledge themselves to protect it against all comers, especially against Stanford students armed with an ax and a can of cardinal paint.

A Californian custom that could be adopted by many other universities, much to the improvement of their looks, is Labor Day, when all the students turn out to beautify the campus. It is like a scene from a utopian romance, the wageless workers, ready to do anything useful, each according to his ability, all duly coordinated and directed by volunteer experts; the civil engineers superintending the grading of roads and cutting of new paths; the arboriculturists the planting and trimming of trees and shrubbery; a season of general cleaning up, clearing out, and putting to rights; a working day of socialistic brevity, for shortly after noon the boys are called from their labors to a bean feast prepared by the girls in the gymnasium, and the afternoon and evening are spent in sports and merrymaking. The value of the work done last Labor Day is estimated at $2800, but the greater gain to the University in the development of an interest in the looks of the campus cannot be calculated in dollars. The only fault to be found with Labor Day as an institution is that it has been placed on a most unfortunate date, in fact the most unfortunate date, February 29.

University of Michigan: The Eastern universities ordinarily provide both instruction and lodgings and charge for both, although in neither case what they are worth. That is, the total expense of the college course is shared between the college and the student. It is also shared in the case of the State university, but in a different way. The university provides the instruction without charge, and the student bears all his personal expenses. This is a pretty theory, but pretty theories, like pretty girls, do not keep their looks as they grow old. Neither plan, in fact, works satisfactorily. College dormitories and dining halls have often proved annoying to manage and expensive to maintain, and in many cases private dormitories and boarding clubs, self-supporting, have proved more attractive to the students than the accommodations provided by the college. On the other hand, private enterprise, given a free field by the State universities, has not furnished the sort of accommodations that the students ought to have. The fraternity houses provide a part of the students with pleasant and comfortable homes, but have brought with them certain evils that are causing anxiety everywhere. The poor student who "baches it" on crackers and prunes, and puts in twenty to forty hours a week at hard labor, is not getting the most out of his college course. And between these is the great body of young people of both sexes, picking up a precarious living in boarding houses, sporadic clubs, and private families of all sorts and conditions. A town which is dependent on a college for its support gets to regarding the students as its prey. It resents any interference with its proprietary rights.

It weaves around the college a network of intertwined interests, like that which in Switzerland protects the tourist industry. [. . .]

There are more undergraduate students at Ann Arbor than at any other university in the country, 4419 in 1908, Pennsylvania following with 3736, then Minnesota 3468, and Cornell 3454. They have been left largely to their own devices, and the devices have not always been of a creditable character. Class scraps and "horsing" have had no accepted restrictions or regulations. Hair-cutting, face-painting, house-raiding, and kidnapping became epidemic. Freshmen were treed and egged and put through such stunts as sophomoric ingenuity could devise. The class rush on "Black Friday" was preceded by a week of general disorder and excitement, seriously interfering with regular work. The student shows and parades sometimes contained features offensive to good taste and propriety. Press reports of such things, exaggerating the disorder and eliminating its redeeming factor, the good-natured boyishness of it all, have given the institution a reputation that, in my opinion, it does not deserve. The Michigan boys do not, I think, behave any worse than those in other universities, but they make more noise about it.

University of Wisconsin: Young people sometimes get the idea, among the other strange notions that come into their heads, that a professor may have chosen the quiet life of the scholar not so much because of his superiority to the world as because of his inability to cope with it.

Then, too, the fact that members of the faculty will have an opportunity to become leaders of men as well as teachers of youth makes the authorities of the university more careful in the selection of its instructors. If a man is a failure, if he does not have ability as well as knowledge, the fact cannot be kept safely hidden within the faculty circle, but is known to the outside world, always too ready to suspect college professors of inefficiency, and the university suffers in consequence. A State university like Wisconsin is set upon a high hill, watched from all quarters by friendly and unfriendly eyes. Its defects are conspicuous and swiftly penalized. This I believe to be a wholesome influence, in spite of the fact that the standards by which the outside world judges university work are frequently incompetent and unfair. For the college professor, as a rule, is too much sheltered from criticism and competition. Good teachers and poor teachers, men who stimulate their students, those who depress them, and those who do not influence them at all, have throughout their lives the same rank, reputation, and salary. There are no tests of efficiency applied to class-room work, and the president of a university has no way of finding out definitely which are his good teachers. If an instructor hands in unusually high marks or low marks, if he "flunks" 60 per cent of a class on examination, if his electives are overcrowded, if he is popular or unpopular with students and faculty, it may mean that he is an exceptionally good teacher or quite the reverse. That is one reason why so much stress has been laid on research in the gaining of position and promotion. It provides an objective test by which all the men working in the same lines may be ranked with remarkable exactness. Administrative and advisory work outside the university provides a similar test of a somewhat different kind of ability. The old-fashioned college was composed mostly of teachers. To these were added during the last generation investigators. Now there are coming in a third class of men, who are largely occupied with professional work in a public or private capacity. That is, the university of the future will be composed of three classes: men who have the genius for discovering truth, men who are especially adapted to imparting it to others, and men who are successful in showing how it may be applied to the problems of life. It is unfortunately rare to find these three forms of ability equally developed in the same individual, so the next best thing is to bring them together in the same faculty, where they mutually strengthen each other and give the institution as a whole an unprecedented power in the community.

University of Chicago: The University of Chicago does not look its age. It looks much older. This is because it has been put through an artificial aging process, reminding one of the way furniture is given an "antique oak finish" while you wait by simply rubbing a little grime into the grain of it. I never understood why this policy was adopted. It could hardly have been for popularity, for your wild Westerner likes things brand new and shiny and smelling of varnish. And he has a prejudice, quite unjustifiable though inherited legitimately enough from the Declaration of Independence, against all things British. But one thing leads on to another. The antique buildings had to have furnishings to match; such, for example, as the chandeliers in the law library with porcelain candles, and the massive lanterns, not giving light but lit up very prettily on the outside by electric bulbs. With the buildings and the furnishings came the caps and gowns in colors and designs unrecognizable by Mr. M. A. Oxon, but nevertheless fine examples of the pseudoantique, and serving to give visible emphasis to the already exaggerated distinction between men who have certain degrees and men who have them not. The gowns should, however, be made thicker, or the outside world may see through the pretentiousness of the pretense. The University of Chicago carries, I think, its ritualism farther than any other American university. It has not as yet a golden mace like Yale, but on the other hand it requires academic costume for both examiners and candidates on the occasion of doctors' examination, which is not the custom elsewhere so far as I know. This devotion to ceremony is particularly curious in a Baptist institution when we consider what iconoclastic and radical folk the Baptists were in their early days. Baptist orthodoxy is unconventionality.

****

The difference between the universities in regard to their undergraduate work is greatly exaggerated, while the difference in their graduate work is insufficiently recognized. The question, "Which college for the boy?" is not of such importance as it is popularly supposed to be. All the universities here considered, and a host of others, provide substantially the same facilities for the cultural and ordinary vocational courses in at least the first two or three years. The ratio of good teachers to poor does not vary much the country through. All the libraries have more books·than the undergraduate can read. Anywhere he can learn more than he wants to. Everywhere he will be subjected to the same temptations. He will find in any of the large universities a sufficient number of associates of any desired moral, cultural, or intellectual qualities. So far as social influences go it makes more difference which fraternity he joins than which university he attends. The reports of the Carnegie Foundation show that there are enormous differences in the average expenditure per student by the different universities, but I do not believe that there is any such difference between the quality of the instruction given or the opportunities afforded, or even any direct relation between the two, so far as undergraduate work is concerned.

On the other hand, too little discrimination is commonly shown in the selection of the institution for advanced work. The differences between the universities increase as one goes up the grades. In the field of research and specialized professional work the general reputation of a university is no safe guide. Yet too often the general reputation is the deciding factor. For example, a man from California may go to Harvard or Yale for his graduate course because of their high renown, yet it may happen that Chicago or Cornell has far superior facilities for the particular work he wishes to undertake. The undergraduate is often blamed for his propensity for electing professors instead of subjects. I am inclined to think he is not altogether wrong in this, but, at any rate, the graduate should elect a professor instead of a university. The graduate student, before he begins his dissertation work, should make diligent inquiry for the most able man in the country in his chosen field and then go after him wherever he may be found. Nothing would do more to raise the standard of the graduate schools everywhere than such a disposition on the part of research students. A new-fledged doctor once suggested to me that this result could be attained most simply by putting the name of professor under whom the research was carried on in place of the name of the university in the title. "For instance," he said, "Ph.D. (Pickering) or Ph.D. (Wilson) means much more than Ph.D. (Harvard) or Ph.D. (Columbia)."

The graduate's trend of thought and life work are largely determined by his research professor, the man who sets his course for his first voyage into the unknown. If the young man realized how much depended upon the personality and perspicacity of this pilot, he would take more pains in the selection. As it is, he is apt to choose his research professor as carelessly and unpremeditatedly as he chooses a wife. One of the benefits that would result from a greater discrimination on the part of graduates would be to give the lesser universities a more even chance to do advanced work of the highest order and to retain their best men. If students would flock from all parts to a man of superior attainments wherever he might be, his honor in his own country would be enhanced and the importance of his work better recognized elsewhere. The drawing power of the great university for professors is not so much a higher salary or a bigger laboratory as it is the chance to multiply one's efficiency by the aid of a devoted band of able young disciples. [. . .]

Personally I am inclined to think that after a student has spent two years in one college the law of diminishing returns begins to apply and that he would be likely to grow faster if transplanted to another environment; but I find few agree with me on this point. Many, however, will assent in the abstract to the statement that six, seven, or eight years in a single institution is too long for the best results. [. . .]

We are assured by the president of one of our greatest universities that the superiority of the educated over the uneducated man consists in the power to discern genuine worth and exceptional ability in other men. This possession of any such superior discernment is not, however, always obvious in presidents, trustees, and other educational authorities. For example, Mr. Carnegie, who had not the advantage of college training, ascribes his industrial success to having been able to pick out for his lieutenants young men of unusual talents and enterprise. He founded the Carnegie Institution for the purpose of doing in science what he had done in the steel business; that is, to discover the exceptional man wherever he might be and set him at the work for which he was peculiarly fitted. But the Carnegie Institution, under the exclusive control of college men, has practically abandoned the search for diamonds in the rough and mute inglorious Darwins buried in country colleges, and is devoting its revenues chiefly to the support of a few permanent establishments for systematic research. I do not say that this is not a more profitable way of promoting science than the endowment of individual genius, but it is a very different thing. The patron we have always with us, but the form of the patronage changes. Formerly the duke or king gave his stipend to a certain person whom he knew and thought would make him a good poet, playwright, painter, engineer, alchemist, or astrologer. In spite of the capriciousness and tyranny of the patron and the sycophancy of the retainer, the system did produce some great names. Nowadays we put faith in institutions rather than in individuals, and our modern Medici subsidize sciences instead of men of science.

The scores of different degrees granted by our universities have mostly lost their significance, those that ever had any, but fortunately the most important of them, the doctorate of philosophy, has a fairly well-defined meaning in any particular field. Between different departments of the same university, however, there is apt to be wide variation in its requirements. In the sciences, for example, it stands for creative ability, for the power to produce whatever one has been studying about. It must be admitted that not all the doctors in science give any convincing evidence of such ability after they get away from their Alma Mater, but while there they are supposed to have done some original work. In the literary departments there is not even a pretense of any such standard. The candidate for Ph.D. in literature is not expected to produce a book, only to learn about it or about something more or less remotely connected with it, such as the printer or the printer's blunders, or the author, or the author's house, or his wife or his manservant or his maidservant or his ox or his ass or anything that is the author's. He is not required to discover something hitherto unknown, but merely to dig up something that had been forgotten. He is not even expected to discover a new author. He simply explains why some celebrated author was worth discovering and how he came to be discovered in spite of the opposition of the academic circles of his day. If one of these candidates would apply his talents and training to the exploration of an unknown field, say the reading of the thousand volumes of new poetry published in 1909 in order to pick out all the verses that show originality and genius, he would do us all a service and demonstrate the possession of a certain degree of critical insight and esthetic taste. This would correspond in science to work in taxonomy, such as going over the herbarium specimens of a particular genus or family in search of a new species, a humble but creditable branch of botanical research which, if successful, might be deemed worthy of being rewarded with a Ph.D. The origination and propagation of a new species by cross-fertilization would, however, be regarded as more completely satisfying the requirements of the degree. At any rate, the doctor in botany knows a flower when he sees it. But I am acquainted with some doctors in literature who not only could not write a good poem, but do not know what poetry is, have no idea what poetry is for, and would not be able to detect it in an unlabeled package.

It is not probable that any reputable department of chemistry would grant its doctorate to a man who presented a dissertation on "The Family, Friends, and Formative Influences of Amadeo Avogadro, Conte di Quadregna," however long and arduous a research this might have involved. No, the chemist has to imitate Avogadro to the best of his ability, not study about him. He must discover a new law, work out a puzzling reaction, or make a lot of new compounds; not find them, but invent them. It is the same in applied science and the fine arts. For an advanced degree in engineering a man must, for instance, be able to construct a bridge, one that will not fall down a-building. The school of architecture will not certify to the competency of a student until he can design a Carnegie library or a triumphal arch. The doctor in music must compose an original symphony or something of the kind.

It seems to me that it would be only fair to require of every candidate for Ph.D. in English literature the writing of a successful novel, a volume of good essays, a poem of distinct merit, an acceptable play, or some contribution to belles-lettres that will meet with the approval of the judicious if not of the public. Even the requirement that the candidate should have a ghost story accepted by *The Black Cat* or a feature page by a Sunday newspaper, would serve to weed out a considerable portion of that teeming department. That is, if literature is a science, it should require original contributions to knowledge like the other sciences. If it is an art, it should require craftsmanship like the other arts. If it partakes of the character of both, it should meet both requirements instead of dodging both by keeping in between. I do not mean to say that the dissertations now presented in literature are necessarily valueless, though it seems to me they often belong more properly to other departments, such as history, sociology, or pure philology. The subject on which a friend of mine worked for some years in one of these universities, "The Use of Sense Adjectives in the Minor Poets of the South," belongs, I should say, in psychology, if anywhere.

Now, this lowering of the standard would not matter so much in any other department. If, for example, the departments of astronomy should cease to require original research, in the sense that this is understood in the other sciences, it would not have much effect upon the university as a whole. The intrinsic difficulty of the subject would prevent its being sought by the leisure class, and even if professors of astronomy should in the future not have the zeal for discovery now so characteristic of them, it would not seriously impair the faculty and student body. But all the students go through the English department, and there they are apt to come under the influence of men who have other ideals than most of their colleagues, who are not doing, and are often not capable of doing, original work; who are not making literature of the day as other men in the faculty are making the philosophy, the politics, the art, and the science of the day. They are critical rather than creative. Their ideal is impeccability rather than originality. [. . .]

The degree of doctor of philosophy is further imperiled by its popularity. Its financial value is too great. College and even high school authorities are disposed to ignore the application of any candidate not having this appendage. They insist that all their teachers shall be doctors, oblivious of the fact that all doctors are not teachers. We have got far away from the original meaning of the title. If those trustees and presidents who regard a Ph.D. as indispensable would take the trouble to go through the catalogues of Harvard, Columbia, and Yale, they would be surprised to find how many names there are, some of the highest renown, which are not followed by these magic letters; in a few cases not even by a modest A.B. or B.S. But so long as Ph.D. is regarded as a necessary teaching degree it will be sought with persistency by those who have no other qualifications for it. And persistency here, as elsewhere, is apt to attain its object. After a while the professors get tired of seeing a man hanging around the seminar or laboratory and will give him a degree to get rid of him.

The most effective check on the tendency to lower the degree is the printing of the dissertations. This ought to be done in all cases and promptly. If delayed, as it often is, for months or years, some other graduate is likely to put down a prospect hole on the same lead and lose his labor through the prior claim. If not deemed worth printing, it may be questioned whether it is worth accepting. By printing it other people will have a chance to form an opinion as to whether it was worth accepting. The requirement of having it in type before the degree is conferred would work little hardship were it not for the insistence upon the bodily presence of the candidate, for no other apparent purpose than to grace the triumphal procession of the president on Commencement Day. Otherwise the candidate could complete his research, take his final examination, and go home or to his new field of labor, assured that his diploma would follow by registered mail whenever his dissertation was published. Under such circumstances its publication would not be unduly delayed or indefinitely postponed, as it often is at present.

But the doctors we are turning out now are not so likely to be deficient in the knowledge of their specialties as they are in that general culture and broadmindedness that are properly regarded as belonging to "a gentleman and a scholar." The making of a doctor is looked upon too much as a departmental, even as a personal, affair. If the major professor is satisfied with him, nobody else feels inclined to interpose very emphatically. This would be all right if the doctor bore the name of the professor as part of his title, but he does not. He stands as the representative of his Alma Mater in his community, and if he is not a man in whom the university can take pride, it is because the university as a whole has refused to assume the responsibility for him.

To correct this, I suggest that a preliminary examination be given after the candidate has been working a year or so in the graduate school, about the time when he begins to settle down on his specific research. Some of the universities are now requiring an examination at this point if for nothing more than to ascertain if he has a reading knowledge of French and German, but I have in mind something more thorough and extensive, a long and informal conference attended by representatives of all the principal departments, to test the candidate's personal fitness for the honor, his range of ideas, and his command over them. If the professor of political economy and the professor of philosophy find that the candidate for Ph.D. in botany cannot converse intelligently with them on their own ground, they should exercise their veto power. If, on the other hand, they find that they cannot converse intelligently with him on botanical subjects, they should resign and go into the insurance business. Nowadays, when the civil service examiners expect mail carriers to know the distance from the earth to the sun, and policemen the capital of Sweden, it is not too much to require of doctors — and of professors — a corresponding extent of information. The university authorities may believe that they are certifying only to a man's knowledge of "The Intracellular Enzymes of Penicillium Camemberti," but the outside world interprets the degree differently, and in five years the specialist in moldy cheese may be arbitrating a strike or, quite unconsciously, teaching pragmatism. We have to allow for the fact that the American system of interchangeable parts is held to apply also to our social and educational machinery.

If such a preliminary examination were held, the final one could be confined to two or three related departments, as now. I have attended the oral examinations of doctors whenever I happened to be in a university during the season, and it was interesting to see the variety of ways of conducting them, even in the same institution. Some are very ceremonious; some quite the reverse. The board of examiners varies in number from three to twenty-five. Sometimes the candidate's research work is the main subject of inquiry; sometimes it is not mentioned. In some departments outside specialists are called in to assist in the examination; in others all persons except the committee are excluded. Prospective candidates may be encouraged or may be forbidden to attend. Personally I am in favor of a greater publicity. If professors and advanced students from the same and especially from other departments would attend freely, it would be of great educational value to them and would not materially increase the embarrassment of the candidate. I suggest also that it might be advisable to make it a rule to invite the attendance of a representative of the same department of some other university to take part in the oral examination and vote on the candidate's qualifications. This, even more than the publication of the dissertation, would tend to keep up the standard. Of course, there is the danger in greater publicity, that the examination would become a mere ceremony, as the disputation became in Germany, and the candidate would merely be put through his paces by his trainer to the admiration of his friends and the wonder of the public. [. . .]

In my fourteen weeks' course in American universities I had the unusual experience of attending more than a hundred class exercises in different subjects conducted by as many different instructors. It was an interesting experience, and valuable. If I had had it before, I would not have spoiled so many roomsful of students in learning how to teach — and how not to. Coming back to the classroom after having left it for five years, and so viewing it from the standpoint of an outsider while retaining a sympathetic comprehension of the difficulties of a teacher, I was struck by the waste of time and energy in the ordinary collegiate instruction. The scholarship of the profession in all its grades is doubtless higher than it ever was. There is no lack of industry, devotion, and enthusiasm on the part of the teachers, but the educational results are not commensurate with the opportunities afforded and the efforts expended. There is too much "lost motion" somewhere in the process. It would be well if the teachers did not know quite so much, if they knew how to tell what they did know better. It is a principle of hydraulics that the flow of water depends on the character of the outlet and the head, and not at all on the amount of water in the tank. In many cases it has seemed to me that the instructor has come into the room without the slightest idea of how he is to present his subject. He rambles on in a more or less interesting and instructive manner, but without any apparent regard to the effect on his audience or the economy of their attention. The methods of instruction are much the same as those used in the universities of the thirteenth century. There is no general appreciation of the fact that the printing press has been invented since then, also the camera and kinetoscope, the typewriter, and the mimeograph; and that for this eye-minded generation there are many more effective methods of conveying an idea than the spoken word. "The power of the spoken word," about which we hear so much nowadays, depends unfortunately upon who speaks it. Born orators are few in our faculties and trained orators are fewer. Many lecturers do not even take pains to speak distinctly enough so they can be heard in their small classrooms without strained attention. Many introduce matter which cannot be conveyed through the ear. I have heard long columns of figures read off to a class, tables of boiling points, population, and the like; also descriptions of complicated apparatus and machinery, details of analytical processes, dimensions of ancient buildings, lists of names and dates, references to readings, sometimes read in such a hurried and indistinct manner that they could not be taken down, sometimes slowly and laboriously written out on the blackboard. Such data, wherever necessary, should be given to the students in printed or typewritten syllabi, and the university authorities should see that such facilities are freely provided for their instructors and utilized by them. The lecture is useful for inspiration and demonstration, but not for information. Facts and figures that the lecturer cannot keep in his own head for fifty minutes are not likely to get into the heads of the students.

The scientific professor has an advantage over his colleagues in being able to use experimental illustrations, but he does not always make the most of his advantage. This is due to the general adoption of the self-denying ordinance, "Use the simplest experiment that will illustrate the point." If simplicity means lack of complexity, this is a good rule, but if it is interpreted as "the most modest and inconspicuous experiment that will illustrate the point," it is false pedagogy. We have gone too far in the avoidance of grandstand plays, forgetting that college students are human beings, and as such are impressed by bigness and noise. I believe that the spectacular experiment can be used with advantage in our large lecture rooms, even though it seems like a return to the much contemned "Wonders of Science" epoch. Pouring a jar of carbon dioxide down on a dozen candles undeniably makes more of an impression than pouring it on one candle, and the game is worth the candles. A professor of chemistry was once commiserating the professor of mathematics on the fewness of his students, and the latter, resenting the implication that popularity was a proof of good teaching, replied: "The trouble with mathematics is that nothing ever happens. If, when an equation is solved, it would blow up or give off a bad odor, I would get as many students as you."

I have heard of a professor of English in one of our universities who evidently felt that his department was under the same disadvantage as mathematics. Finding that his scientific colleagues were getting appropriations of astonishing liberality for illustrative apparatus, he put in his annual report a request for $5000 for an aviary. When the president asked him to explain, he said that it was impossible for him to teach poetry properly unless he had an aviary connected with his classroom. "Then," he said, "when the class is reading Shelley's 'Skylark,' I reach my long-handled net into the cage, catch a lark, and hold it up to them. And when we are studying 'The Rime of the Ancient Mariner,' my assistant will be stationed in the gallery with a crossbow to shoot a real, live albatross on the platform, thus giving the students opportunities for observation that doubtless Coleridge himself never had."

The literary faculty has borrowed and misapplied so many of the methods of scientific research and instruction that it is impossible to say that we may not come to this yet. At any rate, the project shows a commendable enterprise and appreciation of the desirability of stimulating the interest of the students by bringing them into closer contact with reality.

If the lectures could be made more inspiring and stimulating, they could be made fewer and shorter. A flash of lightning makes a more lasting impression than a 16-c.p. incandescent running all night. But the students have not sufficient resistance to stand shocks of lightning for eighteen hours a week, nor could the instructor keep up the necessary voltage. The really eloquent and inspiring speakers in the universities, are not numerous enough to go around, and they are often poor drillmasters and inefficient administrative officers. Their gift could be utilized to the best advantage by having them address large classes once or twice a week and in several different institutions during the year. Then the ordinary and stationary instructors could devote themselves to working with the students at close quarters. That is, should not there be recognized in university work the distinction of function which, in some form or other, has always been made in the ecclesiastical work, the distinction between prophet and priest, revivalist and pastor?

As it is, the professors give too many lectures and the students listen to too many. Or pretend to; really they do not listen, however attentive and orderly they may be. The bell rings and a troop of tired-looking boys, followed perhaps by a larger number of meek-eyed girls, file into the classroom, sit down, remove the expressions from their faces, open their notebooks on the broad chair arms, and receive. It is about as inspiring an audience as a roomful of phonographs holding up their brass trumpets. They reproduce the lecture in recitations like the phonograph, mechanically and faithfully, but with the tempo and timbre so changed that the speaker would like to disown his remarks if he could. The instructor tries to provoke them into a semblance of life by extravagant and absurd statements, by insults, by dazzling paradoxes, by extraneous jokes. No use; they just take it down. If he says that "William the Norman conquered England in 1066," or "William the German conquered England in 1920," it is all the same to them. They take it down. The secret is that they have, without knowing anything about physiological psychology, devised an automatic cut-off which goes into operation as they open their notebooks and short-circuits the train of thought from the ear directly to the hand, without its having to pass through the pineal gland or wherever the soul may be at the time residing and holding court.

One of the unfortunate results of the lecture system is that the professors get so used to talking that they cannot stop. Faculty, departmental, and council meetings are apt to be unduly extended, and in the end the wisdom of the whole body is not equal to the sum of its parts. On account of their ineffectiveness as a branch of administrative machinery, the tendency is to curtail their power and throw more responsibility upon the president, who is, like the Speaker of the House of Representatives, forced to become an autocrat. So far as my experience and observation go, the deliberative bodies of universities, small and large, have substantially the same method of procedure, and I suggest that if the following rules were framed and hung on the wall of the faculty room, it would save time now wasted in discussing the proper order: —

Order Of Business at Faculty Meetings

1. Present motion.
2. Pass it.
3. Discuss it.
4. Reconsider it.
5. Amend it.
6. Amend the amendment.
7. Discuss it.
8. Move to lay on the table.
9. Discuss it.
10. Refer to a committee with power to act.
11. Discuss it.
12. Adjourn.
13. Discuss it.

I have preferred to deal with the wider movements and tendencies of the universities, both good and bad, in connection with the particular institutions in which they happened to be conspicuous, rather than reserve them for the end. This has, I am aware, placed an exaggerated emphasis on certain features in each case and given to my criticisms an unfair incidence. But when the novelist describes the nose of one of his characters, the teeth of another, and the hair of a third, he expects the reader's imagination will credit these personages with the other customary features of normal size and function. I ask a similar indulgence. When I do not have occasion to mention, say, the department of French, the Y. M. C. A., or the gymnasium in any case, it is to be assumed that they are present and doing their proper work. If the reader wishes a complete and authoritative description of a university, with each department given its due space, he should read the catalogue instead of this book.

After all, these universities are very much alike; more alike, doubtless, than they claim to be; more alike, probably, than they should be. For a wider field could be covered if the different universities were more specialized and diversified in their professional and graduate schools. The American university tends to a specific type, very different from that of England, Germany, or France. This type has now been authoritatively defined for us by the National Association of State Universities at its thirteenth annual meeting [For full details of the requirements see the Report of the U. S. Commissioner of Education, 1909, p. 89.]. The "standard American university" must require for entrance to its college department a high school course of four years or its equivalent; it must give in its college of arts and sciences two years of general or liberal work, followed by two years of more specialized work of university character; it must have adequate facilities in at least five departments for three years of graduate work leading to the Ph.D. degree; it must have at least one professional school, such as law, medicine, or engineering, requiring for entrance two years of college work. It will be seen that this is an ideal rather than an average. A strict construction of the detailed specifications would come near ruling out some of these fourteen great American universities, particularly on account of the collegiate requirement for the professional schools. [. . .]

In devoting so much attention as I have to the novel and spectacular work of these universities I have not done justice to the faithful service done in the more ordinary and more essential departments. Notwithstanding that the average professor receives relatively less remuneration and less honor from the community than in past generations, there never were more competent and earnest men engaged in university work. And when we consider how many of them have turned aside from opportunities to make money because they preferred teaching and research, it is hard for them to lie sneered at for incompetency because some of the men they have trained are getting bigger salaries than they. Our universities are "under fire" just now from many quarters, but more often because they are in advance of the age than behind it. They are more efficient in their methods and more ready to meet and even anticipate the needs of the community than ever before. On the whole they fully justify the liberal support they are receiving in all parts of this country.

It was necessary for me to limit my study to a few universities, and I have chosen the more prominent ones because they have the most points of interest and present some novel problems. But it should be understood that there are scores of other institutions in the United States that do just as good work in collegiate education and often in advanced and specialized studies as those here mentioned. In conclusion I can find no words that more exactly express my opinion than those used by James Bryce in his "American Commonwealth": —

"If I may venture to state the impression which the American Universities have made upon me, I will say that while of all the institutions of the country they are those of which the American speaks most modestly, and indeed, deprecatingly, they are those which seem to be at this moment making the swiftest progress, and to have the brightest promise for the future. They are supplying exactly those things which European cities have hitherto found lacking to America; and they are contributing to her political as well as to her contemplative life elements of inestimable worth."

4.2: Reforming Medical Education: Abraham Flexner's 1910 Report for the Carnegie Foundation for the Advancement of Teaching

Though more than a century has passed since its publication, the significance of Abraham Flexner's seminal work on medical education in the United States and Canada is undiminished. Although the work came to be associated with its author, the "Flexner Report" moniker leaves unacknowledged the contribution of another luminary, Henry S. Pritchett, who penned the report's introduction. As president of the Carnegie Foundation for the Advancement of Teaching (CFAT), Pritchett's vision and personality permeated that organization's publications and initiatives. His introduction, a portion of which appears below, illuminates the Carnegie Foundation's motives for publishing the report and provides a succinct overview of its contents. Also included here is chapter IX, entitled "Reconstruction," which envisions the transformation of medical education in the United States and Canada based on the report's findings.

Many aspects of the report, though important, prove too narrowly focused for inclusion in this volume; readers interested in the early history of American medical education, the science-intensive curriculum to which Flexner urged schools to adhere, and the regulatory mechanisms that he advocated will find satisfaction in consulting the source document in its entirety. Two formatting changes should be noted in the excerpts that follow: (1) information from the footnotes has been integrated into the text in brackets or, where indicated, omitted; and (2) the maps that appeared in chapter IX of the original report have not been reproduced here.

Abraham Flexner, *Medical Education in the United States and Canada: A Report to the Carnegie Foundation for the Advancement of Teaching*, Bulletin Number Four (New York: Carnegie Foundation for the Advancement of Teaching, 1910). Reprinted by permission of the Carnegie Foundation for the Advancement of Teaching.

The present report on medical education forms the first of a series of papers on professional schools to be issued by the Carnegie Foundation. The preparation of these papers has grown naturally out of the situation with which the trustees of the Foundation were confronted when they took up the trust committed to them.

When the work of the Foundation began five years ago the trustees found themselves intrusted with an endowment to be expended for the benefit of teachers in the colleges and universities of the United States, Canada, and Newfoundland. It required but the briefest examination to show that amongst the thousand institutions in English-speaking North America which bore the name college or university there was little unity of purpose or of standards. A large majority of all the institutions in the United States bearing the name college were really concerned with secondary education.

Under these conditions the trustees felt themselves compelled to begin a critical study of the work of the college and of the university in different parts of this wide area, and to commend to colleges and universities the adoption of such standards as would intelligently relate the college to the secondary school and to the university. While the Foundation has carefully refrained from attempting to become a standardizing agency, its influence has been thrown in the direction of a differentiation between the secondary school and the college, and between the college and the university. It is indeed only one of a number of agencies, including the stronger colleges and universities, seeking to bring about in American education some fair conception of unity and the attainment ultimately of a system of schools intelligently related to each other and to the ambitions and needs of a democracy.

At the beginning, the Foundation naturally turned its study to the college, as that part of our educational system most directly to be benefited by its endowment. Inevitably, however, the scrutiny of the college led to the consideration of the relations between the college or university and the professional schools which had gathered about it or were included in it. The confusion found here was quite as great as that which exists between the field of the college and that of the secondary school. Colleges and universities were discovered to have all sorts of relations to their professional schools of law, of medicine, and of theology. In some cases these relations were of the frailest texture, constituting practically only a license from the college by which a proprietary medical school or law school was enabled to live under its name. In other cases the medical school was incorporated into the college or university, but remained an *imperium in imperio*, the college assuming no responsibility for its standards or its support. In yet other cases the college or university assumed partial obligation of support, but no responsibility for the standards of the professional school, while in only a relatively small number of cases was the school of law or of medicine an integral part of the university, receiving from it university standards and adequate maintenance. For the past two decades there has been a marked tendency to set up some connection between universities and detached medical schools, but under the very loose construction just referred to.

Meanwhile the requirements of medical education have enormously increased. The fundamental sciences upon which medicine depends have been greatly extended. The laboratory has come to furnish alike to the physician and to the surgeon a new means for diagnosing and combating disease. The education of the medical practitioner under these changed conditions makes entirely different demands in respect to both preliminary and professional training.

Under these conditions and in the face of the advancing standards of the best medical schools it was clear that the time had come when the relation of professional education in medicine to the general system of education should be clearly defined. The first step towards such a clear understanding was to ascertain the facts concerning medical education and the medical schools themselves at the present time. In accordance, therefore, with the recommendation of the president and the executive committee, the trustees of the Carnegie Foundation at their meeting in November, 1908, authorized a study and report upon the schools of medicine and law in the United States and appropriated the money necessary for this undertaking. The present report upon medical education, prepared, under the direction of the Foundation, by Mr. Abraham Flexner, is the first result of that action.

No effort has been spared to procure accurate and detailed information as to the facilities, resources, and methods of instruction of the medical schools. They have not only been separately visited, but every statement made in regard to each detail has been carefully checked with the data in possession of the American Medical Association, likewise obtained by personal inspection, and with the records of the Association of American Medical Colleges, so far as its membership extends. The details as stated go forth with the sanction of at least two, and frequently more, independent observers.

In making this study the schools of all medical sects have been included. It is clear that so long as a man is to practise medicine, the public is equally concerned in his right preparation for that profession, whatever he call himself,—allopath, homeopath, eclectic, osteopath, or whatnot. It is equally clear that he should be grounded in the fundamental sciences upon which medicine rests, whether he practises under one name or under another.

It will be readily understood that the labor involved in visiting 150 such schools is great, and that in the immense number of details dealt with it is altogether impossible to be sure that every minute fact concerning these institutions has been ascertained and set down. While the Foundation cannot hope to obtain in so great an undertaking absolute completeness in every particular, such care has been exercised, and the work has been so thoroughly reviewed by independent authorities, that the statements which are given here may be confidently accepted as setting forth the essential facts respecting medical education and respecting the institutions which deal with it.

In this connection it is perhaps desirable to add one further word. Educational institutions, particularly those which are connected with a college or a university, are peculiarly sensitive to outside criticism, and particularly to any statement of the circumstances of their own conduct or equipment which seems to them unfavorable in comparison with that of other institutions. As a rule, the only knowledge which the public has concerning an institution of learning is derived from the statements given out by the institution itself, information which, even under the best circumstances, is colored by local hopes, ambitions, and points of view. A considerable number of colleges and universities take the unfortunate position that they are private institutions and that the public is entitled to only such knowledge of their operations as they choose to communicate. In the case of many medical schools the aversion to publicity is quite as marked as it is reputed to be in the case of certain large industrial trusts. A few institutions questioned the right of any outside agency to collect and publish the facts concerning their medical schools. The Foundation was called upon to answer the question: Shall such an agency as the Foundation, dedicated to the betterment of American education, make public the facts concerning the medical schools of the United States and Canada?

The attitude of the Foundation is that all colleges and universities, whether supported by taxation or by private endowment, are in truth public service corporations, and that the public is entitled to know the facts concerning their administration and development, whether those facts pertain to the financial or to the educational side. We believe, therefore, that in seeking to present an accurate and fair statement of the work and the facilities of the medical schools of this country, we are serving the best possible purpose which such an agency as the Foundation can serve; and, furthermore, that only by such publicity can the true interests of education and of the universities themselves be subserved. In such a reasonable publicity lies the hope for progress in medical education.

****

The striking and significant facts which are here brought out are of enormous consequence not only to the medical practitioner, but to every citizen of the United States and Canada; for it is a singular fact that the organization of medical education in this country has hitherto been such as not only to commercialize the process of education itself, but also to obscure in the minds of the public any discrimination between the well trained physician and the physician who has had no adequate training whatsoever. As a rule, Americans, when they avail themselves of the services of a physician, make only the slightest inquiry as to what his previous training and preparation have been. One of the problems of the future is to educate the public itself to appreciate the fact that very seldom, under existing conditions, does a patient receive the best aid which it is possible to give him in the present state of medicine, and that this is due mainly to the fact that a vast army of men is admitted to the practice of medicine who are untrained in sciences fundamental to the profession and quite without a sufficient experience with disease. A right education of public opinion is one of the problems of future medical education.

The significant facts revealed by this study are these:

(1) For twenty-five years past there has been an enormous over-production of uneducated and ill trained medical practitioners. This has been in absolute disregard of the public welfare and without any serious thought of the interests of the public. Taking the United States as a whole, physicians are four or five times as numerous in proportion to population as in older countries like Germany.

(2) Over-production of ill trained men is due in the main to the existence of a very large number of commercial schools, sustained in many cases by advertising methods through which a mass of unprepared youth is drawn out of industrial occupations into the study of medicine.

(3) Until recently the conduct of a medical school was a profitable business, for the methods of instruction were mainly didactic. As the need for laboratories has become more keenly felt, the expenses of an efficient medical school have been greatly increased. The inadequacy of many of these schools may be judged

from the fact that nearly half of all our medical schools have incomes below $10,000, and these incomes determine the quality of instruction that they can and do offer.

Colleges and universities have in large measure failed in the past twenty-five years to appreciate the great advance in medical education and the increased cost of teaching it along modern lines. Many universities desirous of apparent educational completeness have annexed medical schools without making themselves responsible either for the standards of the professional schools or for their support.

(4) The existence of many of these unnecessary and inadequate medical schools has been defended by the argument that a poor medical school is justified in the interest of the poor boy. It is clear that the poor boy has no right to go into any profession for which he is not willing to obtain adequate preparation; but the facts set forth in this report make it evident that this argument is insincere, and that the excuse which has hitherto been put forward in the name of the poor boy is in reality an argument in behalf of the poor medical school.

(5) A hospital under complete educational control is as necessary to a medical school as is a laboratory of chemistry or pathology. High grade teaching within a hospital introduces a most wholesome and beneficial influence into its routine. Trustees of hospitals, public and private, should therefore go to the limit of their authority in opening hospital wards to teaching, provided only that the universities secure sufficient funds on their side to employ as teachers men who are devoted to clinical science.

In view of these facts, progress for the future would seem to require a very much smaller number of medical schools, better equipped and better conducted than our schools now as a rule are; and the needs of the public would equally require that we have fewer physicians graduated each year, but that these should be better educated and better trained. With this idea accepted, it necessarily follows that the medical school will, if rightly conducted, articulate not only with the university, but with the general system of education. Just what form that articulation must take will vary in the immediate future in different parts of the country. Throughout the eastern and central states the movement under which the medical school articulates with the second year of the college has already gained such impetus that it can be regarded as practically accepted. In the southern states for the present it would seem that articulation with the four-year high school would be a reasonable starting-point for the future. In time the development of secondary education in the south and the growth of the colleges will make it possible for southern medical schools to accept the two-year college basis of preparation. With reasonable prophecy the time is not far distant when, with fair respect for the interests of the public and the need for physicians, the articulation of the medical school with the university may be the same throughout the entire country. For in the future the college or the university which accepts a medical school must make itself responsible for university standards in the medical school and for adequate support for medical education. The day has gone by when any university can retain the respect of educated men, or when it can fulfil its duty to education, by retaining a low grade professional school for the sake of its own institutional completeness.

If these fundamental principles can be made clear to the people of the United States and of Canada, and to those who govern the colleges and the universities, we may confidently expect that the next ten years will see a very much smaller number of medical schools in this country, but a greatly increased efficiency in medical education, and that during the same period medical education will become rightly articulated with, and rightly related to, the general educational system of the whole country.

In the suggestions which are made in this report looking toward the future development of medicine, it ought to be pointed out that no visionary or impossible achievement is contemplated. It is not expected that a Johns Hopkins Medical School can be erected immediately in cities where public support of education has hitherto been meager. Nevertheless, it is quite true that there is a certain minimum of equipment and a minimum of educational requirement without which no attempt ought to be made to teach medicine. Hitherto not only proprietary medical schools, but colleges and universities, have paid scant attention to this fact. They have been ready to assume the responsibility of turning loose upon a helpless community men licensed to the practice of medicine without any serious thought as to whether they had received a fair training or not. To-day, under the methods pursued in modern medicine, we know with certainty that a medical school cannot be conducted without a certain minimum of expense and without a certain minimum of facilities. The institution which attempts to conduct a school below this plane is clearly injuring, not helping, civilization. In the suggestions which are made in this report as to what constitutes a reasonable minimum no visionary ideal has been pursued, but only such things have been insisted

develop medical schools. (2) Unfortunately, however, our universities have not always been so placed. They began in many instances as colleges or something less. Here a supposed solicitude for youth suggested an out-of-the-way location; elsewhere political bargaining brought about the same result. The state universities of the south and west, most likely to enjoy sufficient incomes, are often unfortunately located: witness the University of Alabama at Tuscaloosa, of Georgia at Athens, of Mississippi at Oxford, of Missouri at Columbia, of Arkansas at Fayetteville, of Kansas at Lawrence, of South Dakota at Vermilion; and that experience has taught us nothing is proved by the recent location of the State University of Oklahoma at Norman. Some of these institutions are freed from the necessity of undertaking to teach medicine by an endowed institution better situated; in other sections the only universities fitted by their large support and their assured scientific ideals to maintain schools of medicine are handicapped by inferiority of location. We are not thereby justified in surrendering the university principle. Experience, our own or that of Germany, proves, as we have already pointed out, that the difficulty is not insuperable. At relatively greater expense, it is still feasible to develop a medical school in such an environment: there is no magnet like reputation; nothing travels faster than the fame of a great healer; distance is an obstacle readily overcome by those who seek health. The poor as well as the rich find their way to shrines and healing springs. The faculty of medicine in these schools may even turn the defect of situation to good account; for, freed from distraction, the medical schools at Iowa City and Ann Arbor may the more readily cultivate clinical science. An alternative may indeed be tried in the shape of a remote department. The problem in that case is to make university control real, to impregnate the distant school with genuine university spirit. The difficulty of the task may well deter those whose resources are scanty or who are under no necessity of engaging in medical teaching. As we need many universities and but few medical schools, a long-distance connection is justified only where there is no local university qualified to assume responsibility. A third solution—division— may, if the position taken in previous chapters is sound, be disregarded in the final disposition. [We shall omit the half-school because it may be considered to divide with the whole school the work of the first two years; it does not greatly affect the clinical output, with which this chapter is mainly concerned.]

(3) We shall assign only one school to a single town. As a matter of fact, no American city now contains more than one well supported university, [Chicago is almost an exception, as Northwestern University is situated at Evanston, a

suburb] —and if we find it unnecessary or impolitic to duplicate local university plants, it is still less necessary to duplicate medical schools. The needless expense, the inevitable shrinkage of the student body, the difficulty of recruiting more than one faculty, the disturbance due to competition for hospital services, argue against local duplication. It is sometimes contended that competition is stimulating: Tufts claims to have waked up Harvard; the second Little Rock school did undoubtedly move the first to spend several hundred dollars on desks and apparatus. But competition may also be demoralizing; the necessity of finding students constitutes medical schools which ought to elevate standards the main obstacles to their elevation: witness the attitude of several institutions in Boston, New York, Philadelphia, Baltimore, and Chicago. Moreover, local competition is a stimulus far inferior to the general scientific competition to which all well equipped, well conducted, and rightly inspired university departments throughout the civilized world are parties. The English have experimented with both forms,—a single school in the large provincial towns, a dozen or more in London,—and their experience inclines them to reduce as far as possible the number of the London schools. Amalgamation has already taken place in certain American towns: the several schools of Cincinnati, of Indianapolis, and of Louisville have all recently "merged." This step is easy enough in towns where there is either no university or only one university. Where there are several, as in Chicago, Boston, and New York, the problem is more difficult. Approached in a broad spirit it may, however, prove not insoluble; cooperation may be arranged where several institutions all possess substantial resources; universities of limited means can retire without loss of prestige,—on the contrary, the respect in which they are held must be heightened by any action dictated by conscientious refusal to continue a work that they are in no position to do well.

(4) A reconstruction of medical education cannot ignore the patent fact that students tend to study medicine in their own states, certainly in their own sections. In general, therefore, arrangements ought to be made, as far as conditions heretofore mentioned permit, to provide the requisite facilities within each of the characteristic state groups. There is the added advantage that local, conditions are thus heeded and that the general profession is at a variety of points penetrated by educative influences. New Orleans, for example, would cultivate tropical medicine; Pittsburgh, the occupational diseases common in its environment. In respect to output, we may once more fairly take existing conditions into account. We are not called on to provide schools enough to keep up the present ratio. As

we should in any case hardly be embarrassed for almost a generation in the matter of supply, we shall do well to produce no doctors who do not represent an improvement upon the present average.

The principles above stated have been entirely disregarded in America. Medical schools have been established regardless of need, regardless of the proximity of competent universities, regardless of favoring local conditions. An expression of surprise at finding an irrelevant and superfluous school usually elicits the reply that the town, being a "gateway" or a "center," must of course harbor a "medical college." It is not always easy to distinguish "gateway" and "center:" a center appears to be a town possessing, or within easy reach of, say 50,000 persons; a gateway is a town with at least two railway stations. The same place may be both,—in which event the argument is presumably irrefragable. Augusta, Georgia, Charlotte, North Carolina, and Topeka, Kansas, are "centers," and as such are logical abodes of medical instruction. Little Rock, St. Joseph, Memphis, Toledo, Buffalo, are "gateways." The argument, so dear to local pride, can best be refuted by being pursued to its logical conclusion. For there are still forty-eight towns in the United States with over 50,000 population each, and no medical schools: we are threatened with forty-eight new schools at once, if the contention is correct. The truth is that the fundamental, though of course not sole, consideration is the university, provided its resources are adequate; and we have fortunately enough strong universities, properly distributed, to satisfy every present need without serious sacrifice of sound principle. The German Empire contains eighty-four cities whose population exceeds 50,000 each. Of its twenty-two medical schools, only eleven are to be found in them: that is, it possesses seventy-three gateways and centers without universities or medical schools. The remaining eleven schools are located in towns of less than 50,000 inhabitants, a university town of 30,000 being a fitter abode for medical study than a non-university town of half a million, in the judgment of those who have best succeeded with it.

That the existing system came about without reference to what the country needed or what was best for it may be easily demonstrated. Between 1904 and 1909 the country gained certainly upwards of 5,000,000 in population; during the same period the number of medical students actually decreased from 28,142 to 22,145, i.e., over 20 per cent. The average annual production of doctors from 1900 to 1909 was 5222; but last June the number dropped to 4442. Finally, the total number of medical colleges which reached its maximum—166 [not including osteopathic schools]—in 1904 has in the five years since decreased about 10 per cent. Our problem is to calculate how far tendencies already observable may be carried without harm.

We have calculated that the south requires for the next generation 490 new doctors annually, the rest of the country, 1500. We must then provide machinery for the training of about 2000 graduates in medicine yearly. Reckoning fatalities of all kinds at ten per cent per annum, graduating classes of 2000 imply approximately junior classes of 2200, sophomore classes of 2440, freshman classes aggregating 2700,—something over 9000 students of medicine. Thirty medical schools, with an average enrolment of 300 and average graduation classes of less than 70, will be easily equal to the task. As many of these could double both enrolment and output without danger, a provision planned to meet present needs is equally sufficient for our growth for years to come. It will be time to devise more schools when the productive limit of those now suggested shall come in sight.

For the purpose here in mind, the country may be conceived as divided into several sections, within each of which, with due regard to what it now contains, medical schools enough to satisfy its needs must be provided. [This chapter now recapitulates and summarizes the more detailed accounts contained in Part II, in which the schools of each state are described and the general state situation discussed.] Pending the fuller development of the states west of the Mississippi, the section east will have to relieve them of part of their responsibility. The provisional nature of our suggestions is thus obvious; for as the west increases in population, as its universities grow in number and strength, the balance will right itself: additional schools will be created in the west and south rather than in the north and east. It would of course be unfortunate to over-emphasize the importance of state lines. We shall do well to take advantage of every unmistakably favorable opportunity so long as we keep within the public need; and to encourage the freest possible circulation of students throughout the entire country.

(1) New England represents a fairly homogeneous region, comprising six states, the population of which is increasingly urban. Its population increased, 1908–9, somewhat less than 75,000, requiring, on the basis of one doctor to every increase of 1500 in population, 50 new doctors. About 150 physicians died. Seventy-five men would replace one-half of these. In all, 125 new doctors would be needed. To produce this number two schools, one of moderate size and one smaller, readily suffice. Fortunately they can be developed without sacrificing any of our criteria. The medical schools of Harvard and Yale are university departments, situated in the midst of ample clinical material, with considerable financial backing

now and every prospect of more. It is unwise to divide the Boston field; it is unnecessary to prolong the life of the clinical departments of Dartmouth, Bowdoin, and Vermont. They are not likely soon to possess the financial resources needed to develop adequate clinics in their present location; and the time has passed when even excellent didactic instruction can be regarded as compensating for defective opportunities in obstetrics, contagious diseases, and general medicine. The historic position of the schools in question counts little as against changed ideals. Dartmouth and Vermont can, however, offer the work of the first two years with the clinical coloring made feasible by the proximity of a hospital, as is the case with the University of Missouri at Columbia; with that they ought to be content for the time being.

(2) The middle Atlantic states comprise for our purpose New York, New Jersey, Pennsylvania, Delaware, Maryland, and the District of Columbia. Their population grows at the rate of 300,000 annually, for whom 200 doctors can care; 230 more would fill one-half the vacancies arising through death: a total of 430 needed. Available universities are situated in New York city, Syracuse, Philadelphia, Pittsburgh, Baltimore. The situation is in every respect ideal; the universities located at New York, Philadelphia, and Baltimore are strong and prosperous; those of Syracuse and Pittsburgh, though less developed, give good promise. Without sacrifice of a single detail, these five university towns can not only support medical schools for the section, but also to no small extent relieve less favored spots. The schools of Albany, Buffalo, Brooklyn, Washington [Except Howard University which, patronized by the government, is admirably located for the medical education of the negro] would, on this plan, disappear,—certainly until academic institutions of proper caliber had been developed. Whether even in the event of their creation they should for some years endeavor to cultivate medicine is quite doubtful. Appreciation of what is involved in the undertaking might well give them pause. Meanwhile, within the university towns already named there would be much to do: better state laws are needed in order to exterminate the worst schools; merger or liquidation must bring together many of those that still survive. The section under consideration ought indeed to lead the Union; but the independent schools of New York and Pennsylvania are powerful enough to prove a stubborn obstacle to any progressive movement, however clearly in the public interest.

(3) Greater unevenness must be tolerated in the south [The south includes eleven states, viz., Virginia, Kentucky, North Carolina, South Carolina, Florida,

Georgia, Tennessee, Mississippi, Louisiana, Arkansas, Texas]; proprietary schools or nominal university departments will doubtless survive longer there than in other parts of the country because of the financial weakness of both endowed and tax-supported institutions. All the more important, therefore, for universities to deal with the subject in a large spirit, avoiding both overlapping and duplication. An institution may well be glad to be absolved from responsibilities that some other is better fitted to meet. Tulane and Vanderbilt, for example, are excellently situated in respect to medical education; the former has already a considerable endowment applicable to medicine. The state universities of Louisiana and Tennessee may therefore resign medicine to these endowed institutions, grateful for the opportunity to cultivate other fields. Every added superfluous school weakens the whole by wasting money and scattering the eligible student body. None of the southern state universities, indeed, is wisely placed: Texas has no alternative but a remote department, such as it now supports at Galveston; Georgia will one day develop a university medical school at Atlanta; Alabama, at Birmingham,—the university being close by, at Tuscaloosa. The University of Virginia is repeating Ann Arbor at Charlottesville; whether it would do better to operate a remote department at Richmond or Norfolk, the future will determine. Six schools are thus provided [A seventh, Meharry, at Nashville, must be included for the medical education of the negro]: they are sufficient to the needs of the section just now. The resources available even for their support are as yet painfully inadequate: three of the six are still dependent upon fees for both plant and maintenance. It is doubtful whether the other universities of the south should generally offer even the instruction of the first two years. The scale upon which these two-year departments can be now organized by them is below the minimum of continuous efficiency; they can contribute nothing to science, and their quota of physicians can be better trained in one of the six schools suggested. Concentration in the interest of effectiveness, team work between all institutions working in the cause of southern development, economy as a means of improving the lot of the teacher—these measures, advisable everywhere, are especially urgent in the south.

(4) In the north central tier—Ohio, Indiana, Michigan, Wisconsin, Illinois—population increased 239,685 the last year: 160 doctors would care for the increase; 190 more would replace one-half of those that died: a total of 350. Large cities with resident universities available for medical education are Cincinnati, Columbus, Cleveland, and Chicago. Ann Arbor has demonstrated the ability suc-

cessfully to combat the disadvantages of a small town. The University of Wisconsin can unquestionably do the same, with a slighter handicap, at Madison whenever it chooses to complete its work there. Indiana University has undertaken the problem of a distant connection at Indianapolis. Four cities thus fulfil all our criteria, two more develop the small town type, one more is an experiment with the remote university department. Surely the territory in question can be supplied by these seven medical centers. Chicago alone is likely to draw a considerable number of students from a wider area. It has long been a populous medical center. Nevertheless the number of high-grade students it just now contains is not large. If the practice of medicine in this area rested on a two-year college basis, as it well might, there would to-day be perhaps 600 students of medicine in that city. Cooperative effort between the two universities there and the state university at Urbana would readily provide for them.

(5) The middle west comprises eight states, Minnesota, Iowa, Missouri, Oklahoma, Kansas, Nebraska, South Dakota, North Dakota, with a gain in population last year of 216,036, requiring 140 more physicians, plus 160 to replace half the deaths: a total of 300. To supply them, urban universities capable of conducting medical departments of proper type are situated in Minneapolis and St. Louis; and both deserve strong, well supported schools. For Minneapolis must largely carry the weight of the Dakotas and Montana; St. Louis must assist Texas and have an eye to Arkansas, Oklahoma, and the southwest. The University of Nebraska, now dispersing its energies through a divided school, can be added to this list; for it will quite certainly either concentrate the department at its own site (Lincoln, population 48,232), or bring the two pieces together at Omaha, only an hour's distance away. The University of Kansas will doubtless combine its divided department at Kansas City. The State University of Iowa emulates Ann Arbor at Iowa City. These five schools must produce 297 doctors annually. Their capacity would go much farther. Oklahoma [Should it be possible for the State University of Oklahoma, by engaging in clinical work at Oklahoma City, to get and to retain a monopoly of the field, the step would doubtless be advisable even now] and the Dakotas might well for a time postpone the entire question, supporting the work of the first two years, which they have already undertaken, on a much more liberal basis than they have yet reached. With the exception of St. Louis, all these proposed schools belong to state universities, and even at St. Louis the cooperation of the state university may prove feasible. A close relation may thus be secured between agencies concerned with public health and those devoted to medical

education. The public health laboratory may become virtually part of the medical school,—a highly stimulating relation for both parties. The school will profit by contact with concrete problems; the public health laboratory will inevitably push beyond routine, prosecuting in a scientific spirit the practical tasks referred to it from all portions of the state. The direct connection of the state with a medical school that it wholly or even partly maintains will also solve the vexed question of standards: for the educational standard which the state fixes for its own sons will be made the practice standard as well. Private corporations, whether within or without its borders, will no longer be permitted to deluge the community with an inferior product.

(6) Seven thinly settled and on the whole slowly growing states and territories form the farther west: New Mexico, Colorado, Wyoming, Montana, Idaho, Utah, Arizona. Their increase in population was last year about 45,000. They contain now one doctor for every 563 persons. In view of local conditions, let us reckon one additional doctor for every additional 750 persons: 60 will be required. And, further, let us make up the death-roll man for man: 60 more would be needed—altogether 120. There are at the moment in this region only two available sites, Salt Lake City and Denver. At the former the University of Utah is situated; the latter could be occupied by the University of Colorado, located at Boulder, practically a suburb. The outlying portions of this vast territory will long continue to procure their doctors by immigration or by sending their sons to Minneapolis, Madison, Ann Arbor, Chicago, or St. Louis.

(7) The three states on the Pacific coast, California, Oregon, Washington, are somewhat self-contained. They increased last year by 53,454 persons, requiring 36 more physicians; 50 more would repair one-half the losses by death: a total of 86. Available sites, filling the essential requirements, are Berkeley and Seattle. The former, with the adjoining towns of Alameda and Oakland, controls a population of 250,000 or more; the medical department of the University of California concentrated there would enjoy ideal conditions. At present the clinical ends of two divided schools share San Francisco, and the outlook for medical education of high quality is rendered dubious by the division. With unique wisdom the University of Washington and the physicians of Seattle [footnote omitted] have thus far refrained from starting a medical school in that state. They have held, and rightly, that in the present highly overcrowded condition of the profession on the coast, there is no need for an additional ordinary school; and the resources of the university are not yet adequate to a really creditable establishment. The

field will therefore be kept clear until the university is in position to occupy it to advantage.

(8) In Canada the existing ratio of physicians to population is 1:1030. The estimated increase of population last year was 239,516, requiring 160 new physicians; losses by death are estimated at 90. As the country is thinly settled and doctors much less abundant than in the United States, let us suppose these replaced man for man: 250 more doctors would be annually required. The task of supplying them could be for the moment safely left to the Universities of Toronto and Manitoba, to McGill and to Laval at Quebec. Halifax, Western (London), and Laval at Montreal have no present function. At some future time doubtless Dalhousie University at Halifax will need to create a medical department. The future of Queen's depends on its ability to develop halfway between Toronto and Montreal, despite comparative inaccessibility, the Ann Arbor type of school. As for the rest, the great northwestern territory will, as it develops, create whatever additional facilities it may require.

In so far as the United States is concerned, the foregoing sketch calls for 31 medical schools [footnote omitted] with a present annual output of about 2000 physicians, *i.e.*, an average graduating class of about 70 each. They are capable of producing 3500. All are university departments, busy in advancing knowledge as well as in training doctors. Nineteen are situated in large cities with the universities of which they are organic parts; four are in small towns with their universities; eight are located in large towns always close by the parent institutions. Divided and far distant departments are altogether avoided.

Twenty states [They are Maine, New Hampshire, Vermont, West Virginia, North Carolina, South Carolina, Florida, Mississippi, Kentucky, Arkansas, Oklahoma, North Dakota, South Dakota, Montana, Wyoming, Idaho, New Mexico, Arizona, Nevada, Oregon. One school will not long content the state of Texas.] are left without a complete school. Most of these are unlikely to be favorably circumstanced for the next half century, so far as we can now judge. Several may, however, find the undertaking feasible within a decade or two. The University of Arkansas might be moved from Fayetteville to Little Rock; Oklahoma, if its rapid growth is maintained, may from Norman govern a medical school at Oklahoma City; Oregon may take full responsibility for Portland. Unfortunately, of the three additional schools thus created, only one, that at Little Rock, would represent conditions at their best. There is therefore no reason to hasten the others; for their problem may, if left open, be more advantageously solved.

To bring about the proposed reconstruction, some 120 schools have been apparently wiped off the map. As a matter of fact, our procedure is far less radical than would thus appear. Of the 120 schools that disappear, 37 are already negligible, for they contain less than 50 students apiece; 13 more contain between 50 and 75 students each, and 16 more between 75 and 100. That is, of the 120 schools, 66 are so small that their student bodies can, in so far as they are worthy, be swept into strong institutions without seriously stretching their present enrolment. Of the 30 institutions that remain, several will survive through merger. For example, the Cleveland College of Physicians and Surgeons could be consolidated with Western Reserve; the amalgamation of Jefferson Medical College and the University of Pennsylvania would make one fair-sized school on an enforced two-year college standard; Tufts and Harvard, Vanderbilt and the University of Tennessee, Creighton and the University of Nebraska, would, if joined, form institutions of moderate size, capable of considerable expansion before reaching the limit of efficiency.

In order that these mergers may be effective, not only institutional, but personal ambition must be sacrificed. It is an advantage when two schools come together; but the advantage is gravely qualified if the new faculty is the arithmetical sum of both former faculties. The mergers at Cincinnati, Indianapolis, Louisville, Nashville, have been arranged in this way. The fundamental principles of faculty organization are thus sacrificed. Unless combination is to destroy organization, titles must be shaved when schools unite. There must be one professor of medicine, one professor of surgery, etc., to whom others are properly subordinated. What with superabundant professorial appointments, due now to desire to annex another hospital, and again to annexation of another school, faculties have become unmanageably large, viewed either as teaching, research, or administrative bodies.

Reduction of our 155 medical schools to 31 would deprive of a medical school no section that is now capable of maintaining one. It would threaten no scarcity of physicians until the country's development actually required more than 3500 physicians annually, that is to say, for a generation or two, at least. Meanwhile, the outline proposed involves no artificial standardization: it concedes a different standard to the south as long as local needs require; it concedes the small town university type where it is clearly of advantage to adhere to it; it varies the general ratio in thinly settled regions; and, finally, it provides a system capable without overstraining of producing twice as many doctors as we suppose the country now

146 Captains of Industry and Erudition

to need. In other words, we may be wholly mistaken in our figures without in the least impairing the feasibility of the kind of renovation that has been outlined; and every institution arranged for can be expected to make some useful contribution to knowledge and progress.

The right of the state to deal with the entire subject in its own interest can assuredly not be gainsaid. The physician is a social instrument. If there were no disease, there would be no doctors. And as disease has consequences that immediately go beyond the individual specifically affected, society is bound to protect itself against unnecessary spread of loss or danger. It matters not that the making of doctors has been to some extent left to private institutions. The state already makes certain regulations; it can by the same right make others. Practically the medical school is a public service corporation. It is chartered by the state; it utilizes public hospitals on the ground of the social nature of its service. The medical school cannot then escape social criticism and regulation. It was left to itself while society knew no better. But civilization consists in the legal registration of gains won by science and experience; and science and experience have together established the terms upon which medicine can be most useful. "In the old days," says Metchnikoff, [*The Nature of Man* (translated by Chalmers), p. 300] "anyone was allowed to practise medicine, because there was no medical science and nothing was exact. Even at the present time among less civilized people, any old woman is allowed to be a midwife. Among more civilized races, differentiation has taken place and childbirths are attended by women of special training who are midwives by diploma. In case of nations still more civilized, the trained midwives are directed by obstetric physicians who have specialized in the conducting of labor. This high degree of differentiation has arisen with and has itself aided the progress of obstetrical science." Legislation which should procure for all the advantage of such conditions as is now possible would speedily bring about a reconstruction quite as extensive as that described.

Such control in the social interest inevitably encounters the objection that individualism is thereby impaired. So it is, at that level; so it is intended. The community through such regulation undertakes to abridge the freedom of particular individuals to exploit certain conditions for their personal benefit. But its aim is thereby to secure for all others more freedom at a higher level. Society forbids a company of physicians to pour out upon the community a horde of ill trained physicians. Their liberty is indeed clipped. As a result, however, more competent doctors being trained under the auspices of the state itself, the public health is improved; the physical well-being of the wage-worker is heightened; and a restriction put upon the liberty, so-called, of a dozen doctors increases the effectual liberty of all other citizens. Has democracy, then, really suffered a set-back? Reorganization along rational lines involves the strengthening, not the weakening, of democratic principle, because it tends to provide the conditions upon which well-being and effectual liberty depend.

4.3: A College Professor's Wife (1905)

Official documents and formal organizational charts of American colleges and universities seldom, if ever, include the role of faculty spouse. Yet anyone who has studied or worked at a campus knows well the crucial and underappreciated contributions spouses—overwhelmingly women—have made to the campus community. College presidents and boards have for years benefited from and often exploited the talents, good faith, and dedication of faculty spouses. Professors' wives often worked as overqualified and underpaid secretarial and staff members on campus. They were expected to host numerous receptions at their private homes without reimbursement. The following account by a professor's wife at a small independent college in the Midwest offers a rare portrait of an academic family, including workload, living conditions, salary, and the demands of socialization into the college town.

Many of the people in our town think that we members of the college faculty dwell on Mount Parnassus; that we eat of the ambrosia of books and drink of the nectar of music and painting. No burdens of ordinary mortals come near us, no sordid struggles engage us ours is a life of high ideals and beautiful thoughts. The color and making of the next ball gown certainly never is discussed, but in place of it there is careful planning to see if a suit and a half for the boys may be gotten out of their father's old one. The latest fad in dinner serving is unheard of, but we professors' wives do try to learn the most attractive way to prepare the famly breakfast without the luxuries of coffee and meat.

An income of $1,100 a year and four children and house rent, a taste for books, art and music, and travel and no struggles, think you?

My day begins at six o'clock the year round with giving or superintending cold baths for the four children and myself. Then there are backs to button and

"A College Professor's Wife," *The Independent* (November 30, 1905) vol. 59, pp. 1279–1283.

hair to comb, and it is easily quarter after seven, our breakfast hour, by the time all are ready.

Bertha, a student who earns her room and board with us during term time, prepares the breakfast of oatmeal and cocoa.

After the meal there are the Professor and two boys to start off to college and school, respectively. Each needs personal inspection a loose button tightened, an application of the whisk broom, or the tie retouched. Then the little girls come with me into the kitchen, and we wash and put away the breakfast dishes, scalding all the milk pails and pans and skimming the cream for the butter. Then we make the beds and put upstairs in order. (Bertha cares for her own room.) The study and other living rooms come next, and when they are dusted and neat, it is time to prepare the vegetables for dinner.

It is while I am getting dinner that Ruth and Mary have their book lessons. We do not care to have our children enter school before the third grade because of the class of children that attend our ward school. The two little girls use a wooden box for a desk, sitting on two lower ones, in a snug corner of the kitchen, where I can teach them as I peel potatoes, pare apples or move about the room mixing a pudding. It takes some time to prepare a meal for seven people, four of them hungry students. One thing that makes it harder is not having any water or sink in the house. By half after twelve the dinner is on the table, and I have spent a morning in careful planning, with quick, sure strokes to get all the work done, and yet have time to stop occasionally, as I have to, to teach the children. They come first, after all.

In winter the dinner consists of a cheap cut of meat, usually beef, that I grind up or steam tender and then cook in all sorts of ways to make a palatable variety, potatoes in various forms, frequently dried beans or peas, baked or boiled, from time to time relieved by parsnips, carrots, turnips, or macaroni, rice and escalloped tomatoes, a large part of the latter being bread crumbs. For dessert, clear fruit is too luxurious, so I prepare it with tapioca; batter pudding, corn starch or bread crumbs in different puddings. I begrudge the time it takes to make these simple puddings, but we cannot afford an apple, orange or banana apiece per diem at winter prices.

During the summer we rarely buy meat, but eat the eggs from our own hens. We also have many fresh vegetables from our garden patch; but we can't touch even canned ones in winter, much less dream of fresh ones. The tomatoes used for escalloping in Winter are some I put up from our own garden.

The dinner over, Bertha takes charge of dining-room, kitchen and door-bell. The Professor takes care of the children, and I have one quiet, restful hour alone, the only one in the twenty-four that I can call all mine. That is not always un-interrupted, as every mother knows. In that hour I have to make my simple toilet for the afternoon and take a nap. A cat nap it is; but oh! it is so much needed, for housework tires me out. Perhaps if the muscles for housework had been devel-oped in girlhood it would not wear on me so much. Then, best of all in my hour, I lie down on the bed and read for twenty minutes—sometimes a full half hour. I read—I devour rather—some rare morsel of rich condensed thought-food, and I digest it later as I sew, enjoying it quietly, deeply.

From two thirty until ten o'clock I sew, stopping at half past five for a half hour's walk with my husband and some of the children, followed by supper at six. If informal callers drop in during the afternoon, I continue sewing, they often bringing theirs with them.

I give half an hour of music to each of the children during the afternoon as I sew. Except for his half hour at the piano or violin, each child lives out of doors all afternoon, no matter what the weather, and a rosy, jolly little group they make. On my constitutional with James the children skip and dance around us as we walk out over the prairie toward the glorious West sky. Then comes the most pleasant meal of the day, supper. Then my husband's class work is over, and we are all hungry from the fresh air, and we have the fun of a foreign language. We have French and German suppers on alternate days, in conversation only, the bill of fare being good American cereals and bread and milk.

After supper, if it lacks seven o'clock, the little girls' bed time, we all gather around the piano and sing some simple songs in English, French and German, or I play while the children dance. The little dances they know I teach them on Saturday mornings, when Bertha takes some of my housework.

At seven, James carries a little girl upstairs on each shoulder and puts them to bed, a privilege he has made his own. In the meantime, I have my talk with the boys. They tell their little confidences more freely being both together, each one helping the other by loving suggestion. They are so unalike that each has great admiration for the other. In half an hour they scamper upstairs and take posses-sion of their father.

By eight o'clock my turn comes. James sits by me as I sew, and we talk alone together for the first time in the day. Sometimes he reads aloud to me, but at half after eight his evening's study begins. If my work is on a garment that does not need turning and shifting about so that I make no motions to divert his attention from his books, I sit silently by him sewing, sewing without a word, glad to be near my faithful, plodding man. When ten o'clock comes, I bid him goodnight and go off to my little Ruth and Mary, leaving him still working. Sometimes a neighbor spends the evening with me, sewing or reading aloud. What a delight to be read to as I sew! Because I loved books and music too well, I hardly knew how to handle a needle before I was married. But the college days and study in Europe help the needle thru hard places now. All this sewing does not mean that I am an atom in a sweatshop system. I means that I am taking the only, the last way possible, to make ends meet on our salary and yet live with my children in their work and in their play. My husband's clothing and my winter under woolens are all that we buy ready made. I make sturdy jackets for James to save the wear on his sacque coat, and keep a piece of carpet in his study chair to save the trousers. Of course, all repairs, relinings and pressing on his clothing I attend to. My coats and dresses are my hardest tasks, harder even than the boys' suits. All of the children's clothing, both outer and undergarments, I alone make, many of them from the sound parts of their parents' clothing. Then there are carpets to mend, comfortables to make, and other household supplies to keep up. The regular weekly stocking darning and other mending for an active family of six is no small item.

Our student helper, Bertha, does her own ironing and bakes the bread twice a week. I frequently help her with the mid-week baking. She cooks breakfast and supper, washes the dinner and supper dishes, and fills the lamps. On Friday afternoon and Saturday morning she gives me two extra hours each for sweeping. In exchange for these services she receives her board and room, well furnished and heated, and enters into the family life as one of us at meals and other times. Often I help her with her lessons during the evening.

One part of the week's work I hire done for me. That is the washing and as much of the ironing as can be crowded into the same day, subject to the discretion of our whimsical dusky Minerva. The rest of the ironing for the family falls to me.

The poorly built house adds to my difficulties as maid of all work. All of the water has to be carried into the house from the cistern pump, ten or fifteen feet from the kitchen doorsteps. There is no sink or waste pipe of any kind, so all the waste water has to be carried some distance from the house and thrown on the ground. When it is below zero those two things amount to hardships, almost, for a family of our size uses a good deal of water. We have no cellar, except a small excavation in the clay soil under our dining room. It is called a cyclone cellar, and might be used as such if we were not in as great danger of drowning—as it is utterly useless for anything but frogs. When we asked our landlord to have it drained he laughed, and answered that he did not think we needed any more piping than the nightly frog songs. That is all that came of it, except, perhaps, a doctor's bill or two, but other interesting features about the house have their part in these little notes, "For services rendered." Rain and snow and wind sift in around the door and window frames and thru the corners of the house, where we can often see light shining at the joint in the mopboard. Certainly they swell the fuel bill. The care of four stoves, three of them heating and one a cook stove, is no small matter. The boys help their father carry the coal from the barn, the only place to store it. Soft coal is bulky and dirty, but anthracite is far beyond our means here in the Middle West. The same strong arms bring in much of the water also.

We pay eighteen dollars ($18) a month for this poorly built, eight small-roomed house, its three lots and barn made of piano boxes and other odds and ends of lumber. We could not hope to rent a better built house, merely a larger one, for more money unless we were willing to go over forty dollars. Families have come to live in our town faster than houses could be properly built, and it is hard on the man who has not capital enough to build for himself. The three lots that go with our leaky house are very useful, for they furnish us a garden of rich soil in Summer and a playground for children and chickens in Winter. The cow and the coal repose in our barn, and each has about equal space in its luxurious proportions. That cow is a big saving of money, but it adds to our labor, for we make our own butter, but we must have it to help those proverbial "ends." There is plenty of prairie south and east of us for pasturage.

Others of the faculty are trying to tie those flying *ends* too. Mrs. A— does about what I do for her three little girls and gives piano lessons to the neighborhood besides. Mrs. B— has her three year old boy and housework, including the washing, and tutors in mathematics and Latin five hours every day, four of the five hours coming after seven o'clock at night, when the little fellow is in bed. Mrs. C—, who has no children, writes book reviews and has charge of the Women's and Children's Page in our paper. All of the wives of the faculty are busy women, trying each in her own way to add to her husband's pittance. Where the men are not full professors, that pittance is less than my husband's.

With all this straining to live comes a wish from the President and Trustees of the college that we mingle more in town society, that it will be good advertisement for the college to be well represented everywhere. Who can afford the evening dress to go? Or the evening's sewing left undone? Who can return invitations? Who has the strength—and this is at the highest premium—who has the strength to spare? Not one of the wives of the Trustees who desire this has ever called on a professor's wife, much less done anything to bring the college people into her circle of acquaintances. We meet them at the college receptions; they always express their interest in the college, and that is all.

The little social life we have is among ourselves almost entirely. We gather informally at a house for a hour and a half or so, chat awhile, then, perhaps have an impromptu entertainment of music, or an account of a book lately read, a bit of a lecture on a topic of general interest; then light refreshments and home by ten o'clock, for the next day's hard work is before us all. There are college lectures, debates and entertainments that those of us who have few or no children attend; but the children mean spending no admission fees, however small. Of course, it would be a real benefit to the students as well as ourselves if we could keep in touch with these broadening influences; but it is in other ways we are forced to help them. It is expected that we subscribe to the football, baseball, glee club, Y.M. and Y.W.C.A., and other college student funds. To some of these we would volunteer to add as liberally as we could, but not to all, when we hardly are clothed warmly enough all Winter. Anyway, we do not like to have the sum we are expected to raise announced to us, with the request that we see that the vote passes in faculty-meeting. If the request, or demand rather, came from the student-body it could be resisted.

There is one way in which James and I rejoice to help the students. Whenever we treat ourselves to a roast of meat we share it with one or two self-supporting students. It is reward enough that they bring us their joy or suffering, even coming back after graduation to share their life-crises with us.

It has been suggested to us not to live in such and such a house because it is not in keeping with the dignity of our position (!). We are to entertain in such and such a way, for we have had the best advantages in social life that this country can boast (!). (I add the exclamation with respect to our superiors.) The discrepancy comes between the ideal and the actual possibilities of our salaries. We who have had comforts, even luxuries, do not avoid them now because we were satiate. True, our tastes and education make us companions of the refined in easy circumstances, but our incomes are those of mechanics. The mechanic may be refined and have lofty ambitions, but he does not *need* travel, close contact with good libraries and large minds, an intimacy with the fine arts and the sciences to keep him ready to help those under him, as a professor does. It is enervating to work by one's self, going over the same ground every year, always alone, with but a new book or two on the subject. Oh! how I long that my husband may have the chance to study under somebody, with some one of his own or greater education and intelligence! If it were but for a Summer it would give him a new impetus. But how is this possible on our $1,100 a year? This is just how it all goes:

Rent	$216.00
Food (including fodder for cow in winter)	300.00
Clothing	125.00
Fuel and light	55.00
Hired help for washing (52 weeks at $1.25)	65.00
Hired help for housecleaning (4 days at $1.25)	5.00
Magazines and books (including technical books for professor and school books for children)	35.00
Church and college contributions	40.00
Life insurance and fire insurance on furniture	105.00
Doctor's and dentist's bills	20.00
Carfare, postage, etc.	30.00
Household furnishings, tinware, garden implements, etc.	40.00
Sundries (Christmas presents and other expenses larger than average)	64.00

Where does the possibility to travel and study elsewhere come in here? To get away from one's cow and vegetable patch must help to quicken a man's wits in itself, to say nothing of our stultifying Summer heat.

It is because we with our needs and tastes are not receiving a living salary that there is a constantly changing element in the faculty, especially among young married men with no children. They consider their connection with our college temporary, taking it as a stepping-stone to larger institutions. They do us a real harm with their inexperience in teaching and their restlessness. An occasional one would not be so detrimental, but it is demoralizing for the students to change instructors in a study every few years, just as the former one begins to understand how to teach it. This spirit of self-interest is more noticeable in the science and music departments than others, it seems to me.

I overheard a conversation between James and Mr. E—, a Ph.D. from Halle, a while ago. They were standing in our little hallway when Mr. E— asked James for a letter of recommendation to a teachers' agency.

"Why do you want one?" James asked.

"Stay here! I'd rust."

"Oh, no, you wouldn't. Men who carry double schedules don't rust."

"Perhaps you can stand grinding all your life for nothing, but I've got to have a better place."

I thought about it afterward. "A better place!" He might find a more remunerative one, but after all, is there a better place than here and time than now, for giving one's best? Are not these hardworking, serious young men and women worth helping as much as their more delicate, high-strung Eastern cousins?

4.4: Jesse Brundage Sears's Report on Endowed Universities (1922)

Indicative of the unprecedented growth, wealth, and popularity of colleges and universities in American life was the federal government's sponsorship of Jesse Brundage Sears's 1922 study of donors, donations, and endowments in U.S. higher education. One revelation provided by Sears's original survey was that funding and planning in higher education were fragmented well into the twentieth century. Sears's concise, carefully documented report conveys a profile of higher education in the United States which had acquired by accident and design a complex and often generous support of colleges and universities from a wide range of sources. It included unprecedented large donations from individuals and from resultant foundations associated with new industrial wealth, from state governments via recurrent tax policies, and from churches and other charitable institutions. The cumulative signaled that the United States was moving toward substantial, enduring investment in higher education in the early twentieth century.

Philanthropy in the Colleges of This Period

Down to 1865 practically every college begun its existence with very small funds, usually with little or no real endowment, and had had to pass through a long financial struggle before it had won a clientage sufficient to guarantee its future.

Jesse Brundage Sears, "Endowed Universities," *Philanthropy in the History of American Higher Education* (Washington, DC: Government Printing Office, 1922) pp. 67–83.

During the period under discussion colleges continued to be founded on that same basis. Drury College began in poverty in 1873 and remained poor until 1892, when a gift of $50,000 laid the foundation of her present endowment of over a quarter of a million. Carleton College, chartered in 1867, began with $20,000 received from the citizens of Northfield and $10,000 received from Congregational Churches of the State. In 1915 this college possessed endowment funds of almost a million dollars. Washburn College, chartered in 1865, was started by small gifts from the Congregational Churches, but by 1915 had developed an endowment of over $360,000. These are but three from the many well-known illustrations of this type.

The Privately Endowed University as a New Type

In addition to this type, however, we see the beginning of a new era in educational philanthropy—an era in which a great and independently endowed university could spring into existence almost at once from the gifts of a single benefactor.

Such schools did not have to go to the public and beg for funds, nor await any sort of social sanction. They secured their charters as corporations, erected their buildings, called together their faculties, organized their curricula, and opened their doors to students. They start, therefore, as educational and philanthropic, and we might also say, social experiments. Can such financially powerful corporations be trusted to keep the faith with America's educational, economic, religious, and social ideals was the question in many minds at that time. . . .

Summary and Conclusions

We may characterize this period in the growth of higher education in America as follows:

The question of State versus private endowments of higher education has been fought through and settled favorably to both methods: the church has continued its work of founding small colleges; several very large institutions (in a sense, a new type) have been founded by the fortunes of single individuals and have not looked to the church for support; a number of large foundations, the aim of which is research and general educational stimulus and supervision, have been created; and a new philosophy of education, which has found expression in the organization, administration and management of our institutions of higher learning has been worked out.

In opening up new territory to higher education during this period, the State has for the most part done the pioneering, thus reversing the custom of pre-Civil War days when the church school led the way.

From a general view of the work of philanthropy in higher education, as gathered from the Reports of the United States Commissioner of Education, we have seen that philanthropy has gradually built up a vast fund for the permanent endowment of higher learning; that from this source, together with annual gifts, philanthropy is still bearing decidedly the larger part of the burden of higher education, though the State is assuming a relatively larger portion of this burden each year; and, that tuition has covered practically the same percentage of the total annual cost from 1872 to the present. . . .

CHAPTER FIVE

Alma Mater
America Goes to College, 1890 to 1920

Within the impressive architecture of new universities and old colleges, American undergraduates created a world on their own terms. For many students course requirements and examinations were the obligatory "price of admission" into the main event of what has been termed "college life." In an era when relatively few Americans were able to attend college, the American public eagerly sought a vicarious glimpse at the real and imagined adventures of being a "college man" or a "college woman." This public curiosity lent itself to coverage in popular magazines, daily newspapers, weekly journals, and movies and newsreels. One of the more appealing activities that bonded student culture and popular culture was college sports. The strength and success of the elaborate undergraduate culture and its student organizations and varsity teams were such that even Woodrow Wilson as president of Princeton observed that in American higher education "the sideshows were running the circus." Most Americans probably agreed with and applauded Wilson's characterization. An important exception was the serious concern and critical analysis provided by Howard Savage and his research associates in their 1929 study of college sports for the Carnegie Foundation for the Advancement of Teaching.

5.1: Student Memoir: Robert Benchley's "What College Did to Me" (1927)

Robert Benchley, class of 1912 at Harvard College, has captured the hearts and memories of generations of undergraduates with his good-natured memoir written in 1927 about how he navigated the course catalogue. Today sociologists and psychologists refer to the "hidden curriculum" to describe and explain the elaborate decision-making process in which students engage, whose goals may—or, may not—be congruent with those of college officials. One view of college is that it is an experience in which late adolescents learn to cope with the numerous obligations and opportunities of a complex organization. Robert Benchley's version of this saga shows imagination and humor. His experience as a member of several undergraduate publications was good preparation for his eventual professional career. During the 1920s and 1930s, Benchley was one of the first and most popular celebrities of several media—as a writer, as a radio personality, and in movies. Some of his strategies and situations will seem dated to contemporary students; however, the kinds of challenges and solutions he describes have remarkable endurance—and inspiration—for college students in the twenty-first century.

My college education was no haphazard affair. My courses were all selected with a very definite aim in view, with a serious purpose in mind—no classes before eleven in the morning or after two-thirty in the afternoon, and nothing on Saturday at all. That was my slogan. On that rock was my education built.

As what is known as the Classical Course involved practically no afternoon laboratory work, whereas in the Scientific Course a man's time was never his own until four p.m. anyway, I went in for the classic. But only such classics as allowed for a good sleep in the morning. A man has his health to think of. There is such a thing as being a studying fool.

In my days (I was a classmate of the founder of the college) a student could elect to take any courses in the catalogue, provided no two of his choices came at the same hour. The only things he was not supposed to mix were Scotch and gin. This was known as the Elective System. Now I understand that the boys have to have, during the four years, at least three courses beginning with the same

Robert Benchley, "What College Did to Me," in *The Early Worm* (New York: Henry Holt, 1927). Reprinted with permission of the estate of Robert Benchley, Nat Benchley, Executor.

letter. This probably makes it very awkward for those who like to get away of a Friday afternoon for the week-end.

Under the Elective System my schedule was somewhat as follows:

Mondays, Wednesdays and Fridays at 11:00:

Botany 2a (The History of Flowers and Their Meaning)

Tuesdays and Thursdays at 11:00:

English 26 (The Social Life of the Minor Sixteenth-Century Poets)

Mondays, Wednesdays and Fridays at 12:00:

Music 9 (History and Appreciation of the Clavichord)

Tuesdays and Thursdays at 12:00:

German 12b (Early Minnesingers – Walter von Vogelweider, Ulric Glannsdorf and Freimann von Stremhofen. Their Songs and Times)

Mondays, Wednesdays and Fridays at 1:30:

Fine Arts 6 (Doric Columns: Their Uses, History and Various Heights)

Tuesdays and Thursdays at 1:30:

French 1c (Exceptions to the verb *être*)

This was, of course, just one year's work. The next year I followed these courses up with supplementary courses in the history of lace-making, Russian taxation systems before Catharine the Great, North American glacial deposits and Early Renaissance etchers.

This gave me a general idea of the progress of civilization and a certain practical knowledge which has stood me in good stead in thousands of ways since my graduation.

My system of studying was no less strict. In lecture courses I had my notebooks so arranged that one-half of the page could be devoted to drawings of five-pointed stars (exquisitely shaded), girls' heads, and tick-tack-toe. Some of the drawings in my economics notebook in the course on Early English Trade Winds were the finest things I have ever done. One of them was a whole tree (an oak) with every leaf in perfect detail. Several instructors commented on my work in this field.

These notes I would take home after the lecture, together with whatever supplementary reading the course called for. Notes and textbooks would then be placed on a table under a strong lamplight. Next came the sharpening of pencils, which would take perhaps fifteen minutes. I had some of the best sharpened pencils in college. These I placed on the table beside the notes and books.

At this point it was necessary to light a pipe, which involved going to the table where the tobacco was. As it so happened, on the same table was a poker hand, all dealt, lying in front of a vacant chair. Four other chairs were oddly enough occupied by students, also preparing to study. It therefore resolved itself into something of a seminar, or group conference, on the courses under discussion. For example, the first student would say:

"I can't open."

The second student would perhaps say the same thing.

The third student would say: "I'll open for fifty cents."

And the seminar would be on.

At the end of the seminar, I would go back to my desk, pile the notes and books on top of each other, put the light out, and go to bed, tired but happy in the realization that I had not only spent the evening busily but had helped put four of my friends through college.

An inventory of stock acquired at college discloses the following bits of culture and erudition which have nestled in my mind after all these years.

Things I Learned Freshman Year

1. Charlemagne either died or was born or did something with the Holy Roman Empire in 800.
2. By placing one paper bag inside another paper bag you can carry home a milk shake in it.
3. There is a double l in the middle of "parallel."
4. Powder rubbed on the chin will take the place of a shave if the room isn't very light.
5. French nouns ending in "aison" are feminine.
6. Almost everything you need to know about a subject is in the encyclopedia.
7. A tasty sandwich can be made by spreading peanut butter on raisin bread.
8. A floating body displaces its own weight in the liquid in which it floats.
9. A sock with a hole in the toe can be worn inside out with comparative comfort.
10. The chances are against filling an inside straight.
11. There is a law in economics called *The Law of Diminishing Returns*, which means that after a certain margin is reached returns begin to diminish. This may not be correctly stated, but there *is* a law by that name.
12. You begin tuning a mandolin with A and tune the other strings from that.

Sophomore Year

1. A good imitation of measles rash can be effected by stabbing the forearm with a stiff whiskbroom.
2. Queen Elizabeth was not above suspicion.
3. In Spanish you pronounce z like th.
4. Nine-tenths of the girls in a girls' college are not pretty.
5. You can sleep undetected in a lecture course by resting the head on the hands as if shading the eyes.
6. Weakness in drawing technique can be hidden by using a wash instead of black and white line.
7. Quite a respectable bun can be acquired by smoking three or four pipefuls of strong tobacco when you have no food in your stomach.
8. The ancient Phoenicians were really Jews, and got as far north as England where they operated tin mines.
9. You can get dressed much quicker in the morning if the night before when you are going to bed you take off your trousers and underdrawers at once, leaving the latter inside the former.

Junior Year

1. Emerson left his pastorate because he had some argument about communion.
2. All women are untrustworthy.
3. Pushing your arms back as far as they will go fifty times each day increases your chest measurement.
4. Marcus Aurelius had a son who turned out to be a bad boy.
5. Eight hours of sleep are not necessary.
6. Heraclitus believed that fire was the basis of all life.
7. A good way to keep your trousers pressed is to hang them from the bureau drawer.
8. The chances are that you will never fill an inside straight.
9. The Republicans believe in a centralized government, the Democrats in a de-centralized one.
10. It is not necessarily effeminate to drink tea.

Senior Year

1. A dinner coat looks better than full dress.
2. There is yet no law determining what constitutes trespass in an airplane.

3. Six hours of sleep are not necessary.

4. Bicarbonate of soda taken before retiring makes you feel better the next day.

5. You needn't be fully dressed if you wear a cap and gown to a nine-o'clock recitation.

6. Theater tickets may be charged.

7. Flowers may be charged.

8. May is the shortest month in the year.

The foregoing outline of my education is true enough in its way, and is what people like to think about a college course. It has become quite the cynical thing to admit laughingly that college did one no good. It is part of the American Credo that all that the college student learns is to catch punts and dance. I had to write something like that to satisfy the editors. As a matter of fact, I learned a great deal in college and have those four years to thank for whatever I know today.

(The above note was written to satisfy those of my instructors and financial backers who may read this. As a matter of fact, the original outline is true, and I had to look up the date about Charlemagne at that.)

5.2: The Popular Press and Women's Colleges: Smith College in 1897

One of the notable developments in American popular culture in the late nineteenth century was the flourishing of high-quality, mass-produced periodicals and magazines—many of which enjoyed national sales and circulation. Improvements in technology steadily fueled additions of sophisticated graphics—including etchings and photographs. Moreover, colleges and universities became one of the favorite, recurring subjects for editors and writers. The proliferation of new women's colleges, especially in the Northeast, became a recurrent subject, especially since many of these institutions were well funded through generous philanthropy and had magnificent campuses that housed an elite constituency—the "college woman." The following profile of Smith College was published in *Munsey's Magazine* in 1897 and includes special attention to the distinctive architecture, ceremonies, events, and activities that characterized a college education in the late nineteenth century.

The claim is justly made for the old town of Northampton, Massachusetts, that it makes provision for a wide variety of earthly needs. It contains a lunatic asylum,

Douglas Z. Doty, "Life at a Girls' College," *Munsey's Magazine* (September 1897) pp. 865–872.

BASKETBALL IN THE SMITH COLLEGE GYMNASIUM.

LIFE AT A GIRLS' COLLEGE.

The Smith girls at work and at play—Their college buildings, their studies and amusements, their secret societies, their customs and traditions.

THE claim is justly made for the old town of Northampton, Massachusetts, that it makes provision for a wide variety of earthly needs. It contains a lunatic asylum, an institute for the deaf and dumb, a water cure establishment—and a girls' college. In addition to these beneficent human agencies, the town is liberally endowed by nature with the gifts at her disposal. Not only is it most picturesquely placed on elevated ground near the bank of the Connecticut River, but it affords a wide view of the Connecticut valley, so that for charms within and without it is a spot to be remembered.

The town, which Smith College has made notable, consists of one principal street stretching out interminably. The college is situated at one end of the village, on an eminence commanding a fine view of the surrounding country. The buildings are well constructed, though unpretentious in comparison to some of the larger American universities. But the whole place is wonderfully attractive and homelike. It has more the appearance of a group of well kept private dwellings than that of a seat of learning, a place for work and study. And they do study, the daughters of "Fair Smith," in a manner that would put the average college man to shame. Yet if any one supposes that these young women are a set of "grinds," that they all wear glasses and masculine collars, and go about continually talking women's rights

6

an institute for the deaf and dumb, a water cure establishment—and a girls' college. In addition to these beneficent human agencies, the town is liberally endowed by nature with the gifts at her disposal. Not only is it most picturesquely placed on elevated ground near the bank of the Connecticut River, but it affords a wide view of the Connecticut valley, so that for charms within and without it is a spot to be remembered.

The town, which Smith College has made notable, consists of one principal street stretching out interminably. The college is situated at one end of the village, on an eminence commanding a fine view of the surrounding country. The buildings are well constructed, though unpretentious in comparison to some of the larger American universities. But the whole place is wonderfully attractive and homelike. It has more the appearance of a group of well kept private dwellings than that of a seat of learning, a place for work and study. And they do study, the daughters of "Fair Smith," in a manner that would put the average college man to shame. Yet if any one supposes that these young women are a set of "grinds," that they all wear glasses and masculine collars, and go about continually talking women's rights and political economy, he is vastly mistaken. They are students, of course—otherwise they would not be at Smith—but they appreciate the maxim that "all work and no play makes Jill a dull girl," and they act upon it with good will.

No one ever accused the Smith girl of being dull. She blends work and fun in such happy proportions that to her life is always interesting. She is neither a bookworm nor an idler, but keen intellectual competition and wholesome physical activity combine to bring out all that is best in her. On any bright day the campus is an extremely interesting sight. From dawn till dark it is always full of life. The girls are continually flitting from one building to another, or meeting in groups on the smooth, well kept lawn.

> Here's a group of just eleven,
> Talking o'er a hard exam. ;
> Here's a group of six or seven,
> Eating ginger snaps and jam!

In pleasant weather the "Smithians" rarely wear any headgear; or if they do, it is nothing but a "Tam-o'-Shanter." When the weather is cold, they slip over their shoulders a warm golf cape, which may be as easily slipped off again on entering a recitation room. The very sensible fashion prevails of wearing skirts that escape the ground by two or three inches, while many of the girls fairly live in their bicycle costumes.

Founded in 1871 by Sophia Smith, of Hatfield, Massachusetts, the college has long since outgrown the capacity of its dormitories, but all about the grounds houses and cottages have sprung up which, during the college year, are devoted wholly to the use of the Smith girls. The campus houses are naturally more in demand than those outside, and there is always a long waiting list of applicants who are anxious to obtain rooms in them.

The outside houses are beyond the jurisdiction of the college authorities, and the girls living in them have greater freedom than those living in the college buildings, for here such rules as "lights out at ten," "no breakfast if late," are more or less rigidly enforced.

A decided innovation in the dormitory life of Smith is the handsome building which has recently been erected outside the campus. It is a massive pile of masonry that conveys the impression of having wandered from its foundation in some large city. It has all the modern conveniences, from steam heat and electric lights to an elevator with a boy in buttons. These "improvements" are all very well in their way; but when a girl surrounds herself with all the paraphernalia of hotel existence, she is apt to find that she is not quite in touch with that democratic spirit which is one of the greatest charms of the life at Smith. The cost of living in such a dormitory is, of course, greater than in the other houses, and so, naturally, the occupants are regarded more or less as a class by themselves—as girls of means. Such a distinction is, of course, made unconsciously, but it exists nevertheless, and results in the formation of "cliques" —always an unfortunate feature of undergraduate life.

In the campus houses such cliques can have no existence. The daughter of the man who owns two or three railroads has no better surroundings and no more comforts than the ambitious girl who is working her way through college. Of the latter there are quite a number, and they exhibit much ingenuity in devising ways and means of self support. One girl is noted for the stylish shirt waists she makes, and her needle is kept busy in this direction. This same girl plays the piano for any dance that may be given. Another almost entirely supports herself with her camera, while a third is correspondent for several newspapers.

The curriculum at Smith is practically the same as that at any first class university, but the pastimes are vastly different. Basketball is the most popular game, and keen is the rivalry between the classes. The contests are held in the seclusion of the college gymnasium. Basketball is not unlike a mild form of football, and, while it avoids the danger of the latter, it is well calculated to arouse the enthusiasm of rival classes to the highest pitch. Boating and tennis are also favorite amusements in their season, and in winter there is skating, in which the Amherst students often join.

One of the first places shown to the visitor is "Paradise." This delightful spot—the name is applied, in a general way, to a pretty sheet of water and the charming, shady walks near by—is the favorite retreat of the Smith girls. On pleasant half holidays one may see many of them wending their way in its direction, laden with sofa pillows and "fudge"—a kind of home made candy, locally in great demand.

The principal secret societies at Smith are the Alpha and the Phi Kappa Psi, to either one of which a girl may be elected after her freshman year. In order to be eligible an undergraduate must possess decided talent for literature, or else be a general favorite.

Graduation time is marked by many time honored observances. The seniors wear white dresses for the last three days of the college year. One of these is known as "Ivy Day," and on it the departing class plants an ivy vine near College Hall. It is a pretty sight to see the "sweet girl graduates," all in white, marching two by two across the green campus.

5.3: Student Memoir: James Thurber's "University Days" (1933)

American humorist James Thurber was born in 1894 in Columbus, Ohio. He was raised and educated in Columbus, attending Ohio State University from 1913 to 1918. He worked as a newspaper writer in Columbus, Paris, and New York before joining the staff of the *New Yorker* in 1927. His contributions to that magazine as both a writer and an artist were instrumental in changing the character of American humor. Thurber left the staff of the magazine in 1935 but continued to contribute to it for the next two decades. In 1940, failing eyesight—the result of a boyhood accident—forced him to curtail his drawing; by 1952, he had to give it up altogether. He continued to write until his death in 1961. Thurber received a Tony Award for *A Thurber Carnival* (1961), and an Emmy Award for Best Comedy was given to *My World and Welcome to It* (1970). Thurber's humor speaks not only for an era but for the confused human condition in general. It has been collected in over thirty volumes of essays, stories, fables, plays, drawings, and cartoons and continues to be reprinted often in textbooks and anthologies. In addition, his work has been adapted for the stage, television, movies, and musical presentations. The Thurber House (www.thurberhouse.org) has awarded the Thurber Prize for American Humor since 1997, honoring contemporary outstanding American humor. Some recipients have been Ian Frazier, Jon Stewart, Alan Zweibel, Joe Keenan, and Calvin Trillin.

James Thurber's 1933 short story "University Days" has provided an enduring and endearing memoir about going to college in America. Whereas many histories of colleges and universities are written "from the top down," reflecting the priorities and preoccupations of presidents, provosts, and professors, James Thurber turned the tables by recalling how a freshman viewed the complex state university. After having graduated from high school in Columbus, Ohio, Thurber entered the Ohio State University during the fall 1913 semester. As with all new students, he suddenly encountered a maze of catalogues, course requirements, mandatory swimming tests, obligatory ROTC drills, a challenging lab course in botany, and orientation talks by an assortment of deans and instructors. Thurber brought the official catalogues and forms to life through an insightful account of undergraduates, professors, and campus administrators. Whether in 1913 or 2013, students and alumni will identify with and recognize the themes of campus life.

I passed all the other courses I took at my university, but I could never pass botany. This was because all botany students had to spend several hours a week in a laboratory looking through a microscope at plant cells, and I could never see through a microscope. I never once saw a cell through a microscope. This used to enrage my instructor. He would wander around the laboratory pleased with the progress all the students were making in drawing the involved and, so I am told, interesting structure of flower cells, until he came to me. I would just be standing there. "I can't see anything," I would say. He would begin patiently enough, explaining how anybody can see through a microscope, but he would always end up in a fury, claiming that I could too see through a microscope but just pretended that I couldn't. "It takes away from the beauty of flowers anyway," I used to tell him. "We are not concerned with beauty in this course," he would say. "We are concerned solely with what I may call the mechanics of flars." "Well,"

I'd say, "I can't see anything." "Try it just once again," he'd say, and I would put my eye to the microscope and see nothing at all, except now and again a nebulous milky substance – a phenomenon of maladjustment. You were supposed to see a vivid, restless clockwork of sharply defined plant cells. "I see what looks like a lot of milk," I would tell him. This, he claimed, was the result of my not having adjusted the microscope properly, so he would readjust it for me, or rather, for himself. And I would look again and see milk.

I finally took a deferred pass, as they called it, and waited a year and tried again. (You had to pass one of the biological sciences or you couldn't graduate.) The professor came back from vacation as brown as a berry, bright-eyed, and eager to explain cell structure again to his classes. "Well," he said to me, cheerily, when we met in the first laboratory hours of the semester, "we're going to see the cells this time, aren't we?" "Yes, sir," I said. Students to right of me and to the left of me and in front of me were seeing cells; what's more, they were quietly drawing pictures of them in their notebooks. Of course, I couldn't see anything.

"We'll try it," the professor said to me, grimly, "with every adjustment of the microscope known to man. As God as my witness, I'll arrange this glass so that you see cells through it or I'll give up teaching. In twenty-two years of botany, I— " He cut off abruptly for he was beginning to quiver all over, like Lionel Barrymore, and he genuinely wished to hold onto his temper; his scenes with me had taken a great deal out of him.

So we tried it with every adjustment of the microscope known to man. With only one of them did I see anything but blackness or the familiar lacteal opacity, and that time I saw, to my pleasure and amazement, a variegated constellation of flecks, specks, and dots. These I hastily drew. The instructor, noting my activity, came back from an adjoining desk, a smile on his lips and eyebrows high in hope. He looked at my cell drawing. "What's that?" he demanded, with a hint of a squeal in his voice. "That's what I saw," I said. "You didn't, you didn't, and you *didn't!*" he screamed, losing control of his temper instantly, and he bent over and squinted into the microscope. His head snapped up. "That's your eye!" he shouted. "You've fixed the lens so that it reflects! You've drawn your eye!"

Another course I didn't like, but somehow managed to pass, was economics. I went to that class straight from botany class, which didn't help me any in understanding either subject. I used to get them mixed up. But not as mixed up as another student in my economics class who came there directly from a physics laboratory. He was tackle on the football team, named Bolenciecwcz. At that time

If I went through anguish in botany and economics—for different reasons—gymnasium work was even worse. I don't even like to think about it. They wouldn't let you play games or join in the exercise with your glasses on and I couldn't see with mine off. I bumped into professors, horizontal bars, agricultural students, and swinging iron rings. Not being able to see, I could take it but I couldn't dish it out. Also, in order to pass gymnasium (and you had to pass it to graduate) you had to learn to swim if you didn't know how. I didn't like the swimming pool, I didn't like swimming, and I didn't like the swimming instructor, and after all these years I still don't. I never swam but I passed my gym work anyway, by having another student give my gymnasium number (978) and swim across the pool in my place. He was a quiet, amiable blond youth, number 473, and he would have seen through a microscope for me if we could have got away with it, but we couldn't get away with it. Another thing I didn't like about gymnasium work was that they made you strip the day you registered. It is impossible for me to be happy when I am stripped and being asked a lot of questions. Still, I did better than a lanky agricultural student who was cross-examined just before I was. They asked each student what college he was in – that is, whether Arts, Engineering, Commerce, or Agriculture. "What college are you in?" the instructor snapped at the youth in front of me. "Ohio State University," he said promptly.

It wasn't that agricultural student but it was another a whole lot like him who decided to take up journalism, possibly on the ground that when farming went to hell he could fall back on newspaper work. He didn't realize, of course, that that would be very much like falling back full-length on a kit of carpenter's tools. Haskins didn't seem cut out for journalism, being too embarrassed to talk to anybody and unable to use a typewriter, but the editor of the college paper assigned him to the cow barns, the sheep house, the horse pavilion, and the animal-husbandry department generally. This was a genuinely big "beat," for it took up five times as much ground as the College of Liberal Arts. The agricultural student knew animals, but nevertheless his stories were dull and colorlessly written. He took all afternoon on each of them, on account of having to hunt for each letter on the typewriter. Once in a while he had to ask somebody to help him hunt. "C" and "L," in particular, were hard letters for him to find. His editor finally got pretty much annoyed at the farmer-journalist because his pieces were so uninteresting. "See here, Haskins," he snapped at him one day, "why is it we never have anything hot from you on the horse pavilion? Here we have two hundred head of horses on this campus—more than any other university in the Western Conference except Purdue—and yet you never get any real low-down on them. Now shoot over to the horse barn and dig up something lively." Haskins shambled out and came back in about an hour; he said he had something. "Well, start it off snappily," said the editor. "Something people will read." Haskins set to work and in a couple of hours brought a sheet of typewritten paper to the desk; it was a two-hundred word story about some disease that had broken out among the horses. Its opening sentence was simple but arresting. It read: "Who has noticed the sores on the tops of the horses in the animal-husbandry building?"

Ohio State was a land-grant university and therefore two years of military drill was compulsory. We drilled with old Springfield rifles and studied the tactics of the Civil War even though the World War was going on at the time. At eleven o'clock each morning thousands of freshmen and sophomores used to deploy over the campus, moodily creeping up on the old chemistry building. It was good training for the kind of warfare that was waged at Shiloh but it had no connection with what was going on in Europe. Some people used to think that there was German money behind it, but they didn't dare say so or they would have been thrown in jail as German spies. It was a period of muddy thought and marked, I believe, the decline of higher education in the Middle West.

As a soldier I was never any good at all. Most of the cadets were glumly indifferent soldiers, but I was no good at all. Once General Littlefield, who was commandant of the cadet corps, popped up in front of me during regimental drill and snapped, "You are the main trouble with this university!" I think he meant that my type was the main trouble with the university but he may have meant me individually. I was mediocre at drill, certainly – that is, until my senior year. By that time I had drilled longer than anybody else in the Western Conference, having failed at military at the end of each preceding year so that I had to do it all over again. I was the only senior still in uniform. The uniform which, when new, had made me look like an interurban railway conductor, now that it had become faded and too tight made me look like Bert Williams in his bellboy act. This had a definitely bad effect on my morale. Even so, I had become by sheer practice little short of wonderful at squad maneuvers.

One day General Littlefield picked our company out of the whole regiment and tried to get it mixed up by putting it through one movement after another as fast as we could execute them: squads right, squads left, squads on right into line, squads right about, squads left front into line, etc. In about three minutes one hundred and nine men were marching in one direction and I was marching away from them at an angle of forty degrees, all alone. "Company, halt!" shouted General Littlefield. "That man is the only man who has it right!" I was made a corporal for my achievement.

The next day General Littlefield summoned me to his office. He was swatting flies when I went in. I was silent and he was silent, too, for a long time. I don't think he remembered me or why he had sent for me, but he didn't want to admit it. He swatted some more flies, keeping his eyes on them narrowly before he let go with the swatter. "Button up your coat!" he snapped. Looking back on it now, I can see that he meant me although he was looking at a fly, but I just stood there. Another fly came to rest on a paper in front of the general and began rubbing its hind legs together. The general lifted the swatter cautiously. I moved restlessly and the fly flew away. "You startled him!" barked General Littlefield, looking at me severely. I said I was sorry. "That won't help the situation!" snapped the general, with cold military logic. I didn't see what I could do except offer to chase some more flies toward his desk, but I didn't say anything. He stared out the window at the far-away figures of co-eds crossing the campus toward the library. Finally, he told me I could go. So I went. He either didn't know which cadet I was or else he forgot what he wanted to see me about. It may have been that he wished to apologize for having called me the main trouble with the university; or maybe he had decided to compliment me on my brilliant drilling of the day before and then at the last minute decided not to. I don't know. I don't think about it much any more.

5.4: Real Estate Promotion and Colleges: "A College among the Orange Groves" (1920)

College building as part of community building has a long tradition in America. By the early nineteenth century real estate promoters worked to attract settlers by extolling the merits of a college as a central feature of an attractive town or city. A good example of this partnership of campus and community is demonstrated in this real estate brochure for the town of Claremont, east of Los Angeles, which highlighted the benefits of Pomona College, along with modern utilities and civilized living. Eventually, as Pomona College worked with various groups to found and cooperate with new institutions to create the "Claremont Colleges," the campus and community came to be known as the "Oxford of the Orange Belt."

"A College among the Orange Groves," Real Estate Brochure (Claremont, CA, 1920).

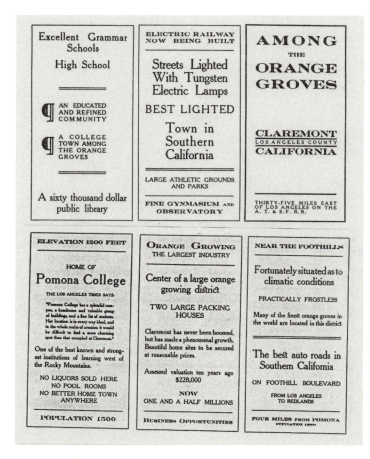

"A College Town among the Orange Groves," real estate brochure
for Claremont College in 1920 (Document 5.4)

5.5: College Sports Reform: Howard J. Savage's 1929 Report for the Carnegie Foundation for the Advancement of Teaching

This report was featured as a front-page headline story in newspapers nationwide in October 1929. Primary author Howard J. Savage and his research team examined the

Howard J. Savage, Harold W. Bentley, John T. McGovern, and Dean F. Smiley, M.D., *American College Athletics*, Bulletin Number Twenty-Three (New York: Carnegie Foundation for the Advancement of Teaching, 1929). Reprinted by permission of the Carnegie Foundation for the Advancement of Teaching.

history, conduct, and values of sports and games in American universities, colleges, and schools; the development of the modern amateur status; the administrative control of college athletics; athletic participation and its results; the hygiene of athletic training; the coach in college athletics; athletic conferences and associations; the recruiting and subsidizing of athletes; and the relation of the press to college sport. The report includes an appendix with statistical materials and excerpts from correspondence to recruit college athletes. A preface by Henry S. Pritchett titled "Athletics, an Element in the Evolution of the American University" begins the volume. *American College Athletics* was undertaken at the request of the Association of American Colleges, the Association of Colleges and Secondary Schools of the Southern States, the National Collegiate Athletic Association, and other representative bodies.

II   Nothing in the educational régime of our higher institutions perplexes the European visitor so much as the role that organized athletics play. On a crisp November afternoon he finds many thousands of men and women, gathered in a great amphitheater, wildly cheering a group of athletes who are described to him as playing a game of football, but who seem to the visitor to be engaged in a battle. He is the more mystified when he discovers that of the thousands of onlookers, not one in a hundred understands the game or can follow the strategy of the two teams. At the end, the vast majority of the onlookers only know, like old Kaspar of Blenheim, that " 't was a famous victory" for one university or the other.

When the visitor from the European university has pondered the matter, he comes to his American university colleagues with two questions:

"What relation has this astonishing display to the work of an intellectual agency like a university?"

"How do students, devoted to study, find either the time or the money to stage so costly a performance?"

III   This study undertakes to answer these questions, not for the foreigner so much as for thoughtful Americans both in and out of the university. In undertaking this study the Foundation has sought sincerely after the facts. It has got information at first hand and has aimed to marshal it, in this report, in such form as will enable the student of education to apprehend the process through which the present athletic situation has come about, and the reaction of this development upon the scholarly and social life of the universities, colleges and schools.

The study has been carried out, and its results are here set forth, in no captious or faultfinding spirit. It has been assumed that there is a legitimate place in the secondary school and in the college for organized sports, that such sports contribute, when employed in a rational way, to the development both of character and of health. The report is a friendly effort to help toward a wise solution as to the place of such sports in our educational system. It has been necessary, in order to render this service, to set forth the abuses and excesses that have grown up. This has been done with the most painstaking effort to be fair, as well as just. A statement with respect to each institution mentioned has been communicated to its officers before going to press.

VI   The college president or teacher interested in the place of organized sports in American colleges and the effects of these upon the intellectual life of his college will desire to go carefully into the details as set forth in the chapters of this report. On the other hand, experience shows that few busy men find the time to read a detailed report. It is also realized to-day, in all fields of public action, that the facts must be presented in a form available to the intelligent layman as well as to the professional student. In the matter of the public health, for example, it is clear that the public must be educated in the knowledge of the fundamental facts concerning health and disease before any great advance in the health of the nation can be effected. The same thing is true of education. The public must gain some clear notion of tendencies, the limitations, and the cost of our school system before any general advance in educational effectiveness is likely to result. I have therefore sought to condense into a single chapter the essential facts brought out by this study, and to indicate their relation to the process of public education as conducted in present-day American universities, colleges, and schools. The great expansion of college sports is not an isolated fact in our educational development. It is characteristic of the transformation through which the college has gone in the last five decades.

To make clear to the reader what has happened, one can scarcely do better than to answer the questions of the European visitor just quoted. What has organized sport to do with the work of an intellectual agency which the university and the college are conceived to be? And how can college boys find the time or the money to maintain so costly a display for popular entertainment?

VII   In brief these questions can be answered in the following terms:

In the United States the composite institution called a university is doubtless still an intellectual agency. But it is also a social, a commercial, and an athletic agency, and these activities have in recent years appreciably overshadowed the intellectual life for which the university is assumed to exist.

In the second place, the football contest that so astonishes the foreign visitor is not a student's game, as it once was. It is highly organized commercial enterprise. The athletes who take part in it have come up through the years of training; they are commanded by professional coaches; little if any personal initiative of ordinary play is left to the player. The great matches are highly profitable enterprises. Sometimes the profits go to finance college sports, sometimes to pay the cost of the sports amphitheater, in some cases the college authorities take a slice of the profits for college buildings.

XIV   The preceding pages have dealt with a complicated situation of which organized athletics are but one factor. It remains to summarize the particular defects and excesses of present-day athletic contests as set forth in detail in the chapters of this report. The game of football looms large in any account of the growth of professionalism in college games. This does not mean that other sports are untouched by the influences that have converted football into a professional vocation.

The unfavorable results upon students through the athletic development may be briefly stated in the following terms:

1. The extreme development of competitive games in the colleges has reacted upon the secondary schools. The college athlete begins his athletic career before he gets to college.
2. Once in college the student who goes in for competitive sports, and in particular for football, finds himself under a pressure, hard to resist to give his whole time and thought to his athletic career. No college boy training for a major team can have much time for thought or study.
3. The college athlete, often a boy from a modest home, finds himself suddenly a most important man in the college life. He begins to live on a scale never before imagined. A special table is provided. Sport clothes and expensive trips are furnished him out of the athletic chest. He jumps at one bound to a plane of living of which he never before knew, all at the expense of some fund of which he knows little. When he drops back to a scale of living such as his own means can afford, the result is sometimes disastrous.
4. He works (for it is work, not play) under paid professional coaches whose business it is to develop the boy to be an effective unit in a team. The coach of to-day is no doubt a more cultivated man than the coach of twenty years

ago. But any father who has listened to the professional coaching a college team will have some misgivings as to the cultural value of the process.

5. Inter-college athletics are highly competitive. Every college or university longs for a winning team in its group. The coach is on the alert to bring the most promising athletes in the secondary schools to his college team. A system of recruiting and subsidizing has grown up, under which boys are offered pecuniary and other inducements to enter a particular college. The system is demoralizing and corrupt, alike for the boy who takes the money and for the agent who arranges it, and for the whole group of college and secondary school boys who know about it.

6. Much discussion has been had as to the part the college graduate should have in the government of his college. In the matter of competitive athletics the college alumnus has, in the main, played a sorry role. It is one thing for an "old grad" to go back and coach the boys of his college as at Oxford or Cambridge, where there are no professional coaches and no gate receipts. It is quite another thing for an American college graduate to pay money to high school boys, either directly or indirectly, in order to enlist their services for a college team. The process is not only unsportsmanlike, it is immoral to the last degree. The great body of college graduates are wholly innocent in this matter. Most college men wish their college to win. Those who seek to compass that end by recruiting and subsidizing constitute a small, but active, minority, working oftentimes without the knowledge of the college authorities. This constitutes the most disgraceful phase of recent inter-college athletics.

7. The relation of organized sports to the health of college students is not a simple question. The information to deal with it completely is not yet at hand. A chapter of the report is devoted to this subject. In general it may be said that the relation of college organized sports to health of the individual student is one dependent on the good sense exhibited by the college boy in participating in such sports, and to the quality of the advice he receives from the college medical officer.

8. For many games the strict organization and the tendency to commercialize the sport has taken the joy out of the game. In football, for example, great numbers of boys do not play football, as in English schools and colleges, for the fun of it. A few play intensely. The great body of students are onlookers.

9. Finally, it is to be said that the blaze of publicity in which the college athlete lives is a demoralizing influence for the boy himself and no less so for his college.

XVI   The process of developing our composite four-story educational structure—elementary school, secondary school, college, and university—was, until recently, highly competitive. The colleges of twenty years ago competed for students in much the same way in which the railroads competed for passengers. Admission requirements were cut as the railroads cut rates. The attractions of athletic distinction were added to the other reasons for choosing a particular college. In some states the colleges depleted the secondary schools in order to fill their own ranks.

The process has been successful beyond all expectations. An artificial market in college attendance has been created beyond the ability of the colleges to supply. The pressure to seek students has gone by. The problem to-day is how to deal with the ever-increasing army of applicants for admission to the college door. The elementary school points the boy to the secondary school, and the secondary school points the youth at eighteen or nineteen to the college. Down the long vista of the years from six to eighteen our educational system points to one door—the college-university.

Consequences of great moment result from this rigid organization.

Many boys and girls whose usefulness and happiness would be best sought in a commercial or industrial trade are carried into the college by the mere sweep of the tide. Insensibly but inevitably the intellectual quality of the college is softened in order to meet the capacity of those who must be cared for. In some institutions, notably in some tax-supported universities, where graduation from any high school automatically admits to the state college, the incoming class is in large measure got rid of in the examinations of the freshman year, a costly process and one entirely unjust to a great number of the youth of both sexes.

In the third place, the program of carrying great masses of young people through college, with little regard to their intellectual fitness, translates itself in terms of cost that is growing at an alarming rate. In no other nation is mass production in higher education attempted at public cost. Aside from the social and intellectual objections to such a process, the financial load will in time become too heavy even for our rich nation.

In this situation the athletic competition has played a minor part. The number of those who go to college or who remain in it for the sake of engaging in its commercialized and highly advertised college sports is relatively small. But as far as it goes the history of inter-college athletics points straight at the fact that our system of public education, democratic as it is, has been evolved in great haste under the stimulus of competition and with all too little of wise thinking either as to the intellectual quality of the higher institution or the economic and vocational needs of the great body of children who enter the elementary school and find therein their ideals of life and their choice of a means of support. We hear much inspiring talk touching the ideals of college life. This is as it should be. But no nation can afford in its educational system to forget that to the great mass of mankind an honest job, performed in good spirit, is the road to moral soundness and to social contentment.

We need now to deal with the educational system as a whole with the purpose both to serve the needs of the great majority who ought not to go to college and to preserve at the same time the intellectual quality of those who can and ought to seek the higher education. Fortunately, justice to the vocational need and ministry to the intellectual aspirations lie along the same path.

The weakness of the American university as it exists to-day lies in its lack of intellectual sincerity. It stands nominally for high intellectual ideals. Its effort at intellectual leadership is diluted with many other efforts in fields wholly foreign to this primary purpose. Inter-college athletics form only one of these.

Our competitive stage of university building ought now to cease. We have more universities in name than we need, if they are to be universities in the sense of sincere scholarship. We have passed the pioneer stage of nation building. Our nation has traveled at a rapid pace this last generation. The duty of to-day is to readapt our public educational system as a whole to a sincere conception of education conceived to meet the actual needs and aspirations of all the people, which shall be sincere alike in the things of the mind and the spirit as well as in those of the daily job. To inaugurate such a fundamental and far-reaching study of what can and ought to be done is the most important national problem that confronts us. The college and the university were merged not as the result of deliberation but hurriedly. Whether they ought to remain permanently united is yet to be determined. Our situation to-day is one of confusion. Thoughtful and able men are concerned both for the American college and for the university. To integrate our composite structure in terms of the intellectual, social, and moral aspirations of the whole people is the vital need that confronts us.

Definitions

Athletics in American colleges and universities form a part of those diversions of college life generally termed either *outside activities*, in the sense that they lie beyond the academic requirements of the institution, or *student activities*, as representing one means whereby students may exercise their abilities and predilections apart from the strictly educational or academic routine. *Extramural athletics* are understood to be those branches of competitive sports and games in which duly authorized undergraduates representing a university, a college, or a school meet in contests representatives of other institutions or organizations. Thus, strictly speaking, a college soccer team which plays against the team of a local amateur club participates in extramural but not intercollegiate athletics. *Intercollegiate athletics* are those branches of undergraduate sports and games in which duly authorized representatives of one institution of higher education meet in contests with those of another. Similar distinctions should be borne in mind respecting school athletics. *Intramural athletics* comprise those games and contests in which duly matriculated students, undergraduates, graduates, or both, contend against other contestants of similar status in the same institution. In the course of an intramural schedule, however, a dormitory team which plays principally against fraternity, other dormitory, and class teams, may undertake a game with a school or some other body that is not an integral part of the institution to which the team belongs.

Mention should also be made of three distinctions which, although too little recognized, have grown in importance since 1913. The first of these distinctions is connoted by the terms *control* and *guidance*. The second is the essential difference between, on the one hand, the regulation of college athletics by faculty members whose professional interests centre primarily upon things of the mind, and on the other, control by faculty members whose professional interests concern the development of the body, or "physical education" in its accepted sense. The third distinction lies between (1) a college program of physical education which includes only such matters as athletic sports and games, intercollegiate and intramural, corrective exercises, and rather perfunctory discussion of certain aspects of social hygiene set forth in a few lectures to large groups, and (2) a college program which includes some or all of these matters, but has for its ultimate and sincere purpose the fitting of young men and women to understand in a general way the relationships of hygiene in the broadest sense of the term to their own lives, to the end that they may intelligently conduct this phase of their own careers.

In the present study *physical education* denotes primarily that phase of college or school instruction which has for its principal purpose the development of bodily strength and well-being and muscular coordination among its participants. The wider implications of the term include, as just indicated, instruction in personal and social hygiene, in exercises calculated to correct physical or nervous defects, and in the use for purposes of instruction of competitive games and contests that until recent years have figured principally as college pastimes. Physical education, therefore, extends its field to deal with mental, physical, social, and moral health. Frequently the terms *educational* and *education* are employed in contrast to commercialism.

Commercialism in sport is the placing of a higher value upon monetary and material returns, whether direct or indirect, from any athletic activity than is placed upon its returns in recreation, health, and physical and moral well-being.

A sentence uttered by Professor Percy Hughes, of Lehigh University, at the dedication of the University of Nebraska stadium, expresses a contrast which is all too often ignored in considering college athletics: "We train the body, only the mind is capable of education." Finally, it must be taken for granted that *sportsmanship*, which in its essential manifestation is merely the operation of the golden rule and of the attitude of the gentleman (in the American sense) in competitive contests, is a desirable social phenomenon. The development of the qualities included in the term "sportsmanship" is possible not alone in all species of contests and games but in all of the other social aspects of life.

"Shopping-Round"

"Shopping-round" is the soliciting by a prospective college athlete of financial assistance in the form of a scholarship or other aid at a college or a private school in exchange for athletic participation, in such a fashion that the offers, real or imagined, from one institution are used to procure offers or overtures from another. The causes and results of this process, as regards the college or university, will be discussed in their appropriate connections. For the moment we are concerned only with its effect upon the schoolboy.

Perhaps the most important single result of "shopping-round" upon the schoolboy's character is the engendering of a purely materialistic attitude at an age when his outlook upon life is naturally quite the opposite. A lad hears tales of "easy money" made by his fellows merely from a game that he plays for fun. Some of these other boys he knows to be less expert than he. Now, a youth of college or school age is rarely supplied so generously with money that he cannot use more, and so, when a means of capitalizing athletic ability presents itself, its temptations are likely to be too strong to be resisted. Not infrequently the reasoning runs thus: Others get subsidies through "shopping-round." Why should n't I? I can use the money as well as anyone else. If money is to be had, I am a fool not to get my share. The boy puts out feelers in the form of letters to coaches or alumni of a few colleges. Much of the lad's character and future career depends upon the replies which he receives to those first communications. If his correspondents answer him sharply and wisely that they and their institutions do not countenance athletic subsidies, he may be brought to realize the implications of his course in time to abandon it. If, on the other hand, a correspondent indicates a willingness to go deeper into the boy's case, the way is open to striking a secret bargain which in time may convert that boy into an athletic impostor, and place the university or college in a position of deceit with relation to other institutions. These remarks are not theoretical. They are grounded in the history of many cases in which precisely these debasing things have happened to scores of youths, schools, and colleges.

The process of corrupting a boy's ideals, as just outlined, is not confined to the private schoolboy and the college. It exists between the public schoolboy and the private school, and the public schoolboy and the college. One of its most astonishing results was the "Intercollegiate Athletic Bureau."

Fundamental Considerations in Intercollegiate Contests

When two institutions compete in athletics the ends involved belong less to the fields usually labeled "educational" than to what one university president has called "the pageantry of college life." There probably are moral values to be developed from a game well played or a race well run, but they accrue less from the final contest than from the period of preparation and training. Partly for this reason, the fundamental purpose of intercollegiate contests ought to be the diversion or development of undergraduates, alumni, other members of the college family, and their guests. As matters now stand, their fundamental purpose is financial and commercial. The monetary and material returns from intercollegiate athletics are valued far more highly than their returns in play, sport, and bodily and moral well-being.

The observation is especially true of football, but it holds good for other branches of athletics as well, except rowing and fencing and, perhaps, squash racquets. Football carries the bulk of the monetary burden. Any other branch than can be so administered as to leave untouched some of the profits from football thereby augments the sums that can be expended on improving athletic facilities and university buildings. This commercial aspect is illustrated in the making of football schedules, especially when they include games to be played on "neutral" grounds. It is almost universal. In New England, traditional rivalry may outweigh it (Amherst, Bowdoin, Wesleyan, Williams), and in some other parts of the East as well. But in Pennsylvania two universities (Pennsylvania, Pittsburgh) reshaped their athletic policies with a view to higher profits from contests. Even in instances where football receipts have reached hundreds of thousands of dollars, games with well-established rivals have been abandoned if they have involved financial loss (New York University and Syracuse; Ohio State and University of Iowa). The Missouri Valley Conference was reorganized to eliminate four financially unprofitable institutions. In the Intercollegiate Conference, the cry is "We've got to have money." The fundamental principles of athletic profits are so well known that the losses occasioned by the Carnegie Institute of Technology-Georgetown football game in 1928 occasioned much newspaper comment. In short, the commercialization of intercollegiate athletic policy in the United States is undeniable. In Canada, university rivalry is no less keen, games are no less enjoyable, and sport is not less well served because its monetary aspects are less magnified. Other powerful materialistic considerations enter into the shaping of athletic policy. The supposed advertising values of success at football and a few other branches has led some institutions to charge certain athletic expenses to advertising, and others to render a naïve and undue regard to the notice which a victorious team or an athletic event attracts (Bellefonte Academy, Centre, Drake, Notre Dame, Southern California). Rowing appears to be the only major branch of intercollegiate athletics from which commercialism is absent. Even in cases where the formalities of bookkeeping do not involve charging expenses of a team to college advertising, the motive of advertising and publicity is often discernible. On the other hand, a college may become self-conscious with respect to losing teams and a defeat at football is regarded as a major tragedy. Alumni testify to great embarrassment because their football does not win from their dearest rival or is not numbered by sports writers and enthusiasts among the outstanding teams of the section (Brigham Young, Columbia, Cornell, Tufts). The exaggeration

the men thus obtained are held so definitely segregated from the rest of the participants in general athletics that it is difficult to understand how coaches, directors, and others can be ignorant of their special status. Incidentally, in this sort of esoteric information resides much of the power of the commercially-minded director or coach. It is paradoxical that the "freshman rule" should have been instituted primarily to protect first-year athletes against too heavy encroachments upon their time and energy during those initial months of a college course which should be devoted to winning a place in the institution and laying a firm foundation in academic work. In the special training regimen that to-day exists for freshman squads, it is common for these young athletes to undergo as great a strain as they would in competing for university teams.

In spite of these defects, the general developments and purposes of American intramural athletics are more salutary than those which motivate intercollegiate contests. Especially worthy of praise in this particular are institutions (Amherst, California, Cornell, Harvard, McGill, Oberlin, Princeton, Stanford, Toronto, Wesleyan, Williams) at which the athletic needs of capabilities of entering students are determined by analysis of individual cases through physical examinations and tactful interviews, and advice is given as to which branches of athletics offer the most opportunities for future success, often as a welcome substitute for the physical training required for a degree. Once enlisted in the branch of athletic exercise appropriate to personal needs, the undergraduate finds his participation enlivened by the hope that he may some day represent the university. His youthful ambitions are stimulated and he is led at all times to do his best. The result is an attempt to enrich his own experience of athletics in a way that can yield much good.

Conversations with many athletes, as well as independent observation, prompts to the belief that, aside from academic requirements, the most common stimuli to competition in intramural sports are, first, loyalty to a group or organization, such as fraternity or club, and, secondly, a desire for relaxation from the rigorous training for intercollegiate contests, coupled with the "instinct" for play. Although expert 'varsity players choose to compete for intercollegiate teams in preference to participating in intramural contests, it appears probable that in most cases their motive is not so much the pleasure of the game as their connections with the larger group,—tinctured in many cases by a craving for publicity. Those who have been questioned in this particular were almost unanimous in their preference for the inter-fraternity or other intramural contests. If enjoyment and recreation are to be sought, it is significant that, with the exception of larger institutions, few of the better intramural teams possess the ability to compete with representatives of other colleges. Occasionally, where an intramural team has displayed unusual talent and has won all or most of its games, efforts are made to arrange contests with extramural rivals.

The tests of a beneficial intramural program can be derived from close scrutiny of experience: the sincerity of the contests and the participants, their spontaneity and voluntary nature, and their persistence, or even their development, from year to year. The great adverse influence is perfunctoriness in administration or in play. Owing to the fact that not a few intramural programs have grown out of the prescription of physical training for a degree, participation easily becomes mere lax credit-seeking on the part of the student, or involves on the part of the director, a bewildered attempt to keep large numbers of men and women occupied.

At a number of institutions, however, it is not so much compulsion as guidance that undergraduate participants in intramural contests need and receive (Amherst, California, Dartmouth in winter sports, Harvard, Oklahoma, Princeton, Toronto, Wisconsin certainly in football). In such instances, and especially at institutions (Emory, Massachusetts Institute of Technology, Reed, Stevens Institute) where intercollegiate games are curtailed or lacking altogether, the competitive tendency and the "instinct" for play have developed and enhanced each other. To achieve such a result at any college, the man or woman responsible for intramural contests needs certain qualities of the good teacher that are rare in their best manifestations: tact, enthusiasm, ingenuity, resourcefulness, and sympathetic understanding of youth. That intramural programs are in the best sense successful at so many universities and colleges should lead the most discouraged critics of intercollegiate athletics to take heart. The pity is that such beneficial results as are now being achieved are allowed to depend universally upon the financial prosperity of football.

Because of the development of intercollegiate competition, not so much in games as in its material and especially in its monetary aspects, its bearings as play have fallen largely into a subordinate position. The task confronting those concerned with the development of intramural athletics involves the restoration of play as recreation and diversion to its appropriate place in college life.

The Inherited Characteristics of Athletics

In a special study of the inheritance of athletes made for the present enquiry, Mr. Richard H. Post and Dr. Charles B. Davenport, Director of the Laboratory of Experimental Evolution of the Carnegie Institution of Washington, at Cold Spring Harbor, Long Island, considered the inherited characteristics of some 587 athletes, belonging to fifty-four American families. Studies in this or related fields had already been made by, among others, Dr. Davenport, Sir Francis Galton in 1869, Dr. F. Bach in connection with 3,457 participants in the Munich Turnfest of 1923, and Dr. O. Schlaginhaufen in 1927. From these previous enquiries and from the newer data of Mr. Post and Dr. Davenport, a few fundamental inferences may be drawn respecting the inherited characteristics of athletes as contributory to their participation in athletics.

Sixty years ago, Sir Francis Galton showed that unusual ability in rowing and wrestling may "run in the family." By anthropometric measurements, Dr. Davenport fifty years later demonstrated that both stature and body-build are family traits. Dr. Bach concluded substantially that "it seems impossible that the sport-types have been formed exclusively by environmental influences. We must rather assume a genotype which directed its possessor to certain bodily exercises." In other words, the athlete's inheritance of physique not only predisposes him to athletics in general, but may even tend to direct him in his choice of branches for participation without his being fully aware of its influence. Thus a long-legged youth becomes a sprinter primarily because of his long legs. A short, stocky, powerful-shouldered man becomes a wrestler partly because of his build. The influences of initial success at some branch or the urgings of a trainer or a fellow-athlete are, from the point of view of genetics, secondary to the initial promptings of inherited physical characteristics. On the other hand, other environmental forces my inhibit or modify this native pre-disposition, and so not all long-legged boys become sprinters nor do all heavily built men become wrestlers.

The inheritance of traits of character is far less easily demonstrable. The studies of Dr. Davenport and Mr. Post have indicated a probability that a father's interest in athletics may result in a son's becoming an athlete, perhaps through the influence of home or other environmental conditions or the removal of prohibitions. Certainly, such qualities as self-assertion, physical energy, control of temper, coolness, fondness for publicity, persistence, and many more besides, are common in varying degree to all men. Some may be inherited in a higher degree than others. Apparently, participation in athletics develops, rather than implants, certain traits of character. After inherited physical conformation has predisposed some persons to athletic exercise, habituation emphasizes and heightens certain characteristics already present.

We turn now to the results of the environment, which, Professor Elmer D. Mitchell says, "is a more potent factor than heredity in the playing of athletic games." Given an inherited tendency to athletics, what conditions encourage the fulfilling of that tendency?

The Future Career as a Motive

In numbers of instances, voluntary participation in college athletics is prompted by considerations respecting the life career that the participant intends to enter. To the successful athlete who decides to capitalize his reputation, three roads are open: playing as a professional, coaching or work as director of physical education, and certain kinds of business.

Professional Athletics

Sharp connection for expert players has enhanced the value of the college athlete as a recruit to professional teams in football, baseball, hockey, basketball, and, in a very few instances, soccer. The influence of such overtures, even when the athlete is supposedly safeguarded from professional inducements and left to complete his college course, is overwhelmingly in the direction of commercializing college athletics. For example, during college games which "scouts" or promoters of professional teams attend in order to discover promising material, the players tend to become self-conscious, and if they make errors of play, they are commonly chided with such jibes as "That will cost you a job for next year," or "That will cost you money." In the South and Mid-West, the professionalizing motive apparently becomes strong in many athletes as early as their high school days, with the result that not a few players of baseball at school enter college merely to play on college teams in hopes of establishing reputations that will attract substantial offers from "scouts" and professional leagues. In such instances, the academic aspects of college or university life are naturally of comparatively minor importance. The awarding of scholarships or other aids to college athletes whose intentions to enter professional athletics as a career are known, is difficult to justify. On the other hand, not a few undergraduates who have received offers from professional teams after graduation have refused them from a variety of motives: previous selection of a different career, the fear of losing social position, parental objection, contrary advice from college officers and coaches, and other reasons. A further motive for professionalizing one's athletic career is discernible in cases of athletes who have entered professional athletics after graduation in order to earn, readily and pleasantly, money to start themselves in business or in training for a profession. Certainly, to all forms of professional athletics, successful participation in college athletics affords a comparatively easy and enjoyable approach.

Payment for Participation in Intercollegiate Athletics

Because the matter of compensation to college athletics receives detailed discussion elsewhere in this study, it is sufficient to note here that the threat, expressed or implied, that a scholarship or subsidy may be withdrawn if the recipient athlete fails in athletic performance is a powerful compulsion to participation. The importance of athletics in the mind of the subsidized athlete necessarily dwarfs the importance of maintaining satisfactory academic standing.

A curious instance of the prevalence of this feeling occurred at a college where no athletics subsidies are in use. An athlete who had been awarded a scholarship on the grounds of his financial need and adequate academic standing, called upon the president and offered to resign his scholarship because, not having been selected as a member of the football team, he was not earning his stipend. Upon the president's asking what that had to do with the matter, the young man replied that it was his understanding that he had been receiving a football scholarship and that he could not continue to accept money that he did not deserve. It took the president longer than a few minutes to set matters straight in the athlete's mind.

Women's Sports

Sports for women, played under women's rules, are usually organized on an intramural basis. Most of the women's colleges, however, permit contests with other institutions of their kind, and some (Bryn Mawr, Wellesley) allow teams of undergraduates to meet teams representing approved women's amateur clubs. Branches of women's athletics include field hockey and basketball, which are the most popular, swimming, running, jumping, gymnastics, volley ball, and more rarely, rowing, golf, and tennis.

Scholastic Requirements and their Administration

In the course of the study much attention has been paid to scholastic requirements for participation in intercollegiate athletics and the strictness or laxity with which they are administered. Some hundreds of academic records of athletes and non-athletes have been examined, transcripts have been freely furnished by university officers upon request, the attendant circumstances surrounded many records have been canvassed, and even preparatory and high school records have been studied. The importance of the matter lies in its bearing upon the standing of the institution and its attitude toward the problems of eligibility and status.

It is possible to say, first, that over the past twenty years American scholastic standards for participation have risen, and, secondly, that there is still room for their improvement. Probably at no other point in the administration of athletics is imitation of good practice so salutary. Yet the mere announcing of standards is not enough. It is their application that matters.

Not a few universities possess scholastic requirements higher than those of the intercollegiate conferences or agreements to which they subscribe (Chicago, Cornell, Harvard, Princeton, Yale), and their enforcement of these standards respecting both admission and collegiate standing is honest, willing, and sportsmanlike. Other institutions (Columbia, Georgia School of Technology, Tulane) possess equally high requirements, which are rather frequently met through tutoring. Although certain Canadian universities have been accused by sister institutions of relaxing requirements for participation (Dalhousie, Queen's, Toronto), we have not found the charge to be justified. Not so, however, in the case of many other institutions.

All such matters are in the hands of faculties. They are not the concern of alumni or of friends of a college. When, therefore, standards are relaxed to permit skilled athletes either to enter a college without due qualifications or to compete in intercollegiate athletics without satisfying academic requirements, these matters also are the affair of faculties. But when the faculty officers concerned with eligibility happen to be athletic enthusiasts as well, the resulting division of responsibility has worked, in an appreciable number of cases, to the impairment of the standards and standing of the institutions.

A collection of examples (Alabama, Boston College, Fordham, Grinnell, Iowa, New York University, Northwestern, Notre Dame, Southern California, Stanford, Wisconsin) drawn from many parts of the United States will illustrate some of the results of conflicts between athletic ambitions and academic standards. The decision of one university faculty in a matter of participation and eligibility was overruled by the president. A trustee of another institution endeavored to persuade a college president to admit a young athlete whose credentials were not sufficient to justify this course. Prominent alumni of a third were embarrassingly insistent in their demand that a scholastically unqualified athlete should be admitted. The double standard that results from different university and conference requirements, non-athletes meeting the higher university requirements and athletes being held to meeting the lower conference requirements, not to mention a tradition of *laissez-faire* respecting a dean's office, results in immediate injustice to non-athletes and lasting injustice to athletes. At certain Southern institutions the practice of checking of players' scholastic records in mid-season has not been followed by the strictest adherence to requirements. At another university an athlete attained scholastic eligibility through the passing of an examination under circumstances that were, to say the least, unusual. The registrar of this same university has in at least three instances received instructions to admit candidates whose records were defective because of "the unusual conditions surrounding the case." The rulings concerning scholastic eligibility at certain Catholic institutions have been widely questioned. It is a pleasure to note that at another Catholic university (Georgetown) a strengthening of eligibility requirements is said to be in process. In two carefully studied cases, one of which is typical of a very large majority of institutions that are members of highly respected conferences, the functions of the university registrar are debased to those of a clerk, with the result that questionable rulings are reflected in questionable practices.

In short, high though the academic standards of participation maintained at certain institutions may be, they represent no universal condition. Faculties, trustees, and even college or university presidents are not as yet united as respects the maintenance of strict requirements in the face of the supposed benefits that can be wrung from winning teams. The fact that all of these supposed advantages are tinged at one point or another with the color of money casts over every relaxation of standards a mercenary shadow. The good repute which a university attains through high academic standards and their honest enforcement is priceless, and it is not to be compared with the cheap and ephemeral notoriety that winning teams may bring.

Academic Records of Athletes

In accordance with a plan outlined in the Twenty-Second Annual Report of the Carnegie Foundation for the Advancement of Teaching, 1927, detailed studies of the academic records of 2,787 athletes and 11,480 non-athletes in fifty-two representative colleges and universities of the United States were made at the institutions by registrars, deans, professors, and others. These results, assembled in the offices of the Foundation, are of sufficient accuracy to be interpreted as follows, due allowances being made for deviations in methods of grading and differences in type and procedure regarding intelligence tests and scores.

Time Spent in College for Degrees

The academic "mortality" of the athletes was lower than that of their fellows; that is, a higher proportion of athletes graduate than non-athletes. But it takes the athlete about half a college year longer, on the whole, to obtain his degree. The figure is probably less serious than at first appears, because in cases where longer than the normal time is required to obtain the credits for a degree, it is the almost universal rule that a semester of attendance is the minimum that can be required. On the average, about 95 per cent of the athletes registered as members of each successive college class returning to college in the following semester, as compared with 90 per cent of the non-athletes.

Scholarship Grades by Sports

Respecting the average comparative scholarship of individual participants in sports by branches, only general tendencies have importance. Wrestlers, cross-country runners, and track men do well,—indeed, far better than the general run of both athletes and non-athletes, especially the wrestlers. Swimmers and oarsmen do better than the average of athletes, but not quite so well as the average non-athletes. Soccer, lacrosse, and baseball players are below the averages of both athletes and non-athletes. Football and polo players stand at the bottom of the list. Athletes rank below non-athletes in scholarship, but the difference in average grades between the two general groups is statistically negligible. Participants in two or more branches of athletics stand on the average considerably below all athletes, as a group, and nearly as badly as football players.

His Relation to Athletics

Just as an ideal occasionally exists between the alumnus and the general affairs of the university, so a corresponding ideal relationship may sometimes be found with respect to athletics. It is manifested by that rare alumnus who sees individual boys as the educational units in college life, who expends his best effort in developing not alone their physical prowess but also their contacts with their fellow students and especially their relationship to the things of the mind and of the spirit. To such an alumnus intellectual endeavor, a knowledge of the past, honesty, right living, industry, and love of athletic games all have their appropriate places in the life of the undergraduate. Such an alumnus is of wholesome influence, even though he can afford to give little in time or money.

On the other hand, the usual current relationship of alumni to athletics manifests itself in two ways: the control of policies, and the recruiting and financing of athletes. Probably not a fifth of all alumni are active in either direction.

Alumni and Athletic Policies

The influence and activity of alumni in formulating the policies of universities and colleges as regards athletics have already been discussed at length in Chapter V. Only a few brief observations need to be added.

In the modern American university, the graduate manager or treasurer and his functions bear witness to the importance of the alumni and the esteem in which they are held. Their influence is felt in the appointment of coaches, the shaping and administering of coaching policies, the erection and size of stadiums, building programs, the provision and distribution of tickets, the making of schedules, and, indeed, in practically all of the extramural relationships of college athletics. Seldom do alumni manifest strong interest in intramural programs or competition. Although many play golf, tennis, squash, and handball, relatively few appear to realize the importance of cultivating in all undergraduates the experience of games that are suitable to his enjoyment and recreation in later life. The present-day attitude of alumni toward athletics is essentially the product of our long-standing emphasis upon extramural competition. It is likely that the growth of intramural games will give future graduates a different point of view.

Football attracts most of the alumni attention. During undergraduate days it draws and keeps the interest of men and women students to an extraordinary degree. After graduation the interest persists but does not manifest itself in active participation. Very few players take part in football games for more than five or six years after graduation. In the United States, contests at football between alumni and undergraduates have little to commend them; the graduates, "fat and scant of breath," endure, with little credit to their zeal, the falls, knocks, and runs of American football, while the student players receive small benefit from meeting a team possessing only antiquated strategy and tactics. That this should be so is one of the principal limitations of American football. True, a few alumni who have formerly played on college teams join local or amateur organizations after graduation. In California, for football, and in New York City, for basketball, athletic clubs provide opportunity and training accommodations for graduate athletes; teams representing these clubs are almost invariably more skillful than undergraduate college organizations. Some college graduates, especially from the Middle West, enter professional football for a few years, and a larger number take up coaching or physical education. But by their thirtieth birthdays the great majority of graduates feel more at home in their seats at a football spectacle than they would in suits upon any field. In Great Britain this is not the case. English Rugby, soccer, and the special football games of certain public schools, once mastered, are not infrequently played almost until middle age. The interest of the American changes early from the active to the passive. Usually it expresses itself in attending games, listening to broadcasts play-by-play, participating in the shaping of college athletic policies, subscribing money for equipment and increased facilities, and in other similar works. Much the same is true of other forms of athletics in American colleges and universities.

The Procurement and Support of Athletes

Although methods and procedure in recruiting and subsidizing college athletes are discussed at length in Chapter X, a word may be said here concerning the motives which lead alumni to these practices. The number of cases in which the entire support of athletes is furnished by alumni are far fewer than those in which a part is given and the athletes are provided with actual or nominal jobs through alumni efforts. Doubtless some alumni have a philanthropic and worthy desire to enable a deserving youth to obtain a college education, but comparatively seldom is this the genuine motive for subsidizing and recruiting. In the course of this study we have never heard it advanced except in defense of dishonest practices, in extenuation of the course of an institution, a group, or an individual, or in a theoretical and academic discussion. The pretended fear of doing injustice to some deserving boy is a bogeyman kept close at hand to justify all such doings. In view of the kindly solicitude that is lavished upon the athlete, the only justice that he is likely to experience is the injustice that falls to any youth who is over-coddled and whose money comes too easily.

The guidance of alumni interest and activity in athletics presents one of the crucial problems of college administration. What is needed is not more interest on the part of graduates, but the direction of this interest to ends that will truly benefit undergraduates. At present, too few alumni look upon athletics as a factor of higher education which prepares for afterlife, where games and outdoor contests ought to play their part. The most active of the alumni in a number of institutions, consciously or unconsciously, tend to make college athletics a preparation for professional athletics.

Certain National Relationships of American College Athletics

In the United States, universities and colleges, although influential, have not dominated athletic and sporting tradition as they have in England and Canada. This fact, as regards the United States, is accounted for by three considerations, which have operated to dilute the effect of university life upon the life of the people: democratic conditions, political, and social; both the vast expanse of territory and the distance between institutions of higher education; and, above all, the nature of the interest that the American people have evinced in college games and contests. This interest is largely ascribable to the emphasis laid by our newspapers upon athletics in college life. Under these conditions, the day has not yet arrived when the college or the university may be regarded as furnishing all of the essentials of an American athletic tradition. That day will be delayed until our college men and women over a period of years act as regards athletics with a "leadership," a sincerity, and a courage of principle that shall command the respect and the active emulation of other Americans.

Our present concern is with only two phases in the national relationships of American college athletics: representative legislative and executive bodies and their functions, and national contests as they involve individual college students as participants.

The National Collegiate Athletic Association

Membership in the National Collegiate Athletic Association, originally organized as the Intercollegiate Athletic Association in 1905, is open to "all colleges, universities, and institutions of learning in the United States."

Three classes of membership are provided: active, which includes some one hundred and fifty universities and colleges; allied, embracing six conferences with about sixty institutional members; and associate, in two classes, the first consisting of schools, the second of "groups of colleges and universities that are organized for the purpose of conducting mutual competition in sports," of which only one, the United States Intercollegiate Lacrosse Association, holds membership. The constituency of the National Collegiate Athletic Association is divided into eight geographical districts, each with its vice-president, who acts as arbitrator of charges concerning amateurism, adviser of the conduct of intercollegiate athletics, and custodian of records, and who reports to the annual convention of the Association concerning the strictness with which the rules have been "enforced" during the year, "modifications or additions to the eligibility code made by institutions individually or concertedly," progress toward uniformity in the activities of intercollegiate athletic associations, of local conferences, of leagues, district competitions if any, and other facts or recommendations which may be of interest to the Association. A council of fifteen members, eight of whom are members of faculties, conducts the affairs of the Association between meetings, and the council elects its own executive committee of five. The Association chooses annually committees to frame the rules in twelve branches of athletics – football, soccer, basketball, swimming, volley ball, boxing, track, wrestling, hockey, fencing, gymnastics, and lacrosse; to preserve college athletic records; to arbitrate; and, under the approval of the executive committee, to publish the rules of various sports. Many of the items of receipt and expenditure in the accounts of the Association concern the preparation and publication of these rules.

The Amateur Athletic Federation

The Amateur Athletic Federation, organized in 1920, comprises two divisions, one for men, the other for women.

In the men's division are included eighteen bodies, among which may be mentioned the United States Army, Navy, and Marine Corps, the American Legion, the National Collegiate Athletic Association, the Young Men's Christian Association, the American Physical Education Association, the Jewish Welfare Board, and the Catholic Boys' Brigade of the United States. The Federation states its "mission" to be "to create and maintain in the United States a permanent organization representative of amateur athletics and of organizations devoted thereto; to establish and maintain the highest ideals of amateur sport in the United States; to promote the development of physical education; to encourage the standardization of the rules of all amateur athletic games and competitions and the participation of this country in the International Olympic Games." Its definition of an amateur and its pronouncement upon the spirit of "Amateurism" are those of the National Collegiate Athletic Association. The constitution provides that "each organization in the Federation shall direct its own activities, conduct its own competitions, and control its own athletes in accordance with the principles set forth by the Federation. Governmental agencies are exempt from all dues. These provisions appear to leave the Military and Naval Academies, as well as the Services, responsible for the formulation and application of their own regulations.

CHAPTER SIX

Success and Excess

Expansion and Reforms in Higher Education, 1920 to 1945

Between World War I and World War II, higher education in the United States enjoyed expansion and diversification. One finally sees signs that the land grant acts of 1862 and 1890 were being fulfilled, marked by the maturation and public support of the great state universities of the Midwest and the Pacific Coast. Junior colleges—local two-year transfer institutions—also started to stake out an important role. Women's colleges in both the public and private sectors flourished in all regions. Historically black colleges and universities extended both educational opportunity and the American tradition of separation and exclusion. The tenacity and growing appeal of "going to college" were demonstrated by the phenomenon of rising enrollments during the Great Depression.

During World War II, American campuses demonstrated remarkable resiliency and service in assisting the effort to win the war. They did so in varied ways, ranging from providing training programs for officers and foreign language instruction for military translators to hosting advanced applied scientific research, such as the Manhattan Project—in which an interdisciplinary team of physicists, chemists, and mathematicians used the locker rooms of the deserted University of Chicago football stadium as its secret laboratory site. National appreciation for higher education was demonstrated in two major federal initiatives: student financial aid for veterans via the GI Bill, and establishment and funding of such permanent federal agencies as the National Science Foundation and the National Institutes of Health. Higher education following World War II increasingly gained stature as a fixture in American society.

Hollywood and Higher Education: The Marx Brothers' 1932 movie
Horse Feathers, publicity still photograph (Document 6.1)

6.1: Hollywood and Higher Education: The Marx Brothers Go to College (1932)

In 1932 only a small number and percentage of Americans attended college. Most adults had never set foot on a college campus, except perhaps to be a spectator at an intercollegiate football game. Nonetheless, images and characterizations of "college life" were central to American popular culture in magazine articles, newspaper coverage, sporting events, and Hollywood movies. Illustrative of this popularity was the 1932 movie *Horse Feathers*, featuring the Marx Brothers—with Groucho as the new president of the financially troubled, fictional "Huxley College."

For all its caricatures and exaggerations, the movie was unusual in that it had some grounding in reality, as the script was written by college graduates—such as S. J. Perlman of Brown University—who as undergraduates had been editors and writers for college humor magazines. Even though the movie makes light of lectures and teaching, at the very least it did include some classroom scenes. The movie is fictional in its portrayal of the campus as an idyllic setting. At the same time the movie is fac-

Horse Feathers (Los Angeles, CA: Paramount Pictures, 1932). Distributed by Paramount Pictures. Norman Z. McLeod, Director; Herman J. Mankiewicz, Producer.

tual in that the student body is affluent and racially homogeneous—and with college women deferring to the mores of a campus world dominated by college men. Many college presidents of the era also identified with such trade-offs as to whether they wanted a powerful football team or an academic campus. Indicative of popular over-statement was a scene in which professors complain that they had not been paid in five years. A more accurate portrayal might have been that pay had been suspended "only" for one year—and, as was the case at many colleges during the Great Depression, professors were paid with credit and scrip. The campus as a haven for drinking reflected the collegiate and alumni response to Prohibition.

6.2: Student Memoir: John Kenneth Galbraith on Graduate School at Berkeley in the 1930s (1968)

John Kenneth Galbraith was a prominent economist whose broad writings and numerous service roles elevated him to the level of a genuine "public intellectual" who was influential and provocative throughout the last half of the twentieth century. He brought to his numerous articles and books an understated yet pervasive wit that gave his discipline of economics a reprieve from being "the dismal science." The following memoir, first published in the *Atlantic Monthly* in 1968, was selected by Irving Stone to be the lead entry in a 1970 anthology of memoirs by famous alumni of the University of California, Berkeley. Galbraith did not disappoint his editor or readers with his recollection of student days at Berkeley in the 1930s. His contribution has special importance in that he wrote from the perspective of a graduate student—a role that has been important yet underrepresented in the heritage of higher education. Galbraith was a famous and longtime professor at Harvard. At the same time one finds in his recollection the power of Alma Mater as he reveals a deep, justifiable love for his studies, explorations, friends, and professors at the University of California, Berkeley.

One day in the autumn of 1930 I was gazing at the notice board in the post office of the main men's residence at the Ontario Agricultural College at Guelph, Canada. It was usually an unrewarding vision but on this day it advertised a number

John Kenneth Galbraith, "Berkeley in the Age of Innocence," *Atlantic Monthly* (June 1969) pp. 62–68. This was republished in Irving Stone, ed., *There Was Light: Autobiography of a University—Berkeley: 1868–1968* (Garden City, NY: Doubleday, 1970) pp. 19–31. Reprinted by permission of the estate of John Kenneth Galbraith.

of research assistantships at the Giannini Foundation of Agricultural Economics at the University of California. The annual stipend was $720 for unmarried scholars. I copied down the details and applied. Some time later I received a letter from George Peterson, associate professor of Agricultural Economics, saying that I had been selected. I was surprised and so were my professors, who detested me and thought the people at Berkeley were crazy. I quickly accepted; in that second year of the Great Depression the monthly salary of sixty dollars, if not princely, was by far the best offer of any kind I had. In fact it was the only offer of any kind I had. From that day on the University of California has engaged my affection as no other institution—educational, public or pecuniary—with which I have ever been associated. One Sunday afternoon in the summer of 1968, with my wife and oldest son (who followed me to be an assistant at the University of California Law School) I strolled across the California campus—over Strawberry Creek, by the Campanile, down by the Library, out Sather Gate. I was taught, as were most of my generation, that no one should allow himself the weak luxury of sentiment or even emotion. To this day when I write "Love" at the end of a letter I always remind myself that it is only modern affectation, in all respects a matter of form. I was suddenly overwhelmed by the thought that I loved this place—the paths, trees, flowers, buildings, even the new ones. I was deeply embarrassed.

In the thirties, for some reason related either to the eccentricities of the California crop year or climate, the University of California opened in August. Accordingly in July of 1931 I borrowed $500 from an aunt, once of the few members in our rural family still to command such capital, and, almost literally, set sail for California. I boarded the steamer which plied between Port Stanley on the north shore of Lake Erie and Cleveland, where, by prearrangement of our local jeweler and oculist, I met his nephew who had a graduate fellowship at California in astronomy. At five o'clock the following morning we set out in the 1926 Oakland automobile my companion had acquired for this trip. The car was in terrible condition and almost immediately got worse. To save money he had bought a five-gallon gasoline tin and a one-gallon container for oil so that we could stock up on these products whenever, as happened in those days, our path led us to a region being ravaged by a price war. Such at least was the theory. About thirty miles out of Cleveland my friend stopped to check the gas (the gauge was broken) and look at the oil. The car absorbed the whole five gallons of gasoline and the whole gallon of oil. For the rest of the trip we averaged around a quarter gallon of gas and a half pint of oil to the mile. To this day I shudder at the cost.

The journey took ten days not counting twenty-four hours at Casey, Iowa, where we laid up with a broken connecting rod. That, too, had a lasting effect. It was raining hard, and as we waited for the repairs, we listened to the local farmers, who used the garage as a club, discuss Hoover. I became a life-long Democrat. It was about six o'clock on the bright summer evening when we got to Berkeley and drove to Bancroft Way to the International House. The hills behind were very bleached and sere but the low sun glistened on the live oaks and the green lawns and the masses of pink geraniums, which elsewhere are only geraniums but in Berkeley are the glory of the whole city. The sun also lit up a vast yellow-buff facade of the International House with the large Spanish arches of the portico below. We passed into the great hall, then gleaming new, and combining the best mission style with the finest Moorish revival. I thought it a place of unimaginable splendor.

Eventually the International House was to prove a bit too expensive even for one who earned sixty dollars a month and was, as a result, one of the more affluent members of the community. My capital had been depleted by that terrible car. But for the first few months at Berkeley this nice Rockefeller benefaction—it had counterparts in New York, Chicago, Paris and Tokyo—housing several hundred students of both sexes from the Unites States and many foreign lands, was to be my window on the Berkeley world. Never before had I been so happy.

The world on which I looked down could not be recognized in important respects by Mario Savio. I must stress that I had just emerged from the Ontario Agricultural College and this could have distorted my vision. Once not long ago I was asked by *Time* magazine about this academy; I replied, thoughtlessly, that in my day it was certainly the cheapest and possibly the worst in the English-speaking world. This was tactless and wrong and caused dissatisfaction even after all these years. (No one questioned my statement that the college was inexpensive.) But at OAC students were expected to keep and also to know and cherish their place. Leadership in the student body was solidly in the hands of those who combined an outgoing anti-intellectualism with a sound interest in livestock. This the faculty thought right. Anyone who questioned the established agricultural truths, many of which were wildly wrong, was sharply rebuked, and if he offended too often he was marked down as a troublemaker. A fair number of faculty members had effectively substituted the affable and well-clipped manner and mustache of the professional countryman for the admitted tedium of science. Unquestionably the place did build health. At Berkeley I suddenly encountered professors who knew their subject and, paradoxically, invited debate on what they knew. They also had time to talk at length with graduate students and even to come up to International House to continue the conversation. I first discovered at Berkeley from Henry Erdman, who had until recently been the head of the Agricultural Economics Department, and Howard Tolley, who had just succeeded him as the director of the Giannini Foundation, that a professor might like to be informed on some subject by a graduate student—not just polite but pleased. So profound was that impression that I never stopped informing people thereafter. The pleasure I have thus given has been very great. (Howard Tolley, after a year or two, went on to Washington to become head of the Agricultural Adjustment Administration under FDR. I shall mention him again in a moment. In 1968, after the elapse of a third of a century, I was back in Berkeley one Sunday to urge the case and, more important, since everyone was persuaded, to raise money for Eugene McCarthy. I was not at all surprised to see Henry Erdman in the front row. He believed strongly in keeping informed.)

Although we had stipends, we agricultural economists were second-class citizens. Our concern was with the prices of cling peaches, which were then appalling, and the financial condition of the Merced irrigation district, which was equally bad, and the prune industry, which was chronically indigent, and other such useful subjects. I earned my research stipend by tramping (sic) the streets of Los Angeles and also Oakland and San Jose to ascertain the differing preferences as to package and flavor—sage, orange blossom, clover—of Mexican, Jewish, Negro and (as we then thought of them) ordinary white Americans, for honey. No differences emerged. This kind of work was not well regarded by the non-agricultural, or pure, economists. Thorstein Veblen was still being read with attention in Berkeley in the thirties. He distinguishes between esoteric and exoteric knowledge, the first having the commanding advantage of being without "economic or industrial effect." It is this advantage, he argues, which distinguishes the higher learning from the lower. Ours, obviously, was the lower.

We suffered from another handicap. Agriculturalists, in an indistinct way, were considered to be subject to the influence of the California Farm Bureau Federation and, much worse, of the opulent and perpetually choleric baronage which comprised the Associated Farmers of California. Actually our subordination was not all that indistinct. Both organizations told the dean of the College of Agriculture and the director of Extension what they needed in the way of research and also conclusions. They were heard with attention, even respect. No one was ever told to shape his scholarly work accordingly; men were available who did it as a matter of course.

The non-agricultural economists, whatever their differences in other matters of doctrine, were united in regarding the farmers, even more than the bankers or oilmen, as an all-purpose class enemy. In time I acquired a certain reputation in economic theory and other branches of impractical knowledge and also a rather circumspect critic of the agricultural establishment. So I was accorded an honorary status as a scholar, my agricultural handicaps notwithstanding. I was then even more happy.

The Department of Economics at Berkeley has never been considered quite as eminent as that at Harvard. The reason is that the best Californians have always been at Harvard. As this is written in the autumn of 1968, of the twenty-three full professors of economics at Harvard no fewer than seven, nearly one third, were recruited at one stage or another in their careers from the University of California at Berkeley. And economics at Berkeley has long had a marked personality. In the early thirties, years before the Keynesian revolution, Leo Rogin was discussing Keynes with a sense of urgency that made his seminars seem to graduate students the most important things then happening in the world. I learned Alfred Marshall from Ewald Grether, who taught with a drillmaster's precision for which I have ever since been grateful. Marshall is the quintessence of classical economics and much of what he says is wrong. But no one can know what is wrong if he does not understand it first. My memory also goes back to M. M. Knight's seminar in economic history, a gifted exercise in irrelevancy. Once Robert Gordon Sproul, then the president of the University, said in one of his booming speeches that, after all, a university was run for the students. Knight, a brother of the noted Frank H. Knight of the University of Chicago, attacked this doctrine for two full sessions. A university, he argued with indignation, was run for the faculty and, to affirm the point, he announced his intention of introducing a resolution at some early faculty meeting to exclude the students from the library. They got in the way.

We graduate students were also fond of Paul Taylor, who spoke out unfailingly for the small farmer in California, Charles Gulick, who spoke out for the farm workers, who then as now aroused great animosity and a measure of righteous anger for wanting a union and a living wage, and Robert Brady, who was the friend of the consumer and other lost causes. Brady taught courses in the business cycle and set great store by exhaustive bibliographic research. One of my friends met this requirement by going to the card catalogue in the library and copying into the appendix of his thesis everything that appeared there under the headings Cycle, Business, and Cycle, Trade. Brady sent over for some of the latter items which were new to him and they turned out to be works on bicycles, tricycles, and motorcycles published by the Cycle Trades of America. We always heard there was quite a scene.

A few years after I left Berkeley I became deputy head of the Office of Price Administration in charge of the World War II price controls. This was a post with unlimited patronage—eventually, as I recall, I had some seventeen thousand assistants. In addition to Richard Nixon and Mrs. Nixon and many other promising people, numerous of my former professors, including Howard Tolley, Harry Wellman (later the acting president of the University) and Robert Brady turned up on our staff. Brady had scarcely arrived before he was assaulted hip and thigh by the Dies Committee—now better known as HUAC—for saying in a book on German fascism that American capitalism was only technically better. To complicate matters further, Dies had got hold of the edition published by the Left Book Club in England. It had something on the cover about not being for public sale. I handled the defense on the Hill with the handicap of knowing that everything I said in favor of Bob would immediately be used against me. Brady later attributed his troubles to the oil companies and said I was their tool. He had proposed that people conserve oil by not draining the crankcase for the duration or ten thousand miles, whichever was less. I did not endorse the idea. This was mostly because with everything else it never got to my attention. But if it had, I might have remembered that Oakland and the way it changed itself and wondered if it would have made much difference.

The graduate students with whom I associated in the thirties were uniformly radical and the most distinguished were Communists. I listened to them eagerly and would have liked to have joined both the conversation and the Party but here my agricultural background was a real handicap. It meant that, as a matter of formal Marxian doctrine, I was politically immature. Among the merits of capitalism to Marx was the fact that it rescued men from the idiocy of rural life. I had only very recently been retrieved. I sensed this bar and I knew also that my pride would be deeply hurt by rejection. So I kept outside. There was possibly one other factor. Although I recognized that the system could not and should not survive, I was enjoying it so much that, secretly, I was a little sorry.

In the ensuing twenty years many of those I most envied were accorded an auto-da-fé by HUAC, James Eastland or the late Joseph R. McCarthy. Their lives

were ruined. Phrases about the unpredictable graces of God kept constantly crossing my mind.

One man who did not get called by Joe McCarthy was Robert Merriman, a vital
and popular graduate student and teaching assistant who came down to Berkeley
from Nevada in the early thirties. As an undergraduate he had been wholesome
and satisfactory and even took an interest in ROTC. But Berkeley had its effect
and so (as he told friends) did the great waterfront strike of 1934, where he saw
soldiers deployed against the strikers. Hugh Thomas' brilliant book, *The Spanish
Civil War* tells the rest of his story. Interrupting a traveling fellowship in Europe
in 1936, Merriman went to Spain, where (one assumes as an uncalculated consequence of ROTC) he commanded the Abraham Lincoln Battalion on the Jarama
and then went on through many battles to be chief of staff of the XV International
Brigade. A major and by now long a veteran, he was killed (possibly executed after
capture by the Nationalists) on the Aragon front in 1938. He must have been the
bravest of our contemporaries; he so impressed Ernest Hemingway that he became
in part the model for Robert Jordan (a professor from Montana) in *For Whom the
Bell Tolls*. The California campus has ornaments for lesser heroes who died nearer
home for more fashionable beliefs. There are some naïve, haunting lines written
by John Depper, a British volunteer, of the Battle of Jarama that might serve:

> Death stalked in the olive trees
> Picking his men
> His leaden finger beckoned
> Again and again.

A year ago in Chicago I was on a television discussion program with Robert
Merriam, a White House aide to President Eisenhower and once Republican candidate for mayor of Chicago against Richard Daley. He said that for many years
he had been investigated assiduously by the FBI because of his name. Merriman
was not completely forgotten.

I would not wish it thought that our life in the thirties was limited to politics and great matters of the mind. One roamed through San Francisco, climbed
Mt. Diablo, went up to the Sierras, where someone was always imagining that
the Depression might make panning gold profitable again, and consumed (I most
diffidently) alcohol stolen from the chemistry laboratories and mixed with grape-
fruit juice and, after repeal, a blended whiskey of negligible cost called, to the best
of my memory, Crab Orchard. I have difficulty in believing that the latter-day

Though we graduate students expected the revolution very soon and planned to encourage it, we did not expect any help from the Berkeley undergraduates. Not that they would oppose—they would simply, as usual, be unaware that anything was happening. A singular accomplishment of American higher education, as one reflects on it, was the creation of a vast network of universities, public and private, which for a century, until the sixties, caused no one any political embarrassment of any kind. In other countries they created trouble from time to time, but not here. A control system which subtly suggested that whatever the students most wanted to do—i.e., devote themselves to football, basketball, fraternities, college tradition, rallies, hell-raising, a sentimental concern for the old alma mater and imaginative inebriation—was what they should do, was basic to this peace. The alumni rightly applauded this control system and so, to an alarming extent, did the faculty. An occasional non-political riot was condoned and even admired; some deeper adult instinct suggested that it was a surrogate for something worse. At Berkeley in the thirties this system was still working perfectly. Coming up Bancroft Way to the International House of an evening one saw the fraternity men policing up the lawns of their houses or sitting contentedly in front. Walking along Piedmont at night one heard the shouts of laughter from within, or occasional bits of song or what Evelyn Waugh correctly described as the most evocative and nostalgic of all the sounds of an aristocracy at play, the crash of breaking glass. Here were men with a secure position in society and who knew it and who were content. On a Friday night they would do their duty at the pep rally shaming the apathetic; on Saturday they would be at the stadium and on Saturday night, win or lose, they joined with the kindred souls of earlier generations, men they did not hesitate to call brother, to whoop it up as a college man was meant to do. The *Daily Californian* was the approving chronicle of this world—of the Big Game, the Axe, the cards turned in unison in the cheering section to depict an Indian or a bear, the campaign to send the band to Oregon to support the team. In 1932 Norman Thomas came to the campus and spoke to a small assembly in a classroom. Neither Hoover nor Roosevelt dreamed of favoring us. Hoover did speak to a vast audience of indigent citizens from the local Hooverville down on the Oakland flats and was cheered uproariously when he told them that, at long last, the Depression was over. They had not heard. Only once was there a suggestion of student involvement. The financial condition of the state of California in those days was appalling. State workers were being paid with tax-anticipation certificates. Even the governor, James (Sunny Jim) Rolph, sensed that something was wrong. In 1932 and 1933 there were threats to cut the University budget. When it seemed that these were serious, the students were encouraged to assemble and ask their relatives and friends to petition their legislators to relent. Perhaps that was the camel's nose, the seed of the Frankenstein. As to persuading the legislature, however, it was considered less important than a promise by the University to retrench voluntarily and to begin with the Agricultural Extension (Farm Adviser) Service. No one said so but we agriculturalists certainly felt that our pragmatic approach to scholarship had paid off for everybody.

In the 1960s Dean Rusk, Lyndon Johnson, General Westmoreland, Lewis Hershey and Ronald Reagan accomplished what not even the most talented of our teachers had ever hoped to achieve. The undergraduates became politically concerned. When the time comes to award honors to those who made our universities the center of our political life, it will be a great injustice if the men of affirmative, as distinct from the negative, influence are featured. Now, I would suppose, Berkeley is the most intense intellectual and political community in the world; perhaps, indeed, it is the nearest thing to a total university community in modern times. As such it would be silly to suppose that it could be altogether tranquil. Often in these past years, following some exceptionally imaginative outbreak on Telegraph Avenue I've heard a colleague say: "You know that sort of thing could never happen here." I've always been too polite to say why I agreed. And the statement could be wrong. As other university communities succumb to the concerns so long a commonplace at Berkeley, they, too, cease to be tranquil.

Not everyone is as restrained as I am about Berkeley. A few weeks ago I shared a seat on an airplane with a young colleague newly recruited, like so many before him, from the University of California. I asked him if he missed it. He replied, "Christ, yes! At Berkeley you worked all morning in the library and then at noon you went out into the sun and there was always a demonstration going on or something. Man, that was living!"

The days passed. During my second year my stipend was raised to seventy dollars a month, allowing me to save a little money and also to have a larger social life. Then in my third year I was sent to Davis, which, for the benefit of non-Californians, is in the Sacramento Valley not far from Sacramento. It is now a full-fledged university but in those days it was the center of agricultural research and instruction too closely associated with orchards, insects and the soil to be carried on at Berkeley. It cultivated, in other words, the lowest of the lower learning. At Davis I was the head of the Department of Economics, of Agricultural

Economics, of Accounting and of Farm Management. I also gave instruction in all of these subjects and, with the exception of one elderly dean, who gave lectures to non-degree students, I was also the total teaching staff in these disciplines. During the year I also had time to write my Ph.D. thesis and I do not recall that I was especially rushed. Certainly such was my love for Berkeley that I went there every weekend. At Davis my pay was $1,800 and I was able (by way of repayment of my own college debts to my family) to send my younger sister to college.

The Davis students were also highly stable. My course in beginning economics was required for some majors. The scholars so compelled tramped in at the beginning of the hour, squeezed their yellow corduroy-clad bottoms into the classroom chairs, listened with indifference for an hour and then, by now conveying an impression of manfully suppressed indignation, tramped out. Only once in the entire year did I arouse their interest. I gave some support to the textbook case for lower tariffs. Coming as they did from the sugar beet fields, olive orchards, cattle ranches and other monuments to the protective tariff, they knew that was wrong and told me so. My best remembered student that year was a boy who had an old Ford runabout and spent his weekends putting up signs on the highways which warned motorists to repent and prepare at a fairly early date to meet their God. In response on an examination to a question about the nature of money, he stuck resolutely to the proposition that it (not the love of money but money itself) was the root of all evil. I tried to reason with him, but in vain. So I flunked him, for his contention seemed to me palpably untrue. That was my only personal encounter in those years with any form of student dissent.

One day in the spring of 1934 I was in Berkeley putting the finishing touches on my thesis. A Western Union boy came into the room with a telegram offering me an instructorship at Harvard for the following year at $2,400. I had not the slightest idea of accepting, for I was totally happy at California. But my rapid advance in economic well-being, plus no doubt the defense of my faith against that student, had made me avaricious and I had heard that one won advances in academic life by flashing offers from other universities. I let it be known over the weekend that "Harvard was after me," and, on the following Monday, went by appointment to see the dean of the College of Agriculture to bargain. I carried the telegram in my hand. The dean, a large, handsome and highly self-confident man named Claude B. Hutchison, who later became the mayor of Berkeley, was excellently informed on all matters in the college and his intelligence system had not failed him on this occasion. He congratulated me warmly on my offer, gave me the impression that he thought Harvard was being reckless with its money and said that, of course, I should go. In a moment I realized to my horror I had no choice. I couldn't now plead to stay at two thirds the price. The great love of my life was over. I remember wondering, as I went out, if I had been right to flunk that nut.

6.3: Federal Student Financial Aid: The GI Bill of 1944

Sociologists have long alerted us to "unintended consequences" and "latent functions." Their message has been especially pertinent to the aftermath of the U.S. victory in World War II. The obvious, primary concern of the United States Congress was how to deal with readjustment from a wartime economy of production and prosperity to a domestic peacetime economy—which suddenly had little demand for tanks, missiles, or bombs. And there also was the problem of how the peacetime economy could absorb literally hundreds of thousands of veterans who had demonstrated loyalty, dedication, patriotism, and diverse skills in a demanding war effort. In Congress a groundswell of appreciation combined with apprehension about the fear of postwar unemployment led to interesting and unprecedented legislation. Well known by its nickname, the "GI Bill," this landmark legislation relied on the cooperation of colleges and universities and generous entitlement funding from the federal government to provide student financial aid and institutional choice for veterans of World War II to attend college and other postsecondary education programs. The GI Bill demonstrated how a quantitative change—in student financial aid and in the number of newly enrolled students—elicited a qualitative change in the character of "going to college" and the American campus.

Chapter IV Education of Veterans

Sec. 400. (a) Subsection (f) of section 1, title I, Public Law Numbered 2, Seventy-third Congress, added by the Act of March 24, 1943 (Public Law Numbered 16, Seventy-eighth Congress), is hereby amended to read as follows:

(f) Any person who served in the active military or naval forces on or after September 16, 1940, and prior to the termination of hostilities in the present war,

Servicemen's Readjustment Act (1944): an act to provide federal government aid for the readjustment in civilian life of returning World War II veterans, June 22, 1944; Enrolled Acts and Resolutions of Congress, 1789–1996; General Records of the United States Government; Record Group 11; National Archives.

shall be entitled to vocational rehabilitation subject to the provisions and limitations of Veterans Regulation Numbered 1 (a), as amended, part VII, or to education or training subject to the provisions and limitations of part VIII.

(b) Veterans Regulation Numbered 1 (a), is hereby amended by adding a new part VIII as follows:

Part VIII

1. Any person who served in the active military or naval service on or after September 16, 1940, and prior to the termination of the present war, and who shall have been discharged or released there-from under conditions other than dishonorable, and whose education or training was impeded, delayed, interrupted, or interfered with by reason of his entrance into the service, or who desires a refresher or retraining course, and who either shall have served ninety days or more, exclusive of any period he was assigned for a course of education or training under the Army specialized training program or the Navy college training program, which course was a continuation of his civilian course and was pursued to completion, or as a cadet or midshipman at one of the service academies, or shall have been discharged or released from active service by reason of an actual service-incurred injury or disability, shall be eligible for and entitled to receive education or training under this part: Provided, That such course shall be initiated not later than two years after either the date of his discharge or the termination of the present war, whichever is the later: Provided further, That no such education or training shall be afforded beyond seven years after the termination of the present war: And provided further, That any such person who was not over 25 years of age at the time he entered the service shall be deemed to have had his education or training impeded, delayed, interrupted, or interfered with.

2. Any such eligible person shall be entitled to education or training, or a refresher or retraining course, at an approved educational or training institution, for a period of one year (or the equivalent thereof in continuous part-time study), or for such lesser time as may be required for the course of instruction chosen by him. Upon satisfactory completion of such course of education or training, according to the regularly prescribed standards and practices of the institutions, except a refresher or retraining course, such person shall be entitled to an additional period or periods of education or training, not to exceed the time such person was in the active service on or after September 16, 1940, and before the termination of the war, exclusive of any period he was assigned for a course of education or training under the Army specialized training program or the Navy college

training program, which course was a continuation of his civilian course and was pursued to completion, or as a cadet or midshipman at one of the service academies, but in no event shall the total period of education or training exceed four years: Provided, That his work continues to be satisfactory throughout the period, according to the regularly prescribed standards and practices of the institution: Provided, however, That wherever the additional period of instruction ends during a quarter or semester and after a major part of such quarter or semester has expired, such period of instruction shall be extended to the termination of such unexpired quarter or semester.

3. Such person shall be eligible for and entitled to such course of education or training as he may elect, and at any approved educational or training institution at which he chooses to enroll, whether or not located in the State in which he resides, which will accept or retain him as a student or trainee in any field or branch of knowledge which such institution finds him qualified to undertake or pursue: Provided, That, for reasons satisfactory to the Administrator, he may change a course of instruction: And provided further, That any such course of education or training may be discontinued at any time, if it is found by the Administrator that, according to the regularly prescribed standards and practices of the institution, the conduct or progress of such person is unsatisfactory.

4. From time to time the Administrator shall secure from the appropriate agency of each State a list of the educational and training institutions (including industrial establishments), within such jurisdiction, which are qualified and equipped to furnish education or training (including apprenticeship and refresher or retraining training), which institutions, together with such additional ones as may be recognized and approved by the Administrator, shall be deemed qualified and approved to furnish education or training to such persons as shall enroll under this part: Provided, That wherever there are established State apprenticeship agencies expressly charged by State laws to administer apprentice training, whenever possible, the Administrator shall utilize such existing facilities and services in training on the job when such training is of one year's duration or more.

5. The Administrator shall pay to the educational or training institution, for each person enrolled in full time or part time course of education or training, the customary cost of tuition, and such laboratory, library, health, infirmary, and other similar fees as are customarily charged, and may pay for books, supplies, equipment, and other necessary expenses, exclusive of board, lodging, other living expenses, and travel, as are generally required for the successful pursuit and

completion of the course by other students in the institution: Provided, That in no event shall such payments, with respect to any person, exceed $500 for an ordinary school year: Provided further, That no payments shall be made to institutions, business or other establishments furnishing apprentice training on the job: And provided further, That if any such institution has no established tuition fee, or if its established tuition fee shall be found by the Administrator to be inadequate compensation to such institution for furnishing such education or training, he is authorized to provide for the payment, with respect to any such person, of such fair and reasonable compensation as will not exceed $500 for an ordinary school year.

6. While enrolled in and pursuing a course under this part, such person, upon application to the Administrator, shall be paid a subsistence allowance of $50 per month, if without a dependent or dependents, or $75 per month, if he has a dependent or dependents, including regular holidays and leave not exceeding thirty days in a calendar year. Such person attending a course on a part-time basis, and such person receiving compensation for productive labor performed as part of their apprentice or other training on the job at institutions, business or other establishments, shall be entitled to receive such lesser sums, if any, as subsistence or dependency allowances, as may be determined by the Administrator: Provided, That any such person eligible under this part, and within the limitations thereof, may pursue such full time or part-time course or courses as he may elect, without subsistence allowance.

7. Any such person eligible for the benefits of this part, who is also eligible for the benefit of part VII, may elect which benefit he desires: Provided, That, in the event of such election, subsistence allowance hereunder shall not exceed the amount of additional pension payable for training under said part VII.

8. No department, agency, or officer of the United States, in carrying out the provisions of this part, shall exercise any supervision or control, whatsoever, over any State educational agency, or State apprenticeship agency, or any educational or training institution: Provided, That nothing in this section shall be deemed to prevent any department, agency, or officer of the United States from exercising any supervision or control which such department, agency, or officer is authorized, by existing provisions of law, to exercise over any Federal educational or training institution, or to prevent the furnishing of education or training under this part in any institution over which supervision or control is exercised by such other department, agency, or officer under authority of existing provisions of law.

9. The Administrator of Veterans Affairs is authorized and empowered to administer this title, and, insofar as he deems practicable, shall utilize existing facilities and services of Federal and State departments and agencies on the basis of mutual agreements with them. Consistent with and subject to the provisions and limitations set forth in this title, the Administrator shall, from time to time, prescribe and promulgate such rules and regulations as may be necessary to carry out its purposes and provisions.

10. The Administrator may arrange for educational and vocational guidance to persons eligible for education and training under this part. At such intervals as he deems necessary, he shall make available information respecting the need for general education and for trained personnel in the various crafts, trades, and professions: Provided, That facilities of other Federal agencies collecting such information shall be utilized to the extent he deems practicable.

11. As used in this part, the term educational or training institutions shall include all public or private elementary, secondary, and other schools furnishing education for adults, business schools and colleges, scientific and technical institutions, colleges, vocational schools, junior colleges, teachers colleges, normal schools, professional schools, universities, and other educational institutions, and shall also include business or other establishments providing apprentice or other training on the job, including those under the supervision of an approved college or university or any State department of education, or any State apprenticeship agency or State board of vocational education, or any State apprenticeship council or the Federal Apprentice Training Service established in accordance with Public, Numbered 308, Seventy-fifth Congress, or any agency in the executive branch of the Federal Government authorized under other laws to supervise such training.

6.4: The Federal Government and Sponsored Research: Vannevar Bush's 1945 Report, *Science: The Endless Frontier*

In 1960 the president of the University of California, Clark Kerr, wrote in glowing terms about the rise of the "Federal Grant University"—an elite, influential group of universities that qualified for federally funded scientific projects. How did this come about? It is no less than an academic mystery story, given that as late as 1940 the

Vannevar Bush, *Science: The Endless Frontier; A Report to the President* (Washington, DC: Office of Scientific Research and Development, 1945).

federal government had little presence in campus-based research, with the important exception of various agriculture grant projects. The answer to the puzzle is found in large part with Vannevar Bush. Bush led by example as a new public figure in American life: a combination of scientist, scholar, inventor, campus administrator, business founder, and government agency director who brought together the remarkable alliance of the federal government, the U.S. military, the scientific community, and the higher education establishment. He was an electrical engineer who had been an effective administrator and professor at the Massachusetts Institute of Technology. During World War II, he was called on by the White House to orchestrate unprecedented projects that called for coordination and cooperation across private and public sectors. This included serving as director of the National Defense Research Committee and, later, the Office of Scientific and Research Development. He accomplished this mission admirably and was featured on the cover of *Time* magazine in the April 3, 1944, issue.

Apart from national service as a director of federal agencies, he was a founder of Raytheon Corporation in the greater Boston area. His diverse and triangulated pursuits exemplified that the academic as entrepreneur and broker had a prominent place in American life—both during and after the World War II effort. Bush's legacy—and tribute—was the appreciation of the president and the United States Congress. This was manifest in the attention they gave to his 1945 report, *Science: The Endless Frontier*. Here one finds that ideas matter, and that the expertise and innovation of the American campus during World War II could be—and would be—incorporated into a long-term domestic economy of research and development which would become the marvel and envy of the world. It would be most obvious in the enthusiastic, generous support the federal government would provide to the National Science Foundation and the National Institutes of Health. Bush, in short, had laid the groundwork for the creation and proliferation of the so-called Federal Grant University—a prestigious circle of research universities.

President Roosevelt's Letter:

The White House
Washington, D. C.
November 17, 1944

Dear Dr. Bush: The Office of Scientific Research and Development, of which you are the Director, represents a unique experiment of team-work and cooperation in coordinating scientific research and in applying existing scientific knowledge to the solution of the technical problems paramount in war. Its work has been conducted in the utmost secrecy and carried on without public recognition of any kind; but its tangible results can be found in the communiques coming in from the battlefronts all over the world. Some day the full story of its achievements can be told.

There is, however, no reason why the lessons to be found in this experiment cannot be profitably employed in times of peace. The information, the techniques, and the research experience developed by the Office of Scientific Research and Development and by the thousands of scientists in the universities and in private industry, should be used in the days of peace ahead for the improvement of the national health, the creation of new enterprises bringing new jobs, and the betterment of the national standard of living.

It is with that objective in mind that I would like to have your recommendations on the following four major points:

First: What can be done, consistent with military security, and with the prior approval of the military authorities, to make known to the world as soon as possible the contributions which have been made during our war effort to scientific knowledge?

The diffusion of such knowledge should help us stimulate new enterprises, provide jobs for our returning servicemen and other workers, and make possible great strides for the improvement of the national well-being.

Second: With particular reference to the war of science against disease, what can be done now to organize a program for continuing in the future the work which has been done in medicine and related sciences?

The fact that the annual deaths in this country from one or two diseases alone are far in excess of the total number of lives lost by us in battle during this war should make us conscious of the duty we owe future generations.

Third: What can the Government do now and in the future to aid research activities by public and private organizations? The proper roles of public and of private research, and their interrelation, should be carefully considered.

Fourth: Can an effective program be proposed for discovering and developing scientific talent in American youth so that the continuing future of scientific research in this country may be assured on a level comparable to what has been done during the war?

New frontiers of the mind are before us, and if they are pioneered with the same vision, boldness, and drive with which we have waged this war we can create a fuller and more fruitful employment and a fuller and more fruitful life.

I hope that, after such consultation as you may deem advisable with your associates and others, you can let me have your considered judgment on these matters as soon as convenient – reporting on each when you are ready, rather than waiting for completion of your studies in all.

Very sincerely yours,
(s) Franklin D. Roosevelt

Letter of Transmittal

Office of Scientific Research and Development
1530 P Street, NW.
Washington 25, D.C.
July 25, 1945

Dear Mr. President:
In a letter dated November 17, 1944, President Roosevelt requested my recommendations on the following points:

(1) What can be done, consistent with military security and with the prior approval of the military authorities, to make known to the world as soon as possible the contributions which have been made during our war effort to scientific knowledge?

(2) With particular reference to the war of science against disease, what can be done now to organize a program for continuing in the future the work which has been done in medicine and related sciences?

(3) What can the Government do now and in the future to aid research activities by public and private organizations?

(4) Can an effective program be proposed for discovering and developing scientific talent in American youth so that the continuing future of scientific research in this country may be assured on a level comparable to what has been done during the war?

It is clear from President Roosevelt's letter that in speaking of science that he had in mind the natural sciences, including biology and medicine, and I have so interpreted his questions. Progress in other fields, such as the social sciences and the humanities, is likewise important; but the program for science presented in my report warrants immediate attention.

In seeking answers to President Roosevelt's questions I have had the assistance of distinguished committees specially qualified to advise in respect to these subjects. The committees have given these matters the serious attention they deserve; indeed, they have regarded this as an opportunity to participate in shaping the policy of the country with reference to scientific research. They have had many meetings and have submitted formal reports. I have been in close touch with the work of the committees and with their members throughout. I have examined all of the data they assembled and the suggestions they submitted on the points raised in President Roosevelt's letter.

Although the report which I submit herewith is my own, the facts, conclusions, and recommendations are based on the findings of the committees which have studied these questions. Since my report is necessarily brief, I am including as appendices the full reports of the committees.

The pioneer spirit is still vigorous within this nation. Science offers a largely unexplored hinterland for the pioneer who has the tools for his task. The rewards of such exploration both for the Nation and the individual are great. Scientific progress is one essential key to our security as a nation, to our better health, to more jobs, to a higher standard of living, and to our cultural progress.

Respectfully yours,
(s) V. Bush, Director

[Excerpts from the report]

Scientific Progress is Essential

Progress in the war against disease depends upon a flow of new scientific knowledge. New products, new industries, and more jobs require continuous additions to knowledge of the laws of nature, and the application of that knowledge to practical purposes. Similarly, our defense against aggression demands new knowledge so that we can develop new and improved weapons. This essential, new knowledge can be obtained only through basic scientific research.

Science can be effective in the national welfare only as a member of a team, whether the conditions be peace or war. But without scientific progress no amount of achievement in other directions can insure our health, prosperity, and security as a nation in the modern world.

For the War Against Disease

We have taken great strides in the war against disease. The death rate for all diseases in the Army, including overseas forces, has been reduced from 14.1 per thousand in the last war to 0.6 per thousand in this war. In the last 40 years life expectancy has increased from 49 to 65 years, largely as a consequence of the reduction in the death rates of infants and children. But we are far from the goal. The annual deaths from one or two diseases far exceed the total number of American lives lost in battle during this war. A large fraction of these deaths in our civilian population cut short the useful lives of our citizens. Approximately 7,000,000 persons in the United States are mentally ill and their care costs the public over $175,000,000 a year. Clearly much illness remains for which adequate means of prevention and cure are not yet known.

The responsibility for basic research in medicine and the underlying sciences, so essential to progress in the war against disease, falls primarily upon the medical schools and universities. Yet we find that the traditional sources of support for medical research in the medical schools and universities, largely endowment income, foundation grants, and private donations, are diminishing and there is no immediate prospect of a change in this trend. Meanwhile, the cost of medical research has been rising. If we are to maintain the progress in medicine which has marked the last 25 years, the Government should extend financial support to basic medical research in the medical schools and in universities.

For Our National Security

The bitter and dangerous battle against the U-boat was a battle of scientific techniques – and our margin of success was dangerously small. The new eyes which radar has supplied can sometimes be blinded by new scientific developments. V-2 was countered only by capture of the launching sites.

We cannot again rely on our allies to hold off the enemy while we struggle to catch up. There must be more—and more adequate—military research in peacetime. It is essential that the civilian scientists continue in peacetime some portion of those contributions to national security which they have made so effectively during the war. This can best be done through a civilian-controlled organization with close liaison with the Army and Navy, but with funds direct from Congress, and the clear power to initiate military research which will supplement and strengthen that carried on directly under the control of the Army and Navy.

And for the Public Welfare

One of our hopes is that after the war there will be full employment. To reach that goal the full creative and productive energies of the American people must be released. To create more jobs we must make new and better and cheaper products. We want plenty of new, vigorous enterprises. But new products and processes are not born full-grown. They are founded on new principles and new conceptions which in turn result from basic scientific research. Basic scientific research is scientific capital. Moreover, we cannot any longer depend upon Europe as a major source of this scientific capital. Clearly, more and better scientific research is one essential to the achievement of our goal of full employment.

How do we increase this scientific capital? First, we must have plenty of men and women trained in science, for upon them depends both the creation of new knowledge and its application to practical purposes. Second, we must strengthen the centers of basic research which are principally the colleges, universities, and research institutes. These institutions provide the environment which is most conducive to the creation of new scientific knowledge and least under pressure for immediate, tangible results. With some notable exceptions, most research in industry and Government involves application of existing scientific knowledge to practical problems. It is only the colleges, universities, and a few research institutes that devote most of their research efforts to expanding the frontiers of knowledge.

Expenditures for scientific research by industry and Government increased from $140,000,000 in 1930 to $309,000,000 in 1940. Those for the colleges and universities increased from $20,000,000 to $31,000,000, while those for the research institutes declined from $5,200,000 to $4,500,000 during the same period. If the colleges, universities, and research institutes are to meet the rapidly increasing demands of industry and Government for new scientific knowledge, their basic research should be strengthened by use of public funds.

For science to serve as a powerful factor in our national welfare, applied research both in Government and in industry must be vigorous. To improve the quality of scientific research within the Government, steps should be taken to modify the procedures for recruiting, classifying, and compensating scientific personnel in order to reduce the present handicap of governmental scientific bureaus in competing with industry and the universities for top-grade scientific talent. To provide coordination of the common scientific activities of these governmental agencies as to policies and budgets, a permanent Science Advisory Board should be created to advise the executive and legislative branches of Government on these matters.

The most important ways in which the Government can promote industrial research are to increase the flow of new scientific knowledge through support of basic research, and to aid in the development of scientific talent. In addition, the Government should provide suitable incentives to industry to conduct research, (a) by clarification of present uncertainties in the Internal Revenue Code in regard to the deductibility of research and development expenditures as current charges against net income, and (b) by strengthening the patent system so as to eliminate uncertainties which now bear heavily on small industries and so as to prevent abuses which reflect discredit upon a basically sound system. In addition, ways should be found to cause the benefits of basic research to reach industries which do not now utilize new scientific knowledge.

We Must Renew Our Scientific Talent

The responsibility for the creation of new scientific knowledge—and for most of its application—rests on that small body of men and women who understand the fundamental laws of nature and are skilled in the techniques of scientific research. We shall have rapid or slow advance on any scientific frontier depending on the number of highly qualified and trained scientists exploring it.

The deficit of science and technology students who, but for the war, would have received bachelor's degrees is about 150,000. It is estimated that the deficit of those obtaining advanced degrees in these fields will amount in 1955 to about 17,000—for it takes at least 6 years from college entry to achieve a doctor's degree or its equivalent in science or engineering. The real ceiling on our productivity of new scientific knowledge and its application in the war against disease, and the development of new products and new industries, is the number of trained scientists available.

The training of a scientist is a long and expensive process. Studies clearly show that there are talented individuals in every part of the population, but with few exceptions, those without the means of buying higher education go without it. If ability, and not the circumstance of family fortune, determines who shall receive higher education in science, then we shall be assured of constantly improving quality at every level of scientific activity. The Government should provide a reasonable number of undergraduate scholarships and graduate fellowships in order to develop scientific talent in American youth. The plans should be designed to attract into science only that proportion of youthful talent appropriate to the needs of science in relation to the other needs of the nation for high abilities.

Including Those in Uniform

The most immediate prospect of making up the deficit in scientific personnel is to develop the scientific talent in the generation now in uniform. Even if we should start now to train the current crop of high-school graduates none would complete graduate studies before 1951. The Armed Services should comb their records for men who, prior to or during the war, have given evidence of talent for science, and make prompt arrangements, consistent with current discharge plans, for ordering those who remain in uniform, as soon as militarily possible, to duty at institutions here and overseas where they can continue their scientific education. Moreover, the Services should see that those who study overseas have the benefit of the latest scientific information resulting from research during the war.

The Lid Must Be Lifted

While most of the war research has involved the application of existing scientific knowledge to the problems of war, rather than basic research, there has been accumulated a vast amount of information relating to the application of science to particular problems. Much of this can be used by industry. It is also needed for teaching in the colleges and universities here and in the Armed Forces Institutes overseas. Some of this information must remain secret, but most of it should be made public as soon as there is ground for belief that the enemy will not be able to turn it against us in this war. To select that portion which should be made public, to coordinate its release, and definitely to encourage its publication, a Board composed of Army, Navy, and civilian scientific members should be promptly established.

A Program for Action

The Government should accept new responsibilities for promoting the flow of new scientific knowledge and the development of scientific talent in our youth. These responsibilities are the proper concern of the Government, for they vitally affect our health, our jobs, and our national security. It is in keeping also with basic United States policy that the Government should foster the opening of new frontiers and this is the modern way to do it. For many years the Government has wisely supported research in the agricultural colleges and the benefits have been great. The time has come when such support should be extended to other fields.

The effective discharge of these new responsibilities will require the full attention of some over-all agency devoted to that purpose. There is not now in the permanent Governmental structure receiving its funds from Congress an agency adapted to supplementing the support of basic research in the colleges, universities, and research institutes, both in medicine and the natural sciences, adapted to supporting research on new weapons for both Services, or adapted to administering a program of science scholarships and fellowships.

Therefore I recommend that a new agency for these purposes be established. Such an agency should be composed of persons of broad interest and experience, having an understanding of the peculiarities of scientific research and scientific education. It should have stability of funds so that long-range programs may be undertaken. It should recognize that freedom of inquiry must be preserved and should leave internal control of policy, personnel, and the method and scope of research to the institutions in which it is carried on. It should be fully responsible to the President and through him to the Congress for its program.

Early action on these recommendations is imperative if this nation is to meet the challenge of science in the crucial years ahead. On the wisdom with which we bring science to bear in the war against disease, in the creation of new industries, and in the strengthening of our Armed Forces depends in large measure our future as a nation.

6.5: Higher Education for American Democracy: The 1947 Truman Commission Report

After World War II various constituencies and advocacy groups edged persistently toward persuading Americans that higher education was no less than a public good. The corollary was that government—local, state, and now federal—had a responsibility to invest in making college education both accessible and affordable. Whereas the 1944 GI Bill concentrated federal resources to address a specific, pressing problem— accommodating and encouraging servicemen to enroll in postsecondary education— the 1947 President's Commission provided a long, comprehensive and visionary report on the potential for an expanded model of higher education to be pursued over several decades. This massive six-volume study, chaired by George F. Zook, the president of the American Council on Education, is remarkable not only for its length and depth but most of all for its prescient and informed discussion of changes in American society in such matters as demographics, civil rights, social justice, economic opportunity, and the growing belief in access to a college education as an important, perhaps indispensable, passport for navigating citizenship and work in American life of the post–World War II period. Although the report did not lead immediately or directly to large-scale programs or legislation, it did shape the conversation and provide the blueprint for myriad innovations and reforms in American higher education well into the twenty-first century. The concise excerpt presented below follows from this firm resolution that the committee presented in its introduction to the full six-volume report: "It is obvious, then, that free and universal access to education, in terms of the interest, ability, and need of the student, must be a major goal in American education."

Toward Equalizing Opportunity

The American people should set as their ultimate goal an educational system in which at no level—high school, college, graduate school, or professional school— will a qualified individual in any part of the country encounter an insuperable economic barrier to the attainment of the kind of education suited to his aptitudes and interests.

This means that we shall aim at making higher education equally available to all young people, as we now do education in the elementary and high schools,

George F. Zook, chair, "Toward Equalizing Opportunity," in *A Report of the President's Commission on Higher Education: Higher Education for American Democracy; Volume I: Establishing the Goals* (New York: Harper and Brothers, 1947) pp. 36–39.

to the extent that their capacity warrants a further social investment in their training.

Obviously this desirable realization of our ideal of equal educational opportunity cannot be attained immediately. But if we move toward it as fast as our economic resources permit, it should not lie too far in the future. Technological advances, that are already resulting in phenomenal increases in productivity per worker, promise us a degree of economic well-being that would have seemed wholly Utopian to our fathers. With wise management of our economy, we shall almost certainly be able to support education at all levels far more adequately in the future than we could in the past.

The Commission recommends that steps be taken to reach the following objectives without delay:

1. High school education must be improved and should be provided for all normal youth.

This is a minimum essential. We cannot safely permit any of our citizens for any reason other than incapacity, to stop short of a high school education or its equivalent. To achieve the purpose of such education, however, it must be improved in facilities and in the diversity of its curriculum. Better high school education is essential, both to raise the caliber of students entering college and to provide the best training possible for those who end their formal education with the twelfth grade.

2. The time has come to make education through the fourteenth grade available in the same way that high school education is now available.

This means that tuition-free education should be available in public institutions to all youth for the traditional freshman and sophomore years or for the traditional 2-year junior college course.

To achieve this, it will be necessary to develop much more extensively than at present such opportunities as are now provided in local communities by the 2-year junior college, community institute, community college, or institute of arts and sciences. The name used does not matter, though community college seems to describe these schools best; the important thing is that the services they perform be recognized and vastly extended.

Such institutions make post-high school education available to a much larger percentage of young people than otherwise could afford it. Indeed, as discussed in the volume of this Commission's report, "Organizing Higher Education," such community colleges probably will have to carry a large part of the responsibility for expanding opportunities in higher education.

3. The time has come to provide financial assistance to competent students in the tenth through fourteen grades who would not be able to continue without such assistance.

Tuition costs are not the major economic barrier to education, especially in college. Costs of supplies, board, and room, and other living needs are great. Even many high-school students are unable to continue in school because of these costs.

Arrangements must be made, therefore, to provide additional financial assistance for worthy students who need it if they are to remain in school. Only in this way can we counteract the effect of family incomes so low that even tuition-free schooling is a financial impossibility for their children. Only in this way can we make sure that all who are to participate in democracy are adequately prepared to do so.

4. The time has come to reverse the present tendency of increasing tuition and other student fees in the senior college beyond the fourteenth year, and in both graduate and professional schools, by lowering tuition costs in publicly controlled colleges and by aiding deserving students through inaugurating a program of scholarships and fellowships.

Only in this way can we be sure that economic and social barriers will not prevent the realization of the promise that lies in our most gifted youth. Only in this way can we be certain of developing for the common good all the potential leadership our society produces, no matter in what social or economic stratum it appears.

5. The time has come to expand considerably our program of adult education, and to make more of it the responsibility of our colleges and universities.

The crisis of the time and the rapidly changing conditions under which we live make it especially necessary that we provide a continuing and effective educational program for adults as well as youth. We can in this way, perhaps, make up some of the educational deficiencies of the past, and also in a measure counteract the pressures and distractions of adult life that all too often make the end of formal schooling the end of education too.

6. The time has come to make public education at all levels equally accessible to all, without regard to race, creed, sex, or national origin.

If education is to make the attainment of a more perfect democracy one of its major goals, it is imperative that it extends its benefits to all on equal terms. It must renounce the practices of discrimination and segregation in educational institutions as contrary to the spirit of democracy. Educational leaders and institutions should take positive steps to overcome the conditions which at present obstruct free and equal access to educational opportunities. Educational programs everywhere should be aimed at undermining and eventually eliminating the attitudes that are responsible for discrimination and segregation—at creating instead attitudes that will make education freely available to all.

CHAPTER SEVEN

Gilt by Association
Higher Education's "Golden Age," 1945 to 1970

The quarter century following World War II has often been called American higher education's "golden age" as a result of the coincidence of prosperity and prestige that the public bestowed upon colleges and universities. In quantitative terms this meant persistent increases in the number and percentage of young men and women who enrolled in some form of postsecondary education, combined with an increase in the average size of a campus and the construction of new institutions, especially public junior colleges and state colleges. Size coincided with increasing complexity of institutional missions and structures, in which the core commitment to four-year undergraduate programs leading to the bachelor's degree was supplemented by greatly expanded offerings in master's degree and PhD programs. To further extend the transformation, doctoral programs often were part of a constellation of federally sponsored research projects and campus-based centers and institutes for advanced scholarship. Institutional proliferation also led to the creation of multicampus systems. Within these structural changes the traditional college life of varsity sports, student clubs, and fraternities and sororities continued to flourish. Federal initiatives, such as the GI Bill of 1944 and the President's Commission Report of 1947, heralded diversification of the composition of a new generation of enrolling students. Colleges and universities in the United States edged away from the scarcity of an elite system toward what was termed "mass higher education," whose watchwords were accessibility and affordability.

One consequence of this structural complexity and intensity of purposes was that the American university came to be known—with both favorable and unfavorable connotations—as the "multiversity" and the "Knowledge Factory." Two documents in this chapter—the December 2, 1964, speech at Berkeley by Mario

Savio (Document 7.5) and the memoir of student activism at Harvard in the late 1960s by Steven Kelman (Document 7.6)—provide snapshots of the generational tensions between students and adults in their roles as administrators, taxpayers, and legislators. In contrast to the optimism of the immediate post–World War II period, the campus mood had changed visibly during the Vietnam War as evidenced by student activism and antiwar demonstrations that overlapped with student dissatisfaction about the impersonality of the large university. Colleges and universities, for a variety of reasons, had lost the consensus of public deference and support which had soared in the two preceding decades. Campus unrest that might have been explained away as an exceptional phenomenon at a handful of extreme universities in 1964 had spread to all regions and to most colleges and universities, especially with the antiwar demonstrations in May 1970—followed by national horror brought about by television and newspaper coverage of the campus shootings by the National Guard at Kent State and Jackson State Universities. For American higher education by 1970, all that glittered was not gold.

7.1: Coeducation and Student Life: Rules and Regulations for Women in Higher Education in 1955–56

One of the first documents given to new students to make them feel part of the campus community was the official student handbook. What was essentially a blueprint for college success presented within its pages the rules and mores of both academic achievement and social engagement at the university level. *The Handbook for Women in Residence* was an example of *in loco parentis*, an educational doctrine that allowed educators and administrators to assume a parental role toward their students. This doctrine, formalized with the rules outlined in the *Handbook*, made a college woman feel as if her campus experience was at the same time an initiation into adulthood and an extension of her teenage years at home—complete with curfews, dress codes, and punishments for bad behavior or academic disappointment.

This document also gives a close look at what it meant to be a woman college student (sometimes called "Betty Co-Ed") after World War II, when the focus of socialization into American adult life was creating nuclear families and happy homes. The following excerpts touch on etiquette, appearance, and social behavior. The document's emphasis on adult control of student conduct gives the reader a glimpse into

Handbook for Women in Residence (Sororities and Residence Halls), University of Kentucky (1955–56).

the "girl world" of the 1950s. Informative as this document is about student rights and responsibilities, it leaves historians of higher education with two questions: First, how rigorously were rules enforced? And, second, were there comparably detailed hand-books intended to control the conduct of men who were enrolled at the university?

In this booklet the House President's Council has not tried to answer any sixty-four dollar questions, but to give you a simple guide for everyday group living. Whether you are an acceptable member of your group will be determined not only by whether you live according to the "letter of the law," but whether you observe the spirit as well. We hope that you will consult this little booklet often and, when in doubt, talk things over with your head resident or student counselor.

We look forward each year with keen anticipation to the return of our old students, and we greet with enthusiasm our new girls. May the year in your residence group pay great dividends in happiness and personal development.

Sarah B. Holmes, Dean of Women

Procedures and Regulations

Room and Board, Tuition, Fees

The cost of room and board in the dormitories at present is $240 per semester. Tuition for Kentucky students is $65.00 per semester, and for out of state students it is $125.00 per semester. Room, board, and tuition are all paid in the line of registration. All three may be paid by one check if it is more convenient. For the rates in sorority houses see pages 27 and 28 of this book.

By vote of the House President's Council, a social fee of two dollars is collected each semester at the time she signs into the residence hall. This fee is used for parties, decorations for Homecoming, materials for floats, etc.

Hall Facilities and Service

Phones and Buzzers

All long distance calls, *including reversed charges, must be placed on the pay phones.* A $5.00 fine will be charged for calling on a regular phone. *Phones in the Halls are not to be used after 11 p.m. on week nights, nor after closing hours on weekends.*

Freshmen do not receive calls during quiet hours. Calls into freshmen halls should be made before 7:30 p.m., and between 10:00 and 11:00 p.m.

Upperclasswomen may answer the phone until closing time. Be considerate and limit the conversation to five minutes.

If there is a buzzer system in the hall, learn the signal and how to answer it correctly for speedy service. Allow the receptionist time to the complete the ring.

Dining Halls

Hours

Breakfast: Weekdays – 6:45 to 8:45; Sundays – 8:30 to 9:30

Lunch: Weekdays – 11:00 to 1:00 p.m.

Dinner: Monday through Fridays – 5:00 to 6:30, Saturdays – 5:00 to 6:00, Sundays – 12:00 noon to 1:30.

No Sunday night supper is served.

If classes interfere with the scheduled dining hall hours, see the hostess in the dining room.

Conserving Food

A second serving may be served on vegetables and bread only. Take the regular serving when going through the line the first time. Go back to serving table for a second serving.

Appearance at Meals

Housecoats may be worn to *breakfast* providing they are *clean and reach to the knee or longer*. Hair must be combed, if in pin curls a scarf must be worn over the hair. Slacks, blue jeans, and *Bermuda shorts* or peddle pushers are permissible in the dining room at breakfast or lunch, but *never* at dinner. *Short* shorts are *never* to be worn in the dining room. Only during exam week may blue jeans be worn to all three meals. This does not mean short shorts.

Sunday dinner is more formal than dinner during the week. Come in heels, hose, and a dress or suit. No scarves are worn at Sunday dinner.

There is no smoking in the dining room.

Care of Halls

Appearance in Residence Halls

At all times, except before the halls open in the morning and after closing hours at night, girls are to be fully clothed when they are in the living and recreation rooms. No slacks, jeans, or shorts are to be worn in the lounges.

A robe or housecoat should be worn at all times a girl is not completely dressed, since a janitor or repair man may be working in the corridors at any time.

Hours

Hours for Callers

The Residence Halls are open to visitors from 10:00 a.m. until closing time. Many individual groups, especially sororities, have set later opening hours.

If a girl's date is late in getting out of the hall she will be penalized as though she were late coming in.

The hall clock is the official time piece and all residents should set their watches by it.

Closing Hours

All houses close Friday and Saturday nights at 12:30; Sunday night at 11:30. Freshmen Halls close at 10:00 Monday through Thursday, the other halls close at 10:30. Freshman halls are closed to visitors at 7:30 p.m. Monday through Thursday. Lights out in freshman halls at 11:00 p.m. Lights out in upperclass halls at 12:00.

One-half hour is allowed students to return to the residence halls after attending recognized special activities such as concerts, plays, etc., which extend beyond closing time. Restricted students, who have night classes, are allowed one-half hour to return to the residence hall after class.

A 1:30 a.m. permission will be given to each hall and sorority house on the night upon which a *formal* dance is given by that particular house. All members of this sorority must spend the night in the sorority house if they wish to have the 1:30 permission. The house will close at 12:30 a.m. as usual on the night of the formal. No dates will be permitted in the lounges after that hour. Only those girls attending the dance will receive the 1:30 permission. *Permission to go home, or to spend the night out of town after a dance or other late function will not be granted.*

Quiet Hours

Freshmen quiet hours are 7:30 to 10:00 p.m. and from 11:00 p.m. to 8:00 a.m. Monday through Thursday. (Freshmen may not receive telephone calls during these hours.) On Friday and Sunday nights Quiet Hours are from 7:30 to 10:30 p.m. and from midnight until 8:00 a.m.

Upperclass quiet hours are from 7:30 to 10:00 p.m. and from 11:00 p.m. to 8:00 a.m. Monday through Thursday. On weekends the halls are to be quiet 30 minutes after closing hours.

Radios and record players should never be played in such a manner that they disturb others. *Do not place radios in the windows.*

Typewriting, after 10:30 p.m., must be done in special rooms.

The piano is not to be played before 10:00 a.m., or after 7:30 p.m. Monday through Thursday, except during relaxation periods. *No practicing is to be done on any musical instrument in the halls.* There are practice rooms in the Art Center for this purpose.

Quiet Hour Courtesies

There should not be an undue amount of noise in the building at any time.

The keeping of quiet hours in the hall will be much more successful if the following courtesies to others are observed:

1. Please refrain from loud talking, loud laughing, slamming of doors, running in the halls, calling down the halls, running or shouting on the stairs, singing and loud talking in the bathrooms, walking in wooden soled shoes, and otherwise creating a disturbance when others are trying to study or sleep.
2. Please keep room doors closed during quiet hours. It helps to eliminate noise.
3. Please respect your fellow student's "Do Not Disturb" signs and sleeping schedules.
4. Please carry group discussions to the recreation room. When a group of girls gather in the hall, or in any room, the noise may be louder than it seems to those talking and laughing.

Calling out of windows is not an accepted means of communication. This rule applies at all times.

General

Alcoholic Beverages

The taking of alcoholic beverages or liquor into student rooms or into the halls, either for use or for storage, is prohibited. Residents who violate this rule, or who return to the halls showing evidence of excessive drinking subject themselves to disciplinary action.

Excerpt from the minutes of the university faculty, December 9, 1946: "The University of Kentucky looks with disfavor on the excessive use of intoxicating liquors and on their use under any conditions which will jeopardize the reputation of the institution.

"No intoxicating liquors are to be brought into any fraternity or sorority house, and the drinking of such liquors or being intoxicated in these houses, is forbidden. The same prohibition applies to all residence halls and to all rooming houses for University students. The serving or drinking of intoxicating liquors at dances or other social functions held by University organizations is forbidden in all areas under the jurisdiction of the group responsible for the function.

"A student adjudged in violation of the above regulations shall be subject to dismissal from the University. An organization which, as such, violates these regulations shall be subject to such penalty as seems appropriate, including if necessary, the withdrawal of its charter."

Campuses

A campus is a penalty imposed for the infringement of one or more rules. This may be given for a week night, or a weekend night, depending upon the seriousness of the offense. It may also be made to apply to day time hours. A campus not kept at the appointed time will be doubled.

When a girl is campused:

She may not receive callers or phone calls.
She must sign in at a designated place every hour, on the hour, from 6:00 p.m. until the time designated by the House Council. (At times the Dean of Women or Head Resident may also impose a campus upon a student for misconduct.)

A campus may consist of the student's being restricted to the upstairs of her hall, or to her room.

Dancing

Dancing is not permitted in the University Residence Halls on Sunday.

Marriage Announcements

Women students who are married without public announcement, during the school year, are required to report such marriage to the Office of the Dean of Women immediately.

Serenades

During serenades lights should be turned out. Students should listen quietly to serenades. Applaud at the end of each song without undue noise.

Standings and Probation

When a student makes below a C average, she is said to be on *Restriction* and is permitted fewer nights out.

Probation is much more serious and should not be confused with *Restriction*.

With the exception of the Colleges of Law and Pharmacy any full-time student who fails either to pass nine semester hours of work during the regular semester (or five semester hours during the summer term) or fails to attain the following standing shall be placed upon probation by the college in which the student is enrolled.

Freshmen – average of 1.4 quality points
Sophomore – average of 1.6 quality points
Juniors and Seniors – average of 1.8 quality points

Probation shall continue until the student attains the scholastic standing specified for his classification in the University. Any student failing to meet the minimum standards specified for two consecutive semesters or terms shall be dropped from the University. The above regulations, with the exception of the minimum number of semester hours required, shall apply to part-time students. A part-time student is required to pass half of his scheduled load.

A student may also be placed on disciplinary probation by the Dean of Women.

7.2: The 1960 California Master Plan for Postsecondary Education

After World War II, California acquired national and worldwide importance as a state that was large in population, prosperous in its economic development, and committed to implementing the ideals of mass higher education which had been advanced by the 1947 President's Commission on Higher Education for American Democracy. Following a period of rapid expansion, California took the lead in providing a model of statewide *coordination* among the numerous systems and institutions. The California Master Plan of 1960 was the blueprint for carrying out the mandate for coherence and cooperation. It was soon renamed the Donahoe Act in honor of Assemblywoman Dorothy Donahoe, chair of the Assembly Education Committee, who died on April 4, 1960. She had authored the resolution (ACR 88) calling for the creation of the Master Plan and had been instrumental in the subsequent negotiations leading to its successful adoption.

The Donahoe Act was memorable because it demonstrated that the complexity of institutions and tiers required planning and coordination if resources were to be used effectively in promoting a state citizenry that was college educated. The resultant Master Plan was shaped in large measure by the influence of Clark Kerr, president of the world-famous multicampus University of California system. It was a model of intrastate diplomacy in that the plan required compromise and conciliation among such major constituencies as the state university and college system, the community colleges, and the inclusion of California's formidable, prestigious independent colleges and universities into the mix of statewide planning.

Undergirding the compacts of intersegmental cooperation was a commitment to affordability. Public higher education in California was characterized by a policy of charging no tuition. And, at the same time, California legislation and state agencies generously funded student financial aid programs that made the price of tuition at private (independent) colleges comparably affordable to the "no tuition" policies in the public segments. The California Master Plan gained national attention, including being featured as a cover story for *Time* magazine. A half century after its passage into law, the California Master Plan persists as the model and inspiration for postsecondary education expansion and planning in numerous nations worldwide. Ironically, celebration of the half-century anniversary coexists today with grave concern as to the efficacy of this distinctive plan for statewide higher education in the twenty-first century.

Donahoe Report: California Master Plan for Postsecondary Education (1960), Senate Bill 33, Section 1, Division 16.5 of the Education Code, Higher Education Chapter 1, General Provisions.

Senate Bill No. 33

Section 1. Division 16.5 is added to the Education Code, to read:

Division 16.5. Higher Education

Chapter 1: General Provisions

22500. Public higher education consists of (1) all public junior colleges heretofore and hereafter established pursuant to law, (2) all state colleges heretofore and hereafter established pursuant to law, and (3) each campus, branch and function of the University of California heretofore and hereafter established by The Regents of the University of California.

22501. It is hereby declared to be the policy of the Legislature not to authorize or to acquire sites for new institutions of public higher education unless such sites are recommended by the Co-ordinating Council for Higher Education and not to authorize existing or new institutions of public education, other than those described in subdivisions (2) and (3) of Section 22500, to offer instruction beyond the fourteenth grade level. Nothing in this section shall be construed to require any further recommendations as a prerequisite to legislative action with respect to state colleges intended to be in operation by 1965 or University of California campuses intended to be under construction by 1962, as set forth in the recommendations contained in the Master Plan for Higher Education printed at page 42, paragraphs 4 and 6, Senate Journal (Regular Session) for February 1, 1960.

22502. Each segment of public higher education shall strive for excellence in its sphere, as assigned in this division.

22503. This division shall not affect the existence or status of the state nautical school.

22504. The provisions of this division shall supersede the provisions of any other law which conflict with the provisions of this division.

Chapter 2: University of California

22550. The Legislature hereby finds and declares that the University of California is the primary state-supported academic agency for research.

22551. The university may provide instruction in the liberal arts and sciences and in the professions, including the teaching profession. The university has exclusive jurisdiction in public higher education over instruction in the profession of law, and over graduate instruction in the professions of medicine, dentistry, veterinary medicine and architecture.

22552. The university has the sole authority in public higher education to award the doctoral degree in all fields of learning, except that it may agree with the state colleges to award joint doctoral degrees in selected fields.

22553. The university may make reasonable provision for the use of its library and research facilities by qualified members of the faculties of other institutions of public higher education in this State.

Chapter 3: The State College System

22600. The State College System shall be administered by a board designated as the Trustees of the State College System of California, which is hereby created.

22601. The board shall be composed of the following four ex officio members: the Governor, the Lieutenant Governor, the Superintendent of Public Instruction, and the person named by the trustees to serve as the chief executive officer of the system; and 16 appointive members appointed by the Governor, except that the members, as of the effective date of this section, of the State Board of Education shall serve ex officio as and among the first appointive trustees. The terms of the appointive members shall be four years, except that the first appointive trustees, including the members of the State Board of Education, shall classify the terms of their offices by lot so that four of the first appointive terms shall expire on the first day of March of each calendar year, commencing in 1961 and ending in 1964. The Speaker of the Assembly shall have the status of a Legislative interim committee on the subject of the State College System and shall meet with the board and participate in its work to the extent that such participation is not incompatible with his position as a Member of the Legislature.

22601.5. Notwithstanding Section 22601, commencing on March 1, 1961, the terms of the appointive trustees shall be eight years, except that the 16 appointive trustees serving on February 28, 1961, shall have new terms of office which they shall classify by lot so that two of the terms of such appointive members shall expire on the first day of March of each calendar year commencing in 1962 and ending in 1969. This section shall become operative only if Senate Constitutional Amendment No. 1 of the 1960 First Extraordinary Session of the Legislature is approved by the electors.

22602. The expiration of a trustee's term of office as a member of the State Board of Education or any earlier vacancy in that office shall create a vacancy in his trusteeship, unless the term ascribed thereto by lot has already expired. In case of any vacancy on the board of trustees, the Governor shall appoint a successor for the balance of the term as to which such vacancy exists.

22603. If the trustees and the Regents of the University of California both consent, the chief executive officer of the State College System shall sit with the Regents of the University of California in an advisory capacity and the President of the University of California shall sit with the trustees in an advisory capacity.

22604. The Trustees of the State College System shall succeed to the powers, duties and functions with respect to the management, administration and control of the state colleges heretofore vested in the State Board of Education or in the Director of Education, including all powers, duties, obligations, and functions specified in Article 2 (commencing at Section 24501) of Chapter 11 of Division 18 of this code, and all obligations assumed by the State Board of Education pursuant to that article prior to July 1, 1961. On and after July 1, 1961, the Trustees of the State College System shall have full power and responsibility in the construction and development of any state college campus, and any buildings or other facilities or improvements connected with the State College System. Such powers shall be exercised by the Trustees of the State College System notwithstanding the provisions of Chapter 2 (commencing at Section 14100) and Chapter 3 (commencing at Section 14250) of Part 5 of Division 3 of Title 2 of the Government Code, except that the powers shall be carried out pursuant to the procedures prescribed by these laws. The provisions of this chapter relating to the transfer of the powers, duties, and functions with respect to the management, administration and control of the state colleges shall become operative on July 1, 1961.

22605. The State College System shall be entirely independent of all political and sectarian influence and kept free therefrom in the appointment of its trustees and in the administration of its affairs, and no person shall be debarred admission to any department of the state colleges on account of sex.

22606. The primary function of the state colleges is the provision of instruction for undergraduate students and graduate students, through the master's degree, in the liberal arts and sciences, in applied fields and in the professions, including the teaching profession. Presently established two-year programs in agriculture are authorized, but other two-year programs shall be authorized only when mutually agreed upon by the Trustees of the State College System and the State Board of Education. The doctoral degree may be awarded jointly with the University of California, as provided in Section 22552. Faculty research is authorized to the extent that it is consistent with the primary function of the state colleges and the facilities provided for that function.

22607. All state employees employed on June 30, 1961, in carrying out functions transferred to the Trustees of the State College System of California by this chapter, except persons employed by the Director of Education in the Division of State Colleges and Teacher Education of the Department of Education, are transferred to the State College System. Nonacademic employees so transferred shall retain their respective positions in the state service, together with the personnel benefits accumulated by them at the time of transfer, and shall retain such rights as may attach under the law to the positions which they held at the time of transfer. All nonacademic positions filled by the trustees on and after July 1, 1961, shall be by appointment made in accordance with Chapter 9 (commencing at Section 24201) of Division 18 of this code, and persons so appointed shall be subject to the provisions of Chapter 9. The trustees shall provide, or co-operate in providing, academic and administrative employees transferred by this section with personnel rights and benefits at least equal to those accumulated by them as employees of the state colleges, except that any administrative employee may be reassigned to an academic or other position commensurate with his qualifications at the salary fixed for that position and shall have a right to appeal from such reassignment, but only as to whether the position to which he is reassigned is commensurate with his qualifications. All academic and administrative positions filled by the trustees on and after July 1, 1961, shall be filled by appointment made solely at the discretion of the trustees. The trustees shall establish and adjust the salaries and classifications of all academic and administrative positions and neither Section 18004 of the Government Code nor any other provision of law requiring approval by a state officer or agency for such salaries or classifications shall be applicable thereto. The trustees, however, shall make no adjustments which require expenditures in excess of existing appropriations available for the payment of salaries. The provisions of Chapter 9 (commencing at Section 24201) of Division 18 of this code relating to appeals from dismissal, demotion or suspension shall be applicable to academic employees. Persons excluded from the transfer made by this section shall retain all the rights and privileges conferred upon civil service employees by law. Personnel of state agencies employed in state college work other than those transferred by this section and who are employed by the trustees prior to July 1, 1962, shall likewise be provided with personnel rights and benefits at least equal to those accumulated by them as employees of such state agencies.

Chapter 4: Junior Colleges

22650. The public junior colleges shall continue to be a part of the public school system of this State. The State Board of Education shall prescribe minimum standards for the formation and operation of public junior colleges and exercise general supervision over public junior colleges.

22651. Public junior colleges shall offer instruction through but not beyond the fourteenth grade level, which instruction may include, but shall not be limited to, programs in one or more of the following categories: (1) standard collegiate courses for transfer to higher institutions; (2) vocational and technical fields leading to employment; and (3) general or liberal arts courses. Studies in these fields may lead to the associate in arts or associate in science degree.

Chapter 5. Co-ordinating Council for Higher Education

22700. There is hereby created an advisory body, the Co-ordinating Council for Higher Education, to be composed of three representatives each of the University of California, the State College System, the public junior colleges, the private colleges and universities in the State, and the general public. The university shall be represented by three representatives appointed by the regents. The State College System shall be represented by its chief executive officer and two trustees appointed by the trustees. Public junior colleges shall be represented by a member of the State Board of Education or its chief executive officer as the board may from time to time determine, and a member of a local public junior college governing board and a public junior college administrator. The junior college governing board member shall be selected by the State Board of Education from a list or lists of five names submitted for its consideration by any association or associations of state-wide coverage which represent junior college governing boards. The public junior college administrator shall be selected by the State Board of Education from a list of five names submitted for its consideration by the California Junior College Association. The private colleges and universities shall be represented by three persons, each of whom shall be affiliated with a private institution of higher education as a governing board member or as a staff member in an academic or administrative capacity and shall be appointed by the Governor after consultation with an association or associations of such private institutions. The general public shall be represented by three members appointed by the Governor. Appointments and removals made pursuant to this section shall be at the sole discretion of the appointing authority specified herein.

22701. The council shall appoint and may remove a director in the manner hereinafter specified. He shall appoint persons to such staff positions as the council may authorize.

22702. The council shall prescribe rules for the transaction of its own affairs, subject, however, to the following requirements and limitations: (1) the votes of all representatives shall be recorded; (2) effective action shall require the affirmative vote of eight members; and (3) the affirmative votes of 10 members shall be necessary to the appointment or removal of the director.

22703. The co-ordinating council shall have the following functions, advisory to the governing boards of the institutions of public higher education and to appropriate state officials; (1) review of the annual budget and capital outlay requests of the university and the State College System, and presentation of comments on the general level of support sought; (2) advice as to the application of the provisions of this division delineating the different functions of public higher education and counsel as to the programs appropriate to each segment thereof, and in connection therewith shall submit to the Governor and to the Legislature within five days of the beginning of each general session a report which contains recommendations as to necessary or desirable changes, if any, in the functions and programs of the several segments of public higher education; and (3) development of plans for the orderly growth of public higher education and the making of recommendations on the need for and location of new facilities and programs.

22704. The council shall have power to require the institutions of public higher education to submit data on costs, selection and retention of students, enrollments, plant capacities and other matters pertinent to effective planning and co-ordination, and shall furnish information concerning such matters to the Governor and to the Legislature as requested by them.

22705. This division shall be known and may be cited as the Donahoe Higher Education Act.

SEC. 2. There is hereby appropriated from the General Fund for the support of the state system of higher education the sum of one hundred thirty-one thousand eight hundred sixty dollars ($131,860) or so much thereof as may be necessary, to be expended as follows:

(a) To the Trustees of the State College System of California for expenses incurred by the trustees pursuant to Chapter 3 (commencing at Section 22600) of Division 16.5 of the Education Code, including planning for the uninterrupted performance of the functions and duties transferred to the board. ———$81,860

(b) To the Co-ordinating Council for Higher Education for expenses incurred by the council pursuant to Chapter 5 (commencing at Section 22700) of Division 16.5 of the Education Code ———$50,000

7.3: Racial Desegregation at State Universities: Commemorative Plaque at the University of Mississippi

The 1954 United States Supreme Court case *Brown v. Board of Education* opened the gate nationwide for federally mandated racial desegregation of public schools. Seeing whether and how this would then play out for public higher education took several years as a result of resistance and inertia. The following document records for historical memory the events of 1963. In addition to the court orders, legal cases, and registrar's records, one also finds historical traces in campus monuments and markers. An excellent source to bring this issue and corresponding events to life is the documentary film *Eyes on the Prize*, especially its episode on civil rights and educational institutions, "Fighting Back."

Although desegregation at two flagship state universities in the South—the University of Alabama and the University of Mississippi—provoked resistance, demonstrations, and even violence by students and some members of the campus community after the 1962 enrollment of James Meredith at Ole Miss, racial desegregation elsewhere in state universities in the South was orderly and calm. By 1970 the unfinished business was for historically white colleges and universities to go beyond desegregation and work to achieve genuine racial integration. This would include not only equity in admissions but also making certain that all students were treated as full citizens within the campus community. This last point warrants emphasis because at many desegregated colleges and universities, compliance by campus administrators and students was grudging and nominal. The first African American students to enroll often encountered exclusion and discrimination within the campus—ranging from dining halls and dormitories, to membership in student organizations, to the right to participate as student-athletes in varsity intercollegiate athletics.

Mississippi Freedom Trail

University of Mississippi

On October 1, 1962, James Meredith broke the rigid

segregation in Mississippi's higher education when he

became the first African American student at the

University of Mississippi. Though federal courts had

ordered his admission, Governor Ross Barnett and

State of Mississippi Freedom Trail Historical Marker in Oxford, Mississippi, on the campus of the University of Mississippi.

other state leaders stood in defiant opposition.
The evening before Meredith enrolled, President
John F. Kennedy deployed to the campus the U.S.
Army and the federalized National Guard to quell
rioting segregationists. The following day agents
of the U.S. Department of Justice escorted Meredith
to the Lyceum Building, where he registered.
He graduated in August of 1963.

7.4: Student Memoir: Jackie Jensen as the "Student-Athlete" following World War II (1970)

Jackie Jensen was one of the foremost athletic stars in the United States in the late 1940s and 1950s. He was most well known to Major League Baseball fans as a star outfielder for the Boston Red Sox who had a high batting average and was a leader in home runs; he was named American League Most Valuable Player in 1958. What has been overlooked in recent years is that he received his start as an All-American football player and baseball player at the University of California, Berkeley, immediately following World War II. He led his Golden Bears to the Rose Bowl and also was the captain and leader of the NCAA championship baseball team. In the NCAA championship baseball game Jensen's opponent was the Yale University team, whose captain and first baseman, George Bush, later served as president of the United States. For all this athletic success, Jensen was modest and grateful. A poignant feature of his memoir is that he makes little mention of his varsity athletics triumphs, opting instead to focus on his appreciation for the professors and courses that expanded his interests educationally. What might have been expected to be a "dumb jock" recollection turns out, instead, to be a subtle reminder of the power of the college experience to shape minds and values.

Jensen's memoir reflects the optimism and enthusiasm of college students nationwide in the post–World War II era. His alma mater, the University of California, Berkeley, was an especially important campus in that era, as it was considered the crown jewel of public higher education in the United States. *Life* magazine, for example, devoted its October 25, 1948, cover story to a lengthy photographic essay of its magnifi-

Jackie Jensen, "Jackie Jensen: Athlete," in Irving Stone, ed., *There Was Light: Autobiography of a University—Berkeley: 1868–1968* (Garden City, NY: Doubleday, 1970) pp. 165–169. Reprinted by permission of the Regents of the University of California.

cent campus facilities, with the title "The University of California: The Biggest University in the World Is a Show Place for Mass Higher Education." It was a place "where professors are famous, equipment fabulous, and educational opportunities almost unbounded." Students paid no tuition thanks to generous state funding. It was truly all-American in its combination of academics and athletics, as a Rose Bowl football team and a national championship baseball team shared the limelight with Nobel laureate professors in a campus setting where "Big was Better."

My life has been and will probably remain influenced more by the world of athletics than by anything else. If I were to describe myself in capsule form, I would have to say, "I am Jackie Jensen, athlete."

In 1946, I regarded Berkeley as a marvelous institution. Its huge gymnasium, the baseball field, the track stadium and Memorial Stadium awed me. The sports complex of the University of California was its most important part to me. It took a full year of convincing by professors, assistant coaches and section leaders before I realized that I would have to discipline myself to study if I were to succeed in athletics.

The Depression years weren't easy for parents, but for youngsters they meant that the playgrounds were active from morning till night. As children, we never owned our own equipment, but the playground supervision and our enthusiasm made up for many luxuries that youngsters today seem to disdain. Competition was fierce between the many playgrounds around Oakland, my hometown, since each was in a different neighborhood and represented a different level of living. I can remember the intense drive I had to beat Crocker Highlands or Piedmont, playgrounds in higher-class communities. Even the games of baseball or basketball against Roosevelt, Belle Vista or McClymonds, in lower-rent areas, were battles—all this at the ripe age of ten or twelve years. Was this when my competitive drives were formed, nurtured and matured for my life ahead? I couldn't really say, although this is a great subject for debate among coaches. When and how do outstanding athletes acquire competitiveness; or were they born with it? For me, I would guess that my two wonderful older brothers would get the credit. I had to be better than they, especially in sports of all kinds, and they made it possible by bringing in the extra money to help my mother support three sons during some very trying years. Today Robert, the middle son, is a highly accomplished and noted artist in the Bay area, and William, the oldest, is a successful businessman in Fresno.

I believe that a turning point in my four years at Cal came when I changed my major from physical education to speech. I knew athletics, but the idea of clearly communicating my feelings and knowledge to others became important to me. Speech courses saved me from a being a quasi-articulate athlete. Through a close and considerate friend, Professor Garff Wilson, I had the thrill of meeting Robert Frost. I couldn't have been more impressed if it had been Babe Ruth! My friendship with the poet continued in later years when I played for the Boston Red Sox. I was never prouder than when he sat in the stands and rooted avidly for us. This friendship opened a way for me that otherwise might not have existed, a way to a world of pleasure apart from sports. Today I am still an athlete, but I am also interested in politics, conservation, art and history. I understand and respect the value of education. It is so rewarding to realize how flexible one can be if he is receptive to a little encouragement by someone or something. In my life it was the University of California that gave me the encouragement.

Baseball is truly a profession. It is as competitive a field as anyone could enter. There is always that young fellow on the bench itching for the moment you relax or slip, so that he can take your place. And once he does, your ball-playing days are numbered. The greatest factor in an active sports career is longevity. When most professional men reach the age when they can begin to reap the harvest of their efforts, the ballplayer must make a great transition to a new field of endeavor. A small number stay on to coach or manage, but the majority must fall back on their education. For a few, investments will create a business life to which they can devote their energies. Others must take up careers completely alien to their backgrounds. My playing days were filled with moments of disappointment and happiness, like any profession. The honors were numerous and rewarding and I'm quite proud of them. To be judged the best of all your colleagues is the pinnacle of success. In 1958, I was awarded that honor when I won the Most Valuable Player Award with Boston. That same year, I was selected as one of the top ten young men in the state of California for its Junior Chamber of Commerce award. An unusual honor? I would say so, for I was the first professional athlete to ever be included among such other recipients as mayors, lawyers, scientists, and explorers. Would I have been considered if I hadn't attended a university? I sincerely doubt it. But, like anyone else, I had my share of disappointments. The day when Casey Stengel told me I had been traded from the fabulous Yankees to the lowly Washington Senators was perhaps the biggest disappointment I can remember. But a year later, the edge was taken off when Casey remarked for the press that "the Jensen trade was the worst the New York Yankees ever made." I wish all of life's letdowns could be made good in this fashion. And could a schoolboy baseball player ever imagine in his wildest dreams that one day he would play in the same outfield with his two biggest heroes—Joe DiMaggio and Ted Williams?

So much for the past. Now I have achieved yet another goal I recorded when I was fifteen: coaching and trying to help youngsters in the world of sports. Trophies and money are empty rewards compared to the satisfaction of contributing to the lives of others. This may sound strange, coming from a man who has known success marked by awards and knows that fame and rewards go together in sports. And I wanted that Most Valuable Player Award so much that I nearly lost it trying *too* hard.

But changes do occur, either by design or fate, as we advance in years and these changes *must* be significant for our own peace of mind. My education and experiences at Cal built a warehouse in my mind, so that I may choose at my discretion the knowledge I need at a given time. I haven't yet used many of the tools that are available in that warehouse, but the inventory is there—and I feel I'm just starting to reap the rewards.

In society, there are "givers" and "takers." The University of California gave what it could to me. Now I have my chance to give in return.

7.5: Campus Unrest and Student Protest: Mario Savio's "Put Your Bodies upon the Gears" Speech at Sproul Plaza, University of California, Berkeley (1964)

Mario Savio was the unassuming yet influential student leader and spokesperson for activism of the campus Free Speech Movement at Berkeley. A native of New York City, where he had been valedictorian of his senior class at Martin Van Buren High School, Savio entered the University of California, Berkeley, as a transfer student in 1963. Savio stands out because his oratory and presence in favor of student activism were in stark contrast to the tradition of political apathy that had been predominant on the American campus for much of its history. All the more remarkable is that his ascent into prominence on campus and in the national media took place outside the elaborate structure of officially approved student organizations and student government.

"Put Your Bodies upon the Gears" speech on December 2, 1964, at the University of California, Berkeley. Original typescript reprinted by permission from Lynn Hollander Savio.

His persistence in presenting a new student point of view toward the official university administration and policies was at a time when the University of California—and especially its historic flagship campus at Berkeley—commanded international power and prestige. These formidable structures did not intimidate or block Mario Savio from having a place on the podium. In short, Mario Savio as a student spokesperson was a true American original.

The focus of Savio's discontent was what came to be called "the impersonality of the multiversity." At one level this indicated student dissatisfaction with educational programs and curricula, in which large lecture halls with little interaction between professors and students were predominant. In the realm of extracurricular activities, Savio joined with an alliance of diverse student organizations to protest when university administrators attempted to intrude on a longtime custom of allowing designated campus areas to be devoted to free speech and dissemination of information, pamphlets, and brochures. Beyond the intramural matters of curriculum and student activities, campus activism at Berkeley extended into larger themes such as civil rights and, eventually, into political protests against what was cast as university complicity with United States foreign policy and the war in Vietnam.

A good source of newsreel footage of Savio's public speeches and leadership is in the documentary film *Berkeley in the Sixties*. Interesting to note, however, is that Savio himself did not agree to be interviewed or to provide a memoir as part of that documentary production. After parting ways with the student Free Speech Movement by 1966, Savio worked at a number of jobs, such as a clerk at a bookstore near campus. Eventually he taught mathematics and philosophy at California State University at Sonoma. Following his death in 1996, he was honored by the Regents of the University of California. The following document is the transcript of his influential, memorable speech on December 2, 1964, on the steps of Berkeley's Sproul Hall—before an estimated crowd of eight thousand. The campus atmosphere and issues associated with Mario Savio in 1964 contrast dramatically with university life at the same place—Berkeley—in 1949–1950, as recalled by Cal alumnus Jackie Jensen in Document 7.4.

You know I just want to say one brief thing about something the previous speaker [ASUC President Charles Powell] said. I didn't want to spend too much time on that because I don't think it's important enough. But one thing is worth considering. He's the nominal head of an organization supposedly representative of the undergraduates whereas in fact under the Kerr directives it derives its authority, its delegated power from the administration. It's totally unrepresentative of the graduate students and TAs. But he made the following statement. I quote: "I would ask all those who are not definitely committed to the FSM cause to stay away from demonstration." All right now listen to this. "For all upper division students who are interested in alleviating the TA shortage problem I would encourage you to offer your services to department chairmen and advisors." That has two things: a strikebreaker and a fink!

I'd like to say, like to say, one other thing about a union problem. Upstairs you may have noticed already on the second floor of Sproul Hall locals 40 and 127 of the painters' union are painting the inside of the second floor of Sproul Hall. Now apparently that action had been planned some time in the past. I've tried to contact those unions. Unfortunately, and it tears my heart out, they're as bureaucratized as the administration. It's difficult to get through to anyone in authority there. Very sad. We're still, we're still making an attempt. Those people up there have no desire to interfere with what we're doing. I would ask that they be considered. And that they not be heckled in any way. And I think that, you know, while there is unfortunately no sense, no sense of solidarity at this point between unions and students there at least need be no, you know, excessively hard feelings between the two groups.

Now there are at least two ways in which sit-ins and civil disobedience, and whatever, at least two major ways in which it can occur. One when a law exists, is promulgated, which is totally unacceptable to people and they violate it again and again and again until it is rescinded, repealed. All right. But there is another way, another way. Sometimes the pull of the law is such as to render impossible its effective violation as a method to have it repealed. Sometimes the grievances of people are more, extend more, to more than just the law, extend to a whole mode of arbitrary power, a whole mode of arbitrary exercise of arbitrary power. And that's what we have here.

We have an autocracy which runs, which runs this university. It's managed. We were told the following: if President Kerr actually tried to get something more liberal out of the regents in his telephone conversation why didn't he make some public statement to that effect? And the answer we received from a well meaning liberal was the following: He said, "Would you ever imagine the manager of a firm making a statement publicly in opposition to his board of directors?" That's the answer! Well I ask you to consider: If this is a firm and if the board of regents are the board of directors and if President Kerr in fact is the manager, then I'll tell you something: the faculty are a bunch of employees and we're the raw materials.

But we're a bunch of raw materials that don't mean to be, have any process upon us, don't mean to be made into any product, don't mean, don't mean to end up being bought by some clients of the university, be they the government, be they industry, be they organized labor, be they anyone! We're human beings!

And that, that, brings me to the second mode of civil disobedience. There's a time when the operation of the machine becomes so odious, makes you so sick at heart that you can't take part. You can't even passively take part. And you've got to put your bodies upon the gears and upon the wheels, upon the levers, upon all apparatus, and you've got to make it stop. And you've got to indicate to the people who run it, to the people who own it, that unless you're free the machine will be prevented from working at all!

That doesn't mean—and it will be interpreted to mean unfortunately by the bigots who run *The [San Francisco] Examiner* for example—that doesn't mean that you have to break anything. One thousand people sitting down someplace not letting anybody by, not letting anything happen can stop any machine, including this machine, and it will stop! We're going to do the following and the greater the number of people the safer they'll be and the more effective it will be. We're going once again to march up to the second floor of Sproul Hall. And we're going to conduct our lives for a while in the second floor of Sproul Hall. We'll show movies for example. We tried to get *Un chante d'amour.* Unfortunately that's tied up in the courts because of a lot of squeamish moral mothers for a moral America and other people on the outside. The same people who get all their ideas out of *The San Francisco Examiner.* Sad. Sad. But Mr. Landau, Mr. Landau has gotten us some other films. Likewise we'll do something, we'll do something which hasn't occurred at this university in a good long time. We're going to have *real classes* up there. There are going to be freedom schools conducted up there. We're going to have classes on [the] First and Fourteenth Amendments. We're going to spend our time learning about the things this university is afraid that we know. We're going to learn about freedom up there. And we're going to learn by doing.

Now we've had some good long rallies. Just one moment. We've had some good long rallies. And I think I'm sicker of rallies than anyone else here. It's not going to be long. I'd like to introduce one last person, one last person before we enter Sproul Hall. And the person is Joan Baez.

7.6: Student Memoir: Steven Kelman on Political Activism at Harvard from 1966 to 1970 (1982)

Steven Kelman gained publicity and notoriety in 1970 as a senior at Harvard College when Houghton Mifflin published his book *Push Comes to Shove: The Escalation of Student Protest*. Kelman's memoir is significant because he reconstructs the atmosphere of selective admissions and intense high school studying followed by the prestige—and pleasures—of being a Harvard undergraduate. A keen participant-observer of politics past and present, his memoir focuses on the campus unrest and student activism of the late 1960s and into 1970. Kelman is the Albert J. Weatherhead III and Richard W. Weatherhead Professor of Public Management in the John F. Kennedy School of Government at Harvard University. His memoir provides a good sequel to the preceding document dealing with Mario Savio as a student activist and leader at Berkeley in 1964. Kelman's story deals with the period a few years later and also provides an East Coast perspective to balance the West Coast events and accounts associated with Berkeley and Mario Savio.

For me, it is most appropriate to begin memories of Harvard with memories of high school. This is so because, among the people with whom I spent the most time in high school, "getting into Harvard" was about the most important goal a person could have.

I was class of 1966 at Great Neck South Senior High School, in Great Neck, Long Island, outside New York City. The high school was mostly Jewish, and over 80 percent of graduating seniors went to college. Harvard took one (or sometimes two) out of our graduating class each year, something we considered terribly unfair, since we were certain that ten of our graduating seniors could easily be among the top students at Harvard. We felt victimized by "geographic quotas" that, we assured one another, were anti-Semitic (without, I think, any great conviction or emotional resentment, since probably none of us had ever personally experienced anti-Semitism in our lives.) We half-growled, half-joked about the groups the Harvard admissions process favored—kids from small towns in Montana and rich prep school types from the right families. (This was before the era of affirmative action for minorities, so that question never came up.)

Steven J. Kelman, "Memoir of Steven Kelman '70," in Jeffrey L. Lant, ed., *Our Harvard: Reflections on College Life by Twenty-two Distinguished Graduates* (New York: Taplinger, 1982) pp. 287–304. Reprinted by permission of Steven J. Kelman.

But the difficulty of obtaining the prize of admission to Harvard made the prize so much the more valuable. There were certainly students at Great Neck South for whom getting into a good college, much less getting into Harvard, was not a preoccupation, but there was a surprisingly large number for whom it was.

My recollections of Harvard are infinitely more favorable than my recollections of high school. A combination of frequent exams (we had five academic courses, and between them we usually had about an exam a week) and the importance of grades for getting into a good college sufficed to give one a more or less standing bout of nervous stomach. Many of my most vivid memories of high school surround tests and grades. I remember students taking up to twenty minutes of class time after a test was handed back to argue over one or two points on the test. (Once a student who was a particularly tenacious disputant announced in chemistry class that he had a headache and wanted to go to the nurse's office, at which point the teacher said, "You stay right here. You've given me a headache all year.") A teacher we had for two straight years in "special" (advanced placement) math made it a practice never to give partial credit for answers in math exams where the student showed by his work that he understood the principle of the problem but made a calculation error somewhere. "Partial credit?" she would ask the class sarcastically, with a salty Nova Scotian accent that was a favorite for student parody, "Would they give an engineer partial credit if he did a calculation wrong and the bridge collapsed?" We laughed, albeit nervously, and we gnashed our teeth. To this day, I have a recurring dream (that, I understand, is relatively common among workaholic types) in which I show up for an exam and realize that I have forgotten to attend the classes all semester or in which I am about to appear in a play and realize that I forgot to learn my lines. The venue of such dreams, to this day, is high school.

By contrast, the academic atmosphere at Harvard during the years I was there (1966–70) was remarkably low-keyed. People never talked about grades. (Generally, one didn't know even one's own roommates' grades.) Exams were infrequent—a midterm and a final in each course. Courses were interesting. On that dimension, I experienced Harvard just as it was in the storybooks: as a chance to have a rewarding intellectual experience while still getting that perpetual knot out of my stomach.

Another way in which it was clear, from freshman year on, that Harvard contrasted favorably with high school was in the lack of social barriers among students. Looking back, it absolutely amazes me how much high school society was a divided society with high walls of insecurity keeping people apart. Our high school newspaper ran a piece once about students at Great Neck South being divided into "beats" (who sang folk music at parties and competed for good grades), "poppies" (who were fashionable and who dated a lot), and "hoods" (who were juvenile delinquents not headed for college). I didn't know a single "hood," and, while I knew some "poppies," I regarded them as socially so superior to me that it was senseless to try to get to know them (especially the girls).

Life in a Harvard freshman dorm (I lived in Matthews South, at the corner of the Yard closest to Harvard Square) was designed to smash such barriers. Suddenly one was placed in close physical and intellectual proximity with kids the likes of whom one had never met before. The strangest thing was meeting for the first time the children of hereditary wealth or hereditary fame, the aristocratic types against whom one had vague prejudices but about whom one knew little.

They *were* different. One guy told me he had only recently learned that not everybody had a coming-out party; he had thought that even in the ghetto modest such parties were held. Others told of summer homes and winter homes and estates their parents lived on when not at either. I wrote an article during my freshman year for *The New York Times Sunday Magazine* on my freshman class; one of the most exhilarating parts of researching the article was talking with "famous children," or, rather, children of famous parents, in the class. It seemed as if, for the first time, I was on the inside looking around rather than on the outside looking in. (As an incidental note, the attention that article received when it came out—and the fact that, to this day, people I meet of my approximate age frequently remember that article—served, and serves, to remind me of the special place Harvard occupies in American life.)

All this was different, but the confrontation with a different world did not, as it had in high school, produce anxiety or insecurity. There were those final clubs, off somewhere, that I knew about and knew I would not be invited to join. But, frankly, it didn't bother me in the slightest. (I endorsed the saw that the people who were upset about not getting into the Porcellian Club were not people like me, who stood completely outside the club system, but those who had "only" made it into the Fly.) The differences were exciting, not depressing.

In a sense, things were made easier because I attended Harvard at a unique moment when, for a brief instant, the cultural role model for significant portions of the Harvard student body—including a not-insignificant number of the aristocrats whose cultural style at an earlier point had dominated—was the New York

Jewish kid, intellectual and radical, perhaps even coming out of a family of 1930s radicals as well.

That in turn, of course, was related to the student politics of the late 1960s. The class of 1970, of which I was a part, caught the wave of student radicalism as it was forming and rode with it until it crested with the Cambodia and Kent State protests in May 1970. The fall of 1966, when I was a freshman, marked the beginning of the dramatic growth of SDS (Students for a Democratic Society). The fall of 1967, with the sit-in at Harvard against job recruiters from Dow Chemical, marked the beginning of the radicalization of SDS. The fall of 1968 marked the beginning of the SDS campaign against ROTC, which culminated in the sit-in and "bust" at University Hall in April 1969. And the spring of 1970 saw trashings in Harvard Square and a shutdown of Harvard following the Cambodian incursion and the Kent State killings. Starting with the fall of 1970—when our class was gone—campuses across the nation began to cool down. If you look at lists of contributions to the Harvard College Fund by class, you will see that there is a marked dip—compared not only with classes before but with classes after as well—in the proportion of members of the class of 1970 who give to Harvard. Our class was prototypical of the student radicalism of the 1960s.

One might have predicted that all this would please me just fine. First, I was addicted to politics. My parents had me out distributing literature for Adlai Stevenson and for local school-board candidates by the time I was four. During the 1956 presidential campaign they dressed me for Halloween in a big diaper, bedecked with Democratic party buttons and a sash reading "Time for a Change." That same year I gave a speech for Stevenson to my third grade class and was depressed that my arguments were not convincing enough to get a majority of my classmates to vote for Stevenson. Given a lifelong addiction to politics, I should have rejoiced in the hyperpolitical environment that Harvard became during the years I was there. Never before (or since) had I been lucky enough to have so many others share my own passion.

The second reason that it might have been predicted that the politics of the late 1960s at Harvard would have pleased me just fine was that I was, by my own definition, a radical. In my junior year in high school, I joined the Young People's Socialist League (YPSL), the youth group of the Socialist party of Norman Thomas and Michael Harrington. I went to Harvard determined to start a YPSL chapter there.

In fact, by the time I graduated I had succeeded in becoming the single undergraduate most hated by SDS. A book I wrote on the Harvard strike, *Push Comes to Shove*, appeared during Cambodia/Kent State, and SDS flooded the campus with leaflets denouncing it. Several months before the book came out, I had entered the competition for undergraduate English language commencement speaker, a competition open to any senior, with the winner selected by some professors in the Classics Department. I won, and when my selection became public a month or so before commencement, SDS began a campaign to have my selection (which they ludicrously saw as an administration conspiracy) annulled. There were threats to storm the commencement stage, and on commencement day a phalanx of faculty members supposedly was there to block the entrance to the stage. The effectiveness of the phalanx was vividly demonstrated when a group of eight demonstrators from a Cambridge community group took over the stage, shortly before it was my turn, to protest Harvard's policies in the city of Cambridge. The takeover did, however, take some of the heat off my appearance. When I finally did give my commencement speech, it was interrupted by virtually constant heckling, and a small number of students walked out. But there was nothing more serious. (My parents commented afterwards that the success of the community demonstrators in storming the commencement stage, outdoors in the vastness of Harvard Yard, hardly inspired their confidence in the security arrangements designed for me.)

Despite my self-proclaimed radicalism and my addiction to politics, the late sixties at Harvard were, politically, a depressing time for me. Depressing, I should add, in an intellectual sense and disappointing in an emotional sense—although still exciting and exhilarating, with the excitement coming from the rush of ideological polemic and the proud feeling that one was standing up for what was decent and right despite hostility and contempt.

The origins of my idiosyncratic response to the politics of Harvard in the late 1960s were, again, in the special nature of my experiences in high school. Great Neck, New York, was an atypical American community. It was an upper-middle-class, predominantly Jewish community where there was a good deal of political activity, much of it on the Left. Many old Communist party members or sympathizers, now older and more settled but still not so different ideologically from what they had been during the 1930s, lived in Great Neck, and their children were my classmates in high school. Several years before the flowering of anti-Vietnam protest movements and of the New Left, the dominant political point of view among the significant number of political activists at Great Neck South was already the kind of radicalism that was to attain similar prominence in many college campuses around the country only by 1970. I remember well the after-school discussions in the Forum Club, a political discussion club that was one of the school's extracurricular activities. In 1963, at the time of the anti-Diem demonstrations in Saigon and two years or so before the antiwar movement began to stir, basically *everyone* was against American involvement in Vietnam. We had a fair number of students who were already then enamored of Mao's China; a pro-Mao book by someone named Felix Greene, *Awakened China*, was eagerly read, and Felix Greene appeared as a speaker sponsored by a local adult group where many of the old Communist party types tended to congregate.

Within the environment I was, already in high school, a dissenter. I defined my politics for myself in the middle of the tenth grade and planted my tree right there. I was a democratic socialist or social democrat in the tradition of the socialist parties of Western Europe. That meant that I was for democracy, against communism, not anti-American. It meant that I supported labor movement and the Democratic party. Like other ideologies on the Left, mine gave me an answer (a sort of informal party line) on most political questions. I proclaimed my political self-definition in an article I wrote during the summer between my sophomore and junior years in high school on the political life of Great Neck South, criticizing procommunism among intelligent high school students. I sent it unsolicited to *The New Leader*, which was a political statement in itself, for *The New Leader* was an old socialist, strongly anticommunist magazine that made the older generation of communist sympathizers see red (no pun intended). *The New Leader* wrote back that it wanted to publish the article, making that day probably the happiest in my sixteen-year-old life. After the article came out, William Buckley wrote a column about it, the local newspaper ran a lead story about it, and I was promptly notorious.

The late 1960s "radicalized" many students, at Harvard and elsewhere. But I wasn't the only one who came to Harvard with ready-made politics. I remember my first weekend in Matthews South, just after my parents returned home after depositing me and some belongings in Harvard Yard. I ate dinner at the Hayes Bickford cafeteria just outside the Yard across Massachusetts Avenue with Mark Dyen, a boy from the dorm. ("The Bick" was later replaced by a Chinese restaurant.) Dyen was from New Haven, and his father taught at Yale. He had spent some time in Indonesia with his parents, and we spent a good part of the evening arguing about President Sukarno: Mark thought he was great, and I thought he was a tinhorn dictator. Dyen also told me about his involvement in efforts to run an independent Left candidate against Congressman Robert N. Giaimo of New Haven, whom I had never heard of before but whom Dyen described to me as an "established liberal." I didn't think people should run candidates against "established liberals," at least not in a general election where it might help elect a Republican. Dyen later became an SDS leader and after that for a short time an underground Weatherman terrorist; now he works for Massachusetts Fair Share, a quasi-populist community organization where many old Harvard SDSers ended up. We became (and remain, I think) fast enemies.

Much of the core of SDS leadership—especially the group that, when SDS factionalized, became known as the New Left caucus—came from hereditary radical, or at least hereditary political, backgrounds not dissimilar to my own. I suspect that all of us who were like that shared a certain feeling of separateness, at some deep emotional level, from the hoards of previously apolitical or nonradical students who became radicalized by Vietnam, or by going away from home and being exposed to new ideas, or by a sense of personal alienation from parents and/or from society, or simply by being at Harvard during a time when our best and brightest were, the common account told us, demonstrating and even occupying buildings. We who brought our politics to Harvard were quicker to engage in obscure polemic, more conversant with Marx, more likely to know where the dividing lines were on such faraway questions as the Kronstadt Rebellion, the role of the Social Democrats in Weimar Germany, or the actions of Ho Chi Minh in 1946. We were, in a sense, more European and less American: we lived and breathed the world where half the people we knew called themselves socialists or radicals, not one where the figure was closer to half of one percent. Something that I think never fully appreciated as I worked to organize a chapter of the Young People's Socialist League on campus was that anyone willing to take the major step of identifying himself, in the United States, as a socialist (even SDS never used the word "socialist" in its name) was unlikely to be sympathetic to the quite restrained and moderate and very out spokenly anticommunist politics the YPSL was offering. In Europe it would have been no problem: there were lots of socialists there, and many of them were quite restrained and moderate and anticommunist. But we were in the United States, not in Europe. And we were not living in a time when people were interested in social change because of an ongoing commitment that did not get born yesterday; we were living in a time when such commitment was born of burning threats and searing alienation.

During the four years I was at Harvard, SDS became both much bigger and much more radical. By junior year SDS regular meetings could go a good way toward filling Burr A, which had a capacity of about two hundred. (I knew the capacity of various lecture halls superbly well because we had to go through the difficult task of trying to estimate meeting and, above all, lecture crowds when scheduling YPSL meetings with the office of the dean of students—more particularly, with Miss Jean Douglas, a short Scottish woman utterly devoted to Dean Watson, who got along with me far better than she got along with other campus radicals, particularly the undergraduate Trotskyist leader, for whom she had a special dislike.) In contrast to SDS meetings, YPSL membership meetings were typically held in various classrooms in Sever that had a capacity of fifty or so. We had speakers fairly frequently, however (more often than SDS did), who drew large crowds. Michael Harrington could fill Lowell Lecture Hall, which had a capacity of eight hundred or so. We got almost two hundred to hear Al Lowenstein speak in Harvard Hall to tell us about his plans, not yet fully formed then, to try to "dump Johnson" in 1968. And—my proudest achievement—we got, with the help of extensive and creative publicity, over a hundred people to pay a dollar each to hear Max Schachtman, of whom nobody had ever heard before, speak on the fiftieth anniversary of the Russian Revolution (his topic: "Workers' Paradise Lost"). Things like that were important to us then.

SDS became bigger. It also became much more radical. A sort of diminishing-astonishment principle was at work within SDS. Some small vanguard scouting party would tentatively stake out some position further and further to the Left. Once the position had been staked out, it no longer seemed quite as daring or unthinkable. Through repetition, gradually it became part of everyday SDS vocabulary. Thus, pro-Castro and pro-Mao positions were advanced very tentatively by some of the more "far out" elements within SDS when I was a freshman, and by senior year they had become the standard line within the organization. Sophomore year, in connection with the sit-in against a Dow Chemical recruiter, tentative talk about the unimportance of "bourgeois civil liberties" began. By senior year, this too became standard. Finally, like a supernova exploding and destroying itself, the now sectarian and factional national SDS organization at its Chicago convention in 1969 divided into several organizations, one of which went underground to bomb buildings and another of which announced that anybody who did not "support" North Vietnam, Albania, China, and Cuba (I think that was the whole list) was "no longer a member of SDS."

Meanwhile, I became—and the friends with whom I associated became—increasingly obsessed with SDS. Although the YPSL leaflets we put out about SDS—filled with accusations of "pro-totalitarianism," "elitism," and "contempt for the American people"—were regarded as hard hitting and even extreme by many students on campus, the leaflets actually reflected mild and sanitized versions of our feelings. Just as we psychoanalyzed the SDS members (in our private discussions) as "crazy" (some were self-hating; others were playing out bad relationships with their parents), so they psychoanalyzed us as being resentful of them because the YPSL was never able effectively to challenge them as a student organization. I can't render definitive judgment on the quality of our psychoanalysis of them, but I think I can say that their psychoanalysis of us was wrong. We thought that their political views were evil and that, if adopted in America, they would make our country a terrible society. Their growth on campus made us obsessive because it made us despair for the future of America. But, given the trends in the country at large at the time, we were quite proud of ourselves that we amassed about sixty dues-paying members and twenty genuinely active members for the organization. We had more active members than the Young Democrats (which dissolved after Humphrey was nominated in 1968) or the Young Republicans.

Looking back on the feelings we had then, several things stand out. We certainly overestimated the threat SDS posed to the future of Western Civilization. I remain convinced that its leaders were as bad as we thought they were, but I think we didn't need to be as worried about them as we were. Our obsession with them honored them by overrating their importance. Second, I think we tended too much to take the idealistic mood—of which the growth of SDS was a twisted but nonetheless unmistakable product—too much for granted. We assumed that students would be idealistic and concerned and that it was all right to devote most of our attention to the twisted forms such idealism was taking. The current vogue of reactionary chic—the opposite of the 1960s' radical chic—testifies all too vividly that such concern and idealism cannot be taken for granted. Third, I am amazed and amused, looking back on those years, at just how sectarian all of us were. We in the YPSL as well as those in the various SDS factions genuinely did have a "line" on most political questions, a "correct" answer that it was important to adopt, even in its details. We could argue at length about—and be very worried about—slight changes in wordings in a resolution. The YPSL nationally, and the top leadership of the Harvard chapter locally, had a complex position on Vietnam that was very careful to avoid a call for unilateral or unconditional

such services, that was all right). There was a history and literature tutor who drove all the way down to New York to cast a ballot against Mayor John V. Lindsay (voting absentee didn't give him the same thrill) and who bordered on being a racist. Arthur Waldron, my roommate for a year, was an anglophile who persisted in wearing a suit with a pocket watch to dinner most nights and dreamed of becoming the first American to master both Russian and Chinese, thus ensuring a successful career in the CIA. (I found out when I visited Hong Kong in 1971 that any number of foreign service officers knew both Russian and Chinese well. Arthur went on to get a Ph.D. in Chinese history at Harvard.) We spent a perhaps disproportionate amount of our time around the dinner table telling SDS horror stories.

The high point of student radicalism at Harvard was, of course, the student strike in April 1969. SDS had been preparing for it during the entire academic year with a campaign to get ROTC off campus; several weeks before the strike, the Progressive Labor faction of SDS began a campaign against Harvard's activities in Cambridge, which they saw as part of a plan to make Cambridge into an "Imperial City" (which I promptly dubbed "Emerald City"). In the week or so before the building occupation, my friends and I began feeling increasingly desperate because there seemed to be no way to stop SDS from taking over a building. We discussed among ourselves having a group of students link arms in front of the entrances to University Hall, so that SDS would have to commit violence against us in order to get in. I cannot recall why the idea was rejected, but it was. The night of the University Hall takeover the YPSL executive committee met all night in my room in Adams House B entryway to draft a statement. We sent representatives to some meeting of "moderate" students going on in the Yard at the same time, using the student ID of a freshman member, Rob Patullo, because the Harvard police had closed off the Yard to all but the freshmen who lived there.

For me, the strike was a time of exhaustion and depression over what had happened at Harvard, mixed with a certain weird exhilaration. YPSL put out reams of leaflets—literally tens of thousands—distributed in connection with the various mass meetings at Harvard Stadium and distributed in the Yard. Officially, we supported the initial three-day strike endorsed the morning after the University Hall "bust" at the student meeting in Memorial Church. Actually, most of our inner circle did not really even support that brief a strike; I can't remember whether we actually pronounced the phrase at the time, but I know that my attitude took off on the statement of the American commander who talked about destroying a village in Vietnam in order to save it. We supported the strike in order to try to destroy it. We officially opposed continuing the strike beyond the original three days.

That summer and fall, I wrote *Push Comes to Shove*, an account of student radicalism at Harvard that culminated in the strike. It came out in May 1970, just a month before I graduated, and it got a fair amount of attention. While Harvard was on strike over Cambodia, I was traveling around the country promoting the book. The book was severely critical of the pro-SDS stance *The Harvard Crimson* took. Instead of assigning one of the more blatantly pro-SDS editors to review the book, they gave it to Jim Fallows, outgoing president of the *Crimson*. Although Fallows had been involved in something the *Crimson* tried to organize called the Conspiracy against Harvard Education, he had generally been a relatively retiring and fair-minded type. Fallows succeeded in penning an absolutely vicious review. At one point (this was before the gay liberation movement rendered such comments unacceptable) he suggested that my hostility to SDS might be due to an unrequited homosexual love for Mike Kazin, an SDS leader in the class of 1970.

I was out of the country for two years after graduating, and in September 1972 I returned to Harvard to attend graduate school in political science. One of the magazines to which I took out a subscription on my return was *The Washington Monthly*, of which Fallows was a contributing editor. I found that, in spite of myself, I liked much of what he wrote. Sometime in early 1973 I got a letter from Fallows. He had been looking through the mailing labels at the magazine to see who in Cambridge subscribed. He came upon my name and address, and he wrote to apologize for his review of *Push Comes to Shove*. The review was one of the most embarrassing things he had ever done, he concluded. I wrote back that I appreciated his letter very much and accepted his apology. In 1977 in Berlin, I attended a conference at which Fallows, then President Carter's chief speech writer, was also present. We hadn't seen each other since graduation. He told me he was very hesitant about ever going back to Cambridge, because there were so many unpleasant memories associated with it in his mind. I told him that was funny, because I didn't feel that way. We talked more about Harvard in those days, and I felt a bond growing as between two people who have been through a difficult experience together. But I also realized how the 1960s were finally becoming part of the past, something one talked about in terms of "how things were then." It was, in a sense, on that day in Berlin that the 1960s at Harvard ended for me.

CHAPTER EIGHT

Coming of Age in America
Higher Education as a Troubled Giant, 1970 to 2000

Higher education in the United States between 1970 and 2000 was in the peculiar situation of having attained international prestige and respect—while at the same time being subjected to a succession of reports emphasizing criticisms and uncertainties within the campus and from external constituencies. Campus unrest and student activism, as noted in documents for chapter 7, were partially responsible for this malaise. However, the 1971 Newman Report (Document 8.1) did not dwell on that cause, opting instead to look at systemic problems as colleges and universities tried to fulfill universal access to postsecondary education. Affordability increased with the 1972 reauthorization of the Higher Education Act, particularly owing to Congress's funding and approval for need-based Basic Educational Opportunity Grants (BEOGs), later named Pell Grants. Student financial aid increased as a subject of intense public and legislative debate. By 1978 Congress had shifted priority to student loans as the major program for financial assistance—a strategy that appealed to many members of Congress who faced reelection because it was a convenient way to regain voter support from a large number of state taxpayers whose college-bound children seldom were eligible for the federal need-based Pell Grants.

Illustrative of the transition—with both gains and problems—from mass to universal access was the coming of age of the public community colleges as a presence in postsecondary education, especially with their hallmark commitment to being accessible as a "port of first entry" for underserved constituencies. At the same time, all colleges devoted increasing attention to "first-generation" students—newcomers to the campus who were the first in their family to attend. Problems with the abuses of big-time college sports persisted as a hardy perennial in higher education, as indicated in Document 8.6 with the 1991 report of the Knight Foundation Commission. In taking stock of American higher education at the end of the twentieth century, the ability to provide access surpassed the record of colleges and universities in promoting achievement, retention, and graduation for all its students.

8.1: The Campus Condition: The 1971 Newman Report on Higher Education

The American penchant for appointing blue-ribbon commissions to make recommendations on social and institutional problems was nowhere more evident than in the publication of the 1971 *Report on Higher Education*. Known as the Newman Report in honor of the commission chair, Frank Newman (who was vice president of Stanford University), this 130-page publication gave a provocative prognosis of what ailed higher education nationwide. Chapter titles suggested the sources of discontent as the commission urged the American public to wrestle with the "paradox of access," the paralysis of the "lockstep" in college curricula, the growth of bureaucracy, and the credentials monopoly. In terms of equity and social justice, the commission devoted complete chapters to "barriers to women" and the "unfinished experiment in minority education." The conclusion left little room for complacence, as the prescription was that higher education leaders should be "changing course" to diversify and make more responsive the institutions, programs, and financial aid for going to college in America.

Preface

Several commissions have examined the state of higher education within the past few years. Their recommendations, ranging from expanding community colleges to spending more for research in the graduate schools, are intended to strengthen and extend the existing system.

We have taken a different approach. We believe that it is not enough to improve and expand the present system. The needs of society and the diversity of students now entering college require a fresh look at what "going to college" means.

Frank Newman, chair, *Report on Higher Education* (Washington, DC: Department of Health, Education and Welfare, March 1971).

As we have examined the growth of higher education in the postwar period, we have seen disturbing trends toward uniformity in our institutions, growing bureaucracy, overemphasis on academic credentials, isolation of students and faculty from the world—a growing rigidity and uniformity of structure that makes higher education reflect less and less the interests of society.

Rather than allow these trends to continue, means must be found to create a diverse and responsive system. We must enlarge our concepts of who can be a student, and when, and what a college is. We need many alternate paths to an education.

Why has there been so little attention devoted to these problems?

Many of the most important studies have written about higher education in terms of needs of institutions. Less attention has been paid to the problems as seen by students, or by the society which must support higher education.

The most prestigious colleges and universities have received most of the attention. The difficulties of the less selective institutions, which are more severe, have largely been ignored. There is a widespread assumption that the responsibility of the system is to provide opportunities for successful students, rather than insuring an exciting and useful education for every student at every step.

The Impact of the New Student: It is still common to think of the typical college entrant as the student who has done well in high school and is excited by the prospect of college. We expect that he will enjoy college life, be generally successful in his studies, and, with reasonable luck, go on to graduate school.

Yet the colleges and universities must now serve a whole new range of students. More young people now graduate from high school and more of these go on to college. Gradually, the public has come to assume that everyone who wants to go to college should be able to do so.

With today's more diverse student body, there may be no such thing as a "typical" entering student. If there is, he is a member of the majority who enter but never graduate. He did only moderately well in high school. Pressured by his parents, concerned about the credential he needs for better job opportunities, and swept along by the general assumptions of his peers, he enters a nearby community college or a large 4-year college. His hopes that this will be a significantly different and more exciting experience than his high school studies soon vanish. Within 6 months he has dropped out. His main gain is the name of an institution that he can put in the space on the application form where it says "College attended _____."

Not only must the system serve students of much more diverse backgrounds, but many students as well whose expectations of college are changing. In part, this results from the profound social changes under way in the United States (and in much of the world). This social change is characterized by a questioning of traditional assumptions, by a loosening of social constraints, and by a pushing against inhibitions everywhere. Universities and colleges have found themselves directly in the path of this revolution, and have been the first to feel its effects. Students want the university as their champion and their target, simultaneously.

While large numbers of students have found traditional academic programs uncongenial, a great many others find that the university or college community represents a life style of great appeal. Many, including numbers of the best students, view the outside world with deepening suspicion and hostility. Some stretch out their programs, others drop out but remain clustered in the shadow of the university. Rather than considering the university as an educational center, these students see it as a haven.

The process of change in the student body is far from complete. A vast range of potential students remains outside. Despite the growth in the proportion of the population going to college, traditional and artificial limits persist as to *when* in a person's life he may be a college student, and as to *what type* of person meets the established requirements. Minorities are still underrepresented. Women are openly discriminated against. Arbitrary restrictions and a lack of imaginative programs limit the opportunities for those of beyond the normal college age and of those for whom attendance at a conventional campus is impractical.

The Need for New Ways of Going to College: Behind the comforting statistics of growth are uncomfortable signs that the present system has failed to adapt. It provides for neither differing institutions nor differing styles of learning. Moreover, we have been losing the limited diversity that has existed.

The modern academic university has, like a magnet, drawn all institutions toward its organizational form, until today the same teaching method, the same organization by disciplines, and the same professional academic training for faculty are nearly universal. The shortcomings of the academic university as a model for all other institutions have been obscured by the dazzling success of the best known examples.

Not only is one campus more and more like the next, but increasing numbers of campuses are parts of larger systems. As the only institutions capable of expanding rapidly enough to meet the postwar demand, public multicampus systems have grown rapidly, until today they dominate higher education. Without quite realizing it, the States have built bureaucracies that threaten the viability and autonomy of the individual campus.

We believe that there is a compelling need for new approaches to higher education—not only new types of colleges with new missions, but also new patterns of going to college. Only when basic changes occur will many segments of the American population find attendance at college a useful learning experience. The creation of new types of institutions, valuable in themselves, will have a second benefit—their competition can be an important pressure for reform of the existing institutions.

The Limits of Present Reform: The 1950's and 1960's were decades of unprecedented development and remarkable accomplishment in American higher education. There was a vast growth in numbers of students, faculty members, and facilities. Access to college widened steadily. Inequality of opportunity among economic classes and ethnic groups, long a factor preventing social mobility, was at last widely recognized as a national concern, and steps were taken toward correction. Greater opportunity was accorded each undergraduate to influence his own curriculum. Graduate education developed a level of scholarly excellence that became the envy of the world.

The value to the United States, and, in fact, the world, of the great liberal arts and science centers, of students absorbed in studies for the sake of those studies alone, of scholarship and research in every field cannot be doubted. But these achievements should not cause us to blunt our criticisms. It is precisely because of the success of American higher education that our Task Force has felt more searching inquiry and more fundamental reform are needed, lest we attempt to meet the future with only the plans from the past. It is because of its strength and vitality that our system can safely undertake change.

There has been reform, and its pace has been accelerated by the advent of student protest and the demands of minority groups. However, virtually all postwar reforms have been based on the assumption that growth, inner diversification of curriculums, and changes in governance will provide the needed solutions.

We are convinced that the probable success of these kinds of reform is limited, for they leave unaffected the institutionalized past decisions as to what higher education is all about. The system, with its massive inertia, resists fundamental change, rarely eliminates outmoded programs, ignores the differing needs of students, seldom questions its educational goals, and almost never creates new and different types of institutions.

The forces that shape the system of higher education are powerful and subtle. The overemphasis on the college degree as a credential, the struggle for prestige within the academic world, the resistance of bureaucracy, the limitations of present methods of funding all play a significant role.

How will new forms of learning and new institutions arise in the face of these pressures? What will make higher education more likely to reflect the real needs of the society it serves rather than its own internal interests?

We believe that only an intensive national effort can bring about sufficient change before the present opportunities for serious reform are lost.

The Paradox of Access

In higher education, growth has been used traditionally as a measure of progress. The number of students enrolled, the number of institutions in existence, and the amount of money being spent on higher education all indicate remarkable growth.

> Between 1955 and 1965, the number of high school graduates increased more than 85 percent; the number of those graduates going on to college increased 110 percent. Today more than half of our young people enter college; yet 20 years ago less than 25 percent entered.
>
> In the last two decades the total number of institutions of higher education has increased from 1,850 to nearly 2,500, and average enrollment has doubled.
>
> Total higher education outlays, public and private, have been increasing at two-and-one-half times the rate of increase in the Gross National Product—which has itself grown nearly fourfold since 1950.

The common plea of educators is that this growth be nurtured until we reach the goal of access to a college education for every young American, a goal finally within reach in several States.

Yet access alone does not automatically lead to a successful education. It measures only the exposure of a particular age group to whatever educational institutions there are, and not the quality of the experience they are likely to find there. When the Task Force looked behind the growth statistics, they were found

Table 1. Variation in graduation rates according to selectivity of institutions

Type of institution	Percentage of students graduating within 4 years at initial institution	Percentage graduating within 10 years at some institution	1st-time, full-time enrollments, fall 1969	Percentage of all 1st-time, full-time enrollees
15 most selective private universities	80–85	90–95	20,000	1
Large State universities	35–45	60–70	239,000	15
State colleges	15–25	35–50	322,000	21
Public junior colleges	[1]20–25	[2]15–30	457,000	29

[1] Graduation from the 2-year program in a 2-year period.
[2] Graduation with a 4-year degree after transfer.
NOTE: - Remaining categories of institutions are: less selective private universities (73,000 first-time enrollees, or 5%); 4-year private colleges (266,000 first-time enrollees, or 17%); 2-year private colleges (55,000 first-time enrollees, or 4%); and small State universities (116,000 enrollees, or 7%), or a total of 1.55 million first-time, full-time enrollees.

to mask a major phenomenon: the surprisingly large and growing number of students who voluntarily drop out of college.

Table 1 summarizes estimates of graduation rates by type of institution.

These figures indicate that of the more than one million young people who enter college each year, fewer than half will complete 2 years of study, and only about one-third will ever complete a 4-year course of study. For example: at the University of Texas no more than 30 percent of entering students graduate in 4 years; after a 5th year the total is still less than 50 percent. The California State College system recently reported that, as an average for all campuses, only 13 percent of entering freshmen graduate in 4 years from the college they enter; the highest was 17 percent, the lowest only 8 percent.

The Significance of "Dropping Out": "Dropping out" is a pejorative term, and, we think, unfortunately so. Individuals should be able to "drop out" of college without social stigma. Indeed, we feel that many students are too reluctant to leave college, and that "hanging on" and "drifting" are themselves major problems in higher education.

Yet the fact that enormous numbers of students do drop out is an index of utmost significance, and, we believe, an index which has escaped public notice and educational debate. Laymen are generally astonished to hear that most students who attend college never finish. Educators themselves are often surprised when confronted with the numbers involved. But more importantly, both lay-men and educators assume that to the extent "dropping out" is a problem, it is an individual, not an educational, problem. Girls wish to marry, boys want to get jobs, and "many students are not suited for college," anyway.

This view is at best only half-true. Many students do leave college for personal reasons, such as shortage of money or the desire to get a job. But the majority of dropouts cite dissatisfaction with college and the desire to reconsider personal goals and interests as the major reasons for leaving school. After reviewing the studies on dropping out and interviewing scores of students, we are convinced that "dropouts" reveal an educational problem of considerable proportions. Col-lege is failing to capture the attention and engage the enthusiasm of many stu-dents. For some, it is a decidedly negative experience.

What makes this problem so acute is that the great expansion in higher edu-cation in recent years has been in just those institutions where dropout rates are the highest—in so-called unselective institutions. Selective institutions have rig-orous admission procedures that, in effect, screen *in* only those who are likely to succeed. At such institutions, "dropping out" occurs in advance of admissions.

In interpreting these findings, we can assume that society fulfills its obliga-tion simply by providing the opportunity for as many as possible to enter college. Success cannot and should not be guaranteed. High dropout rates are not incon-sistent with our commitment to broad access, but rather reflect the maintenance of rigorous academic standards and our insistence that a college degree represent real achievement.

Or we can assume that society's obligation (and its own self-interest, as well) is to provide more than just the chance to walk through the college gate—that there must also be access to a useful and personally significant educational experience.

These two assumptions by no means exclude each other. Some dropouts, for example, are flunk-outs; some clearly are not, or need not be, within alternative teaching-learning formats. Some who drop out may indeed never have been "col-lege material" in the first place. But in the absence of some specification of what is meant by "college," the question must be asked whether different and differing types of colleges would meet student needs more effectively than do the present forms. In the few examples we have found in which the college format has been adapted to meet the needs of a particular group of students who would normally have had a high attrition rate, strikingly lower dropout rates have resulted. In a broader formulation, the question is really what kind of a total "system" of higher education this Nation wants.

Barriers to Women

The higher education community prides itself on its leading role in the fight to end intolerance in American society. Yet with regard to women, colleges and universities practice a wide range of discriminatory practices. These institutions view women primarily as wives and mothers and their education as preparation for these functions.

The Task Force has identified three major types of barriers which block full participation by women in higher education: first, overt discrimination by faculties, deans, and others acting in official capacities; second, practical institutional barriers, such as rigid admission and residence requirements, and a lack of campus facilities and services, which makes participation in higher education incompatible with many women's other interests and activities; and third, the ingrained assumptions and inhibitions on the part of both men and women which deny the talents and aspirations of the latter.

The unique role of higher education gives it extraordinary leverage to either help or hurt women's chances for equality of opportunity. When colleges and universities deny women the chance to gain skills and credentials, they increase the likelihood that women will not receive equal opportunities in all other social institutions for the rest of their lives.

Higher education exerts another kind of leverage as well. Colleges and universities take upon themselves the task of forming and sanctioning the attitudes and practices which educated people will thereafter consider reasonable. If it is fairness which they sanction, all women are helped; but if it is discrimination they sanction, all women are hurt, educated or not.

The Present Extent of Inequality: Comparisons of the participation and attainment of men and women in higher education reveal a clearly unequal pattern.

> Although, in high school, women earn better grades and higher test scores than men, fewer enter college, and they attain only 41.5 percent of the bachelor's and first professional degrees.
> Although women in college earn better undergraduate records than men, fewer enter graduate school.

Most of the degrees earned by women are in a few fields of study, such as education, the humanities, and the health professions. Thus, aggregate figures on attainment of women exaggerate their opportunities in higher
education.

Even within those fields considered acceptable, women are confined to subordinate functions. While virtually all the nursing graduates are women,
they represent only eight percent of graduating physicians.

If there were any assurance that the denial of equality is rapidly becoming a
thing of the past, there could perhaps be some complacency. But it is not merely
residual; in some ways, it is increasing. The proportion of 18- and 19-year-old
males enrolled in higher education increased 20 percent between 1950 and 1966,
but the participation of females increased only 11 percent. The percentage of
master's degrees obtained by women reached its peak in 1930 at 40.4 percent and
declined to 38 percent in 1968, while the percentage of doctor's degrees obtained
by women reached its peak in 1930 at 15.4 percent, and was down to only 12.6
percent in 1968.

We believe that it is not the case that opportunities exist for women which they
simply decline to exercise. Rather, we find that there are specific barriers which
block their progress and which will not disappear without conscious effort.

Discrimination Against Women as Students: The first such barrier is outright discrimination against women as students, especially at the graduate level. Although
few admissions officers or members of graduate fellowship committees would
confess to discrimination on the basis of race, many openly argue that women
should be denied opportunities because they are women. For example, the Academic Senate of the University of California, Berkeley—an institution renowned
for its commitment to civil liberties—recently received the following report of an
interview between a social science department chairman and a woman candidate
for graduate study:

"I suppose you went to another college?"

"I attended U.C. Berkeley."

"But you didn't finish?"

"I was graduated with a B.A."

"Your grades weren't very good?"

"I was named to Phi Beta Kappa in my junior year and was graduated
summa cum laude."

"You have to have 16 to 18 units of X. You don't have that, do you?"

"As my transcript shows, I had 18 units of X, mostly A's, one or two B's."

"I'm going to disallow all 18 because they were so long ago. You understand that, don't you? There's no point in trying to replace the undergraduate course in order to qualify. You could not do it part-time; you would have to take 18 units in one year. Then you would probably not get into graduate school. If you did, you would meet so much hostility that I doubt if you would stay in. Most women do not finish their work, and we couldn't take a chance on you. We don't want women in the department anyway, and certainly not older women. This may be unfair to you in light of your record, but we just are not going to chance it."

Women's Education as a "Poor Investment": In order to justify discrimination against women in higher education, the argument is often made that their education is a poor investment of educational resources. The argument has two parts: first, it is argued that women are much less likely to complete their training than men; second, it is argued that women who do complete their training are much less likely to use it because they are likely to marry, become housewives, and give up any idea of a career.

Both parts of the argument have much less basis in fact than is usually supposed. What basis there is seems clearly attributable to artificial obstacles that unnecessarily stand in the way of women completing and using their education, rather than to some innate disposition of women regarding their educational and career goals.

The facts tend to contradict the view that women are poorer risks than men in their disposition to complete training. The percentage of entering undergraduate students who graduate in 4 years is about 15 percent higher for women than for men. As for graduate students, the record for completion is so poor for male students in the fields of the humanities and social sciences (the fields most open to women) that it is absurd to make comparisons unfavorable to women. The available data suggest, if anything, that women do about the same as men: women constituted 30 percent of graduate and professional students in 1967, but earned 35.8 percent of the master's and first professional degrees awarded in 1968.

Two points may account for the impression department chairmen seem to have that women are less likely to complete their training. First, in our society, most women move where their husbands' educational and career opportunities take them. The result is that women must often transfer from one institution to another to complete their training. Women thus *are* less likely to complete their training at the institution where they began. If, in some field, they are less likely to ever complete it, this might be attributed in large measure to the unwillingness of accessible institutions to accept them as transfer students and give them the support which a nontransferring male student would receive as a matter of course.

The second part of the "poor investment" argument seems also unsupported by the facts. In 1968, 42 percent of all women of working age were in the labor force. Women who complete their training do, in fact, tend to use it, and the more training they have, the higher are their rates of participation. Fifty-four percent of the women who have bachelor's degrees are in the labor force, and 71 percent of those who have 5 or more years of higher education are working. More than 90 percent of women who received doctorates in 1957–58 were employed in 1964, and 79 percent of them had not interrupted their careers in the intervening years. Moreover, there is a strong correlation between the number of years of higher education and the likelihood that a woman will be working in her field of major study, i.e. the field where educational resources have been most intensively invested in her training. Nor do women Ph.D.'s let marriage interfere with their productivity. Those who are employed full time publish slightly more than either men Ph.D.'s or unmarried women Ph.D.'s.

Discrimination Against Women in Academic and Professional Life: In one sense, the "poor investment" argument is self-fulfilling. The normal incentives of prestige and money for active participation in professional fields are, to an important extent, withheld from women, especially married women.

Higher education discriminates against women as employees even more than it does as students. A 1966 Office of Education study estimated that, on college faculties, women comprised 32 percent of instructors, 20 percent of assistant professors, 15 percent of associate professors, and 9 percent of full professors. A substantial part of these differences is due to the fact that women are made to wait longer for promotion. Women who do achieve that rank of full professors wait 2 to 5 years longer than men in the biological sciences, and as much as 10 years longer in the social sciences. Moreover, married women must, overall wait 5 to 10 years longer than single women.

In professional and business life there is similarly less economic reward. Starting salaries tend to be lower. A survey conducted in November 1969, regarding jobs and salaries expected to be offered by 206 companies to June 1970 college graduates, showed a differential in the salary offer to be made to men and women with the same college majors in a wide variety of fields.

Women can only look forward to dropping still further behind as their careers progress. The difference in median salaries for men and women is more than $3,000 in chemistry, physics, mathematics, economics, and the biological sciences. Women similarly average lower salaries than men in each of the academic ranks. In this sense, women's education is a poorer investment than men's, for they are denied the same income as a return on investment. They do, however, earn much better salaries, compared to other women, the more years of higher education they have completed.

A common myth is that opportunities for women in American society, though not equal, are opening up and that discrimination is steadily declining. When we see that the share of master's and doctor's degrees earned by women was higher between 1920–1940 than it was during the decade of the 1960's; and that women's median salary income, as a percent of men's, decreased by 5.7 percent from 1955 to 1968 (from 63.9% to 58.2%); and that the plight of the woman in education and the job market has not improved, but worsened; and when we add to this the information that there are fewer women elected to public office at all levels today than during those same previous decades, we get an overall view that the American woman is not only failing to hold her own, but is losing ground.

The Lockstep and the Lockout: The prevailing college and university structure presents an array of practical hurdles for women. The problems of access and the educational lockstep that we have noted create barriers that are particularly difficult for women. The fact that these barriers exist today is due, in part, to a failure to analyze and understand the needs of women and, in part, to a lack of consensus that they should be removed.

Rigid policies and practices pressure women into making a choice between marriage and children or advanced study and a career, causing many women to lose out permanently. Women who take time out to marry and work or to raise children for several years find it extremely difficult to return to academic life. Residence requirements, the inability to transfer credits, insistence on full-time study, lack of child-care facilities, and inadequate health services are most frequently cited as problems that keep women from undertaking or completing their undergraduate and graduate studies. Women are frequently discriminated against in obtaining fellowships and travel grants and such amenities as married-student housing.

A recent AAUW survey exploring sex discrimination on the college campus reveals that only 5 percent of the schools reporting provide any kind of day-care services for children of students. Evidently, colleges that are willing to spend enormous sums on athletic facilities, used principally by men, recoil at the thought of establishing such facilities as a nursery where women can leave their children in order to attend classes.

One inevitable and damaging result of this combination of discrimination and lack of adequate facilities is that women students are encouraged to conclude that they should think of themselves only as potential wives and mothers, or, at best, as teachers or nurses. Several studies confirm that even very talented women students are affected by what Mary Bunting, the president of Radcliffe, has called the "climate of unexpectation" for women, and that their aspirations decline as they go through college.

The most formidable barrier to full participation by women in higher education is the assumptions of both men and women about the role of women in our society. These assumptions are internalized by individuals and incorporated into the structure of our institutions without being obvious. Instead, they appear to be the natural outgrowth of what society believes to be women's proper responsibilities.

An important fact about the barrier created by these assumptions is that there is, as yet, no consensus that it should be removed. While some Americans regard discrimination against women as gross injustice and detrimental to the whole society, others see it as a perfectly natural division of social roles based upon inherent differences between men and women. There is today a deep concern about the decline of family life as the main focus of American society. Consequently, any discussion of equalizing opportunities for careers for women unleashes powerful and deeply held feelings among many people.

It is becoming apparent that the prevailing view of women's appropriate role in society has been based on ignorance and misunderstanding, on a failure to think of women as individuals with intellects which need stimulation and egos which need satisfaction, as among men. We are belatedly realizing that when women's minds are awakened by an excellent education, they are not going to be completely fulfilled by merely being gracious shadow-figures for their husbands, if they choose to marry. Lack of outside, independent interests often has a detrimental effect on the husbands and children of able, intelligent women as well as on the women themselves. As with minorities, the corrosive effect of repression and lack of opportunity for women goes far beyond the individual.

Colleges and universities have an unparalleled opportunity to affect the status of women. Their role in the transmission of values and the preparation of men and women for careers makes this opportunity a responsibility that these educational institutions must not ignore if they are to be responsive to the needs of society.

8.2: Federal Student Financial Aid: Basic Educational Opportunity Grants Program (Pell Grants) from the 1972 Reauthorization of the Higher Education Act of 1965

The BEOG program was the linchpin of a multifaceted constellation of scholarship grants, loans, and work-study programs that were generously funded and focused on making undergraduate education accessible and affordable, especially to young women and men from historically underserved constituencies. Although federal programs for student financial aid had been established through various, sporadic initiatives by the late 1960s, it was the 1972 reauthorization of the Higher Education Act of 1965 that provided the setting for a large-scale, enduring program. The BEOG eventually was renamed as "Pell Grants," in honor of U.S. senator Claiborne Pell (D-RI), who had been the longtime advocate and architect of the program. The BEOG was distinctive in that it was a federal grant that did not require repayment by the student; furthermore, it was defined and administered according to a new lexicon of financial aid terminology—and coordination with families, colleges, and state agencies.

Public Law 92-318—June 23, 1972
Part A—Grants to Students in Attendance at Institutions of Higher Education
Statement of Purpose: Program Authorization
Sec. 401. (a) It is the purpose of this part, to assist in making available the benefits of postsecondary education to qualified students in institutions of higher education by—

Higher Education Act Reauthorization: Creation of the BEOG (Pell Grants) (1972). Public Law Higher Education Act of 1965, Title IV, Part A, Subpart 1; 20 U.S.C. 1070a. Amendments: Public Law 92-318-June 23, 1972. Pages 247–251.

(1) providing basic educational opportunity grants (hereinafter referred to as "basic grants") to all eligible students;

(2) providing supplemental educational opportunity grants (hereinafter referred to as 'supplemental grants') to those students of exceptional need who, for lack of such a grant, would be unable to obtain the benefits of a postsecondary education;

(3) providing for payments to the States to assist them in making financial aid available to such students; and

(4) providing for special programs and projects designed (A) to identify and encourage qualified youths with financial or cultural need with a potential for postsecondary education, (B) to prepare students from low-income families for postsecondary education, and (C) to provide remedial (including remedial language study) and other services to students.

Sec. 411. (a) (1) the commissioner shall during the period beginning July 1, 1972 and ending June 30, 1975, pay to each student who has been accepted for enrollment in, or is in good standing at, an institution of higher education (according to the prescribed standards, regulations, and practices of that institution) for each academic year during which that student is in attendance at that an institution, as an undergraduate, a basic grant in the amount for which that student is eligible, as determined pursuant to paragraph (2).

(2) (A) (i) The amount of the basic grant for a student eligible under this subpart for any academic year shall be $1,400, less an amount equal to the amount determined under paragraph (3) to be the expected family contribution with respect to that student for that year.

(B) (i) The amount of a basic grant to which a student is entitled under this subpart for any academic year shall not exceed 50 per centum of the actual cost of attendance at the institution at which the student is in attendance for that year.

8.3: Missions and Functions of Community Colleges: The 1981 Report of the California Postsecondary Education Commission

This document gives insight into two distinctive institutions: the public community college, the focus of the report; and state coordinating councils, the source of the

Missions and Functions of the California Community Colleges (Sacramento: California Postsecondary Education Commission, May 1981).

report—in particular, the California Postsecondary Education Commission (CPEC). En-rollment at public community colleges nationwide had grown from 269,031 in 1963 to 1,663,216 in 1980. California was an important state for community colleges, as its 112 campuses in 1990 enrolled over 1.5 million students. California's vast com-munity college system was distinctive in that it charged no tuition and was generous and flexible in allowing enrollment, admission, and reentry. These customary policies faced reevaluation, along with the numerous missions of the community colleges, in the aftermath of California's 1978 Proposition 13, which froze property taxes and, eventually, reduced one of the major revenue sources for the public two-year colleges. CPEC was illustrative of the role assigned to state coordinating agencies as part of overall statewide planning—namely, to raise significant questions about policies and practices which individual institutions and systems were unlikely to raise themselves. The document presents a good example of the high-stakes discussions that were fos-tered by the tapering of public support for higher education by the 1980s. Historically most attention has been focused on established four-year colleges and universities. By the late twentieth century, however, community colleges warranted central inclusion in policy discussions since by 1980 they had come to enroll more than one-third of all college students.

Preface

The California Postsecondary Education Commission is charged by the Legisla-ture, among its other responsibilities, to serve "as a stimulus to the segments and institutions of postsecondary education by projecting and identifying societal and educational needs and encouraging adaptability to change." As part of this function, the Commission plans to issue discussion papers periodically on im-portant issues facing postsecondary education in California. The present paper, the first in the series, has been prepared by the staff of the Commission for con-sideration by groups interested in the California Community Colleges. It contains only one explicit widespread conclusion and no recommendations. Its intent is to stimulate widespread discussion of directions and priorities for the Commu-nity Colleges in the 1980s, from which recommendations might well flow in the future.

Issues of mission and function cannot be isolated from those related to fund-ing, particularly when requests for funding for education and other State-supported functions exceed projected State revenues. However, the genesis of the paper was not the budgetary problems faced by the Community Colleges and the State. Instead, the questions about the effectiveness of the Community Colleges in meeting the increasingly diverse educational needs of the adult population in California lead to its conception, on the assumption that unless the colleges make programmatic choices and set budget priorities they will probably do many things less well and some things unsatisfactorily in the future.

Although this paper is addressed to the Community Colleges, it has implications for other segments of education—the schools on the one hand, and other postsecondary institutions on the other—because of the interrelationship of functions among them and the Community Colleges. Some subjects receive less attention in the paper than might have been expected because they are now being debated by the Legislature—for example, adult education—or are being considered by Commission staff in other studies—for example, remedial education. The major purpose of this paper is to stimulate discussion of a wide range of educational issues which cut across missions and functions, without dealing with each specific function which the Community Colleges perform.

Questions about the Traditional Missions of the California Community Colleges

In 1976, the most important conclusion of a Commission study of California Community College students which was submitted to the Legislature was that "continuing education for part-time, adult students has become the dominant function of the Community Colleges, with no resultant neglect of the occupational, transfer, and general educational functions for more traditional students." Now, five years later, the validity of that conclusion is in doubt. Both research reports and writings about the Community Colleges question whether these traditional missions of offering transfer programs, occupational preparation and general education are suffering in comparison with continuing education.

A few examples will illustrate the current questioning of Community College missions and functions for the 1980s.

Transfer Programs

The number of Community College students transferring to the University of California has been declining, as has the persistence and academic performance of these transfers. A 1980 report from the University's task force on retention and transfer concludes in its Executive Summary, "If we continue on the present downward spiral, many Community Colleges will not articulate with the University of California, because they will not be able to afford to offer the vocational and community service programs their students demand as well as the breadth and quality of program that will prepare students for the University of California." And a 1979 report prepared by the California State University and Colleges revealed that less than one in three Community College students who transferred to the State University and Colleges in the Fall 1975 term had graduated from the campus where the students first enrolled after <u>three</u> years on campus, and only 34 percent of them had graduated from any campus in the system.

General Education

The general education function of the California Community Colleges has recently been subjected to new examination and debate, in large part as a result of impending changes in the graduation requirements of the State University involving general education and related requirements for transfer students. In a report to the Commission in March which explored current issues in general education, including implication of these changes for articulation, the Commission staff concluded:

> . . .The current activity regarding general education within the Community Colleges seems largely to be a reaction to the proposed changes within the State University system rather than the direct result of any desire for constructive change initiated by the Community Colleges themselves. The Community Colleges also need to assume a position of active leadership in the area of general education while recognizing the need for flexibility and compromise if the State's system of higher education is to work on behalf of the students.

The direction in which Community College missions and functions such as these might proceed for the 1980s can perhaps best be sketched in terms of six major issues confronting the Community Colleges: (1) overcoming the myth of the "two-year college," (2) rethinking open enrollment within open admission, (3) improving articulation with the secondary schools, (4) reconsidering student affirmative action, (5) providing remediation, and (6) assuring transfer. All of these issues are interrelated. However, because of their complexity, they will be discussed individually.

Overcoming the Myth of the "Two-Year College"

The fundamental issue relating to Community College missions and functions concerns the limits, if any, that are desirable on their offerings and clienteles. Although the Community Colleges continue to offer one- and two-year curricula leading to certificates, degrees, and transfer, their image as "two-year" postsecondary institutions offering instruction at the thirteenth and fourteenth grade levels for college freshmen and sophomores no longer suffices. They do not offer courses for upper division or graduate credit, but they enroll students holding associate, baccalaureate, and advanced degrees, most of whom are not working for degrees or certificates. At the same time, they offer instruction below what is regarded as "college level," to help both high school graduates and dropouts with deficiencies in basic skills to increase their ability to succeed in college-level instruction.

Only a minority of Community College students complete programs prescribed by the faculties. About one-third of them enroll for only one term, and fewer than 20 percent graduate or are still enrolled by the end of their third year. About three-fourths enroll part time, and the modal student workload is one course. The colleges are authorized to offer both credit and noncredit courses, but many use only the credit mode. Students may not "audit" courses, but provisions for withdrawing from courses without penalty are quite liberal for students who do not want credit or who are failing. Although the commitment of the State is to two years of free public education in the Community Colleges, there is no prohibition against students enrolling throughout their lifetime, without respect to the number or levels of degrees held (or none at all). And there is now relatively little congruence between most of the colleges' catalogues and the institutions they purport to describe.

Rethinking Open Enrollment Within Open Admissions

The current Community College practice of open enrollment and open admissions tends to attract some students who cannot do the assigned work because of inadequate skills but were not counseled prior to enrollment, others who are capable of succeeding but do not want to work for course credit, and still others who need to have the courses taught at the college level for degree or transfer credit.

The basic question of open admissions is the viability of an open-door philosophy, without conditions. At issue is the extent to which the Community

Colleges should adapt their course requirements and teaching methods to the declining levels of basic skills exhibited by their students, when an open-door policy prevails in enrolling anyone at least eighteen years of age in almost any course, as well as in the college at large. California has had a long-standing commitment to making opportunity for postsecondary education available to all high school graduates through the Community Colleges, with the further opportunity to earn a baccalaureate degree available to anyone successfully completing a transfer program.

This commitment was affirmed in the 1960 *Master Plan for Higher Education in California* and in subsequent legislation. The Legislature also made provision for the admission of any applicant at least eighteen years of age "who, in the judgment of the board or of the president. . .is capable of profiting from the instruction offered." Although the law calls for this judgment of capability to be made, the Community Colleges have assumed that any adult who applies is able to benefit in some way from their offerings. At best, this assumption offers open-ended opportunity to students who would be ineligible for admissions to other postsecondary institutions but whose potential for success in college exceeds what would have been predicted from their high school record. At the other extreme, the benefits are said to include the experience of failure on the part of students who were unrealistic about their ability to succeed in college, and socialization for those who had little expectation of succeeding.

The issue at this time is not whether to abandon the philosophy of open-door admission to the Community Colleges but instead to improve the way in which it is implemented with respect to both high school graduates and dropouts. The first question related to implementation may be summarized as that of *advisement*: Should systematic evaluation of student basic skills be made a condition for enrollment, using high school transcripts or test results, or both, followed by counseling and placement in courses, for all first-time students? A second question relates to *screening*: Should some type of screening be instituted of students enrolling in *credit* courses and programs, while retaining open admission to the colleges of all applicants at least eighteen years old? Consider each of these questions in turn.

Assuring Transfer

The viability of the Community Colleges' transfer function came into question most dramatically with the publication last year of the University task force report on *Retention and Transfer*. The issue involves the volume of transfer students from individual colleges, particularly to the University; the readiness of these transfer students to undertake upper division work, in terms of their basic skills and preparation for the major; and articulation of courses and programs, including general education.

It is most unlikely that the Community Colleges would give up their transfer function. However, it is not clear that the broad articulation agreements of the past will continue to work in the 1980s, under which any Community College student with a grade-point average of C or better in fifty-six units of college work would have an opportunity to transfer into a baccalaureate program. The University and the State University are raising their expectations concerning the preparation of first-time freshmen for University-level work. To the extent that the four-year segments are successful in bringing this about, the vitality of the Community College transfer function may be reduced in at least two ways. First, the level of competition for grades in upper division courses will probably increase as a consequence of better preparation for University work on the part of first-time freshmen, particularly if the Community Colleges take no comparable action to raise expectations about pre-college preparation. Community Colleges will need to increase the quality of competition for grades in transfer program courses, to insure that potential transfer students are prepared to compete with "native" students in upper division courses. Second, the University and the State University will probably divert to the Community Colleges freshmen who are unable or unwilling to meet the higher standards at entrance, with some likelihood that the four-year segments may then find it necessary to raise expectations concerning the preparation of transfer students. Stated another way, open enrollment in University-transfer courses of students with low levels of basic skills may have a negative effect on the achievement levels of students who are preparing to transfer, if instructors try to meet the needs of all students enrolled in their classes. The danger appears to be greater in large Community Colleges where a small number of University-transfer students may receive little attention from counselors and faculty teaching transfer courses than in small institutions where a very small number of transfer students may be more easily identified for special attention.

(At the present time, Community College students who were not eligible for State University admission as freshmen may transfer to the State University with an average of C (2.0) in at least fifty-six semester units of credit which the Community Colleges have certified as baccalaureate-level work. Good information about performance after transfer is not yet available statewide, except for State University graduation rates which appear to be indicative of unsatisfactory performance, and the results of limited testing of the writing skills of transfer students.)

Some would argue that the issue to be discussed should be the need for the University and the State University to modify their policies, practices, and programs so as to attract and retain larger numbers of transfer students from the Community Colleges. The Commission and the segments have been charged by the Legislature from time to time to identify barriers to such transfer and to make recommendations for reducing or overcoming them. It appears unlikely that either the University or the State University would make any significant changes which would grant more responsibility for transfer and articulation to the Community Colleges at this time. Instead, the faculty of these systems appear to be moving in the direction of tightening standards and requirements for both transfer and "native" students seeking traditional baccalaureate degrees. However, the possibility of a new kind of degree for transfer students from technical and other "high-level" occupational programs in the Community Colleges may be an issue worthy of exploration, particularly in light of increased student interest in all segments in programs which prepare them for employment.

Conclusion

The California Community Colleges gained their reputation as a full partner in higher education in the 1960s by absorbing a major portion of the increase in lower division enrollments and preparing many of these students for transfer to the University and the State University. This reputation extended to the function of preparing large numbers of students for transfer who were not able to meet freshman admission requirements for the University and the State University when they graduated from high school but who could gain eligibility in the Community Colleges. The Community Colleges also became known during this era for their excellence in vocational and technical programs leading to degrees and certificates.

The fundamental problem now facing the Community Colleges is their ability to cope with the ever-increasing diversity of their students. During the last twenty years, the Community Colleges—faculty, programs, services—have changed more slowly than the characteristics of their students. There is a reluctance in the Community Colleges to establish priorities among student clienteles, programs, and services; and they may be increasingly unable to do everything well by being continually more efficient and more productive. If choices and priorities are not made, the result will probably be to do everything less well and some things unsatisfactorily.

The increasing diversity of the student population in the Community Colleges may be illustrated by a series of three simple images. In the early 1960s, at the time of the *Master Plan for Higher Education in California*, the Community College student population could be depicted as a bell-shaped curve, with a large majority of the students fitting the description, "young, Caucasian, high school graduates, enrolled full time in programs leading to degrees, certificates, and transfer." Some who were called "late bloomers" were at the lower end of the curve—students who had done poor work in high school but showed potential for succeeding in college-level work. Others were at the other end of the curve—"defined adults" and others enrolled part time who probably had not been to college elsewhere.

By the time of the Commission's study, *Through the Open Door*, in the mid-1970s, the curve had flattened to the shape of a rectangle, with large increases in the numbers of students who were educationally and economically disadvantaged, many of them from ethnic minority groups, and with a critical need for remedial programs and services. Increases at the other end were similar in size—more students over the age of twenty-one, with diverse short-term objectives for enrolling, and often with a substantial amount of postsecondary education in another type of institution.

During the 1980s, the Community College student population may come to resemble a bi-modal curve, with two large concentrations of students: at one end, those with serious educational handicaps, including the developmentally disabled, as well as the non- or limited-English speaking, refugees, unemployed workers, and others from the lower strata of society whose needs for postsecondary education can be met only at a relatively high cost—and at the other, relatively well-educated adults for whom education is part-time, irregular pursuit, including "reverse transfers" from the University, with a wide range of interest in almost anything the college offers, without respect to credit. Students who constituted the majority in the 1960s have not diminished in numbers. Instead, the growth of other student constituencies has been so large as to make the majority a minority in the 1980s, at a time when fewer young people may be enrolling in degree and transfer programs. These new student constituencies have increased the demand for community education, English as a second language, short-term vocational training, and instruction in the creative and performing arts, as well as the more traditional general education and occupational courses.

Much of the public still tends to view the Community College as a two-year, sometimes "junior" college, with transfer and occupational programs, rather than a community-based institution with education programs for all adults. There is a certain safety in the old image, at least with respect to continued public funding with no student charges. However, the issues facing the California Community Colleges lead to the conclusion that these institutions need to debate their multiple functions more fully as a prelude to evolving a statement of common mission for the 1980s and beyond.

8.4: The Changing Profile of College Students in the 1980s

College and university officials have benefitted from increasingly systematic and sophisticated demographic data about their applicants and, ultimately, about high school students who chose to enroll for undergraduate studies. Russell Schoch, a longtime outstanding writer about higher education, sorted through detailed, complex reports from offices of institutional research to provide alumni and the general public an informed profile of the changing composition of university students. His focus was on the University of California, but the resultant story had nationwide implications.

Remember Joe College? The young man, who, after working hard and succeeding in high school, arrived in Berkeley, where he found a place to live and set out to sample the rich and incredibly varied intellectual feast at the University of California. Joe was independent, strongly self-motivated, and academically well prepared; he was able not only to sample the intellectual wares but also to settle down, about junior year, to a major field of study, which he pursued with diligence and increasing confidence in order to graduate a neat four years after his arrival.

Joe doesn't live here anymore. Perhaps, in truth, he never did. But now he can't. Times have changed, things have changed, Berkeley has changed.

Russell Schoch, "As Cal Enters the '80s, There'll Be Some Changes Made," *California Monthly* (January–February 1980). Reprinted by permission of Russell Schoch.

The University of California at Berkeley has, in effect, changed its shape. From being a "top heavy" institution, with an emphasis on graduate and upper-division (junior and senior) courses, the balance has shifted to the "bottom," to the lower division of undergraduate education, the freshman and sophomore years. In Master Plans and in actuality during the 1950s and 1960s, the ratios looked like this: 45 percent of Berkeley students were in graduate school, 33 percent were in upper-division courses, 22 percent were in the lower division. What exists as the 1980s begin is an inversion of that shape and of those percentages: now the lower division has increased to 36 percent of the student body (from 6,000 students in 1971 to 11,000 currently), the upper division claims 34 percent, and the graduate division 30 percent. The pyramid has turned upside down.

These facts and figures come from a fascinating document presented to the campus community in December by Berkeley Vice Chancellor Ira Michael Heyman. Titled a "Draft Long-Range Academic Plan Statement, 1980–85," it was put together in advance of a University-wide Campus Plan that is scheduled to be assembled from reports from all University campuses by the late spring.

"The Berkeley campus finds itself at a critical juncture in its development," wrote Heyman in the report. "During the 1960s it experienced rapid and extensive growth." This was followed by the 1970s, "ten years of continuous retrenchment," with cuts in faculty, research, and academic support budgets, with continuous inflationary erosion, and with the tightening up made necessary by reductions in state funding following the passage of Proposition 13.

"At the close of the 1970s, with its enrollment above its planned ceiling, Berkeley finds itself with barely sufficient academic resources to fulfill its many responsibilities. In the 1980s it faces the additional problem of renewing more than 50 percent of its most eminent faculties as the bulge in the professoriate recruited in the 1950s reaches retirement."

So much for the gloomy background. Now for some present and future gloom. The most significant entry here is the problem of enrollment. The Berkeley campus was designed to peak at 27,500 students; last fall it admitted 29,300, creating crowded classrooms and dormitories, a bloated and strained educational faculty. The solution seems obvious: cut back the students.

But Berkeley is caught in a trap, similar to the kind that novelist Joseph Heller called Catch-22: in order for it to do what it wants, it must do what it doesn't want to do. Under current state policy, when enrollments decline, so does state funding. This means, for example, that if Berkeley were to cut back its "excess" number of students—trimming 1,800 to bring the total to 27,500—this would cause "a cut of at least one hundred faculty positions and funds for the support of departmental operations, library book collections, computer time, and other academic services on the order of $2–3 million." Catch-22.

A modern university of Berkeley's size and complexity is, it turns out, a very delicate instrument. This is made clear in the 38 single-spaced pages of the Draft Plan, in which no easy solutions are available and in which problems seem to intertwine in almost incestuous fashion. For instance: the students' shift in interest, well documented over the past five years or so, from general academic subjects to scientific, technological, and professional subjects—a seemingly innocent shift, one in tune with the changing economic times—has helped create parking problems, housing shortages, and overworked libraries.

How? Well, those students who have turned from the humanities to the sciences are now taking courses that offer fewer units of credit (even if the work required is equal to, or exceeds, what they were doing before the shift). Fewer units per student, spread over a fairly large number of students, brings down the average unit load. This wouldn't bother anyone except for the fact that state funding is apportioned in the basis of student unit loads—and when those averages decline, the University must add students. Or lose funds. Add students and you add strains on the facilities—including parking, housing, and the libraries.

The Draft Plan points out this problem and calls for the Academic Senate to reform and equalize the course-unit system.

Other problems, however, are not so clearly and simply attacked. These other problems are part and parcel of the new "shape" of education—the growth of the lower division—at Cal. Things have bogged down: students are taking fewer units, taking longer to graduate, graduating at lower rates, and dropping out at higher rates, especially during the first two years of study. In addition to the "revolving door" situation—more students coming in, fewer leaving four years later with a degree—there now exists, and will continue to exist, the long-awaited demographic decline, a drop in college-age students throughout the state and nation.

In order to keep its enrollment at a satisfactory level—both in quality and in quantity—Berkeley will have to more actively recruit and work to assimilate a different kind of student. A greater proportion of students in the years ahead will differ from Joe College not only in ethnic background but also in quality of academic preparation.

Predictions for the seven Bay Area counties that traditionally feed Cal show a changing ethnic mix in the years to come. By 1986, according to data in the Draft Plan, totals will change from current figures in the following way: Anglo graduating seniors will decline by 12 percent, Blacks will decline by 10 percent, Hispanic graduating students will be roughly the same in number, while Asian high school graduates will increase significantly—by 46 percent.

More significant, educators everywhere, including Cal, are beginning to meet in full force the "TV generation," students raised not on traditional cultural fare but on the more popular stuff available in the marketplace and, during the last decade, served up in the secondary schools. In the polite, but severe, words of the Draft Plan, a growing proportion of students arrive today "weak in their substantive preparation for intellectual work of high standard. Typically, they have only a rudimentary acquaintance with the literature and ideas that have shaped contemporary civilization."

Thus, a pattern emerges: larger numbers of poorly prepared students are entering Cal and finding the going—and the staying—rough. It is time, says the Draft Plan, to recognize what the lower division now is for more and more students: "a difficult and, for many students of all backgrounds, a traumatic transition between the often permissive and unstructured atmosphere of high school and the disciplined regime of major study."

One matter emphasized by the report is that there has been little "programmatic recognition" of the new shape of Cal's educational operation. For example, although the number of students has grown significantly, as have their academic problems, the proportion of regular faculty attention devoted to the lower division has not increased at all—in fact, in recent years it has dropped off slightly.

What is to be done? The Draft Long-Range Academic Plan Statement, which was purposely circulated to stimulate discussion and proposals, has a major proposal of its own. It calls for the creation of a new academic-administrative framework: a Division of Undergraduate Studies headed by an academic dean, assisted by an appropriate number of associate deans. "This division, which will parallel the Graduate Division, will assume responsibility for undergraduate student recruitment, admissions, advising, support service and educational development functions presently dispersed throughout the campus academic and student affairs units. It will also work with the principal academic officers with respect to lower division curricula and staffing."

The new Division, in short, would be charged with insuring that admissions standards and standards of educational performance after admission are maintained.

Thus: many problems, but the beginning of solutions. In a press conference called to prevent the Draft Plan, Vice Chancellor Heyman stressed the "draft" quality of the report—he hopes to hear about it—and also expressed buoyant optimism about the prospect of solving the problems his report outlines. "After all," he said, "there are a lot of very smart people around here."

8.5: Student Memoir: Rosa Maria Pegueros, "Todos Vuelven: From Potrero Hill to UCLA" (1995)

Whereas Russell Schoch's student profile presented in Document 8.4 relies on statistical databases, this document provides an excellent supplement and contrast: the perceptive memoir by a single student. Rosa Maria Pegueros, who received her PhD from UCLA, is professor of history at the University of Rhode Island specializing in modern Latin American history, particularly women's history. Her individual story is especially important in its attention to the kinds of experiences and issues that faced undergraduates who were the first in their family to go to college. An added benefit of her memoir is that she discusses geographic differences, as well as differences between her undergraduate years and subsequent experiences as a PhD student.

Todos vuelven. No importa lo lejos que estemos, siempre estamos con nuestro pais, con nuestra tierra en el alma, en la mente. (Ruben Blades)

(Everyone comes back. It makes no difference how far we wander, we always have our country, our land, in our souls and our minds.)

La Selva *(The Jungle)*

Vince and Richard became trash collectors like their fathers; Joe became a store manager for Sears; Bobby is now captain with the San Francisco Police Department; Ricky teaches high school. I was much too bookish for the boys I dated in high school; they married women who stayed at home. I became a lawyer and a historian.

Rosa Maria Pegueros, "Todos Vuelven: From Potrero Hill to UCLA," in C. L. Barney Dews and Carolyn Leste Law, eds., *This Fine Place So Far from Home: Voices of Academics from the Working Class* (Philadelphia: Temple University Press, 1995) pp. 87–105. Reprinted by permission of Rosa Maria Pegueros.

I was born in San Francisco and grew up on Potrero Hill in the eastern part of the city, south of Market Street. Market Street was known as "the slot" because it housed the underground cables for the trolleys. Running diagonally across the city, it has historically been the dividing line in San Francisco between the middle- and lower-class neighborhoods. South of Market is to San Francisco what the lower east side is to Manhattan. During the last ten years, Potrero Hill has been gentrified; gay people and young professionals have moved in to renovate the houses and open small businesses as industry has moved out of the city. During the 1950s when I was a child, The Hill was a working-class neighborhood along the bay waterfront, surrounded by the huge Kilpatrick and Langendorff bakeries, the Safeway coffee-packing plant, the Hexol disinfectant factory, the Hamm's brewery, the old Seal Baseball Stadium, as well as other factories, slaughterhouses, tuna canneries, and shipyards. Throughout my childhood, the stench from the slaughterhouses and canneries filled the air. It was impossible to get the fetid taste out of one's mouth. At night, we slept with the clamor of trains coupling noisily in the nearby train yards.

Whenever I rode the bus out of Potrero Hill, I would think to myself, "I'm going out of the jungle." To me, The Hill—my jungle—was safe and dark, thick with hardship, connections, and complexity. Beyond The Hill, the world was pellucid; it was if I were looking into a limpid pool where every fish, every anemone, every occupant of the deep was in clear view. I even thought that people with blue eyes could see things more clearly.

My earliest memory is of a sunny June day, sitting between my parents in the cab of the Atlas Paper Company truck as my father drove across the San Francisco Bay Bridge to Vallejo to deliver his load. I was five years old and had not yet started school. My father worried aloud because his teamsters' local was about to go on strike. My mother argued against his participation in the strike. She refused to understand that he, too, hated the picket line but that as shop steward, the nominal head of his union at his warehouse, there was no question that he would take part. I came to dread the month of June because it was always a time of worry, when the local's contract would be up and the union would vote to strike. My father would have to walk the hated picket line, and we would have to depend on our savings and the strike fund.

I grew up knowing that union membership meant we would have good health care and money for education. Christmas meant Santa and presents at the union hall; summer brought picnics sponsored by the local. We lived by one cardinal rule: We must never cross a picket line. I was so naive I believed that everyone respected it. Once, as an adult far removed from my father's gaze, I crossed the picket line at a movie theater. I felt so guilty that I have never done it again.

In those days, Potrero Hill was predominantly Italian. My friends were already second-generation San Franciscans; their grandparents had been immigrants. Unable to speak English, Mama felt snubbed by our Italian neighbors. Her response was to be insular, overprotective of her children, and critical of the few friends I brought to the house. I spoke little English when I started first grade at St. Teresa's School, but I had already taught myself to read from Spanish comic books. They had brightly colored cellophane covers and plots in which someone was always crying "¡Auxilio!" (Help!) My only Latina classmate, a girl whose parents, like my mother, came from Santa Ana, El Salvador, refused to speak Spanish and avoided me because I embarrassed her. Forbidden by the Irish immigrant Sisters to speak Spanish, I quickly learned English.

My father, who is Mexican American, had no relatives but his mother; I grew up surrounded by my mother's relatives and their friends in the Salvadoran immigrant community of San Francisco. While I was grounded in its rituals and mores, I knew little about my mother's family history until I was in graduate school and broke the taboo against inquiring into what had happened in El Salvador. As a child, I was discouraged by my mother and her family from asking questions; their reply to any inquiry was usually, "Why do you want to know? That is in the past." I had not even been told about the pivotal event in modern Salvadoran history, La Matanza, the massacre of thirty thousand Indians and peasants in the western provinces of El Salvador in 1932.

My great-grandfather, el abuelo (grandfather) Aurelio, was a highly educated man who fled his native Cuba at the turn of the century during the Spanish-American war. He settled in El Salvador after traveling throughout the world, earning his law degree, and becoming an architect along the way. Even though he was a Jew, he used his skills to build Santa Ana's cathedral, as well as a maternity hospital, theater, and other public buildings, and he brought the railroad to Santa Ana, the second largest city in the country. Mysteriously, his belongings, collected from travels all over the world, suddenly disappeared and the family was dispersed. As a child, I wondered what terrible calamity could have befallen this prosperous family to cause el abuelo's house to be emptied and razed. My great-grandfather's estate was lost long before I was born. During my childhood, my mother's family was poor though not starving. They had fled El Salvador for

Guatemala only to be caught there in the revolution of the late 1940s; a few years later, my mother and her sisters moved to San Francisco, leaving their mother and brothers in Guatemala.

They say that all beginnings are hard. My mother's arrival in San Francisco was no exception to this rule. Coming from a Guatemalan household where she had had a measure of comfort, she found herself running a sewing machine at the Levi Strauss factory. Fortunately, her sisters, both nurses, were soon employed at St. Joseph's Hospital in San Francisco, and they got her a job in the hospital cafeteria. She was not particularly happy at the hospital. The nursing Sisters, all German immigrants, were kind, but she hated the work. Within a short time after her arrival, she met and married my father.

My mother has had a hard life. Fleeing revolutions, she came to the United States to live the immigrant's dream, only to find that the streets were not paved with gold. Closely tied to her family, she saved every cent she could spare to send to them. We were never impoverished, but neither was anything wasted. Every outgrown item of clothing was packed into duffel bags and sent to Guatemala. My mother sent enough money to her brothers in Guatemala to put one through law school and to help her brothers with their educations.

My father's background was far more humble. My paternal grandmother, Carlota, fled Mexico during the Mexican Revolution; little is known of her family. She was a wily yet undisciplined woman who outlived five husbands in turn. I remember her as angry and abusive. My grandfather, a merchant seaman, seldom saw his only son; when he did, he beat him with whatever was at hand. He died in 1932 at the height of the Great Depression, when my father was only twelve years old. As the depression deepened, my grandmother could not earn enough to support herself and her son. After years of fishing off the San Francisco pier and raiding the trash cans behind grocery stores for wilted cabbage leaves that his mother would make into soup, Dad lied about his age to get a job as a truck driver. Until this day, my father cannot abide the smell of cabbage or fish: for him, they are the stench of poverty.

I am their oldest child. My mother was so ill during her pregnancy and after my birth that her doctor said she should have no more children, so for the first four and half years of my life, I was an only child. Then my younger brother was born and soon after a sister and another brother. The fact that there is such an age gap between my siblings and me, eleven years between me and my youngest brother, means that I had no allies as I was pushing at the borders of acceptable behavior for a Latina. Of course, there was no way to know if I would have had any help if we had been closer in age, but as it was, they were too young for me to be interested in them. We are far closer now as adults than we were as children.

To my family, I was an oddball: bookish, self-absorbed, reaching beyond my family to make friends with people who were different from anyone in our immediate circle, falling in love with classical music when I chanced to hear it. Both of my parents were bewildered by my love for books. My mother, blind in one eye and partially blind in the other from a childhood accident, uses her eyesight for sewing, crocheting, and other utilitarian handicrafts, but she seldom reads a book and only occasionally a newspaper. She often said to me, "You can't eat books; you can't marry books. What are you going to do with all those books?" They worried that my solitary devotion to learning would injure my health. "You'll get consumption!" an uncle once warned me.

My father, working twelve to fourteen hours a day for almost fifty years, had neither the time nor the energy to read. When he saw me reading, he fretted about my future. "Pegueros," he'd say, "I worry about you. You have no ambition; all you want to do is read." Still, they were persuaded by a door-to-door salesman to purchase an *Encyclopedia Britannica Jr.*, as well as the set of children's classics that came with it, including *Black Beauty*, *Treasure Island*, *Robinson Crusoe*, and a children's version of Shakespeare. These books whetted my appetite for more literary riches. After listening to me beg for months, my father took me to the public library when I was nine years old; it changed my life. If I was lacking a wide circle of friends, I was rich in my fantasy world. Language seemed to explode in my brain. I discovered *Grimm's Fairy Tales*, the wonders of science, and the comfort of poetry. I hurried to the library every day after school, neglecting my homework while I indulged myself in the treasures the library offered. The nuns would write concerned letters to my mother, but since she did not read English, I would write a response for her without showing her the missive. This continued until I was in the sixth grade and the Sisters determined that I was a discipline problem who should be kept back. I confounded them, however, when they gave us our first Stanford-Binet tests. My score was far above that of my classmates. The Sisters didn't know what to do with me, so they made me take them again.

The Sisters could hardly be blamed. Each teacher was assigned fifty children of differing capabilities and had to manage without teacher's aides, enrichment materials, or any of the modern-day accoutrements. They had neither time nor the training in pedagogy to ponder why one student never did her homework. I was bored; I had understood the lesson in class and had little need to reinforce it by doing the homework. The lure of the library books was too strong. Grudgingly promoted to the seventh grade, I had the luck to be assigned to a teacher who recognized my abilities, guided my reading, and enrolled me in classes for gifted children at a local public high school.

One of these, a summer class in journalism, sealed my fate. Never had I experienced anything so pleasurable as writing for publication. My identity began to come clear. I imagined myself a famous author. I even decorated a room—"my study"—in the basement with prints by Cézanne and Utrillo and slowly began to fill my bookshelves. I read anything the librarians would let me take home, from the best of children's literature to magazines like *Popular Mechanics* and *Scientific American*. By the time I graduated from St. Teresa's at age thirteen, I was a budding intellectual, loving books, ideas, and music to the exclusion of almost everything else.

Although I had always loved books, I was just beginning to realize that a university education was to be the fulfillment of my dreams, but to attain that goal, I had to do some basic planning. My choice, Presentation High School, was a college-preparatory school. It was across San Francisco, an hour's bus ride away from my home. Located on the edge of the infamous Haight-Ashbury district, it was adjacent to Lone Mountain College and the Jesuit-run University of San Francisco. My mother preferred that I go to a local Catholic girls' high school that was a mere fifteen-minute bus ride away, but its curriculum did not prepare its students for college. It was the first real test of my willingness to defy her. I locked myself in the basement and blockaded the door. I swore not to come out until she gave in. We screamed at each other through the door; I knew that I was earning a beating for myself by my obstinacy. I negotiated my conditions: no beating and the right to apply to the school of my choice. After a day, she gave in to me.

Presentation High School, a girls' school operated by the same order that ran my grammar school, the Sisters of the Presentation of the Blessed Virgin Mary, was better than I imagined. It was a world of women, free from the hormonally induced preening and posturing that goes on in a coeducational high school. The library was larger than our local public library. We were encouraged to excel in every area of our endeavor. It had a reputation for academic excellence. Eventually, I became editor of the high school newspaper and president of the speech club, winning prizes in oratory and debating tournaments throughout California. I learned photography and darkroom work. I had my first experiences doing political work when I helped one of our Sisters collect food for the nascent Farm Workers Union. Later, I worked on Bobby Kennedy's presidential campaign.

During my time there, I became acutely aware of class differences among my classmates. As a child, the phrase *working class* had puzzled me because all of the adults I had ever met worked for a living. *Old money, nouveau riche, capital gains, the stock market* had no meaning for me. That there existed an upper class that lived off the interest from inherited wealth or investments was simply beyond my imagination. Nor had I realized that there was a middle class that went to work every day and lived very comfortably from their income. In fact, when I watched the 1950s TV series *Leave It to Beaver*, the Cleaver family looked very wealthy to me. I used to wonder just how many rooms their house had. I had no clear idea what a den was for, except perhaps for the father to hide out from the rest of the family.

At Presentation, as at St. Teresa's, we were required to wear uniforms, and the Sisters also restricted other displays of wealth that could have set us apart. Nevertheless, making friends often brought the reality of class differences home to me. I remember my amazement when I went home with a friend after school, only to be driven home in her father's Mercedes. My father had never had a new car, and I had never seen a car with a polished wood dashboard and leather seats nor had I imagined such luxurious automobiles existed. I visited another friend whose house had plush wool carpets. I shall never forget the feeling of my feet sinking into the thick pile; for a few moments, I sprung gingerly forward and back until her mother saw me and asked what was wrong. Once I suffered the embarrassment of a friend being denied permission to come to my house because her mother said it was "on the wrong side of the tracks." Nonetheless, my academic success, aided by the strict determination of the Sisters to treat us impartially, led me to believe that I could earn a college degree.

While my father worked so his children would have the life he hadn't had, it never occurred to him a daughter would want anything more than a high school diploma. Thus, when I told my father that I was applying to college, he was stunned. Even though my parents had put us in Catholic schools because they did not trust the quality of the public schools, my decision to continue with my education was a surprise to both of them. My father cried as he told me that he didn't have the money to pay for any more schooling for me, but I had never expected him to pay for my college tuition. By the time I announced my intention to take the entrance exams, the librarian at our local public library gave me a job that would finance my college education.

The fire that destroyed Atlas Paper Company, my father's employer, on the day after I graduated from high school was a pivotal event in my life. I had not expected my father's financial support while I went to college, but the fire could have delayed or even ended my college plans until the family was again on its feet. I wept all that awful night, fearing that I would have to go to work full time, terrified that my dreams had gone up with the paper warehouse, and I worried about my family's survival. Fortunately, my father was given full-time work by a car-parking corporation. My worries were unfounded. However, since in 1968 there were student riots at San Francisco State University and at the University of California at Berkeley (Cal), he vetoed my decision to go to either of those state universities, leaving me only with the choice of the Jesuit-run University of San Francisco. While he was never able to help me with the tuition, I continued to live at home, and he did give me the money for my school books. I knew this meant a tremendous sacrifice for him, with my younger brothers and sister in Catholic schools all needing tuition, books, and school uniforms. He worked twelve hours a day, arriving home exhausted and covered with grease, but I never heard him complain or express the slightest resentment.

Mama was not happy about my choice. She worried that I would not make enough money to finance it and that going to college was an impractical decision. She urged me to take a secretarial or nursing course. Ultimately, faced with a personality as stubborn as her own, she grudgingly accepted my choice. Despite her opposition, my mother's dignity, frugality, and rectitude coupled with her belief in us enabled me to envision the unimaginable. Her brother in Guatemala had become a judge; my great-grandfather had been a lawyer and architect. Now she found herself defending my choice to her sisters and other immigrant friends, all of whose children went directly to work in blue-collar jobs upon graduating from high school. I was oblivious to the criticism. I never thought about my cousins or family friends or considered that I had chosen an unusual path. I just loved my books, loved learning, and loved to stay awake late at night to write essays and to create something original.

The University of San Francisco was across the street from my high school, but in many ways it was a world away. Presentation had seven hundred students; USF had several thousand. For the first time, I met non-Catholics, foreign students, and people of great wealth. I felt like a child in a candy store. Rather than focusing on attaining a good grade point average, I took classes in everything that had ever interested me.

I soon found that my twenty-hour-per-week library job was not enough to pay for the tuition, which was raised every semester I was in college. Within a short time, I was working in the library, holding a cafeteria job that gave me two meals a day, and grading papers for pay. I saved an additional fifteen cents a day by walking the two miles from the university to my job at the library instead of taking the bus. At the end of the month, I would have $3.50 to spend on a book— my splurge. My rigorous work schedule made it impossible for me to study very much.

I encountered some prejudice from my classmates, usually expressed in insinuations that I had displaced other, more qualified students. Most of my professors, the majority of whom were Jesuits, were bemused by me, but a few were openly hostile. Once, my Greek professor, in his cups, took it up himself to phone my father to tell him not to waste his money on my education because I would never be more than a C student. My father was devastated. In tears, he told the priest that he would have to take it up with me since I was paying my own tuition. I was hurt beyond words. The fragile acceptance I had won from my father for my academic work had nearly been destroyed by a drunken cleric.

Most of my teachers were supportive, however. My algebra professor, who was also the dean of students, secured a three-hundred-dollar scholarship for me from the American Business Women's Association, telling them that I really needed the money. Fortunately, he didn't tell them that while diligent, I was about the worst student of algebra he'd ever had. It was my only scholarship in college; I applied for no others because I thought they ought to be reserved for the truly needy. I don't suppose it ever occurred to me that I was about as needy as they got at that school. It was also a matter of pride. Having to endure snubs and snide remarks about "affirmative action students," even though I wasn't one, I declined to give my critics any ammunition.

Mostly Jesuits or unmarried men, our professors were generally gentle, loving souls who had a great deal of time for us. (I had only two women professors during my entire undergraduate education.) My happiest memories are of the long, rainy winter days in San Francisco, arguing over Plato or Aristotle in our tiny classes. The largest philosophy class numbered fifteen people. My favorite professor, Dr. Vincent Moran, was a bachelor, and he gave us much of his leisure time. His home, located two blocks from the university, was a haven for intellectual discussion, classical music, and good art. Never did I experience a hint of prejudice from him because I was a woman or a Latina. His greatest contribution to my education was his careful attention to my papers. I wanted to follow his footsteps, to earn my doctorate in philosophy at the Pontifical Institute of Medieval Studies at the University of Toronto, but my dreams had limits. I could not imagine how to finance such an ambition.

In an abortive attempt to fund my graduate school career, I enlisted in the United States Marine Corps. The recruiter gave me a written promise that I would be stationed in Germany for at least two years of my four-year enlistment. I reckoned that I would learn German, then stay on in Germany after my enlistment was up, using the GI Bill to earn a doctorate in philosophy at Heidelberg. I had to give up that dream when the Marines discovered that, unknown to me, I had arthritis. I had always thought that my legs hurt because of my running. Moreover, as I entered my senior year, I was warned by my department chair to forego the pursuit of an academic career because there were virtually no tenure-track positions available.

I was completely ignorant about the hierarchy among colleges. I had never heard of Harvard, Princeton, or Yale. In my naïveté, I thought that by going to USF, I had "made it." I didn't understand that even though its tuition seemed almost prohibitive to me and though it produced San Francisco's mayors and police chiefs, in the estimation of those in the ivory towers of academe it was a third-rate school. As a junior, I told Father Albert J. Smith, a Harvard alumnus and one of my mentors, that I wanted to do graduate work at Yale. He laughed. I was so wounded I could not even ask why he was laughing. His derision made me realize that in the great scheme of things, the University of San Francisco was not even a player. Father Smith had always been very kind to me, and I had always excelled in his classes. In retrospect, I realize that I cannot assess how much of his reaction was racism, classism, or sexism. Was he laughing because in 1970 there were no women professors in our philosophy department and few elsewhere? Was he laughing because USF couldn't compete with the academic superpowers? Was it because, despite my academic success, he could not imagine a Latina in the halls of an Ivy League school or because he knew I could never afford it?

He taught me a bitter lesson: Being working class means never knowing with certainty why someone is laughing at you. If you are a member of an ethnic minority, it is impossible to separate the disadvantages of class from those of race or ethnicity. If you are a woman, these considerations are further complicated by gender.

Throughout my undergraduate career, I struggled with the fact that my friends at UC-Berkeley or UC-Davis looked down their noses at USF. Since my education was so hard won, I wanted to believe that it was the best. Many of my professors had taught in the great European universities. If the most effective undergraduate education is in small classes where there is direct contact with the professors, why were the overcrowded state universities considered superior? During my five years at USF, I never had to attend a lecture with four hundred other students; my papers were graded and our classroom discussions led by professors rather than teaching assistants. It was ironic that I was at USF during the years when the state campuses were in continual turmoil due to the protests against the Vietnam war; there were threats to withdraw San Francisco State's accreditation, and Cal was on the verge of being shut down. Yet the intense, uninterrupted education I earned at USF was looked down upon when I applied to graduate school at UCLA in the early 1970s. It took years for me to understand that the reason USF was considered inferior to Stanford, UC, and the others is because universities are judged by the research conducted therein rather than by the effectiveness and caring of their teachers.

It is in this regard that I feel the most alienation from my profession, an alienation that arises from the values with which I was raised. While I enjoy research and writing, I place a greater value on teaching than on research. Much of the research that I see seems to me a waste of time, an exercise in hair splitting. Responsibility for educating the next generation is unimportant to many professors in the large research institutions because the priority placed on research is structural, and gifted teachers are seldom rewarded as generously as gifted researchers.

I believed it when my teachers told me I could pull myself up by my bootstraps, but I was misled, in a well-intentioned way, by the American credo of individualism as well as by the efforts of the nuns at the Catholic schools I attended. The Sisters at little St. Teresa's School and at Presentation High School did their best to minimize the class differences among us. Without a political consciousness, their teaching led us to believe that we faced "a level playing field." No one warned us that Mexican Americans, African Americans, and Native Americans had been systematically excluded from housing, employment, and higher education. When we failed, when we could not find housing or jobs, we blamed ourselves in the naive belief that we had only to work a little harder to grasp the brass ring. Despite pervasive rhetoric about a color-blind society, since my siblings and I entered the world of work, we have not been allowed to forget that we are Latinos. My sister Hilda works as a social worker in the San Francisco Department of Social Services, Children's Services Section. Her ability to speak Spanish is an essential part of her job. When my brother Manuel was in the Coast Guard, he was routinely berated by his commanding officer for being a "stupid beaner," a common anti-Mexican slur. After his enlistment was up, he joined the San Francisco Fire Department but stood to lose his job if white firefighters had succeeded in undoing the affirmative action program. My brother Kenneth scored very high in the written and physical examinations for the California Highway Patrol, but he was never called. I realize now that even though our teachers' encouragement was couched in rhetoric about excellence, their expectations for us were low. The bootstrap philosophy is entirely adequate if that is all you want. But if you aspire to something more than just making a working-class living, then pulling yourself up by the bootstraps rarely suffices by itself. I was fooled into believing that equality was the logical by-product of higher education. Now that I have become a university professor, with far more education than anyone from home, I struggle with the task of reconciling the standards expected of academics with my own values.

The Deep Blue Sea

I was twenty-two. I had earned a bachelor's degree, but I didn't have the means to get the doctorate that I coveted. It was then I moved to Los Angeles.

For all its cosmopolitan trappings, in some ways San Francisco is a small town masquerading as a big city. Born and raised in the city, I found it impossible to walk around without meeting an old friend or classmate, a relative or a neighbor. When you live in the city, there is little need to go outside of it. In describing this phase of my life, I am struck by the irony of being a San Franciscan choosing to leave the city where others come to find themselves; the city that was to others a place for freedom and openness was limiting for me, both because of the constraints of my Latino upbringing and the expectations of my working-class parents. I had to leave San Francisco as certainly as others flee Big Pine, Wyoming, or Wichita, Kansas.

When I left San Francisco, my life, which had been following an orderly, linear, if somewhat rocky road, changed dramatically. In attending college, I had chosen a road different from that chosen by my peers and different from what my parents had planned for me. In leaving the city to go to Los Angeles, I left roads altogether to explore the vast depths of the ocean that is Los Angeles. The summer of my twenty-third year, when I moved to Los Angeles, was the real beginning of my adulthood. I put down roots in Los Angeles and forged a circle of friends. Hot while San Francisco is cool and foggy, vast while San Francisco is small and manageable, choking with smog, cars, and people who are seldom at peace with each other, Los Angeles is a wonderful, terrible place. Free to travel anonymously, I could be whoever I chose to be; I could walk the streets in Westwood or Hollywood, never meeting a soul who knew me. Instead of having to share a bedroom with a sister who resented my books and my clutter, I could re-create myself in a little house with book-lined walls, live with whomever I chose, without a phone or a television. For the first time, I was in charge of my own life. Even a small choice, like my decision to buy a dog, was an occasion for celebration. In Los Angeles, I could be an individual instead of the protected eldest daughter of Latino immigrants. For the first time, as we say in California, I had my own space.

How does one distill twenty years of adulthood into a few paragraphs? I married, I bore a daughter, I graduated from law school but quickly quit the legal profession because I was completely unsuited for it. I became a card-carrying feminist and civil libertarian. I worked as a social worker with the homeless, and I was partially disabled for two years after being beaten by a policeman. I spend little time on that period on this essay because I lived this nesting time in a middle-class environment far from my working-class youth. It was an odyssey where I doggedly ran away from myself and everything that tied me to my working-class roots. I had converted to Judaism in college, and some time after moving to Los Angeles I married a Jew. It was the easiest thing in the world to drop my Hispanic surname to adopt his name. For a few years, I deepened my understanding of Jewish history and tradition by attending a variety of Jewish colleges. It was during that time that I fell in love with the study of history. Indeed, for a while, I practiced an Orthodox form of Judaism. Tradition gave me a way out. Of course, my father expected me to take my husband's name. As easily as I slipped out of my name, I slipped into a middle-class life. I strove to feel at ease with my new identity, and I thought that I had succeeded until Passover in 1977.

My husband, Yehuda Lev, and I were attending a Passover seder at the home of some very close friends. As is their custom, they had invited a large number of people to the seder, including some newcomers to the community whom they scarcely knew. I was seated between Yehuda and our host's father. Next to him sat a young woman, a social worker who worked in East Los Angeles, an old Mexican American community.

The social worker was complaining about her job to anyone who would listen. It was clear that she hated it in general and that she particularly detested her Mexican clients. She said that she was sick and tired of working with those dirty, lazy, greasy Mexicans who were always beating their wives and the women who were too stupid to leave them. Yehuda glanced at me with alarm; my friend's father squeezed my wrist gently under the table. It was Passover and I didn't want to make a scene, so I struggled to control myself. Then she turned to me and said, "Oh, you have such long, beautiful hair and such pretty dark eyes; are you Sephardic?"

Without raising my voice, I glared at her and replied stonily, "No, I'm Mexican. My father works twelve hours a day and has never hit my mother; my whole family bathes every day." Then I stood up and walked out.

Outside, gasping and crying in the cool spring air, I realized that I couldn't run away from who I was nor did I want to. I had taken what seemed to me the easy way out, allowing others to mistake me for generic Mediterranean. Shortly thereafter, I took back my own name—over my father's objections!—and set out to discover how to integrate my working-class past with my middle-class present.

My Passover dinner experience was bitter, not only because I was furious at hearing my own people degraded, but also because I held Jews in high regard. I had adopted Jewish culture, taking back for myself the religion of my great-grandfather. I love Jewish culture deeply, and it was this that enabled me to isolate that bigoted woman from my Judaism. Nevertheless, I had to find a way to integrate the two halves of myself.

The Elysian Fields

Education is learning to use the tools the race has found indispensable. (Josiah Royce)
[Legend engraved in the marble arch over the proscenium at Royce Hall at UCLA]

The University of California at Los Angeles is a splendid place. Standing on the terrace on the third floor of Royce Hall, I survey a campus that looks as though it could be in the Italian hills. The red-tiled roofs, the jacaranda trees with their delicate lavender blossoms, and Lombardine architecture lend power to this image. The physical beauty of the campus is a soporific that drugs you, making you forget the ugliness outside. In my program at UCLA, I found a real peer group. I was happy there.

I came to UCLA to become a historian. Modern women live to their eighties; at thirty-eight, when I started graduate school, I was squarely in middle age. If I were a nineteenth-century pioneer, I might be dead by this age. Instead, I am embarking upon a new career. Pursuing a doctorate in Latin American history long after the time, some would say, that I left the working class forces me to address questions that I thought were long settled.

As an older student, I experienced graduate school as a process of infantilization. I was told to trust my professors' judgment and came for a while to distrust my own. My economy of motion, developed by long experience, was undermined. Instead of doing only what needs to be done, graduate students are put through meaningless exercises and rituals, often for no better reason than that our professors had to do them. Yet the process is a socialization to a culture that is in a state of transition. The current "downsizing" of the university and the attrition of faculty due to aging mean that within a decade the university will have a very different appearance. Large numbers of women have acquired higher degrees. While the number of minority faculty is small, there are still many more of us than there were a decade ago.

Returning to school as adults, we find ourselves having to curb our disagreements with the administration or with powerful professors because outspokenness could bring punitive "ratings" (the system by which assistantships and fellowships are determined) or denial of access to academic jobs or funding. Some of us are veterans of struggles for civil rights and/or civil liberties, but we are denied access to our own files because of an archaic system that values secrecy over the civil rights of a student to know who is judging him or her and what is being said. I came back to school as a confident adult, secure in my ability to manage a life balanced between work and love, only to have my priorities questioned and even displaced by a profession that places little importance on being a successful *person*.

As a mother, I found it particularly frustrating that, in order to maintain my academic credibility, I almost had to keep my daughter in the closet. When it became known that I had a child, one of my professors gave me an evaluation that criticized my "inability" to devote myself wholeheartedly to the historical profession—this because I had to leave a seminar immediately at the end of class to pick up my daughter from day care. On another occasion, a professor criticized me for devoting too much time to extracurricular activities such as taking care of my daughter. I have noticed that young women without children or older women whose children are grown get more support from their professors than women with children at home. Furthermore, I have never heard the extracurricular activities of any of my male classmates criticized in their evaluations. Presumably a devotion to racquetball or chasing women is above reproach.

Nevertheless I have been fortunate. My entire graduate career has been financed by the University of California. I have had research and teaching assistantships in the History Department and in the women's studies program and fellowships of various kinds. I have also had the solid backing of my committee. Moreover, I have had my husband's love as well as his moral and financial support. I believe that my law degree helped me in the eyes of those making the decisions, in addition to helping me to develop the tenacity to endure despite many bureaucratic obstacles to success. But other Latinas have not had my good luck.

While the university administration worries aloud about "minority retention," little, it appears to me, is done about it, if the rate of attrition among Latinas in my department is any measure. The university is designed to "help those who help themselves." Unfortunately, this is a culturally biased issue. Little is done by the university to help people of color to adapt to the graduate school or to stay there when the pressures from home are overpowering. I have had several Latina students ask me for advice because they were being subjected to overwhelming pressure from their families to contribute to the family income. University officials forget that success is predicated not only on native ability and hard work but also on a supportive home environment and a hospitable atmosphere at school. As a Latina, I have enjoyed the official approval of the administration as evidenced by the financial support for my work, but I have seen little personal support from professors, particularly male professors, or in support services from the university. To be fair to UCLA, there is a limit to what the university can be expected to do for adults. But in light of its willingness to impose other rules—for instance, requiring the recipients of student loans to come to a meeting explaining their obligations—I do not understand why there is not a more active effort to help its minority and working-class graduate students.

One of the biggest personal obstacles I faced in pursuing my education was my deep reluctance to incur debt. The middle and upper classes are accustomed to manipulating debt to their advantage, but for a working-class person debt is a ball and chain. My father has always paid his bills in cash or has used credit cards only to pay them off monthly. He so feared debt that he refused even to take out a veteran's home loan. The house my parents own was left to them by his mother. While I am aware that many of his friends owe several thousand dollars in educational loans, I was terrified of incurring such debt.

The other obstacle I encountered in graduate school was the resentment of some of my classmates. Over the years, pointed articles against affirmative action were left anonymously in my mailbox in the history department. Many of my women colleagues (not women in my own field, however) have expressed their anger that there "just isn't anything [funding, jobs] out there unless you're a minority." Once, waiting for an elevator, I overheard a discussion carried out in stage whispers between two graduate students in medieval European history. "Oh, I had two good interviews, but I'll never get a job," said one. "There are just too many minorities and women after these positions." I bit my tongue to keep from asking him how many Mexican medievalists he knew. One classmate has told me many times in both subtle and overt ways that he doesn't expect to find a good job because he's "just a historian, not a specialist in African history before the Civil War or some such rot." Another male graduate student in our department complained recently that he had lost a second job to "an affirmative action hire." I suppose the affirmative action candidate was to blame when he failed to fulfill his contract by not finishing his dissertation. This kind of hostility and harassment has forced other Latino scholars out of academe. In truth, the university has traditionally expressed all sorts of preferences, for example, for veterans, for athletes, or for the children of alumni. I believe that increasing the number of minority and working-class faculty is a valid goal, and I will not allow myself to be harassed out of a dream that I have had all my life.

Society benefits when all social classes are represented in higher education. While we all aspire to a higher standard of living, not everyone has the opportunity to make large amounts of money in our chosen life's work, nor is higher education a guarantee of higher wages. A professor who understands only those students from comfortable circumstances will seldom do justice to those whose struggle for education is the end of a long and difficult road. The participation of working-class and minority faculty in higher education assures that the university reflects the diversity of viewpoints found in the society at large.

My circle of graduate students created its own support network. Most of the women are from working-class backgrounds. Four of us are Latinas, three are Jewish (two of the Latinas are Jews, one by choice), and one is of Central European /

French/Native American origin. During our years in graduate school, we shared our joys and frustrations, joined together to face difficulties, held teaching assistantships at the same time and shared our resources, coached each other through examinations, and critiqued our dissertations as they were being written. We believe that our ad hoc support system made it easier for us to succeed. The university's insensitivity to the needs of nontraditional students, the low priority it has given to the special issues they present, and its ineptitude in dealing with diversity doomed the others. Without a good support system, they dropped out.

When I was first in graduate school and I railed against the hierarchical nature of the university, one of my professors, a woman, told me, "But you CHOSE this. This is the way it is." It's true that I chose a life of learning; I *didn't* choose the medieval autocracy that goes with it. Before I started at UCLA, I had thought that the greatest difficulty I would face in graduate school would be learning to study again. Even though I had street smarts from working as a social worker with homeless people and from studying law, nothing prepared me for the labyrinth of academic politics. The political questions that I face arise not from the work of research and writing, with which I became adept as a lawyer, but from the experience of maneuvering through the maze and from teaching a college class as an academic from the working class.

I am no longer the naive working-class girl that I was at seventeen. My education, values, and choice of leisure pursuits are far removed from those of my family and the milieu from which I came, but the values and experiences that inform my thinking are solidly working class. When I step into the voting booth, my choices reflect my lifelong bond with the labor movement, my commitment to feminism, and my concerns about poor and working people, not out of altruism but because in my heart I continue to be the teamster's daughter who won't cross a picket line and who worries about strikes every June, the parking lot manager's daughter who was too proud to apply for a college scholarship, the Catholic schoolgirl whose opportunities were created by the Sisters and an all-girls high school.

While I was a graduate student, dependent upon grants that were announced in June for the next year's livelihood, June was always an anxious time. It was in graduate school that I recognized the characteristics that distinguish the working class from the middle class. The first of these is the middle class's material security. Even when it is having cash-flow problems, the middle class always knows that there will be money for essentials, for plentiful food on the table and a home that's big enough for one's family. There may not be enough for the trip to Europe—this year—but eventually it will work out. In my family, there were never any leftovers because our food had been carefully rationed. Trips to Europe, new cars, expensive jewelry were for other people, not for us.

Applying for grants, I was acutely aware of the items that were missing from my applications. For instance, my middle-class colleagues could point to a year's study in Mexico during college when their interest in our field was sparked by a particular experience. Others could point to travels in Central and South America with their parents. A close friend of mine reported attending a national meeting of the recipients of a major grant; all of them, herself included, were the children of academics. She jokes that as an adolescent she rebelled by going to Brown University instead of Harvard. I wish I'd had that choice.

Middle-class people are not at the mercy of the system in important life decisions, but we were faced with the choice of attending a poor public school or squeezing every penny to attend a slightly less poor Catholic school. We went to the Catholic school and received an education that made it possible for us to be upwardly mobile. Manipulating the system is a given for the middle-class. If there had been magnet schools when I was a child, we wouldn't have known about them.

As a college student, I didn't apply for a scholarship because I thought that financial aid was scarce and that it should be kept for the "truly needy." I didn't realize that anyone needier than I was would not have had the education to qualify for the university in the first place. At UCLA, I saw that the attitude of my mostly middle-class students was quite different from what mine was as a student. They believed they were entitled to support and complained bitterly when it was not forthcoming; I was always insecure about my right to higher education. As a graduate student, I knew that if the university ceased to fund me, it would be nearly impossible for me to finish my doctorate.

Being working-class, I always felt that I was in the university at the sufferance of others, as if I should apologize for filling the space. Later, as an instructor in a college classroom, I was sensitive to the shy working-class students who believed deep down that they didn't belong in it. When I took these students aside, shared my own struggles with them and urged them to utilize the remedial tutoring services offered by the university, I understood the pride that kept them from availing themselves of those programs. They trusted me because they knew that I know what it's like. Nevertheless, I maintained good relations with my non-Latino, non-working-class students. No one chooses the class into which she or he is born. Why should students born into comfort or even wealth and privilege be resented or disparaged? Seeing me as their teacher was a lesson in itself. Furthermore, I wanted to teach them that what they might do with their wealth and privilege is more important than living a comfortable and unexamined life.

I share the memory of having slept in the same bed with all my siblings; I know what it feels like to want desperately to get an education when all your friends are already working at adult jobs; I have written my school papers on a noisy manual typewriter late at night in a room where my sister was trying to sleep. I understand the Latina women who face pressure from families who don't understand why they are going to school when they could be out working and contributing to the family income.

Like my parents, my greatest commitment is to see that my daughter receives a first-rate education. Toward that end, we sent her to a Jewish day school that is known for its academic excellence. It is very American, I'm told, to want for one's children better lives than we had ourselves. But my working-class background makes me yearn for something more. I want all of our young people to have better lives. I believe deeply that our society should make decent education for all children one of its highest priorities. Through my teaching, I intend to do my part.

I do not want anyone to think that I would have traded one minute of my long pursuit of an education for someone else's easier life. I am nobody's victim. I would have liked guideposts and role models along the way (it would have been less scary), but I prevailed even without them. I look upon my experience as a boxer regards the miles of running, the hours of pounding a punching bag, and the years of sparring with partners in a ring. Having to work so hard and come so far has made my resolve rock-hard. I know who I am and what I believe. When I stand before my students, they learn that hard work can lead to triumph. Marriage and education have changed the material conditions of my life, but they cannot change my internal landscape. They cannot take from me the lessons I learned on the way to my doctorate. My lifestyle may be middle class, but my heart and soul are Latina and working class. I want to offer the benefit of my experience to young people who come from circumstances like my own as well as to those who have known only privilege.

Novelist Henry James once told his sister-in-law, "Tell them to follow, to be faithful, to take me seriously" (Edel 554). Artists, musicians, and academics who emerge from the working class have a particular tentativeness, a special need to be taken seriously. I have come a long way from the boys on the hill, the factories, and the slaughterhouses, but I am never quite sure that I am being taken seriously. These days, ensconced in my tenure-track job in New England, so far from home, I am living the dream I dared to dream while hoping that I will someday feel as comfortable on an academic panel as in my kitchen.

8.6: College Sports Reform: The 1991 Knight Commission Report

College sports continued to surge as a highly publicized and commercialized activity between 1970 and 2000. It also was a campus activity with soaring expenses, surpassing revenues even at many high-powered programs that enjoyed sellout crowds. Problems of fiscal fitness were mild headaches, however, compared to the inability of academic leaders, including presidents, to provide an educational or ethical compass for these extravagant varsity sports teams. The Knight Foundation's Commission, headed by former newspaper editor Creed Black, brought together numerous nationwide constituencies to rekindle serious consideration of reform. The 1991 report, *Keeping Faith with the Student-Athlete*, at the very least represented a groundswell of support to restore presidents to their rightful place as institutional representatives—and perhaps as institutional leaders—within the National Collegiate Athletic Association deliberations. And, as the Knight Commission report title suggests, the concurrent aim was to try to bring college sports back into the domain of being a genuine student activity. All this attention and concern tended to affirm the warning that not all problems have solutions.

Introduction

At their best, which is most of the time, intercollegiate athletics provide millions of people—athletes, undergraduates, alumni and the general public—with great pleasure, the spectacle of extraordinary effort and physical grace, the excitement of an outcome in doubt, and a shared unifying experience. Thousands of men and women in the United States are stronger adults because of the challenges they mastered as young athletes.

But at their worst, big-time college athletics appear to have lost their bearings. With increasing frequency they threaten to overwhelm the universities in whose

Knight Commission Report, *Keeping Faith with the Student-Athlete: A New Model for Intercollegiate Athletics* (March 1991). Reprinted by permission of the Trustees of the Knight Foundation.

name they were established and to undermine the integrity of one of our fundamental national institutions: higher education.

The Knight Commission believes that intercollegiate athletics, kept in perspective, are an important part of college life. We are encouraged by the energy of the reform movement now under way. But the clamor for reform and the distinguishing signals of government intrusion confirm the need to rethink the management and fundamental premises of intercollegiate athletics.

The Commission's bedrock conviction is that university presidents are the key to successful reform. They must be in charge—and be *understood* to be in charge—on campuses, in conferences and in the decision-making councils of the NCAA.

We propose what we call the "one-plus-three" model, a new structure of reform in which the "one"—presidential control—is directed toward the "three"—academic integrity, financial integrity and independent certification. With such a model in place, higher education can address all of the subordinate difficulties in college sports. Without such a model, athletics reform will continue in fits and starts, its energy squandered on symptoms, the underlying problems ignored.

This is how these recommendations can help change college sports:

Presidential Control

1. Trustees will delegate to the president—not reserve for the board or individual members of the board—the administrative authority to govern the athletics program.
2. Presidents will have the same degree of control over athletics that they exercise elsewhere in the university, including the authority to hire, evaluate and terminate athletics directors and coaches, and to oversee all financial matters in their athletics departments.
3. The policy role of presidents will be enhanced throughout the decision-making structures of the NCAA.
4. Trustees, alumni and local boosters will defer to presidential control.

Academic Integrity

1. Cutting academic corners in order to admit athletes will not be tolerated. Student-athletes will not be admitted unless they are likely, in the judgment of academic officials, to graduate. Junior college transfers will be given no leeway in fulfilling eligibility requirements.

2. "No Pass, No Play" will be the byword of college sports in admissions, academic progress and graduation rates.
3. An athlete's eligibility each year, and each academic term, will be based on continuous progress toward graduation within five years of enrollment.
4. Graduation rates of student-athletes in each sport will be similar to the graduation rates of other students who have spent comparable time as full-time students.

Financial Integrity

1. Athletics departments will not operate as independent subsidiaries of the university. All funds raised and spent for athletics will go through the university's central financial controls and will be subject to the same oversight and scrutiny as funds in other departments. Athletics foundations and booster clubs will not be permitted to provide support for athletics programs outside the administration's direct control.
2. Contracts for athletics-related outside income of coaches and administrators, including shoe and equipment contracts, will be negotiated through the university.
3. Institutional funds can be spent on athletics programs. This will affirm the legitimate role of athletics on campus and can relieve some of the pressure on revenue-producing teams to support non-revenue sports.

Certification

1. Each year, every NCAA institution will undergo a thorough, independent audit of all academic and financial matters related to athletics.
2. Universities will have to withstand the scrutiny of their peers. Each NCAA institution awarding athletics aid will be required to participate in a comprehensive certification program. This program will verify that the athletics department follows institutional goals, that its fiscal controls are sound, and that athletes in each sport resemble the rest of the student body in admissions, academic progress and graduation rates.

The reforms proposed above are designed to strengthen the bonds that connect student, sport and higher learning. Student-athletes should compete successfully in the classroom as well as on the playing field and, insofar as possible, should be indistinguishable from other undergraduates. All athletes—men or women, majority or minority, in revenue-producing and non-revenue sports—should be treated equitably.

In order to help presidents put the "one-plus-three" model into effect, the Commission proposes a statement of principles to be used as the basis for intensive discussion at each institution. Our hope is that this discussion will involve everyone on the campus with major responsibilities for college sports. These principles support the "one-plus-three" model and can be employed as a starting point on any campus wishing to take the recommendations of this document seriously. We recommend incorporating these principles into the NCAA's certification process and using that process as the foundation of a nationwide effort to advance athletics reform. Ideally, institutions will agree to schedule only those colleges and universities that have passed all aspects of the certification process. Institutions that refuse to correct deficiencies will find themselves isolated by the vast majority of administrators who support intercollegiate sports as an honorable tradition in college life.

CHAPTER NINE

A New Life Begins?

Reconfiguring Higher Education in the Twenty-First Century

During the first decade of the twenty-first century, American colleges and universities balanced the abundance of growing enrollments, international acclaim for advanced research and scholarship, and immense popularity of varsity sports competition with persistent problems of financial strains, legal disputes, and incomplete achievements in social justice and equity. Student loan debt combined with rising prices of tuition dampened the optimism of affordability that had been central to the national agenda for the preceding half century. These national trends were juxtaposed against images of and information about changes in higher education elsewhere. Universities in the United States remained high in all worldwide rankings, yet the relative gains in quantity and quality of universities in Europe and Asia injected seeds of doubt into the American higher education community about its primacy. Some of this angst was unwarranted overreaction. Given that higher education in the United States had been spared the disruption as well as destruction that faced universities in many nations during World War II, it was reasonable (if not inevitable) that over time higher education in these afflicted nations would show signs of recovery—and, hence, gains in relative standing with universities in the United States. For decades the United States, through federal programs and philanthropic foundations, had sponsored exchanges, visiting fellowships, and numerous initiatives that deliberately promoted improvements in universities in many nations, characterized by goodwill and cooperation with universities in the United States. Hence, it was good news that a genuine international community of scholars often hosted and promoted by the United States led to higher education growth and success internationally.

Testimony to the innovation and vigor of higher education in the United States was that between 1990 and 2010 many developing nations adopted the templates of the 1960 California Master Plan for their own national policies and planning. In making such belated transplants, ministers of education outside the United States often overlooked subsequent developments in California related to the original Master Plan—namely, initial enthusiasm for the quest to combine excellence with mass and universal higher education was followed by disappointments and decreased funding. The corollary was that great expectations for the California Master Plan were eventually accompanied by some tapering in support from taxpayers and legislators at the state and national levels. Outside the United States, innovations such as the Bologna Process and the Erasmus Plan in Europe indicated some gratitude to the United States for its support and examples—along with the reminder that there was little room for colleges and universities in the United States to be complacent.

9.1: College Spending in a Turbulent Decade: Findings from the Delta Cost Project, 2000–2010

In contrast to the optimism and prosperity that translated into generous funding for higher education after World War II, a theme at the start of the twenty-first century was that colleges and universities faced a bleak future in terms of public support from state governments and taxpayers. The problem was exacerbated by rising costs of higher education which surpassed the rate of inflation year after year. Although public higher education was the sector most threatened by these trends, all colleges and universities focused on strategies to increase revenue streams, whether by raising tuition, increasing private fund-raising, or lobbying for enhanced state support. The gravity of the financial situation was fueled by competition among institutional categories—including the addition of a growing, confident group of for-profit colleges. The Delta Cost Project of the American Institutes for Research contributed several reports that were central to policy deliberations at the state and national levels. Their particular value was that analysis was no longer confined to a single campus or disparate, fragmented information. These reports were comprehensive and systematic, covering higher education nationwide. One problematic trend was that each year, many institutions spent

College Spending in a Turbulent Decade: Findings from the Delta Cost Project; A Delta Data Update, 2000–2010 (Washington, DC: American Institutes for Research, 2012). Reprinted by permission of the Delta Cost Project of the American Institutes for Research.

an increasing percentage of revenue dollars on noninstructional costs. Colleges and universities in the United States took justifiable pride in their resilience and innovation that succeeded in attracting funding. However, by 2012 the viability of these approaches was met with increasing concerns as to whether the familiar models of financing higher education, public and private, were sustainable.

Two years after the onset of the Great Recession, nonprofit colleges and universities found themselves struggling with their finances. Average per-student spending on academics declined in fiscal year (FY) 2010, and despite per-student spending cuts to prerecession levels at four-year institutions, students shouldered a larger share of the cost this time around. Even in private nonprofit colleges, average educational spending per student declined for the first time in a decade. However, it is higher education's most accessible institutions—community colleges—that took the greatest financial hit in 2010. As funding failed to keep pace with historic increases in enrollment, educational spending per student plummeted to its lowest level in a decade.

These are some of the key findings in this annual update to the Delta Cost Project's Trends in College Spending report series—a series of data briefs highlighting patterns and trends in institutional revenues, spending, subsidies, and outcomes for public and private nonprofit colleges and universities between 2000 and 2010, with particular attention given to changes between 2009 and 2010.

Across higher education, 2010 was indeed a difficult year, with effects of the recent recession widely apparent. Huge enrollment increases took a toll on institutional resources, and even when aggregate revenues and spending increased, colleges and universities often found themselves serving more students with less. The findings show that:

Community colleges suffered the greatest financial hardships in 2010. Historic enrollment increases, combined with sharp losses in per-student revenues from state appropriations and meager increases in net tuition revenue, resulted in significant cuts to academic spending per full-time equivalent (FTE) student. Community colleges concluded the decade spending less per student than they had ten years earlier.

All types of institutions spent less on the academic mission in 2010, but cuts in public four-year institutions appeared more strategic than those in the private nonprofit sector. Education and related spending declined, on average, across all types of public and private institutions from 2009 to 2010. But public four-year institutions were largely able to preserve spending on instruction and student services, while private institutions implemented widespread cuts.

Historic declines in state and local funding per FTE student could not be recouped by increases in net tuition. Public funding per student for higher education reached a decade-long low in 2010. Sharp increases in net tuition revenues were not enough to offset these losses, and for the first time, public research and master's institutions generated more revenue from net tuition than from state and local appropriations.

Private institutions constrained education spending for the first time in a decade, even as their revenues continued to increase. Despite a strong rebound from sharp investment portfolio losses in 2009, all types of private nonprofit institutions spent less on average education and related expenditures in 2010. Even well-funded private research universities, which historically have remained insulated from the economic realities affecting other institutions, were not immune from cutbacks in 2010.

Institutional subsidies reached a decade-long low across most types of institutions, as students covered a larger portion of educational costs. Students at public four-year institutions paid roughly half toward the full cost of education. At private institutions, the student share of costs jumped sharply, in contrast to smaller annual increases across most of the decade.

Colleges and universities did not increase degree productivity—nor degree production costs—in 2010. Though degree productivity was flat or declining in 2010, it has improved since the beginning of the decade at four-year institutions; but so has the cost per degree.

Enrollments

Enrollments were woven into much of the back story of higher education finance in 2010. As often occurs in economic downturns, postsecondary enrollments swelled as traditional college-age students and experienced workers facing a difficult labor market turned to colleges and universities to improve their skills and earn new credentials.

Postsecondary enrollments increased substantially in 2010, often at rates not seen in the previous ten years. Although FTE enrollments increased much faster than average at most types of public and private four-year institutions (2.5 percent to 3.5 percent), the majority of new students selected colleges offering easy access and affordability. Public bachelor's institutions grew twice as fast as other four-year institutions. Because of their small market share, however, they enrolled far fewer new students.

Community colleges, with their open admission policies and abundance of short-term certificate programs, accommodated the most new students in higher education, adding 450,000 new FTE students in 2010. Single-year FTE enrollments rose an average of 12 percent, which is nearly twice the rate observed for community colleges in any other year during the previous decade. Only two- and four-year for-profit institutions grew faster than did community colleges (26 percent), but they added fewer new students.

Revenues: Where Does the Money Come From?

Top-line revenues often obscure what is actually going on within institutions. Colleges and universities are multi-function enterprises that draw in revenues from various sources (such as tuition, grants, contracts, and auxiliary services like bookstores and dining halls). Many of these revenues, however, are earmarked for purposes other than academics.

Funding for the academic mission of colleges and universities declined at public four-year institutions in 2010, even though total revenues were steady or rising. At public institutions, most funding for academics comes from tuition and state and local appropriations. Combined revenue from these two sources declined in 2010 by an average of 2 percent to 5 percent at public four-year institutions compared to a year earlier. Meanwhile, revenues from other university functions (including contracts and grants and auxiliary enterprises) increased, which boosted the bottom line even though these funds are typically unavailable for general instruction.

Public institutions faced historic declines in state and local appropriations per student in 2010. For the second consecutive year, public colleges and universities were operating with less state money when measured on a per-student basis. But the cuts in FY 2010 were much larger than in other years during the decade, averaging single-year declines of 9 percent to 13 percent at public four-year institutions and 15 percent at public community colleges. These declines, which averaged between $600 and $1,000 per student, resulted in the lowest per-student state and local funding in the decade across all types of public institutions.

For the first time in higher education, net tuition brought in more revenue than did state and local appropriations at the average public research and master's institutions. In response to declining state and local appropriations, net tuition revenue per student rose sharply at public four-year institutions in 2010 (5 percent to 7 percent, on average), roughly double the increases in many recent years. Nevertheless, net tuition rose more slowly in 2010 than it did following the 2001 recession, and it did not increase enough to offset losses in state and local appropriations.

Funding from state and local appropriations is cyclical, but the overall trend presses downward. Just a decade ago, public funds for higher education exceeded tuition revenues from students by roughly $3,000 to $5,000 per student; but by 2010, the gap between state appropriations and tuition had shrunk to roughly $500 per student in public four-year institutions.

Funding for community colleges continued to fall further behind other public institutions. Top-line revenues were unable to disguise the long-standing financial difficulties faced by community colleges. They were the only public institutions at which average total operating revenues per FTE student declined in 2010 and *also* were lower than a decade earlier. Community colleges suffered the deepest cuts in state and local appropriations per student in 2010, with funding reduced by approximately $1,000 per student; however, they also limited the new money coming from net tuition revenue more than did other types of public institutions. Efforts to keep community colleges accessible and affordable while accommodating more than 40 percent of new higher education students—often the most economically or academically disadvantaged—have significantly eroded the resources they have to devote to each student.

Private nonprofit colleges and universities regained their footing in 2010 as financial markets recovered and their investment returns once again turned positive. Private nonprofit institutions recovered from a difficult year in 2009, as the average investment portfolio made a significant turnaround and contributed to large increases in total operating revenues for 2010. However, these gains may not have fully erased prior losses which may have had implications for spending. Nevertheless, much of the fluctuation in portfolio income represented "paper" gains and losses, and the impact on annual operating budgets was probably smaller than it appeared.

Excluding these volatile investment returns, operating revenues at private nonprofit institutions grew between 1 percent and 2 percent in 2010, which is generally consistent with past increases. Private master's and bachelor's institutions received much of their new revenue from increases in net tuition, while private research institutions instead relied upon grants, contracts, and revenue from auxiliary enterprises and other sources.

Spending: Where Does the Money Go?

Educating students is the common thread that weaves across all colleges and universities, but it takes more than just faculty to run institutions. Student services (such as admissions, registrar services, and student counseling) are often key to a successful college experience. And other support functions (including academic and institutional support and operations and maintenance) contribute indirectly by providing an infrastructure that supports learning. Institutions may also engage in sponsored research and public service activities or in hosted auxiliary operations, such as food service, book stores, and sometimes even hospitals.

By isolating spending related to higher education's academic mission, it is easier to make reasonable comparisons across institutions. Education and related spending (E&R) is the common metric used to measure the full "production cost" of education, capturing only spending related to academics. Total spending includes all university functions, while education and general spending (E&G) includes all spending except that for auxiliaries, hospitals, and other independent operations.

All types of institutions cut average spending on the academic mission in 2010. The 2010 E&R spending declines were the first cuts that public four-year institutions experienced since the 2008 recession began. E&R spending per FTE student declined by an average of 1 percent to 2 percent across public and private four-year institutions in 2010, bringing spending back to roughly 2007 and 2008 levels. It is not unusual to observe a delayed financial impact from an economic downturn, which could persist for several years; similar patterns of reduced spending were evident after the 2001 recession.

Community colleges experienced per-student cuts for the second consecutive year, though the 8 percent decline in 2010 was far more severe than the reduction of the year before (2 percent). These cuts brought average community college E&R spending to its lowest point in a decade.

Private nonprofit institutions also cut spending in 2010, which was unprecedented over the previous decade. But these cuts were also unexpected because private nonprofit institutions' revenues continued to increase in 2010. The pull-back in spending was perhaps related to broader concerns about the economy or to the significant hit these institutions' investment portfolios took in the prior year.

Spending cuts at public four-year institutions appeared more strategic than were the widespread cuts implemented at private institutions. Facing budgetary pressures in 2010, public four-year institutions typically preserved spending on those functions directly related to students' education—including instruction, student services, and academic support—while cutting spending in other "overhead" functions, such as operations and maintenance and institutional support. However, the severe funding deficits faced by community colleges contributed to widespread cuts across all categories of institutional spending.

Private institutions were less strategic than were their public sector counterparts and largely cut spending across the board—despite increased revenues. The academic mission was not protected, with spending on instruction cut by 1 percent to 2 percent and with spending on student services holding steady or declining. Sponsored research, which is typically financed through external grants and contracts, was spared cuts.

For most of the decade, the portion of educational spending devoted to instruction declined; but it increased at public institutions in 2010. Even though public and private four-year institutions have, on average, made new investments in instruction, student services, and overhead since the beginning of the decade, the relative weight of these investments has gradually shifted. Over most of the decade, the instruction share of E&R spending declined, on average, across institutions. Private institutions typically offset this decline with investments in student services, while public institutions offset reduced educational spending on instruction with related spending increases for student services and overhead (public bachelor's and community colleges shifted more to overhead; research and master's institutions favored student services).

With widespread declines in E&R in 2010—particularly in terms of support functions—institutions devoted a larger share of spending to both instruction and students services, rather than to overhead functions. Public institutions favored instruction over student services, while private nonprofit institutions continued to shift a large share of spending to student services.

Total expenditures increased at public four-year institutions, boosted in part by spending on research and auxiliaries; but total spending declined at private nonprofit institutions. Again, top-line spending trends can sometimes be deceptive. Although E&R spending declined across higher education, at public four-year institutions broader measures of spending (total operating costs and E&G) held steady or rose in 2010. Spending on research and/or auxiliaries seems to account for the boost. Spending on the public service mission has continued to sustain a decade-long decline across all types of institutions except research universities. At private institutions, spending was lower in 2010 regardless of the granularity at which it was observed.

Only community colleges spent less per student at the end of the decade on nearly all spending measures. Most types of institutions spent more on E&R, E&G, and total operating expenses in 2010 compared to five years before, when institutions were still recovering from the fallout of the 2001 recession. Community colleges, however, were the only group of institutions spending less per student, on average, on each of these aggregate spending measures by the end of the decade. Community colleges also spent less in nearly all standard expenditure categories compared to 2000.

Higher Education Subsidies

The full production cost of providing an education is typically a shared expense, funded partly through student tuitions and partly from institutional subsidies. At public institutions, these subsidies come from state and local appropriations; at private institutions, they come from other institutional resources, such as gifts, grants, and endowments.

Students across higher education continued to pay a larger share of the full cost of education in 2010, with private institutions showing the largest subsidy shift in a decade. Students have traditionally paid a majority of the full educational costs at private colleges and universities. But as a consequence of rising tuition revenues and declining E&R, the average net tuition share of costs jumped significantly at those institutions in 2010 (by 2–3 percentage points; see Figure 3), far exceeding increases in most of the previous ten years (except 2004). Though increases were even larger at public institutions, both in dollars and proportion (averaging 3–4 percentage points), the increases were generally smaller than those seen following the 2001 recession.

In just a decade, the share of educational costs paid by students at public institutions has increased sharply. At public four-year institutions, students paid roughly half of the full E&R cost in 2010, a 15–18 percentage point increase since

2000; students at community colleges faced smaller proportional increases over the decade, paying a little more than one third of the full E&R cost in 2010. Private school students inched close to "full pay," with net tuitions averaging 70 percent to 90 percent of education costs. But with less room for cost shifting, the net tuition share of cost increased by only 4–8 percentage points over the decade.

Average subsidies declined across all types of institutions in 2010, and for the most part revealed the largest average cuts in a decade. With E&R declining and net tuition increasing across higher education, declines in average subsidies were also widespread in 2010. Average subsidies were cut by $500 to $700 in public four-year institutions (7 percent to 10 percent) and by nearly $1,000 in community colleges (14 percent). While all the cuts were large compared to other years, the declines in community college subsidies were significantly larger than at any other point in the decade. Subsidies also declined at private institutions (by 7 percent to 19 percent), and private research institutions posted their first meaningful cuts in the decade; they also averaged the largest dollar declines in higher education ($1,000).

At both public and private institutions, net tuition increases in 2010 were entirely the result of cost shifting to replace institutional subsidies. As in 2009, increases in net tuition revenue largely offset declines in institutional subsidies. But it appears that even these new tuition revenues were not enough to offset other revenue declines, so E&R costs were cut in 2010. Though cost shifting has been prevalent in recent years, this is the first time in recent years that students at four-year institutions have borne the full impact of cost shifting (e.g. paying more even though spending was cut), and it is also the first instance of cost shifting at private research institutions.

Spending and Results

Performance in higher education can be evaluated using different degree-related outcome measures. Degree productivity, measured as the number of degrees awarded per 100 FTE students, shows changes in degrees and certificates in the context of changes in enrollment. And the cost per degree/completion measures E&R costs against outcomes, rather than enrollments.

More degrees were granted across all types of institutions in 2010, but degree productivity was flat or declining. Average degree productivity did not improve in either the public or private sectors in 2010. Public bachelor's and community colleges had the largest declines, producing one less degree per 100 FTE students that the year before. With certificates included, community colleges were down almost two completions per 100 FTE. But it was rapidly rising enrollments that dampened the degree productivity ratios. There was a robust increase in the overall number of degrees awarded, which grew by more than 3 percent in public four-year colleges and universities and 8 percent in community colleges, which are among the highest growth rates in the latter half of the decade.

Over the course of the decade, average degree productivity improved at most types of institutions (except at public and private bachelor's colleges). In community colleges, the boost came solely from increases in certificates. At the end of the decade, private research and master's institutions posted the highest degree productivity among all types of institutions.

Cost per degree/completion declined in 2010 at most types of institutions, but was still higher than 5 and 10 years ago. Declines in E&R, coupled with increases in the numbers of degrees and certificates, translated into 1 percent to 2 percent declines in the cost per completion at most types of public and private four-year institutions (see Figure 4). Declines in community colleges were twice as large, continuing a decade-long slide in the cost per completion. Community colleges are the only group of institutions in which the cost per completion was lower in 2010 than at the beginning of the decade, a phenomenon resulting from the growth in less costly and shorter-term certificate programs. The greatest cost increases over the decade were in private research and master's institutions.

Looking Ahead

Though it is difficult to predict the future—or the present, as it may be—because of inherent lags in data collection and reporting, the prevailing view is that the Great Recession has ushered in a new era in higher education finance. Public support for higher education may not return to previous levels as states continue to face financial difficulties and other competing budgetary commitments. But at the same time, strained financial resources have a way of shining the spotlight on spending priorities and may encourage colleges and universities to further organize their resources in ways that support better outcomes for students.

There is no other comprehensive data source that can provide more timely information on higher education spending than the Delta Cost Project Database. However, more recent information on enrollment, tuition prices, revenues, and degree production from other sources hint at what college and university spending may look like in FY 2011.

The wave of new college students that arrived on college campuses at the end of the decade appeared to have receded in 2011, with enrollment growth returning to normal levels. Growth also slowed at for-profit institutions, though these providers will probably continue to change the landscape of higher education as busy students are drawn to their convenient and non-traditional settings— whether they are easy-access office buildings or online courses that transcend time and location. Many traditional brick-and-mortar institutions are also adopting these changes as they strive to offer more flexible programs, courses, and instructional methods.

One steady trend in higher education is that college prices continue to go up: average tuition and fee increases for 2011 mirrored those in recent years. These price increases were consistent with new revenue data showing that net tuition revenues per FTE student grew at similar rates in both 2010 and 2011. At the same time, public support for higher education appeared to continue its decline, though educational appropriations per FTE decreased only half as fast in 2011 as during the previous two years, perhaps reflecting the slowdown in new student enrollments.

Taken together, these data suggest that funding for the academic mission at public institutions may have had a soft landing in 2011. Despite differences in the data sources, the historical patterns are durable; current trends from these other sources show little change in total education revenues between 2010 and 2011, with increases in student revenue fully offsetting declines in public funding. Nevertheless, we expect to see that students continued to pay for more of their educational costs.

Private institutions may have seen a brighter 2011 as financial returns on endowment portfolios continued to rise in FY 2011 at nearly double the rate of 2010. The average three-year return on investments turned positive again; however, it was still below the average spending rates of educational institutions, suggesting that damage from the downturn had not yet been fully restored.

Despite financial difficulties at the end of the decade, the corresponding increase in enrollments added many new college graduates. The number of degrees granted at public institutions climbed sharply in 2011, exceeding the already strong growth exhibited in 2010.

It is perhaps best to look ahead with cautious optimism. The current outlook may not be rosy, but financial stabilization will provide a more solid footing upon which higher education can move forward. Still unclear is whether all institutions will fare equally, or if community colleges will remain at the bottom of this financial roller coaster. And we have yet to see how colleges and universities may further adjust their spending patterns to adapt to this financial reality that is likely here to stay for awhile.

9.2: Curriculum and the Culture of a Campus: A Clash between Students and the President at the University of Chicago (1999)

Course catalogues and official transcripts hardly tell the whole or most important story about the academic life of a particular college. Social and behavioral scientists who study campus culture and student life have identified the concept of "the hidden curriculum"—the unofficial, unwritten code that shapes academic life within a college or university community. It is no less than the compact that students and professors negotiate and then obey—as each constituency goes about its work (and play). At some universities the "hidden curriculum" may be one of avoidance and coexistence—in which the faculty tacitly agree not to press students too hard intellectually, on the conditions that students in turn behave in a civil manner, attend class, and do some acceptable minimal level of academic work. The University of Chicago differs from this model in that its ethos and compact place undergraduate education at the center of a research university that has a full array of PhD programs and advanced professional schools. The Chicago curriculum and its "Common Core" for undergraduates are demanding, marked by heavy reading loads and intense debates in which they are treated as mature scholars. It is a student culture that involves self-selection in the application and admission process. For generations of University of Chicago students, alumni, and faculty, there is unabashed and unapologetic pride for this intellectual tradition. The following document gives an account of a clash between students (along with alumni and faculty) and the president over a presidential initiative to increase enrollments and alter graduation requirements, which the students perceived as an affront to the well-established (and well-protected) customs of the university's aca-

Ben Gose, "University of Chicago President's Plan to Resign Doesn't Quiet Debate over His Agenda," *Chronicle of Higher Education* (June 18, 1999). Reprinted by permission of The YGS Group.

demic life. Whereas the student riots at Oxford in 1354 in Document 1.1 dealt with issues of food and drink, for University of Chicago students in the late twentieth century, the concern was over food for thought.

Hugo F. Sonnenschein is stepping to the sidelines, but the controversy over the expansion he has planned for the University of Chicago shows no sign of abating.

Mr. Sonnenschein, the university's president since 1993, announced this month that he would resign in June 2000 to return to teaching economics. Both supporters and critics describe him as a skilled fund raiser who has helped make possible an ambitious—and badly needed—building program.

But he also has pushed for two changes that have been sharply criticized by some students, faculty members, and alumni—a reduction in the number of required courses in Chicago's fabled "Common Core" curriculum, and an expansion in the size of the undergraduate population.

Though debate over the changes has raged for at least three years, the criticism of Mr. Sonnenschein intensified this spring. A Chicago alumni group established a World-Wide Web site, describing the expansion plans as a cynical effort to attract wealthy students. Seventy-four faculty members, a small portion of the university's total but including some of its luminaries, sent a letter to the Board of Trustees, warning that Chicago's intellectual tradition was "being put at risk by its present leadership." Ten prominent scholars from around the country followed with a similar letter to the board.

Meanwhile, about 1,700 students attended a "fun-in," a parody of the president's concern about students who focus excessively on academics, where they performed such sketches as "The Great Books in One Minute." And just before Mr. Sonnenschein announced his resignation, the student government, in a report on the university's future, said, "We believe there is an acute leadership crisis, primarily on the level of the president."

The former Princeton University provost, who will join Chicago's economics department next year, said in a statement that he had accomplished his goal of renewing the university's "capacity to support excellence, now and in the very long term." He added: "I have come to feel that it is time for another president, one who is less a symbol of change and who has less reason to initiate change, to carry the momentum forward."

His critics did little to disguise their glee. "I wouldn't say the 'fun-in' took down the president," said Aleem Hossain, a junior who helped organize the event. "But I would say that his resignation validates our concerns."

Jerry L. Martin, president of the American Council of Trustees and Alumni, the Washington-based group that organized the letter-writing campaign by prominent scholars, said Mr. Sonnenschein's decision had important national implications. "There's been a serious erosion of standards in colleges and universities, and alumni are beginning to fight back. It turns out they can win." Mr. Martin said he had spoken with three Chicago trustees who had expressed doubts about Mr. Sonnenschein's leadership.

In an interview, Mr. Sonnenschein said that he was not asked to resign, and that the board had always given him its full support. "I want the opportunity to do more research and teaching before I retire," said the president, who is 58. "The only way to do that was to make the change now."

Howard Krane, the outgoing chairman of the board, and Edgar Jannotta, the incoming chairman, said in a joint statement that they had "regretfully accepted" Mr. Sonnenschein's announcement.

"He initiated many changes to strengthen the University both academically and financially," the trustee leaders wrote. They said they would plow ahead with his plan to expand the undergraduate population from 3,800 to 4,500 over a 10-year period.

Two days after announcing his resignation, Mr. Sonnenschein spoke to about 200 Chicago graduates who were here for Alumni Weekend. He proudly described several construction projects, including a $35-million athletics center that will house a new swimming pool. The current swimming facility was built in 1904, he noted, as if it were an example of financial woes.

The expansion in the number of undergraduates, Mr. Sonnenschein has maintained, will improve the university's financial standing. The current ratio of undergraduates to graduates at Chicago is roughly one-to-one, far lower than at most other private institutions, including those in the Ivy League. That ratio limits Chicago's revenue stream, because many graduate students receive free tuition plus stipends.

The additional revenue provided by the expansion will help pay for first-rate libraries, better salaries for professors, and more-generous stipends for graduate students, Mr. Sonnenschein said in the interview. "What we're doing now, by every objective fact, is building a future that provides for these things."

Four faculty members who oppose Mr. Sonnenschein's policies also spoke during Alumni Weekend, at a roundtable discussion in Mandel Hall. Marshall Sahlins, an emeritus professor of anthropology, said the president's depiction of the university as a campus in dire need of funds—at a time when its endowment is well over $2.5-billion—was wrong-headed.

"This is not a football poll," Mr. Sahlins said. "If you have enough money to do what you want to do, it's just as good to be 16th [in the ranking of institutions by endowment size] as fifth."

All four professors also expressed opposition to the reduction in the core curriculum, from 21 courses to 18. The reduction, approved by the faculty last year, will come in courses classified as "humanities, civilizations, and the arts" and "science and mathematics." For students whose test results allow them to skip the three-course language requirement, the core could shrink to a total of 15 courses.

Herman Sinaiko, a humanities professor, predicted that the reduced requirement would lead to the demise of course sequences that last for three straight quarters—a full academic year. The year-long sequences are much more than "survey courses," he said; they prepare students to "become independent critics of each of the major intellectual domains," including the humanities. But as such sequences wither away, the core will lose its uniqueness, becoming "something like the standard distribution requirements that exist in every college in the U.S.," he said.

But other professors noted that the number of three-quarter sequences is already declining, in part because fewer faculty members are interested in teaching them.

John W. Boyer, dean of the college and a professor of history, said the changes in the core would make it easier for students to complete the requirements by the end of the second year, rather than stretch them out until graduation. "General education is most effective when it comes in the first two years," he said.

While many student leaders have denounced the changes, it's not clear that many of their classmates share that sentiment. Next year's sophomores can choose whether to graduate under the old core or the new one. So far, about 85 per cent of the sophomores-to-be are choosing the new, reduced requirements, according to Mr. Boyer.

Nonetheless, many Chicago students continue to revel in the stereotype that they are library-shackled intellectuals. They fear that the softening of the core and Chicago's more-aggressive marketing campaign—not to mention indulgences such as the new swimming pool—are intended to lure more of the dread "well-rounded" students. A satirical tabloid distributed at the fun-in featured a chart projecting a sharp drop in the enrollment of "nerds" by 2005.

Michael Behnke, a vice-president who oversees admissions, rejected the notion that Chicago was going after a different type of student. He cited the university's new viewbook, "The Life of the Mind," which includes this disclaimer: "Warning: Study in this university is known to cause thinking, occasionally deep thinking. Typical side effects include mild temporary anxiety followed by profound long-term satisfaction.

"We make very clear to prospective students what kind of place we are," said Mr. Behnke, who was hired away from the Massachusetts Institute of Technology in 1997 to improve Chicago's marketing.

The challenge, he said, is that the university is not well known among the public, even though it is highly regarded in academe. Chicago sent out a record number of brochures this year, and added additional campus-visitation programs.

So far, the effort is working. The number of applicants rose 24 per cent this year, to 6,854, and Chicago admitted only 49 per cent of them, down from 60 per cent a year ago. Average SAT scores are up. Mr. Behnke said Mr. Sonnenschein deserved much of the credit: "He hired me and made sure I had the resources I needed."

The president is also credited with getting Chicago's fund raising back on track. Since he took over, in 1993, Chicago's endowment has risen at roughly the same rate as those of a nine-institution peer group that includes Princeton, Stanford, and Yale Universities. From 1958 to 1993, Chicago's endowment had increased at just one-sixth the rate of the peer group, after adjusting for inflation.

"Mr. Sonnenschein has put into place some significant things here at the university," said Lorna P. Straus, an anatomy and biology professor, who is spokeswoman for the executive committee of the college faculty. "Some of the things that were laid at his door"—such as blame for the reduction in the core curriculum— didn't belong there, she added.

But she did not fault him for stepping down now. "I can't help but believe that the pressure was great," she said, "and that he couldn't have found every day a bed of roses."

9.3: Faculty Memoir: A Conversation with Professor Laura Nader (2000)

Professor Laura Nader joined the faculty at the University of California, Berkeley, in 1960 with an appointment in the anthropology department. Well known as a published scholar and dedicated teacher, she has initiated Berkeley students into the life of the mind and conscience for over a half century. Her work emphasizes intense discussion on essential principles of civil society and public policies—ranging from health care to working conditions, voting and consumerism, and fundamental issues gleaned from "the anthropology of daily life." The following document is author Russell Schoch's extended conversation with Professor Nader in 2000, in which she reflects on the approaches and issues she has encountered, past and present. As interviewer Russell Schoch notes, "An Anthropologist urges us to challenge the assumptions that guide our lives. For her, it's a family tradition."

In 1960, when Laura Nader became the first woman faculty member in Berkeley's anthropology department, things were a bit different. For example, when she and other women faculty wanted to attend a meeting north of the Great Hall in the Faculty Club, they had to crawl through a window. (The Great Hall was for men only.) "I'm kind of amazed that we did that," Nader says now. "We just laughed about it at the time." How and why people do some of the strange things they do without a second thought has been a focus of Nader's work for decades.

This fall, the prominent anthropologist has a few things to celebrate: her 40th year at Berkeley; being chosen to present, in November, the Distinguished Lecture to the American Association of Anthropology; and the fact that her younger brother, Ralph Nader, is the Green Party candidate for the President of the United States.

The four Nader children were born and raised in Winsted, Connecticut, children of immigrants from Lebanon. "My parents were by my best teachers," Laura says. Her father was a businessman. "But what he liked best," she says, "was talking to the customers in his restaurant about politics, about the town, about good wages for the workers, about health and safety." At the dinner table, she recalls, her father asked his children questions about issues of the day. "We were never

Russell Schoch, "A Conversation with Laura Nader," *California Monthly* (November 2000) pp. 28–32. Reprinted by permission of Laura Nader and Russell Schoch.

treated like kids that didn't know anything; he wanted us to form opinions. He'd say to us, 'If you don't have any answers, what are your questions?'" Her mother, a former school teacher, educated the children in her own way. "She taught by story-telling."

Nader says that her parents "were alert to what was happening in the world," a trait Laura and her siblings share. "My dad left Lebanon for political reasons," she says, "and when he came to the land of the free, he took it seriously. So I guess we were raised that way—to believe that you should be involved in public issues."

After a moment's reflection, she adds, "Public issues are the key. I don't think of my father as being 'political.' And I would never say that Ralph is political. He's interested in public issues, the issues we all need to think about: health and safety and quality of life." Something else the Nader children were raised to do, she says, is "to question assumptions."

Nader attended Wells College, in upstate New York, spending her junior year abroad, in Mexico. She earned her Ph.D. in anthropology under Clyde Kluckhohn at Harvard, based on fieldwork among the Zapotec people in the Sierra Madre mountains of Oaxaca, Mexico. She also has done fieldwork in Lebanon among the Shia Muslims, in the United States among consumers of products and services, and spent a short period in Morocco studying the use of courts during Ramadan. She sums up her intellectual career as the pursuit of an interest in law, justice, and control, and how they are connected to power structures. These are, she says, "everyday problems for everyday people."

Laura Nader has taken on specialists in the fields of law, children's issues, nuclear energy, and science, questioning the assumptions under which these experts operate. She believes a good liberal arts education should lead citizens precisely to ask questions rather than being steamrolled by those in control. A few years ago, when she was addressing experts in nuclear energy at Lawrence Livermore Laboratory, encouraging them to think differently about their practice, one member of the panel passed a note to another (who later passed it to her): "Can't you shut this woman up?" Although many have asked that question, the answer is clearly no.

Nader is soft-spoken but direct, her gaze steady as she asks tough questions about why people think as they do. "The final colonization," she has written, "is the colonization of the mind." Since the early 1980s, she has taught an undergraduate course in anthropology called "Controlling Processes," and has published two volumes of essays by her students on how control penetrates their everyday lives through ideas and institutions. She was interviewed about these and other matters in her third-floor office in Kroeber Hall.

Q&A

You've been called "an anthropologist of everyday life." What does that mean?
I suppose it's an anthropologist who does ethnography. To me ethnography is the key—the serious study of everyday life in context. So, in the 1950s, when I went to southern Mexico, I was studying how the Zapotec organize their lives, what they do with their problems, what they do when they go to court. And when I came back to this country, I started looking at American equivalents, at how Americans solve their consumer and service complaints.

But then one thing led to another, and I began to examine dominant paradigms. The study of the everyday became, for me, a study of how people think. It occurred to me that people are trapped by mind-sets, by their mode of thinking, by invisible processes we sometimes call culture.

Can you give an example?
While serving on the Carnegie Council on Children, I noticed that psychologists have somehow convinced the population that the way children turn out is wholly connected to what their parents do when the children are young—that the parents are somehow totally responsible for raising their children.

I was seeing good parents losing their children in the 1960s, and the notion came apart. It didn't make sense to think that parents are somehow totally responsible when there are so many things operating outside the family that affect children. Certainly the corporate world has an enormous effect: It feeds and clothes children and provides them with music and entertainment. But the poor parents came to feel solely responsible. And so we pursued the questions of how people think about children, and what does the government and the corporate world have to do with raising America's children?

One of my students interviewed executives who market to children. What's between the market and the child? The parents. You should see the stuff they teach children about their parents! "Parents are too old, they don't know anything, they're stupid." And if marketers can get children to think of their parents in these ways, then the kids become the companies' salesmen—nagging their parents to buy them things. I was amazed by that, by the processes that were consciously used to separate offspring from parents, for the benefit of corporations.

As a parent, were you trapped by that kind of thinking?
No, I wasn't. But I realized that my rearing of children was defensive: Don't do this, don't do that; you can't go to this party, there's drug use there, and so forth. I could see I wasn't doing what my mother did—raise us in a small town where the society agreed that parents should be supported.

Today, when they go off to college, freshmen are told that they should stand on their own two feet, that they shouldn't call their parents—they're babies if they do that. It's been said at Berkeley. And this was said to the parents of new students when my daughters went to college, at Smith. The president said, "Don't call your parents; and parents, you should let your daughters grow up."

Wait a minute! *Who* are you supposed to call, if not your parents? I stood up and said: "You're making the argument that, in order to grow up, these young women have to cut the cord from their parents. Could you not make the opposite argument, that if they cut the cord with their parents, they will never grow up?" I then offered my own advice: "Stay in your children's lives. Because nobody cares about your children like you do."

Let's talk about a course you teach, called "Controlling Processes." What is that about?
Controlling processes are the modes people invent in order to manage certain segments of the society in predictable ways. I differentiate between social and cultural control; the two add up to controlling processes.

It's hard to talk about mind control if you live in a society that believes in free will. All students understand what social control is: If you go through a red light, a policeman comes along and says, "You've got a ticket." But to tell students, for example, that they are spending their money in certain ways because they're being manipulated—their minds are being manipulated—that's harder to grasp. And that's cultural control.

Can you give an example?
In a recent course, a student was sitting in the second row. As I was lecturing, every once in a while I'd hear him saying, "Wow!" I wondered, "What had I said to elicit such a response?"

Then he turned in his paper. "When I came to Berkeley as a freshman," he said, "my father had just gotten fired and my mother only had a part-time job. I should have been poor. But I lived in a nice apartment, I had a VCR and a car, and by the end of my freshman year, I was $14,000 in debt. Let me tell you how it happened."

And then he wrote about how the credit-card companies come on campus and teach these young kids to be debtors. They give them credit cards that you and I could never get. His paper was about how he had been conned and how he came to acquiesce.

I think what was happening to him in class, and as he wrote his paper, was that he was beginning to think that, yes, this has long-term consequences. He could end up taking his first job, for example, not because it was the job he most wanted but because he needed it in order to pay off his debt.

Let me compare that to what happened when I was growing up. Starting in kindergarten, the local banker would take the whole class to deposit our quarters in savings accounts.

Isn't that a controlling process?
It is. That's why I say controlling processes are double-edged; they can take you down one road or another road. You should be aware of which road you're being taken down.

When I was young, I was aware that the banker was teaching us to save, because he taught us that explicitly. Controlling processes are not all bad, but they are usually hidden. What was being hidden from my student was the road he was being taken down: long-term debt and how he would have to deal with it. All he was presented with was the notion that he could have anything he wanted.

And that's what advertising and marketing are teaching young and older people as well: satisfy your appetites! Now! It's hedonism. All the stuff that Huxley talked about in *Brave New World*, a novel, along with Orwell's *1984*, that I have students read at the beginning of the class. After they list the controlling processes in those novels, I ask them to find one in their own lives—I never define the process for them; I ask them to find one and write a paper about it. And they do: cults, mind-controlling drugs, advertisements, standardized tests, political rhetoric . . . Once they examine how control works, they understand very well how to recognize controlling processes. And once they're able to do that, they're able to think more freely.

It sounds like "critical thinking" is something you value and teach.
Exactly. Let me give you one example of what happens when people abandon critical thinking. Eight or nine years ago, at the Reagan National Airport in Washington, D.C., a pilot was getting ready to take off. He saw ice on the wings. But the control tower said there was no ice on the wings. *The pilot saw the ice with his own eyes, but he believed the control tower.* He took off, and the plane crashed, and everyone on board died.

That tragic incident has always struck me. We're not taught to listen to our own drum beating, we're taught to listen to someone else's drum.

How critical are students today?
Students today come into class mostly without opinions. They want to know what *I* think. They're afraid to come forth with what they think, or to be critical. And if they disagree with me, they don't want to say it. They're taught not to disagree. You're not supposed to be "negative," you're supposed to just sit there and take notes.

Contentious thinking is not being encouraged as much as I think it should be. You ought to be allowed to be contentious, to argue, to have different opinions. Many students feel liberated when I say that, because they feel they've been squelched. If they disagree with somebody—for example in areas that are tense, like feminism or race or ethnicity—they feel they can't say what they think.

If you go to Boston and get on the subway, you hear people saying things that would make people freak out if they were said on the campus; they tell ethnic jokes. My father used to tell them to the ethnics themselves—Polish jokes to the Poles, Jewish jokes to the Jews. And everybody would laugh and tell one on him! Today that would be considered insulting.

This sounds like "political correctness."
It's very P.C. P.C. is part of this whole thing of what you can and cannot say. You mustn't ruffle anyone's feathers.

Berkeley is often criticized for being P.C.
P.C. charges are always leveled at the left, not the right. But there are things you can't say on the right.

For example?

The Gulf War. You couldn't criticize the Gulf War, which I consider a right wing act because it was the right wing of this country that carried it out, and everybody had to fall in line and not criticize the harm that could have been prevented.

Last year, I asked my class, "How many of you know that more people have died as a result of the Gulf War and the sanctions than died in Nagasaki and Hiroshima?"

A student of mine did a paper on this. She wanted to find out whether what I said was true or not. She found that over a million children have died as a result of the bombing, the destruction of Iraq's infrastructure, and the sanctions. Most Americans don't know that. It's not politically correct to ask or talk about it.

We seem to be a trusting society.

Right. One of the questions I ask students is: "Why is there not an opposite word for paranoia?" I invented such a word; I call it "trustanoia." America suffers from trustanoia.

Did you ever play trust games in school?

No.

Neither did I. That tells us how old we are. But today, when children go to school, they are taught to trust. They play a game where they fall back and have to trust that somebody's going to catch them.

Troy Duster [professor of sociology at Berkeley] told me that, in the black community, among others, the father says, "Jump and I'll catch you." But he doesn't. "Don't ever forget that lesson!"

One might ask, "Why teach people to distrust?" Well, there may be good reasons to distrust others. You should know when to trust and when to distrust. In other words, you have to use your own judgment—not like the pilot who listened to the control tower and crashed.

For alumni, whose formal education is over, what advice do you have?

If their education "took," then they should be asking questions.

I think a lot of people in this country, Cal graduates included, feel that there's something wrong and that they've lost control. And in order to regain control, they must start to ask questions and to participate.

And I think America's been flattened. We've been flattened by what I describe as "harmony ideology"—you mustn't be contentious, you mustn't raise issues; and by fear—fear of loss of jobs, fear that you won't be able to afford what your parents were able to afford, and so forth.

What can people do?
First, people have to recognize what the issues are. I can make a list of issues for me: I happen to be very concerned about basic things—like the quality of water, food, and air, nuclear proliferation, the changing nature of nature. But other people certainly have other issues of concern. And they should be talking to each other! Everybody talks about whether their computer is up or down, or how much e-mail they've gotten, or about the television shows they're watching. But that's all small talk; there's little conversation about the wider world they live in.

When people do get interested and involved in issues, something wonderful happens – they come alive! Because, basically, they discover themselves. I see it in my class all the time.

What makes a good teacher?
I asked a colleague of mine at Santa Cruz, who had just won a teaching award, what he did to deserve that. He said, "I *seduce*." And I thought, "Oh, now I know what I do. I *irritate*." Because my students, especially freshmen, are asleep. And I want to wake them up.

No student comes out of my course without having exercised critical thinking. That's why they say the course has changed their lives. Not because they have a dogma they've picked up from class, but because they've learned to see the invisible. They've learned to make the invisible visible.

That's pretty powerful.
It is powerful. And that's what education should be about. And that's what good teachers do, here and elsewhere.

Another of your topics of study is what you call "central dogmas." Have you ever been caught up in one?
Yes. It was while I was writing a paper on gender, and it took me ten years to write the paper because of the central dogma I was caught up in: "Things may be bad now for women, but they're better than they were."

You know what shook me out of that? It was a study by four of my campus colleagues on the place of women faculty at Berkeley. They found that, in 1887, women made up 3.5 percent of the faculty. And in 1968, the percentage was almost identical. In between, it had gone up to something like 18 percent. So it was a yo-yo model.

That really shook me up! Because I had believed in progress. I wrote a paper comparing women in the Islamic Middle East with women in Euro-American societies. My argument was that the way they keep women controlled in both societies is to represent the *other woman* as being in worse shape.

So we say, "You think it's bad here? Look at Bangladesh." And others say the same thing. "You think it's bad in Egypt? Look at the rape rate in the United States." So they point out what's lacking in our society, and we point out what's lacking in theirs. And, regardless of who says who's got the better status, how we portray the other is a mode of control.

When I went to Morocco in 1980, I discovered there were many more women faculty at the University of Rabat than there were at Berkeley. That wasn't supposed to be, because they were Muslim, and everyone knows that all Muslim women are subjected—that's a central dogma.

The point is that I was being shaken out of participation in the central dogma of progress and progressivism, that it's always somehow better now and here than then and there.

You have a reputation for being contentious and feisty.
Well, I wouldn't have it any other way. I was raised in a feisty family in a feisty town in New England, where you had town meetings and you are supposed to be feisty. Besides, in a country that's democratic, you're supposed to ask questions, challenge assumptions. My brother Ralph once remarked that we live in a time when an expression of candor is viewed as an act of courage.

How would you characterize the current environment at Berkeley?
I think that universities, especially today, are very conformist. Berkeley faculty are scared. I remember when Chancellor Tien came to speak to the Academic Senate on budgets. He asked, "Are there any questions?" Silence! There's a self-censorship here; and if you ask questions—which I did at that meeting—people sort of look at you.

You've written that "There is little room for disgust and outrage in the American university. The university buries emotions, and faculty look for 'balanced' opinions." Is that true?

Oh, yes. And I find it more so as the university gets corporatized. How many economists in this University teach courses on inequality?

How does this affect education for the University of California?

Well, it becomes more of a trade school. The first question I ask in Anthro 3 is, "How many students are here to get a job?" Most hands go up. I'm not saying that jobs aren't important. I am saying that there's something that happens to you as you're going through the educational process if getting a job is what's primary in your mind.

You weren't interested in the early retirement, "the golden handshake," which you could have taken in the early 1990s.

No. As I said at the time, "I don't take bribes." And I think there should be different ages, different generations, around the University.

And different points of view?

That's right. You want to know what drives me absolutely out of my mind? Facilitators. I never like meetings where there are facilitators. I was just at such a meeting in Santa Barbara. We weren't allowed to say "but." You couldn't say, "Yes, but. . ." You had to say something positive. This was a meeting of grown people discussing ecological issues!

I remember a meeting on children a few years ago, here on campus. A facilitator wrote things on the board he thought were important. I asked, "Why don't you ever write anything I say on the board?" He said, "You're usually off the track." And I said, "But isn't that the point—to find out what different people think?"

People have the mistaken impression that our democracy will blossom via incremental consensus. But, in fact, if you look at history, advances in human civilization often come about through leaps and by means of creative—yet often fierce—disagreements.

9.4: College Sports Reform: The Problems of Presidents and Rising Expenses in the Knight Commission Report of 2010

In October 2009 the Knight Commission on Intercollegiate Athletics convened a symposium in Miami, Florida, to bring together a mix of college and university presidents, athletics directors, conference officials, some professors, television network executives, journalists, and other influential figures in the enterprise of college sports. The focus was on the convergence of two disturbing findings: first, that spending on intercollegiate sports was spiraling upward and far outpaced spending on educational and instructional programs within colleges; and, second, the finding from surveys and interviews that college and university presidents acknowledged that they had little control over these excesses. The symposium—and its resultant 2010 report, whose excerpts compose the following document—was the latest in a succession of timely initiatives by the Knight Commission to bring attention and information about college sports reform into the public forum. The credibility and influence of the Knight Commission were enhanced by the fact that it was not hostile or indifferent to college sports. To the contrary, it had been a longtime advocate and leader for promoting excellence in programs for student-athletes in harmony with sound educational values and institutional priorities. Its periodic reports, as ongoing sources of information and insight, were strengthened by databases, reference materials, and interactive resources through which interested individuals and groups could learn about understanding— and changing—the conduct of intercollegiate athletics programs. As such, the Knight Commission's 2010 report and its array of discussions and resources represented a distinctive American tradition: an educational nonprofit foundation committed to public forum and public policies among institutions—voluntary associations and initiatives relying on informed discussion and goodwill among constituencies which were alternatives to government regulation. It has been an organization whose publications have raised significant questions that any college or university would unlikely be able to pursue on its own.

At the nation's most prominent universities, intercollegiate athletics have always played a dual role in campus life. On the one hand, they are managed for the benefit of student-athletes. On the other, they inspire the interest and passions of thousands, if not millions, of fans. For most teams at most institutions, these

Knight Commission on Intercollegiate Athletics, *Restoring the Balance: Dollars, Values and the Future of College Sports* (June 2010). Reprinted by permission of the Trustees of the Knight Foundation.

roles can be reconciled. But in high-profile sports, tensions often surface between the core mission of universities and commercial values.

These tensions have grown significantly over the past two decades. The pursuit of television contracts and slots in football bowl games, together with the quest to win championship tournaments in basketball, have had a destabilizing influence on athletics programs. Among other worrisome developments, the intensely competitive environment at the top levels of college sports has prompted four rounds of realignment among athletic conferences since 1994; a bidding war for prominent coaches; and accelerating expenses across the board.

The growing emphasis on winning games and increasing television market share feeds the spending escalation because of the unfounded yet persistent belief that devoting more dollars to sports programs leads to greater athletic success and thus to greater revenues.

In fact, only a tiny number of college athletics programs actually reap the financial rewards that come from selling high-priced tickets and winning championships. According to a *USA Today* analysis, just seven athletics programs generated enough revenue to finish in the black in each of the past five years. This reality is often obscured by headlines about money in college sports, such as the recent 14-year, $10.8 billion television rights deal for the NCAA men's basketball tournament, and yet another round of conference realignments and expansions designed to increase television market share.

Nevertheless, the pursuit of those elusive goals by many programs creates a cost spiral that causes athletics spending to rise at rates often exceeding those on academic spending. At many universities, institutional spending on high-profile sports is growing at double or triple the pace of spending on academics. This is due to much more than multimillion dollar salaries for football and basketball coaches. Less-publicized trends also play a significant role, including a steep increase in the number of expensive non-coaching personnel devoted to individual sports.

In some instances, there are legitimate reasons for athletics spending to outpace education-related spending on a per-student basis. Health insurance for student-athletes is a unique and large expense, for example. But expenses like this cannot account for the lopsided spending patterns seen at some universities. Median athletics spending per athlete at institutions in each major athletics conference ranges from 4 to nearly 11 times more than the median spending on education-related activities per student.

At most institutions, these expenditures require a redistribution of institutional resources. Because sports revenues so often fall short of meeting the needs of athletics programs, almost all programs must rely on allocations from general university funds, fees imposed on the entire student body, and state appropriations to meet funding gaps. This is a significant concern at a time when economic woes have devastated state budgets and institutional endowments alike. Conflicts over funding between academics and athletics are growing.

Indeed, reliance on institutional resources to underwrite athletics programs is reaching the point at which some institutions must choose between funding sections of freshman English and funding the football team. And student-athletes in non-revenue sports risk seeing their teams lose funding or be cut entirely. These threats extend well beyond universities with high-budget athletics programs: it is clear that the spending race that too often characterizes major football and basketball programs is creating unacceptable financial pressures for everyone.

In brief, if the business model of intercollegiate athletics persists in its current form, the considerable financial pressures and ever-increasing spending in today's college sports system could lead to permanent and untenable competition between academics and athletics. More broadly, this model could lead to a loss of credibility not just for intercollegiate sports but for higher education itself.

The current financial downturn should be a wake-up call for all programs. It has significantly refocused academic priorities and even forced some institutions to ratchet back spending on sports—primarily by paring teams in lower-profile sports, thus curtailing opportunities for student-athletes. However, even with this new reality, top programs are expected to have athletics budgets exceeding $250 million by 2020, based on data from the past five years. Even for the largest and best-positioned universities, a $250 million athletics budget serving an average of 600 student-athletes is untenable.

In the Commission's view, addressing misplaced spending priorities requires answering some searching questions: Are financial incentives at the national, conference, and institutional levels rewarding behaviors that are aligned with the core values of higher education, institutions' educational missions, and amateur athletic competition? Or are they creating a "winner take all" market in which there are very few winners? More often we see the latter.

Changing course will not be easy. But we know that some institutions have been able to achieve a healthy balance between academic and athletics spending.

We believe that the reforms laid out in this report are achievable and can help all college athletics programs do the same.

Presidents of universities with major football programs clearly recognize the need for change. In a 2009 Knight Commission survey, a large majority said that they believe today's revenue and spending trends are not sustainable for athletics programs as a whole. Nearly half expressed concern about the proportion of institutional resources being used to support athletics programs, and a similar proportion said they feared that economic pressures might force them to discontinue a sport.

Presidents also understand the urgency of acting together. To be sure, some institutions have been able to achieve financial stability, taking advantage of significant revenue opportunities while exercising prudent management. But it is clear that the vast majority of Division I institutions will not be able to do so without a shared structure that provides athletics programs and universities with the information, expectations, and incentives needed to achieve a better balance in their spending priorities.

The Commission believes that the first step among the many actions needed to redress the imbalance in athletics spending is to make financial data in intercollegiate sports, both for public and private institutions, readily available to the general public and to trustees, state legislators, students, parents, and the media. Academic reform hit a tipping point when graduation rates for student-athletes were first shared publicly. We believe the same will be true for financial reform when there is far greater openness about spending on college sports—in absolute dollars, in growth levels, and in comparison to academic budgets.

We applaud the NCAA's good work over the past five years in improving the accuracy of financial data and organizing that information into a database accessible to all presidents. These valuable efforts provide a solid foundation on which to build. But much more needs to be done.

We believe that more data, better data, and more transparent data will mean greater accountability for college sports, both on campus and in the public eye.

After all, at a time when all of U.S. higher education is under unprecedented pressure to be more transparent to the public and more accountable for the results it achieves, intercollegiate athletics cannot expect to be immune to the same standards. Moreover, as with other parts of higher education, heightened scrutiny of college sports should not be viewed as a threat but as an opportunity.

With the spotlight already on intercollegiate athletics, more effective disclosure of finances—and of financial priorities—will enhance the long-term prospects of college athletics by ensuring that they remain part of, not apart from, the central mission of colleges and universities.

Our recent survey of college presidents shows that they are united in their desire for greater transparency in athletics spending. Given the diversity and complexity of the challenges they face, however, they are understandably wary of one-size-fits-all solutions. Backers of constructive change face a considerable practical challenge—marking a path to financial reform in a system characterized by great diversity in resources, funding models, institutional practices, and state laws. These concerns are legitimate, but we believe they can be overcome.

In the recommendations that follow, the Commission outlines in the pages that follow how the influence of big money in high-profile college athletics can and must be reduced. We aim not only to foster much-needed discussion but, above all, to stimulate reform.

9.5: European Expansion of Higher Education: The Bologna Process (1999)

In the decades immediately following World War II, universities in the United States were able to ascend in terms of both prosperity and prestige. By 1960 universities in Europe and Great Britain looked to American colleges and universities as leaders both in advanced scholarship and PhD programs and in fulfilling commitments to achieve affordable, accessible mass higher education. Part of this acknowledgment took the form of learning from the U.S. example and establishing new initiatives to expand postsecondary education. One fruit of this labor was the signing in 1999 of a compact called "The Bologna Process." It indicated that cooperation and flexibility for students to cross national boundaries and for European nations to commit to improving universities' courses and curricula made higher education integral to broader programs of economic development and political cooperation. For higher education officials in the United States the news of such initiatives as the Bologna Process had a mixed response. On the one hand, it was good news that higher education in Europe and Great Britain was recovering and gaining momentum—and funding. On the other hand, relative gains elsewhere prompted college and university advocates in the United

The Bologna Declaration of 19 June 1999: Joint declaration of the European Ministers of Education.

States to take stock of their own situations. It was an antidote to complacency and a recognition that higher education had matured as an increasingly global and international endeavor. It meant that all nations competed for and rewarded academic talent in their respective quests for social and economic development. Subsequent innovations in Europe, such as the "Erasmus Plan," gave a twenty-first-century revival to historic continental academic rights such as the freedom for students to wander in their choices of university enrollments and degree programs.

The European process, thanks to the extraordinary achievements of the last few years, has become an increasingly concrete and relevant reality for the Union and its citizens. Enlargement prospects together with deepening relations with other European countries, provide even wider dimensions to that reality. Meanwhile, we are witnessing a growing awareness in large parts of the political and academic world and in public opinion of the need to establish a more complete and far-reaching Europe, in particular building upon and strengthening its intellectual, cultural, social and scientific and technological dimensions.

A Europe of Knowledge is now widely recognised as an irreplaceable factor for social and human growth and as an indispensable component to consolidate and enrich the European citizenship, capable of giving its citizens the necessary competences to face the challenges of the new millennium, together with an awareness of shared values and belonging to a common social and cultural space.

The importance of education and educational co-operation in the development and strengthening of stable, peaceful and democratic societies is universally acknowledged as paramount, the more so in view of the situation in South East Europe.

The Sorbonne declaration of 25th of May 1998, which was underpinned by these considerations, stressed the Universities' central role in developing European cultural dimensions. It emphasised the creation of the European area of higher education as a key way to promote citizens' mobility and employability and the Continent's overall development.

Several European countries have accepted the invitation to commit themselves to achieving the objectives set out in the declaration, by signing it or expressing their agreement in principle. The direction taken by several higher education reforms launched in the meantime in Europe has proved many Governments' determination to act.

European higher education institutions, for their part, have accepted the challenge and taken up a main role in constructing the European area of higher education, also in the wake of the fundamental principles laid down in the Bologna Magna Charta Universitatum of 1988. This is of the highest importance, given that Universities' independence and autonomy ensure that higher education and research systems continuously adapt to changing needs, society's demands and advances in scientific knowledge.

The course has been set in the right direction and with meaningful purpose. The achievement of greater compatibility and comparability of the systems of higher education nevertheless requires continual momentum in order to be fully accomplished. We need to support it through promoting concrete measures to achieve tangible forward steps. The 18th June meeting saw participation by authoritative experts and scholars from all our countries and provides us with very useful suggestions on the initiatives to be taken.

We must in particular look at the objective of increasing the international competitiveness of the European system of higher education. The vitality and efficiency of any civilisation can be measured by the appeal that its culture has for other countries. We need to ensure that the European higher education system acquires a world-wide degree of attraction equal to our extraordinary cultural and scientific traditions.

While affirming our support to the general principles laid down in the Sorbonne declaration, we engage in co-ordinating our policies to reach in the short term, and in any case within the first decade of the third millennium, the following objectives, which we consider to be of primary relevance in order to establish the European area of higher education and to promote the European system of higher education world-wide:

Adoption of a system of easily readable and comparable degrees, also through the implementation of the Diploma Supplement, in order to promote European citizens employability and the international competitiveness of the European higher education system.

Adoption of a system essentially based on two main cycles, undergraduate and graduate. Access to the second cycle shall require successful completion of first cycle studies, lasting a minimum of three years. The degree awarded after the first cycle shall also be relevant to the European labour market as an appropriate level of qualification. The second cycle should lead to the master and/or doctorate degree as in many European countries.

Establishment of a system of credits—such as in the ECTS system—as a proper means of promoting the most widespread student mobility. Credits could also be acquired in non-higher education contexts, including lifelong learning, provided they are recognised by receiving Universities concerned.

Promotion of mobility by overcoming obstacles to the effective exercise of free movement with particular attention to:

for students, access to study and training opportunities and to related services

for teachers, researchers and administrative staff, recognition and valorisation of periods spent in a European context researching, teaching and training, without prejudicing their statutory rights.

Promotion of European co-operation in quality assurance with a view to developing comparable criteria and methodologies.

Promotion of the necessary European dimensions in higher education, particularly with regards to curricular development, inter-institutional co-operation, mobility schemes and integrated programmes of study, training and research.

We hereby undertake to attain these objectives—within the framework of our institutional competences and taking full respect of the diversity of cultures, languages, national education systems and of University autonomy—to consolidate the European area of higher education. To that end, we will pursue the ways of intergovernmental co-operation, together with those of non governmental European organisations with competence on higher education.

We expect Universities again to respond promptly and positively and to contribute actively to the success of our endeavour.

Convinced that the establishment of the European area of higher education requires constant support, supervision and adaptation to the continuously evolving needs, we decide to meet again within two years in order to assess the progress achieved and the new steps to be taken.

Signed by:

Austria, Belgium (French community), Belgium (Flemish community), Bulgaria, Czech Republic, Denmark, Estonia, Finland, France, Germany, Greece, Hungary, Iceland, Ireland, Italy, Latvia, Lithuania, Luxembourg, Malta, the Netherlands, Norway, Poland, Portugal, Romania, Slovak Republic, Slovenia, Spain, Sweden, Swiss Confederation, United Kingdom.

Scripps College Seal of "La Semeuse": *Incipit Vita Nova* (Document 9.6)

9.6: Higher Education: A New Life Begins

Studying American higher education from the seventeenth century into the twenty-first century brings together a complex amalgam of information and images. Good scholarship is useful in that it is thoughtful about significant issues, both past and present, that our colleges and universities face. The coincidence of a rich heritage and great success in American higher education coexists with clear evidence of unfulfilled promises and unfinished business at hand. Since it is customary for students who complete their degrees to leave Alma Mater with a ceremony called "Commencement," this anthology of historical documents closes with a comparable perspective of vitality and renewal. The inspiration for connecting the documents of the past to the present and future of colleges and universities is *Incipit Vita Nova*, from the seal of Scripps College, founded in 1926 as a college for women, as a member of the historic Clare-mont Colleges in California. The postscript for this anthology, with the image of "La Semeuse"—"she who sows the good seed of thought, of action, of life"—is the legacy that might guide higher education in the twenty-first century as "A New Life Begins."

Incipit Vita Nova (Scripps College Seal of "La Semeuse"). Reprinted by permission of Scripps College.

Credits

Many documents included in this anthology are in the public domain. For materials outside this category, in compliance with copyright laws of the United States and in cooperation with protocols of archives and literary executors, I have compiled the following list of official reprint permissions that have made publication of this anthology of documents possible:

Charter for The College of Rhode Island (1764) and *The Laws of the College in Providence in the State of Rhode Island* (1783), reprinted by permission of the Brown University Archives.

Charter for the University of Georgia (1785) reprinted by permission of the *Georgia Review* and with the cooperation and consent of the Archives of the University of Georgia.

Jean Evangelauf, "Where Did U.S. Public Higher Education Begin? Georgia and North Carolina Claim the Honor," *Chronicle of Higher Education* (October 23, 1985); and Ben Gose, "University of Chicago President's Plan to Resign Doesn't Quiet Debate over His Agenda," *Chronicle of Higher Education* (June 18, 1999), with reprint permission from The YGS Group, Inc.

The Commonwealth of Massachusetts, *An Act to Incorporate Mount-Holyoke Female Seminary* (1836), reprinted by permission of the College Archives of Mount Holyoke College.

Abraham Flexner, *A Report on Medical Education in the United States and Canada: Bulletin Four* (1910); and Howard J. Savage et al., *American College Athletics: Bulletin Twenty Six* (1929), reprinted by permission of The Carnegie Foundation for the Advancement of Teaching.

Stephen J. Wright, "The Black Colleges and Universities: Historical Background and Future Prospects," *Virginia Foundation for the Humanities Newsletter* (1987), reprinted by permission of the Virginia Foundation for the Humanities.

Robert Benchley, "What College Did to Me," in *The Early Worm* (New York: Harper, 1927), with reprint permission from Nat Benchley (grandson and literary executor).

James Thurber, "University Days," from *My Life and Hard Times* by James Thurber. Copy-

Index